SAGE Brief Guide to
BUSINESS ETHICS

SAGE Brief Guide to
BUSINESS ETHICS

Los Angeles | London | New Delhi
Singapore | Washington DC

Los Angeles | London | New Delhi
Singapore | Washington DC

FOR INFORMATION:

SAGE Publications, Inc.
2455 Teller Road
Thousand Oaks, California 91320
E-mail: order@sagepub.com

SAGE Publications Ltd.
1 Oliver's Yard
55 City Road
London EC1Y 1SP
United Kingdom

SAGE Publications India Pvt. Ltd.
B 1/I 1 Mohan Cooperative Industrial Area
Mathura Road, New Delhi 110 044
India

SAGE Publications Asia-Pacific Pte. Ltd.
33 Pekin Street #02-01
Far East Square
Singapore 048763

Executive Editor: Lisa Shaw

Acquisitions Editor: Deya Saoud Jacob

Editorial Assistant: Megan Krattli

Production Editor: Eric Garner

Typesetter: C&M Digitals (P) Ltd.

Proofreader: Carole Quandt

Cover Designer: Gail Buschman

Marketing Manager: Helen Salmon

Permissions Editor: Karen Ehrmann

Printed in the United States of America

Library of Congress Cataloging-in-Publication Data

Sage brief guide to business ethics.

p. cm.

Includes bibliographical references.

ISBN 978-1-4129-9721-8 (pbk.)

1. Business ethics.

HF5387.S236 2012 174′.4—dc22 2011006042

This book is printed on acid-free paper.

11 12 13 14 15 10 9 8 7 6 5 4 3 2 1

CONTENTS

PREFACE

Commerce is by its very nature a normative enterprise. It is concerned with creating value for owners and other constituencies, ranging from the firm's immediate stakeholders, such as employees, customers, and suppliers, to the entire society within which the business operates. As a field of study, business ethics aims to specify the principles under which businesses must operate to behave ethically. Thus, business ethics focuses on issues such as those that have recently attracted so much public scrutiny: executive compensation, honesty in accounting, transparency, treatment of stakeholders, and respect for the environment. These are, in fact, perennial questions that accompany the long history of human economic activity and that will also be present through an indeterminate future.

Although defining business ethics has been somewhat problematic, several definitions have been proposed. For example, Richard De George defines the field broadly as the interaction of ethics and business, and although its aim is theoretical, the product has practical application. Manuel Velasquez defines the business ethics field as a specialized study of moral right and wrong. Unfortunately, a great deal of confusion appears to remain within both the academic and the business communities, as other related business and society frameworks, such as corporate social responsibility, stakeholder management, sustainability, and corporate citizenship, are often used interchangeably with or attempt to incorporate business ethics. This *Brief Guide to Business Ethics* is not designed to offer any easy answers about what business ethics is or to oversimplify any of the complex relationships between these frameworks. Rather, its aim is to provoke thought and raise questions about the key concepts in the field—about the history of these concepts and they way in which they have continued to evolve over time, about the key scholars and practitioners who have shaped our understanding of these concepts, and about the many ways in which they relate to and interconnect with each other.

FORMAT

This guide to business ethics provides key terms and concepts related to business ethics in a short, easy-to-use format. It is intended to act as a companion for business ethics courses or as a reference for students and practitioners who would like to learn more about the basics of business ethics.

The text is divided into seven sections that contain important keywords that relate to those sections: *What is Business Ethics?; Theories of Ethics; Ethics of Business and Management; Employee and Human Resources Issues; Consumer Issues; and Ethics of Advertising, Marketing, and Public Relations.* Each keyword entry is a comprehensive essay written by a scholar of business ethics. Entries address such critical topics as ethical decision making, international business ethics, ethics of finance, and consumer and employee rights, and include a list of references and suggested readings. In the back of the book, you will also find three appendixes. Appendix A, Problematic Practices, includes entries on businesses and industries that have encountered ethical issues as well as key incidents that have shaped the way we think about business ethics today. A correlation table in this appendix also provides suggested pairings between the problematic practices and the entries in the text, so that instructors have an idea of which concepts are illustrated in the problematic practices entries. Appendix B provides a list of business ethics organizations and—for further exploration and research—Appendix C provides a list of key business ethics periodicals.

ACKNOWLEDGMENTS

We would like to acknowledge and thank Robert Kolb, editor of SAGE's award-winning *Encyclopedia of Business Ethics and Society,* whose contributions provided the foundation for this companion text.

—The Editors of SAGE

PART I

What Is Business Ethics?

Business Ethics

BUSINESS ETHICS

Although defining business ethics has been somewhat problematic, several definitions have been proposed. For example, Richard De George defines the field broadly as the interaction of ethics and business, and although its aim is theoretical, the product has practical application. Manuel Velasquez defines the business ethics field as a specialized study of moral right and wrong. Unfortunately, a great deal of confusion appears to remain within both the academic and the business communities, as other related business and society frameworks, such as corporate social responsibility, stakeholder management, sustainability, and corporate citizenship, are often used interchangeably with or attempt to incorporate business ethics. Relative to other business and society frameworks, however, business ethics appears to place the greatest emphasis on the ethical responsibilities of business and its individual agents, as opposed to other firm responsibilities (e.g., economic, legal, environmental, or philanthropic).

A BRIEF HISTORY OF BUSINESS ETHICS

The subject of business ethics has been around since the very first business transaction. For example, the Code of Hammurabi, created nearly 4,000 years ago, records that Mesopotamian rulers attempted to create honest prices. In the fourth century BCE, Aristotle discussed the vices and virtues of tradesmen and merchants. The Old Testament and the Jewish Talmud discuss the proper way to conduct business, including topics such as fraud, theft, proper weights and measures, competition and free entry, misleading advertising, just prices, and environmental issues. The New Testament and the Koran also discuss business ethics as it relates to poverty and wealth. Throughout the history of commerce, these codes have had an impact on business dealings. The U.K. South Sea Bubble of the early 1700s, labeled as the world's first great financial scandal, involved the collapse of the South Sea Company. During the 19th century, the creation of monopolies and the use of slavery were important business ethics issues, which continue to be debated until today.

In recent times, business ethics has moved through several stages of development. Prior to the 1960s, business was typically considered to be an amoral activity; concepts such as ethics and social responsibility were rarely explicitly mentioned. During the 1960s, a number of social issues in business began to emerge, including civil rights, the environment, safety in the workplace, and consumer issues. During the late 1970s, the field of business ethics began to take hold in academia, with several U.S. schools beginning to offer a course in business ethics by 1980. From 1980 to 1985, the business ethics field continued to consolidate, with the emergence of journals, textbooks, research centers, and conferences. From 1985 to 1995, business ethics became integrated into large corporations, with the development of corporate codes of ethics, ethics training, ethics hotlines, and ethics officers. From 1995 to 2000, issues related to international business activity came to the forefront, including issues of bribery and corruption of government officials, the use of child labor by overseas suppliers, and the question of whether to operate in countries where human rights violations were taking place. From approximately 2000 until today, business ethics discussion has mainly been focused on major corporate scandals such as Enron, WorldCom, and Tyco, leading to a new phase of government regulation (e.g., the Sarbanes-Oxley Act of 2002) and enforcement.

This current "scandal" phase of the business ethics field has tremendously enhanced its popular use. For example, a search in Google using the term *business ethics* (as of November 2005) generates over 88 million hits. Hollywood continues to portray important business ethics issues or dilemmas in movies such as *Wall Street, Quiz Show, Boiler Room, Erin Brockovich, The Insider,* and *Jerry Maguire* and even in children's films such as *Monsters, Inc.*

MORAL STANDARDS AND BUSINESS ETHICS

Although the field of business ethics covers a broad range of topics, the core of the field is based in moral philosophy and its use of moral standards (i.e., values, principles, and theories) to engage in ethical assessments of business activity. A literature review indicates that five moral standards have been applied in the field of business ethics to a greater extent and with greater consistency than others. Two moral theories are particularly dominant in the business ethics literature: utilitarianism and deontology. Utilitarianism, often expressed as a teleological or consequentialist framework, is primarily based on the writings of Jeremy Bentham and John Stuart Mill. Deontology

3

(i.e., duty-based obligations) is often expressed in terms of "Kantianism" (or more specifically as the principle of the categorical imperative), being primarily based on the writings of Immanuel Kant. In addition to utilitarianism and deontology, two other moral theories (typically considered deontological in nature) have been used extensively in the business ethics field: moral rights and justice (e.g., procedural and distributive). The fifth moral theory receiving attention appears to be moral virtue, being primarily based on the writings of Aristotle. The predominant use by business ethicists of these moral theories points toward their importance in the field. Other important moral standards that are also used (although to a somewhat lesser extent) in the field of business ethics include moral relativism, ethical egoism, and religious doctrine.

There have been several means by which moral standards have been applied in business ethics. Some of the more apparent ways are (1) individual ethical decision making; (2) organizational ethical decision making (e.g., policies and practices); (3) the moral evaluation of business systems (e.g., capitalism) and the marketplace (e.g., competition); (4) the relationship between business and society (e.g., corporate social responsibility); and (5) specific issues in business (e.g., affirmative action and discrimination, conflicts of interest, privacy, whistle-blowing, executive compensation, consumer protection or marketing, and international business). In conjunction with the above are the uses made of moral standards with respect to both teaching and research in business ethics.

BUSINESS ETHICS AS AN ACADEMIC FIELD

Richard De George might be considered the first to attempt to distinguish business ethics as a separate field of study. De George suggests that business ethics is a field to the extent that it deals with a set of interrelated questions to be untangled and addressed within an overarching framework. He argues that the framework is not supplied by any ethical theory (e.g., Kantian, utilitarian, or theological) but by the systematic interdependence of the questions, which can be approached from various philosophical, theological, or other points of view.

Despite business ethics being a relatively recent distinct field of study, several typologies have emerged. There appear to be five general approaches: (1) a normative and descriptive approach, (2) a functional approach, (3) an issues approach, (4) a stakeholder approach, and (5) a mixed approach. For example, in terms of the normative/descriptive approach, academic business ethics research is often divided into normative (i.e., prescriptive) and empirical (i.e., explanatory, descriptive, or predictive) methodologies. A functional approach attempts to divide the subject of business ethics into separate functional areas such as accounting, finance, marketing, or strategy. Others attempt to categorize business ethics by using an "issues" approach—in other words, by discussing issues such as the morality of corporations, employer-employee relationships, or other contemporary business issues. Another approach attempts to discuss the subject of business ethics from a stakeholder perspective (i.e., in relation to which stakeholder is most directly affected). For example, business ethics issues might be framed based on the following stakeholders: owners, employees, consumers, suppliers, competitors, the government, the natural environment, and the community. Finally, a mixed approach draws on aspects of several of the approaches (e.g., normative/descriptive, issues, and stakeholder) and appears to be the most popular approach used by business ethics academics. For example, quite often business ethics textbooks will commence with a normative discussion of moral theory and business systems. The discussion will then turn to a more mixed normative/descriptive discussion of the specific issues. In addition, many of the issues are tied to stakeholders, typically involving employees and customers.

In terms of business ethics research, in a review of the first 1,500 articles published in the *Journal of Business Ethics* from 1981 until 1999, Denis Collins found the presence of the following major business ethics research topics: (1) prevalence of ethical behavior, (2) ethical sensitivities, (3) ethics codes and programs, (4) corporate social performance and policies, (5) human resource practices and policies, and (6) professions—accounting, marketing/sales, and finance/strategy.

MAJOR EARLY CONTRIBUTORS TO BUSINESS ETHICS

Several important early contributors to the field of business ethics, mainly through their initial textbook publications, include Norman Bowie, Richard De George, Manuel Velasquez, Thomas Donaldson, W. Michael Hoffman, Patricia Werhane, John Boatright, and many others too numerous to mention. John Fleming conducted a study in 1987 to determine among other things the most referenced authors, books, and articles in business ethics. The top five referenced authors were (1) Milton Friedman, (2) Christopher Stone, (3) Thomas Donaldson, (4) Peter French, and (5) Alasdair MacIntyre. The top three referenced books were (1) Christopher Stone, *Where the Law Ends;* (2) Thomas Donaldson, *Corporations and Morality;* and (3) John Rawls, *A Theory of Justice.* The top three referenced articles were (1) Brenner and Molander, "Is the Ethics of Business Changing?"; (2) Peter French, "The Corporation as a Moral Person"; and (3) Milton Friedman, "The Social Responsibility of Business Is to Increase Its Profits."

BUSINESS ETHICS TODAY

Based on early efforts, the field of business ethics continues to flourish in both academia as well as the business community. For example, a search (as of November 2005) using the database ABI/Inform for the term *business ethics* found in scholarly journal articles generates over 11,000 hits. Several important academic journals now exist, including *Journal of Business Ethics, Business Ethics Quarterly, Business & Society, Business Ethics: A European Review,* and *Business & Professional Ethics Journal,* among others. Business ethics conferences are held annually, including those conducted by the Society for Business Ethics and the European Business Ethics Network. Every 4 years, the International Society of Business, Economics and Ethics organizes a World Congress on Business Ethics, often portrayed as the "Olympics of Business Ethics." Research centers such as Bentley College's Center for Business Ethics, Wharton's Zicklin Center for Business Ethics Research, or the Ethics Resource Center based in Washington, D.C., continue to support research efforts in the field of business ethics. Surveys suggest that approximately two thirds of the top U.S. business schools now teach business ethics as either a mandatory or an elective stand-alone course. In the corporate world, the growth of ethics officers as well as the Ethics & Compliance Officer Association, ethics programs (e.g., codes of ethics, ethics hotlines or helplines), ethics audits and reports, ethical investment, and even corporate business ethics awards highlight the growing practical importance of the field. Consulting efforts in the business ethics field appear to have grown significantly as well due to the various corporate scandals and the desire of firms to avoid them in the future.

Yet despite the growth of business ethics and the apparent acceptance of its importance among many, several issues are being debated. For example, can business ethics be taught? What factors actually influence ethical behavior? What should a firm's ethical obligations (i.e., beyond the law) consist of?

Does ethical behavior actually improve the firm's financial performance? Is a firm capable of being held morally responsible, or only the firm's agents? How can business ethics best be integrated into a firm's corporate culture? These issues, as well as many others, remain to be examined and debated by those active in the business ethics field.

—Mark S. Schwartz

Further Readings

Beauchamp, T. L., & Bowie, N. E. (2004). *Ethical theory and business* (7th ed.). Upper Saddle River, NJ: Pearson.

Boatright, J. R. (2003). *Ethics and the conduct of business* (4th ed.). Upper Saddle River, NJ: Prentice Hall.

Collins, D. (2000). The quest to improve the human condition: The first 1,500 articles published in the *Journal of Business Ethics. Journal of Business Ethics, 26*(1), 1–73.

De George, R. T. (1987). The status of business ethics: Past and future. *Journal of Business Ethics, 6,* 201–211.

De George, R. T. (2006). *Business ethics* (6th ed.). Upper Saddle River, NJ: Pearson.

Donaldson, T., Werhane, P. H., & Cording, M. (2002). *Ethical issues in business: A philosophical approach* (7th ed.). Upper Saddle River, NJ: Pearson.

Fleming, J. E. (1987). Authorities in business ethics. *Journal of Business Ethics, 6*(3), 213–217.

Goodpaster, K. E. (1997). Business ethics. In P. H. Werhane & R. E. Freeman (Eds.), *Encyclopedic dictionary of business ethics* (pp. 51–57). Cambridge, MA: Blackwell.

Richardson, J. E. (2005). *Annual editions: Business ethics 05/06* (17th ed.). Guilford, CT: McGraw-Hill.

Velasquez, M. G. (2006). *Business ethics: Concepts and cases* (6th ed.). Upper Saddle River, NJ: Pearson.

PART II

Ethics and the Individual

Human Nature

Human Rights

Trust

Integrity

Ethical Decision Making

HUMAN NATURE

PART II: Ethics and
the Individual

Human nature may be defined as the essence of the human species and consists of all the characteristics and behaviors that are inherent in human beings. While inquiries into human nature have occupied philosophers both classical and contemporary, practical men and women frequently attribute one or another experienced injury or benefit to some element of human nature and make decisions informed by their own hopes and fears. Advocates of business ethics often look to human nature to explain abuses or to propose a path of change.

WHAT MAKES A HUMAN BEING?

Humans are distinguished from animals by their ability to use tools, develop language, and reason. These last two are closely connected in that the practice of logic is intertwined with the structure of language. While rhesus monkeys have been taught to use sign language and domesticated animals are capable of understanding spoken words, the development of a formal language is unique to human beings. Indeed, humans have created a diversity of spoken and written languages, and the vocabularies of these languages reveals commonalities and differences among cultures. Written language permits a more detailed historic record and enhanced opportunities for self-consciousness and specialized labor.

In biological terms, the "human" is a mammal, large brained, has an "s"-shaped spinal column, an erect posture, opposable thumbs, an omnivorous diet, binocular vision, speech, practices bipedal locomotion, and dwells on the ground. The human or hominid is preceded in the mammalian chronology by pongids (apes or monkeys). Pongids and hominids share several characteristics with humans: their group living, their careful socialization of children, and their capacity for learning, among others.

The human brain is supple and responds to environmental challenges through reconfiguring its neural pathways. An individual's loss of a sense leads to a process in which the other senses compensate, and a new synthetic understanding of the environment emerges. Damage to the brain stimulates a reassignment of functions among the healthy parts of the brain. The individual's need to process information and interact with the environment stimulates the development of appropriate areas of the brain. The chemistry of the brain is thus altered. Nurture and broad experience may affect nature.

Humans live in groups, not as isolates. Human survival is crucially dependent on primary and secondary groups, from the dyad and nuclear family to larger kinship patterns. Families depend on an overarching organization or complex of organizations, ranging from the tribe and confederations of tribes, to the political structures of the city and nation-state. Pongids share the primary and secondary group structures in which humans live, but they lack the more complex political and economic institutions that characterize human experience.

One basic need satisfied by social organization is continuity in food supply. Participation in social organization with this purpose is not optional. A primary function of the economic system is to assure the availability of food and accommodations and, beyond this, to guide the distribution of wanted goods consistent with cultural values.

Religion has emerged among humans to explain and guide shared experiences of birth, illness, death, love, hurt, and disaster. These explanations are organized into a superstructure that provides reasons, names, and rationales, confers membership, allocates power, and promulgates a charter to order society. Religions proliferate but societies have more recently turned to secular forms of organization in which the influence of religion can still be discerned. Religions constitute one of the oldest forms of social organization and continue to shape business practice, political movements, and statecraft. Religion is an important element of culture that stands along with biology in explaining human behavior.

DETERMINANTS OF HUMAN NATURE

Biology

Biologists have documented much of the human genome and, in doing so, have revealed fundamental elements of human nature. In a very real but limited sense, the genetic code accounts for human nature. Human DNA provides the biological basis for human consciousness, from which derives the human capacity for learning and the complex knowledge transmitted by culture. While the ancient Greeks speculated about fixed forms and ideas determining human nature, contemporary scholars find evolving intelligences, in dialogue with one another and interacting with the environment.

Human evolution is the process through which humans emerge within nature. That humans are animals has led some to claim that humans are inherently violent and aggressive, as some animals appear to be. Evolution is often described as the "survival of the fittest," which is taken by "Social Darwinists" like the 19th-century sociologist Herbert Spencer and his contemporary disciples to mean that humans necessarily struggle with one another, with some destined to lose. Konrad Lorenz argued that humans possess an aggressive instinct but proposed means to subdue it.

Charles Darwin did not intend that evolution be equated with violent competition. Rather, he emphasized the question of reproductive advantage. That is, the evolution of a species is the consequence of the development of characteristics that contribute to differential reproductive success in the local environment. Reproductive success is not necessarily a function of violent competition within or between species. The 19th-century social critic Petr Kropotkin and modern evolutionary biologists have demonstrated that cooperation within and between species also plays a critical role in promoting the survival of offspring. As discussed below, animals and humans have been said to practice a reciprocal altruism in which cooperation emerges as a strategy for survival.

Consider as well the process of symbiosis. Species may evolve in such a way as to intimately depend on conditions produced by other species and may even live within their bodies. This is far from Thomas Hobbes's and Spencer's war for survival.

Culture

Humans are unique in regard to the role played by culture, rather than biology, in shaping individual behavior. Culture is the set of values and customs in which individuals are socialized and that bind a community together. Cultural values shape but do not determine behavior because individuals and groups have the capacity to examine their culture's assumptions and subject them to analysis. Socrates counseled that "the unexamined life is not worth living." Descartes explored the uncertainties of his own existence, and every generation brings a new round of questioning.

Moreover, cultures may coexist, merge, or fragment. Cultures and nations may share boundaries but varied cultures may also blend in a single nation. Shared beliefs and behaviors rather than physical location or political jurisdiction characterize cultures.

The logical structure embedded in many of the languages of the world facilitates questioning. The concept of opposite or negation invites an experimental mind to invert culturally transmitted propositions. Any culture, however conformist, inspires movements of dissent and reformulations of received doctrine. No culture is fully stable.

It is possible almost everywhere to find borderlands where cultures mix and traditions bend or erode. Authority and challenges to it coexist in the borderlands and throughout the contours of cultural evolution.

Clyde Kluckhohn, a cultural anthropologist best known for his survey of the many definitions of culture, called culture an abstract description of the trends toward uniformity in the words, deeds, and artifacts of a human group. Kluckhohn and other anthropologists have noted that cultures are dynamic and are characterized by processes reinforcing both stability and change. Geography and legal jurisdiction shape but do not determine cultural change.

Anthropologists have found considerable differences among the peoples of the world in their practice of gender roles, in their construction of race and class, in their conception of the individual and the collective, in their interpretation of family responsibility and the extended family, in their treatment of elders and assessment of tradition, in their assessment of the proper relations between workers and managers (laypersons and clergy, amateurs and experts), and in their attitudes toward progress. Kluckhohn found these questions to be central to the differentiation of cultures: the conceptions of inherent good or evil in human nature; the perceived relationship of humans and nature; the emphasis on past, present, or future; the conception of life as being, becoming, or doing; and the patterns of emphasis in primary relationships.

Management scholar Geert Hofstede sought to apply the concept of culture to a business context. He surveyed the global population of IBM managers to illuminate national differences in values. He found national differences on the acceptance of power differentials (power distance), individualism (vs. collectivism), masculinity (vs. femininity), the tolerance of uncertainty, and future (or present) orientation. GLOBE researchers at the Thunderbird School of Management amended his model, identifying nine cultural dimensions: performance orientation, assertiveness, future orientation, humane orientation, institutional collectivism, in-group collectivism, gender egalitarianism, power distance, and uncertainty avoidance.

From an anthropological perspective, patterns of uniformity and divergence are of equal interest. The Hofstede and GLOBE models appear to emphasize uniformity rather than change and differentiation. They also assume the narrow vantage point of the multinational manager and cultural variation is understood in relationship to the constituent parts of a multinational enterprise. However, the multinational enterprise is perhaps too culturally specific to serve as a framework for comprehending cultural variation.

The United Nations Universal Declaration of Human Rights emerged from a process in which representatives from the world's nations debated the notion of rights in the aftermath of World War II. That such a document was written with broad international support underscores the possibility of communication and understanding across cultures. Beneath the evident cultural differences on dimensions like individualism and collectivism across the globe, there are underlying problems about the relationship of the individual to the group. Even violations of the Declaration reveal similar patterns of social control and resistance across cultures and nations.

Diversity: Relationships of Gender, Race, Class

The wide variation in cultural practices across the globe and the visible differences among races and genders have inspired theories of difference and inequality. Explorers and scholars who recorded differences among races and cultures in the 18th, 19th, and 20th centuries, in many cases, assumed a fixed hierarchy of ability and intelligence. These views are increasingly contested by egalitarian perspectives that emphasize the complexity of language and belief systems in disparate civilizations. French anthropologist Claude Levi-Strauss studied the religions and other beliefs of so-called primitive societies and discovered similarities in the detail and complexity of understanding and argument. Franz Boas and more contemporary anthropologists have questioned the concept of race, noting that race accounts for minuscule differences in the genetic code and that there are far greater genetic differences within rather than between the races.

In the United States and many other industrialized nations, women increasingly participate in the labor force. Despite this, there are persistent disparities in income and occupational distribution. While feminists, professional groups, and trade unions agitate for corrective action, there remain significant constituencies who argue for a return to traditional gender roles.

DEBATE OVER ESSENTIALISM

The ancient Greeks and particularly Plato and Aristotle contributed profoundly to the historical development of ideas about human nature. In various ways, they advanced the argument that human nature is fixed and personal qualities unalterable. Plato and Aristotle argued that human beings, animals, and things were expressions of underlying forms. For Plato, the material world known by sensation was merely a shadow of a more fundamental reality of unchanging forms or ideas perceived by the intellect or reason. Most important among forms is "goodness," accessible only to reason.

On the other hand, Aristotle saw form and matter as intertwined. According to Aristotle, humans share the same underlying form but differ in their material manifestations. The human soul or mind consists of the distinctly human faculties including consciousness and reason. From the material world come individual differences.

Aristotelian philosophy validates experience as a source of knowledge. Aristotle believed that the forms manifested in all living and inanimate things are accessible to the human mind through experience coupled with reason.

Like Plato, Aristotle embraced inequality among humans and rationalized a rigid class system. Aristotle specifically endorsed slavery as natural and argued that most slaves were mentally inferior to their masters. He placed humans at the peak of a hierarchy of all life-forms but suggested that some humans were brutish or animal-like, particularly non-Greeks.

Aristotle identified human fulfillment with the exercise of reason in a life of activity and social engagement. He proposed practical wisdom, moderation, courage, and justice as principal virtues to guide living. Virtue lies in the mean between extremes, and extremes of wealth and poverty produce manifold injustice.

Platonic and Aristotelian philosophies continue to shape modern thinking. Plato's notion of the separation of mind and body or "dualism" is reflected in Christian teaching about the soul's independence from flesh. Contemporary arguments about the superiority of reason to emotion recall his work.

Platonic idealism has an analog in the free market model in neoclassical economics. Many economists view the market as the underlying reality of economic life even as they de-emphasize the violations of neoclassical assumptions posed by the details of corporate power and the experience of individuals and groups at work. Institutionalists, Marxists, and other dissenters within economics have sought to counterpose the social realities of poverty and exploitation with the abstract formalism of economic models. Economists' adherence to the ideal of free markets, like Platonic idealism, is rooted in a preference for mathematical structures over subjective experience.

Aristotle's conception of human differences, characterization of human virtues, and empiricism have been influential. Modern conservatives find in Aristotle a justification of aristocracy in the political and economic realms. On the other hand, Robert Solomon and others have developed paradigms of multiple virtues in business ethics relying on Aristotle's works.

Forms in Platonic and Aristotelian philosophy represent means to explain what is common and what is different among humans, animals, and things. Contemporary scientists struggle with the same questions and have found that the DNA code constitutes a modern equivalent for form among living things. However, DNA does not determine all aspects of human nature or individual differences. For example, it is probably only one of many factors influencing intelligence.

Scholars and practitioners continue to debate the relevant contributions of nature and nurture to intelligence. The Intelligence Quotient is premised on the notion that there is one fundamental kind of intelligence that has a fixed and unequal distribution among the human population. Critics such as Howard Gardner now argue that there are multiple forms of intelligence, including social and emotional varieties, that depend on context and are not necessarily correlated. Others have suggested that apparent cultural differences in intelligence are an artifact of testing, in which culturally specific approaches to reasoning are privileged. Most important, critics find considerable evidence for the notion that individuals have multiple paths of intellectual development open to them and that they are not handicapped by a fixed amount of intelligence.

Given the near-universality of complex hierarchies in the business world and the phenomenon of the "pecking order" among animal species, it is tempting to say that hierarchy and inequality are embedded in human nature. From Plato and Aristotle to contemporary ethologists such as Desmond Morris, this has been the view. Others condemn this notion as an anthropomorphic fallacy. Dominant chimpanzees or roosters do not claim superiority relative to the others in their group. Their dominance is highly constrained and relates to the ordering of events rather than to the quality of existence. It is only among humans that hierarchy rations access to necessary goods.

Counterposed to the essentialist views of Plato and Aristotle are models of a malleable and flexible human nature. Jean-Jacques Rousseau, Karl Marx, John Dewey, and even the 20th-century management scholar Douglas McGregor argued that the reconstruction of social institutions could initiate new patterns of human development. Rousseau argued that humans were essentially good but corrupted by existing civilizations. He called for a new social contract informed by the "general will," freed of corrupting sectarian interests. Karl Marx imagined an emancipated human nature of unlimited capacity following socialist revolution and the transition to communism. Dewey believed democracy to be the key to the enhancement of ordinary individuals' abilities. McGregor argued that a more participatory approach by managers would uplift and fulfill most workers. The debates about the scope of human malleability and improvement are embedded within contemporary political discourse.

BEHAVIORS BASED IN HUMAN NATURE

Self-Interest Versus Altruism

One of the most important debates in business ethics revolves around the relationship of self-interest, competition, profit-maximizing, and human nature. The obverse question is the relationship of altruism inherent to human nature. What are the relative shares of altruism and self-interest in the fundamental nature of the human actors?

Some argue that examples of altruistic behavior abound in nature. Care for family members is a characteristic seen in a wide variety of species. The careful protection of eggs by penguin parents is a remarkable demonstration of willing self-sacrifice. Of course, biological urges are supplemented by cultural traits in human society; the balance of cooperation and competition in animal nature does not determine the balance in human nature.

The care shown by a parent for a child is often explained as selfish in that it helps preserve the parent's genes. However, the wolf pack's embodiment of extended family and the human concern for community and humankind (described in robust form in Kristin Monroe's *Heart of Altruism*) cannot easily be construed as self-interest. It is noteworthy that neither narrow self-interest nor broad social solidarity, strictly defined, requiring either a developed personality or a science of politics, is present in the animal world.

Economists Samuel Bowles and Herbert Gintis posit that strong reciprocity and basic needs generosity are fundamental human motives. They contend that anthropological research and game theory suggest that people are not stingy, but that their generosity is conditional on context. By strong reciprocity, they mean a propensity to cooperate and share with others in a similar position, even at personal cost. By basic needs generosity, they mean a virtually unconditional willingness to share with others and assure them some means of subsistence. Evolutionary biologists find evidence of reciprocal altruism as an evolved behavior. Anthropologists find altruism and self-interest embodied in varying combinations in existing and ancient cultures.

Some have argued that altruism is linked to a particular formulation of self-interest. Altruistic service to others requires a healthy self, without which one's service may lack consistency and effectiveness. Someone who fails to attend to his or her health and other needs cannot be reliably helpful to others. Sustainably altruistic behavior, whether for business leaders, philanthropists, community activists, or helping professionals, cannot involve self-destruction. Altruism may be linked to a conception of self-interest that is broadly construed so as to be consciously embedded in the social. The altruist judges the welfare of others to be intertwined with his or her own interests.

Despite the long tradition of writing and argument that humans are inherently social (supported by Plato and Aristotle and their Christian interpreters among others), individualistic conceptions of human nature have grown in influence in the United States and Western Europe since the 18th century. Social contract models like that of Thomas Hobbes and John Locke played a critical role in the revolt against monarchical absolutism and feudal privilege; individual rights and reason were key to this process. Both Hobbes and Locke hypothesized that humans were equal in the state of nature but endorsed a civil society of individualism and unequal property relations. Individualistic ideas were a potent solvent that shook the feudal order to its foundations. Canadian political theorist C. B. Macpherson identified a contradiction in the "possessive individualism" of Hobbes and Locke between the logic of individual liberty and exploitative property relations.

The 18th-century political economist Adam Smith was one of the great architects of the capitalist system. One of his important contributions was to link individualism to a self-regulating natural order. His best known work, *The Wealth of Nations,* introduced the concept of the "invisible hand" guiding the self-interested behavior of economic actors toward the public good. Modern individualists continue to pay tribute to Smith's conception of the invisible hand. Objectivists like Ayn Rand add to Smith's embrace of markets a belief in the moral superiority of capitalists.

Despite Smith's celebrated role as an exponent of laissez-faire capitalism, he did not argue that selfishness was a sufficient explanation of human behavior. He worried that self-interest often led businessmen to conspire against the public and called attention to "sympathy" as a motive coexisting with selfishness. Indeed, he raised questions about the morality of individual capitalists.

Utilitarian philosopher Jeremy Bentham contributed much to the classical model of "economic man," the individual as utility maximizer practicing a hedonistic calculus. In this analysis, market transactions generate the greatest happiness of the greatest number, and no other motives need constrain self-interest. However, even within utilitarianism more complex views of human nature have emerged. John Stuart Mill found happiness to be something more than the sensation of pleasure. Mill's emphasis on the quality of happiness and his concern for workers' conditions in free markets led him to contemplate means to introduce a measure of solidarity in economics, thereby adding to self-interest as the primary human motive. Smith and Mill considered together reveal a developing argument for social responsibility to restrain capitalist excess within the classical economic paradigm.

Capitalists and socialists, reformers, reactionaries, and revolutionaries of all stripes have posited views of human nature that validate their political analyses. Capitalists find self-interest everywhere. Socialists find altruism prominent in both "primitive" and civilized societies. Ayn Rand and modern objectivists continue to argue for an atomistic individualism and interpret human interaction as a form of rational contracting.

Good and Evil

War and violence have bedeviled humanity throughout recorded history. While Rousseau posited a noble savage and Marxian socialists have forecast human perfectibility, Saint Augustine and succeeding generations of Catholic and Protestant thinkers have asserted the principle of original sin.

Immanuel Kant thought the human mind capable of discerning moral duties or categorical imperatives through the application of reason. Because reason is an inherent human capacity, the perception of duty is embedded in human nature. This does not mean that humans will always do that which is good. Their capacity to reason provides the opportunity to make choices, and these choices may reflect selfish interests and violate duty.

The 20th-century Protestant theologian Reinhold Niebuhr elaborated a view of human nature in which good and evil coexist and define the arc of human practice, and democracy is justified as a constraint on evil and a means to develop the good. Niebuhr warned of the children of light and the children of darkness, both of whom do evil as they dwell in illusion. The children of light assume that human nature is perfectible and fail to recognize the damage they do as they aggressively pursue what they regard as the good. The children of darkness know of no law apart from their own will and narrow interest. Niebuhr held that powerful corporations routinely abuse their power, both through the naïve optimism of the children of light and the manipulative cynicism of the children of darkness. Niebuhr's moderate pessimism about human nature led him to argue for extensive regulation of corporations, but he also warned of abuses in the exercise of governmental power.

Reason and Emotion

Philosophers from classical to modern times have cited reason as the faculty that distinguishes human beings from animals. It must be conceded that primates have the capacity for physical problem solving, but they lack the ability to consider abstractions and formulate principles. This gives humans the capacity to distinguish self-interest from group and societal interests and to choose rules for decision making.

While Plato and other dualists considered emotion to be inferior to reason, and others have linked emotions and the flesh to moral corruption, emotion plays a critical role in human behavior. It cannot be so easily distinguished from reason. Emotion provides information. When one experiences emotional pain, one recognizes a peril in the path of decision making. Pleasure reveals a favorable association. Emotions illuminate some of the personal and social consequences that derive from one's choices and situation. One is free to employ reason in the consideration of emotion. While Jeremy Bentham was probably a reductionist in his construction of a hedonistic calculus for human behavior, it is equally suspect to dismiss pleasure and pain as irrelevant to human action.

The Life Cycle

A challenge posed by human nature to the business world is the recognition of the life cycle. The utilitarian model premised on economic man fails to fully acknowledge the ways in which humans mature and develop distinct needs (rather than wants). Humans are distinguished from other mammals by their survival long past child-bearing years. Older humans have much to contribute to society based on their experience, and children have much to learn from society, but neither reality is fully reflected in any company bottom line. Industrialized societies now face difficult questions relating to the funding of private and public pensions given widespread employer pressure to attenuate historic commitments to retirees. The elderly face increased poverty and exclusion.

SOCIAL RESPONSIBILITY AND SOLIDARITY

Business leaders, scholars, and the public at large vigorously debate about whether corporations owe society anything more than profit-maximizing. The advocates of profit-maximizing and of social responsibility often turn to conceptions of human nature to explain their positions. If rational self-interest is a sufficient explanation of human behavior, then corporate social responsibility receives little reinforcement from human nature. Classical notions of the social contract and contemporary economic models reinforce the notion of the atomistic individual. If, on the other hand, altruism is sustainable at the individual and group levels, then there may be a variant that is appropriate to the business enterprise. A third possibility is that human nature leaves individuals and groups with a wide array of choices and in no way determines the configuration and practice of business enterprise.

Of the three propositions, the weakest appears to be monistic interpretation of human nature and business practice as self-interested. Certainly anthropologists' survey of human behavior and social institutions finds multiple patterns of self-interested and altruistic behavior. Individuals' loyalty to tribes, businesses, or movements cannot be fully explained by self-interest. It should be noted that profit-maximizing corporations depend on considerable self-sacrifice from employees.

Social psychologist Lawrence Kohlberg describes the process of ethical development according to which an individual learns to behave according to the dictates of successively broader communities, from the family to peer groups and ultimately global humanity. Parental approval and avoidance of punishment determines the behavior of the child, but abstract principles may guide the decisions of adults.

Underlying this process is an expanding social consciousness. Humans see the consequences of their actions and derive lessons from what they see. They easily perceive their dependence on immediate and extended families. As they mature, they may increasingly identify commonalities with other individuals and families. They observe an array of "experiments" in which individuals and families pursue varied options with respect to patterns of cooperation and conflict with relevant others. As a result, they forge bonds of identity linking the local, regional, national, and perhaps global networks.

Regardless of one's values and background, one has the potential to embrace a consciousness of kind with global dimensions. This is true of the

Human Nature

hard-nosed business conservative as well as the international unionist. What distinguishes the two is the choice of others with whom to identify. In neither case is the individual self-sufficient.

Social consequences may extend to considerations of the natural world. Humans cannot sever their relations with the natural world, but they can learn better how to evaluate the natural consequences of their actions. The human capacity to perceive consequences, experiment as to behaviors, identify with others, and invent ways of living and working together provide the intellectual and social context for conceptions of social responsibility.

Behavioristic psychologists like James McConnell and B. F. Skinner viewed human behavior as a set of responses to stimuli in which conscious choice is absent. This perspective recognizes few differences between rats and humans and omits culture as a significant element of human existence. On the other hand, if one accepts the notion of consciousness, one can see in cultural variety the multiplicity of social choices humans have made as well as the consequences. One might speak broadly of a "consciousness of kind" (following Giddings), ranging from familial (nuclear, extended) to group, nation, species, and nature. This "consciousness of kind" follows the contours of association and solidarity through which individuals and groups demonstrate their identity with and fidelity to others.

There is considerable opportunity for choice in the way in which business institutions reflect individual, group, and societal priorities. The multiple paths to corporate social responsibility depend on choices as to the institutionalization and reconciliation of the self-interests and altruistic concerns that coexist in human nature.

Consider Kant's maxim that one should treat others as ends and never solely as means. This categorical imperative has been interpreted by some to require the overhaul of organizations. Labor cannot merely be a factor of production and thus a means but must become an end as well. Producer cooperatives, employee ownership, collective bargaining, and employee involvement may be more consistent with Kantian ethics and represent means to reconcile the self-interested and altruistic motives in human nature.

—David Carroll Jacobs

Further Readings

Bentham, J. (1996). *An introduction to the principles of morals and legislation.* Oxford, UK: Clarendon Press.

Bowles, S., & Gintis, H. (1998, December-January). Is equality passe. *Boston Review, 23.* http://bostonreview.mit.edu/BR23.6/bowles.html

Broadie, S., & Rowe, C. (2002). *Aristotle, Nicomachean ethics, translation, introduction, and commentary.* Oxford, UK: Oxford University Press.

Gardner, H. (1993). *Frames of mind: The theory of multiple intelligences.* New York: Basic Books.

Giddings, F. H. (1896). *The principles of sociology: An analysis of the phenomena of association and of social organization.* New York: Macmillan and Co.

Hobbes, T. (2005). *Leviathan: Parts one and two* (A. P. Martinich, Ed.). Peterborough, Ontario, Canada: Broadview Press.

Hofstede, G. (1980). *Culture's consequences: International differences in work-related values.* Beverly Hills, CA: Sage.

Jacobs, M. (1972). A tentative model for religion. *Anthropos, 67,* 196–208.

Javidan, M., Dorfman, P., De Luque, M., & House, R. (2006). In the eye of the beholder: Cross cultural lessons in leadership from Project GLOBE. *Academy of Management Perspectives, 20*(1), 67–90.

Kant, I. (2005). *Groundwork for the metaphysics of morals* (L. Denis, Ed.). Peterborough, Ontario, Canada: Broadview Press.

Kluckhohn, C. (1965). *Mirror for man.* Greenwich, CT: Fawcett.

Kohlberg, L. (1981). *Essays on moral development.* San Francisco: Harper and Row.

Kropotkin, P. (1972). *Mutual aid: A factor of evolution.* New York: New York University Press.

Lévi-Strauss, C. (1966). *The savage mind.* London: Weidenfeld & Nicolson.

Lorenz, K. (1996). *On aggression.* New York: Harcourt, Brace & World.

McGregor, D. (1985). *Human side of enterprise: 25th Anniversary printing.* New York: McGraw-Hill.

Mill, J. S. (1873). *Autobiography.* New York: Holt, Rinehart & Winston.

Monroe, K. R. (1996). *The heart of altruism: Perceptions of a common humanity.* Princeton, NJ: Princeton University Press.

Niebuhr, R. (1972). *The children of light and the children of darkness: A vindication of democracy and a critique of its traditional defense.* New York: Scribner.

Plato. (1992). *Republic* (G. Grube, Trans.). Indianapolis, IN: Hackett.

Rand, A. (1967). *Capitalism: The unknown ideal.* New York: New American Library.

Rousseau, J.-J. (2003). *Emile, or, Treatise on education* (W. H. Payne, Trans.). Amherst, NY: Prometheus Books.

Smith, A. (2003). *Wealth of nations.* New York, NY: Bantam Classic.

Solomon, R. (1992). *Ethics and excellence: Cooperation and integrity in business.* New York: Oxford University Press.

Spencer, H. (1970). *Social statics; the conditions essential to human happiness specified, and the first of them developed.* New York: Robert Schalkenbach Foundation.

Stevenson, L., & Haberman, D. L. (2004). *Ten theories of human nature.* New York: Oxford University Press.

HUMAN RIGHTS

Basic human rights are moral rights that apply to all persons in all nations, regardless of whether the nation in which a person resides acknowledges and protects those rights. It is in this sense that basic human rights are said to be *inalienable.* Human rights can also be aspirational in the sense of specifying the ideal rights to which individuals ought to be entitled. The 1948 *Universal Declaration of Human Rights* is aspirational in this sense. To think about human rights in a meaningful way, it is helpful to answer certain philosophical questions about their nature. Three of the most basic questions are the following: How can human rights be justified? What basic human rights exist? How do human rights differ from other rights, such as legal rights? Let us consider each question in turn.

PHILOSOPHICAL FOUNDATIONS

Human rights are rights enjoyed by humans not because we are members of the species *Homo sapiens* but because fully functional members of our species are persons. Personhood is a metaphysical category that may or may not be unique to *Homo sapiens.* To be a person one must be capable of reflecting on one's desires at a second-order level, and one must be capable of acting in a manner consistent with one's considered preferences. The capacity to reflect on one's competing preferences and to act in a manner consistent with one's second-order preferences is a key feature of personhood and one that distinguishes persons from mere animals. It is in this sense that the idea of personhood is properly understood as metaphysical rather than biological.

Rights theorists with a wide range of commitments readily agree that persons enjoy a basic right to individual freedom and that other persons have a duty not to restrict or constrain the freedom of others without strong justification. Sometimes, as in the case of John Locke, this right is merely assumed or asserted. Modern rights theorists such as Robert Nozick, Loren Lomasky, and Onora O'Neill typically ground this claim in Kant's second formulation of the categorical imperative, which holds that one must treat other persons always as an end and never as a means only. Kant provides a sustained defense of the doctrine of respect for persons, and he and his interpreters specify in detail its practical implications. Respecting other persons requires that one refrain from interfering with their decisions and actions. Typically, one person is justified in limiting the freedom of another only when her own freedom is unjustly restricted by that person. One traditional way of capturing this sense of a liberty right is that individuals should be free to as much liberty or freedom as is compatible with like liberty or freedom for all.

There is little controversy among rights theorists regarding the plausibility of a negative right to liberty or freedom. However, there is significant controversy over whether or not there are positive rights to certain economic and social goods. Positive rights entail not merely negative obligations on the part of others to refrain from certain actions, but a positive obligation to fulfill the right of the rights holder. One positive basic right that is often defended is the right to physical well-being. For example, if individuals have a right to economic aid or health care to ensure their physical well-being, then others have a duty to provide them with such assistance. The state may be called on to fulfill these duties, but in weak or corrupt states such duties may be neglected. And in states where market values trump consideration for positive human rights, such rights may also be neglected. Under such conditions the burden of fulfilling such obligations seems to fall on individuals, but most individuals are not well positioned to meet such obligations. Furthermore, even in cases where the state does meet such alleged obligations, traditional libertarians would argue that it is illegitimate to tax some citizens in order to ensure the well-being of others. Have we then reached an impasse?

Arguably, there are at least two philosophically sound reasons for thinking that we can move beyond this apparent impasse. First, there is an influential and persuasive argument that holds that the distinction between negative and positive rights is unsustainable. Second, there is a widely influential set of positive arguments that can be used to support both a right to freedom and minimal welfare rights, such as the right to subsistence or well-being. Let us consider each argument in turn.

Henry Shue has famously argued that the very distinction between negative and positive rights that the preceding analysis presumes is artificial and inconsistent with social reality. For example, consider the right to physical security (i.e., the right not to be harmed). It is possible to avoid violating a person's right not to be harmed by refraining from certain actions. However, it is not possible to protect a person from harm without taking proactive steps. At a minimum, Shue argued, law enforcement agencies and a criminal justice system are required so that individuals are not left to defend themselves against forces that they are unable to defeat on their own. The existence of these social institutions is predicated on positive actions in the forms of design, implementation, administration, and taxation. In this way, it can be seen that the protection of a prototypical negative right requires positive actions and not merely the avoidance of particular actions. Since negative rights entail both negative and positive duties, the notion of negative versus positive rights loses its meaning. There are only rights and corresponding duties; but the duties that correspond to these rights are both negative and positive. There is, then, Shue concluded, a strong argument against a theory of rights that includes negative but not positive rights.

Much of the most important and influential work on human rights has been produced by Kantians. Rather than beginning with rights claims, Kantians begin with obligations or duties to respect other persons. These duties constrain the pursuit of ends, whether they are self-interested goals or projects pursued on behalf of other parties such as shareholders. Respecting persons involves both negative obligations, such as refraining from using others as mere tools via physical force, coercion, or manipulation, and positive obligations, such as supporting physical well-being and the development of basic human capacities. When they stand in the appropriate relationship to an obligation bearer, persons have rationally justified rights-claims against them. Rights take the form of side-constraints that bound the moral space in which agents may pursue ends without unjustified interference by other agents or institutions. For example, a minor child has legitimate rights-claims against her parents regarding her physical well-being and the development of her human capacities by virtue of her relation to them. The morally legitimate ends of parents do not include actions that substantially undermine the physical well-being or normal development of their child. Similarly, a convenience store owner has a rights-claim against those in his community to be free from assault and robbery. The morally legitimate ends of other community members do not include actions that would undermine the freedom of the store owner.

Wherever corporations conduct business, they are already in special relationships with a variety of stakeholders, such as workers, customers, and local communities. In their global operations and in their global supply chains, corporations have a duty to respect those with whom they have relationships.

Corporate managers, then, have obligations to both ensure that they do not illegitimately undermine the liberty of any persons and the additional obligation to help ensure that minimal welfare rights to physical well-being and the development of basic human capacities are met within their spheres of influence. For example, corporations have sufficient power and coercive influence to ignore the labor and environmental laws in many developing nations. These host nations typically lack the police and judicial infrastructure necessary to enforce such laws. Host nation governments may also be fearful that if they enforce their own laws, then the corporations may move their operations to nations that are willing to ignore local laws. However, such laws are essential for the protection of the basic rights of the citizens of developing nations. For this reason, it has been argued that corporate managers have an obligation to ensure that local host nations' laws are respected.

HUMAN RIGHTS VERSUS LEGAL RIGHTS

Human rights are moral rights that apply to all persons in all nations, regardless of whether the nation in which a person resides acknowledges and protects those rights. Human rights attach to persons and not merely to citizens. Human rights differ from legal rights in that, unlike legal rights, the existence of human rights is not contingent on political institutions. This is true despite the fact that the enforcement of human rights typically does rely on institutional mechanisms.

Many nations grant their citizens certain constitutional or legal rights via foundational documents or legal precedent. However, the rights that are protected vary among nations. Some nations ensure that the rights of citizens are protected by effective policing and an independent judiciary. Frequently, however, poor citizens and disfavored groups are not provided with the same level of protection for their legal rights as the economic and political elite. Persons who are deprived of their rights do not thereby cease to have those rights. Employers may deny employees or other stakeholders their inalienable right to freedom and well-being, whether or not local governments are complicit, but in doing so they in no way diminish the legitimacy of the claims of their employees to those rights. However, by virtue of their failure to properly respect these stakeholders, such employers succeed in diminishing their own standing in the community of rights holders.

In the weak and failed states where many multinational corporations operate, they are often the most powerful institutions in existence. In such cases, corporate managers are uniquely situated to help ensure that the basic rights of individuals within their spheres of influence are protected. Many corporations have embraced this obligation. For example, Mattel ensures that all the factories in its global supply chains meet basic human rights standards. Nike provides microloans to community members in the areas where it has large contract factories, thus providing additional help to improve the economic well-being of these communities. And Adidas ensures that the basic rights of workers in its contract factories are respected while using its occupational safety expertise to help noncontract factories in those same communities improve working conditions.

ARE HUMAN RIGHTS A WESTERN CONCEPT?

At this point in our discussion, it is worthwhile to consider an objection to the foregoing argument concerning human rights. This criticism stems from the observation that the idea of human rights emerged from the Western philosophical tradition but is taken to be universal in its applicability. The claim is then made that human rights are of less importance in the value systems of other cultures. For example, it is argued that "Asian values" emphasize order, discipline, and social harmony, as opposed to individual rights. In this view, the freedom and well-being of individuals should not be allowed to interfere with the harmony of the community, as might be the case, for example, when workers engage in disruptive collective action in an effort to secure their rights. This view might also be used to defend the claim that the moral norms that govern Asian factory operations should emphasize order and discipline, not such basic rights as freedom and well-being.

Several points may be made in reply to this objection. First, Asia is a large region with a vast and heterogeneous population. As Amartya Sen and others have argued, to claim that all, or even most, Asians share a uniform set of values is to impose a level of uniformity that does not exist at present and has not existed in the past. Second, in secular, democratic Asian societies such as India, respect for individual rights has a long tradition. Indeed, there are significant antecedents in the history of the civilizations of the Indian subcontinent that emphasize individual freedom and well-being. For example, Amartya

Sen has noted that in the third century BCE, the Emperor Ashoka granted his citizens the freedom to embrace whatever religious or philosophical system they might choose, and at the same time he emphasized the importance of tolerance and respect for philosophical and religious beliefs different from one's own. Third, even if it was the case that Asian cultures shared a uniform set of values that de-emphasized human rights, this would not by itself provide good reasons for denying or disrespecting the rights to freedom and well-being. This is because the justification of human rights provided above is grounded in rational arguments that are valid across cultures.

The critic is likely to retort that such a view reflects Western prejudices grounded in Enlightenment ideals. This response is unpersuasive. Diverse intellectual traditions have emphasized the importance of values derived from reason, rather than mythology, traditionalism, mere sentiment, or some other source. For example, in the 16th century, the Mughal emperor Akbar arranged to have philosophers representing diverse religious and philosophical beliefs engage in rational discussions regarding the merits of their competing views and sought to identify the most persuasive features of each view. In so doing, Akbar was able to emphasize the power and force of rational analysis. Given that a similar emphasis on rational analysis concerning values may be found in the histories of other non-Western cultures, the claim that such analysis is uniquely Western is unpersuasive.

—Denis G. Arnold

Further Readings

Arnold, D. G. (2003). Philosophical foundations: Moral reasoning, human rights, and global labor practices. In L. P. Hartman, D. G. Arnold, & R. E. Wokutch (Eds.), *Rising above sweatshops: Innovative approaches to global labor challenges* (pp. 77–100). Westport, CT: Praeger.

Arnold, D. G. (2008). *The ethics of global business.* Malden, MA: Blackwell.

Donnelly, J. (1999). Human rights and Asian values: A defense of "western" universalism. In J. R. Bauer & D. A. Bell (Eds.), *The East Asian challenge for human rights.* Cambridge, UK: Cambridge University Press.

Dworkin, G. (1988). *The theory and practice of autonomy.* Cambridge, UK: Cambridge University Press.

Frankfurt, H. (1988). *The importance of what we care about.* Cambridge, UK: Cambridge University Press.

Hartman, L., Arnold, D. G., & Wokutch, R. E. (2003). *Rising above sweatshops: Innovative approaches to global labor challenges.* Praeger: Westport, CT.

Human Rights

Inoue, T. (1999). Liberal democracy and Asian orientalism. In J. R. Bauer & D. A. Bell (Eds.), *The East Asian challenge for human rights*. Cambridge, UK: Cambridge University Press.

Lomasky, L. (1987). *Persons, rights, and the moral community*. New York: Oxford University Press.

Melden, A. I. (1977). *Rights and persons*. Berkeley, CA: University of California Press.

Nozick, R. (1974). *Anarchy, state, and utopia*. New York: Basic Books.

O'Neill, O. (2000). *Bound of justice*. Cambridge, UK: Cambridge University Press.

Sen, A. (1999). Human rights and Asian values. In T. Machan (Ed.), *Business ethics in the global marketplace* (pp. 37–62). Stanford, CA: Hoover Institution Press.

Sen, A. (2000, July 20). East and West: The reach of reason. *The New York Review of Books, 47*(12), 33–38.

Shue, H. (1996). *Basic rights: Subsistence, affluence, and U.S. foreign policy* (2nd ed.). Princeton, NJ: Princeton University Press.

TRUST

T rust is essential for establishing and maintaining mutually advantageous, even amicable, relationships in business or other cooperative social arrangements. A violation of trust will severely test and may end the relationship. There is an old saying that trust arrives on foot but leaves on horseback.

THE DEFINITION PROBLEM

Despite nearly unanimous agreement on the importance of trust as a lubricant for expediting market exchanges and as a glue for cementing cooperative relationships in that market, scholars have failed to achieve consensus on its definition. They have tended to focus on different aspects of trust observed through different disciplinary lenses in a wide variety of contexts, from individual (micro) to organizational (meso) and even societal (macro) levels of analysis and at different stages of development.

Virtually all definitions of trust include two conditions. (1) *Vulnerability*— The person who trusts someone else voluntarily places valued assets at risk when entering into a one-time exchange or an ongoing relationship with another party. (2) *Expectation of reciprocal regard or treatment*—The prospect of mutual gain from cooperative behavior gives rise to an obligation to treat each other fairly, that is to say, without opportunism or guile, and with some expectation of goodwill in the face of vulnerability. Even where trust may appear blind, as in the case of an infant's dependence on its mother, there is an implicit expectation of unqualified goodwill. Blind trust of a stranger may be either foolish or saintly, but it is hardly rational. Consider the case of hiring a babysitter. Parents place their children at some risk when they invite a stranger to serve as a caregiver while they are away. They can mitigate this risk by investigating the background and qualifications of the sitter. They might check on the certification of the candidate by a professional babysitters' association. In the absence of such macro-level institutional assurance, they could ask for letters of reference, either from previous clients or from reputable persons who could attest to the candidate's sterling character and love of children. References from known parents in the neighborhood would weigh more heavily than the word of strangers. Hiring a relative would be even more reassuring, given the strong ties of family feeling. Direct evidence of the sitter's qualifications could be gathered once employment commenced. Especially cautious parents might set up a secret "baby cam" to monitor electronically the sitter's behavior in their absence, possibly providing a live feed to a security firm. However, this kind of covert monitoring would seem better suited to allaying distrust. Trust is most likely to arise from the sitter's personal interactions with the family while providing impeccable care. This history of trust-based behavior can cement a long-term employment relationship and even develop the affective bonds of friendship. Thus, trust arises both from the prospect of vulnerability and from efforts to mitigate that risk by forging bonds of reciprocal benefit and regard.

DIFFERENT DISCIPLINARY PERSPECTIVES ON TYPES AND LEVELS OF TRUST

In general, psychologists have tended to focus on the internal cognitive attributes of those who confer and seek trust, primarily at the interpersonal (micro) level of interaction. Economists have tended to think of trust in terms of ways of minimizing mistrust in economic transactions at the interpersonal or firm (meso) level of analysis. Sociological treatments have focused primarily on the meso (network) and macro (societal) levels of analysis, where trust is treated as an organizational or institutional variable embedded in relationships. Philosophers have devoted remarkably little attention to trust, other than as a desirable indirect outcome of principled action after considering what is right, just, and fair in governing relationships. The recent emergence of turbulent, hypercompetitive market conditions has stimulated considerable cross-disciplinary interest in finding ways of mobilizing trust over time within knowledge-creating networks. A convergence of perspectives on trust across disciplines and at different levels of analysis points to the need for better understanding of the role of ethical, trust-based governance within networks in efforts to develop and sustain a dynamic competitive advantage over time. Thus, much of the definitional confusion can be resolved by recognizing that different disciplines tend to focus on the trust phenomenon at different levels of analysis and from either static or dynamic (stages of development) perspectives. Special attention will be devoted to the treatment of trust within the discipline of economics since this treatment underlies transaction cost assumptions about the role of corporate governance mechanisms for minimizing mistrust in hierarchical relationships.

THE TRANSACTION COST ECONOMICS PERSPECTIVE ON TRUST

When complete contracts govern discrete market transactions—where the terms of one-time economic exchanges are specified, costs and benefits to both parties are measurable, and the contract is enforceable under the law—there is little need for trust. Under such circumstances, valued resources of the buyer and seller are hardly at risk. Trust has potentially greater scope when contracts are "incomplete" or "relational." Such contractual relationships are open-ended and emergent over time, where the terms are not specified fully and thus are subject to learning-based clarification or renegotiation as the exchange relationship unfolds. Institutional economist Oliver Williamson argues that incomplete or relational contracting is much more common than is complete contracting, particularly at the meso level, where business firms are engaged in ongoing economic exchange relationships. This insight gives rise to the "transaction cost-based" theory of the firm, whereby Williamson and others argue that managerial monitoring of underspecified relational contracts, backed by corporate governance mechanisms to control for potential managerial opportunism, tends to minimize transaction costs of hierarchical relationships inside the firm.

Since Williamson defines opportunism as the pursuit of self-interest with guile, it becomes quickly apparent that trust is severely circumscribed within the transaction cost-based theory, as well as in the closely associated "agency theory" of corporate governance. Agency theorists, such as Michael Jensen and William Meckling, argue that the innate opportunistic, self-serving inclinations of human nature must be taken into account by the design of managerial control and incentive systems within the firm. They propose dealing with the "agency problem" (where managers are inclined to serve their own, rather than the ownership, interest) by more closely aligning the interests of managerial agents and shareholder principals. Taking maximization of shareholder value as the unitary purpose of the firm, agency theorists seek closer interest alignment between agents and principals by improving transparency in financial reporting, minimizing conflicts of interest, and designing executive compensation schemes weighted toward bonuses and stock options that pay for superior *financial* performance. Managers are paid to think and act like owners. Such structural remedies seek to recognize and compensate for the inherent *untrustworthiness* of human nature. Many economists are inclined to regard trust as more of an irrational, idiosyncratic, emotional state of mind, which cannot assure efficient and profitable market transactions. Indeed, most of the control and incentive schemes offered by agency theorists and transaction cost economists seem more intent on deterring outbreaks of self-interest with guile, rather than on enhancing trust. Thus, deterrence-based "trust" is the outgrowth of efforts to diminish distrust by controlling for the potential of opportunism, rather than a form of trust, per se.

TRUST AS AN EMBEDDED SOURCE OF SOCIAL CAPITAL

Alternatively, a growing number of scholars have come to argue that trust has real economic value because it not only reduces monitoring and control costs in business transactions but also encourages cooperation, information sharing, and the joint creation of new knowledge, generated within or among firms—hence the recent interest in a "knowledge-based" (similar to a "resource-based") theory of the firm. The work of Janine Nahapiet and Sumantra Ghoshal is especially helpful in developing this argument. If the firm is a social community specializing in creating and transferring knowledge with speed and efficiency, then the key to developing the dynamic competitive capabilities of this network must lie in efforts to invest in and improve returns on a community's *social capital.* This term first appeared in studies of how and why some urban or regional communities developed networks of strong and weak ties that enabled trust and cooperative enterprise to emerge, innovate, and flower into collective action. The operative word here is *developed*—drawing attention to learning processes that enable forms of trust to evolve over time, strengthening and becoming more *embedded* in social relationships. As trust in social relationships builds, social capital accumulates from the cohesiveness and solidarity of strong ties and from the new information and multiple perspectives available in weak ties.

A DEVELOPMENTAL PERSPECTIVE— FROM CALCULATIVE TO RELATIONAL TRUST

Efforts across scholarly disciplines to arrive at a comparative and developmental framework of trust focused on aspects of *calculative* and *relational* trust. Calculative (sometimes called calculus-based) trust arises from the context of shallow or short-term dependence or interdependence between trustor and trustee, primarily at the interpersonal or organizational level of analysis. It is associated with treatments of rational decision-making processes in economic exchanges. A potential exchange relationship is evaluated to determine whether the likely return from cooperation outweighs the risk to valued assets placed in the hands of the trusted party. A positive evaluation of risk and return is based not only on the strength of deterrence safeguards (to reduce distrust) but also on the availability of evidence attesting to the credibility and competence of the trusted party. Given the shallowness or absence of a direct personal connection, trustworthiness is determined from indirect evidence, such as letters of reference or credit reports that attest to a person's or an organization's reliability, competence, and reputation for fair dealing.

The evolutionary stages of trust are mirrored in changes in the terms and conditions of the "prisoner's dilemma" game—a classic role-playing simulation of game theorists in which each "prisoner" must evaluate the costs and benefits of a self-interested or a cooperative strategy. When neither prisoner has any information about the motives of the other, then the winning strategy is to rat out the other prisoner in exchange for a reduced sentence. In the absence of information about the other prisoner's intentions, blind trust is foolhardy. However, Robert Axelrod has shown that a cooperative "tit-for-tat" strategy based on trust followed by verification of reciprocal regard offers more gains or, at least, reduced losses for both parties over time. By extending this game to an infinite number of plays, others have shown that a tit-for-tat strategy of building trust and cooperation over time has a higher payoff than do strategies of either unconditional opportunism or one-sided altruism. Thus, over the long run, self-interested rationality discovers the net benefit of at least some degree of cooperation with others. It is at this point of learned self-awareness of the value of working and living together with others over time that calculative trust begins to fade into relational trust.

Relational trust builds from a history of direct, personal interactions over time, where both parties demonstrate a willingness to forego the possibility of short-term gain from a default of contractual or moral obligations. Relational trust can arise out of the earlier stage of calculative trust, though some authors prefer to think of these as discrete forms of trust. The initial rational assessment of costs and benefits associated with an opportunity for cooperative exchange can be enriched by the growth of more emotional ties of friendship.

Thus, relational trust is also known as "affective trust," where a handshake, or even a hug, can take on new meaning as the relationship deepens. Relational trust may evolve into an even deeper form, frequently called "identity-based trust." Over time, the reciprocal perception of "I" and "thou" can be transformed into the shared identity of a "we" relationship. Under conditions of deep interdependence, equivalent to a marriage, partners feel that they can act with the other party's interests in mind since their interests are virtually synonymous. Such deep emotional ties are not irrational since they typically are built over time from a history of mutual advantage and shared regard. Moreover, a violation of trust in a marriage or a friendship can be devastating to the relationship. Even so, a violation of calculus-based trust tends to be more damaging since shallow relationships built on rational calculations and indirect evidence tend to be more fragile when they are not supported by subsequent facts on the ground. Relational trust is more resilient because emotional bonds tend to stretch before they snap. An act of contrition followed by sincere efforts to renew commitment to the other can restore relational trust over time. Trust, but verify. In other words, honesty is the best policy, both in personal relationships and in business dealings, over the long or short run.

What is the connection between ethics and trust? Social scientists have been reluctant to trace a link between behavioral manifestations of trust and the normative realm of ethics. They prefer to describe and predict what "is" in the "real world," whereas moral philosophers are more concerned with deriving normative rules that point the way toward achieving an idealized "good life." The failure of philosophers to agree on a set of decision rules (Kantianism, utilitarianism, pragmatism, virtue ethics, and social contracting, among others) for deriving ethical norms has not improved prospects for integrating the realms of "is" and "ought." Economists, as reluctant and partial converts to the possibility that trust (as opposed to the deterrence of distrust) may have some economic value, are even more reluctant to confer on ethics a role in economic decision making. Business ethicists ask corporate executives to suspend their laser-like focus on profit whenever an ethical dilemma arises that requires consideration of the rights, values, and interests of nonowner stakeholders in the firm. When the bilateral obligations of principal-agent relationships are supplanted by the more complex, multilateral demands of a multistakeholder network, prospects for enacting a straightforward economic "rationality" dim. Economists resist normative calls for a more comprehensive corporate citizenship practice, to the extent that such calls appear to be driven by emotional appeals to altruism, rather than to the "rational" pursuit of self-interest. Management scholars, noting the growing role of intra- and inter-organizational cooperation in leveraging competitive capabilities, have drawn attention to the importance of trust in developing and sustaining productive relationships. However, they have been less successful in showing how management practices that create and maintain trust relate to ethical governance.

Remarkably, even moral philosophers have not considered the trust/ethics connection very carefully. LaRue Tone Hosmer, a notable business ethicist, observed that philosophers tend to regard trust in relationships as a fortuitous by-product of the responsible application of ethical judgment. However, trust becomes a central concern and an essential output of ethical decision making in the "good life" when all members of a community come to realize that they can't achieve their own ends without taking into account the rights and interests of others. Ultimately, ethical norms guide the actions of men and women of *goodwill,* who voluntarily assume the risks and responsibilities of working out productive relationships according to the principles of fairness and justice. Thus, trust necessarily arises from an amalgam of self-interested and other-regarding motives, neither of which is sustainable separately for long in the real world.

TRUST IN ETHICAL GOVERNANCE PROCESSES

In the *Academy of Management Review* special issue on trust, Blair Sheppard and Dana Sherman relate different processes for producing trust to the kinds of risks associated with the shallowness or depth of dependent and interdependent relationships. Thus, in a context of shallow dependence, a calculative trust assessment of the risk of a party's unreliability in living up to the terms of a short-term exchange relationship is reinforced by deterrence-based safeguards against opportunistic violation of a reasonably complete contract (a lawsuit, regulatory action, etc.). In a context of deep dependence, however, such as one in which risk to the welfare of a child is involved, deterrence threats are reinforced by claims of obligation that are binding, not only on the party who may harm the child but also on those in a social network who may be aware of the potential for harm. When harm does occur, blame is placed not only directly on the perpetrator but also indirectly on anyone who should have exercised an oversight responsibility. Thus, in situations of deep dependence, the expectation of procedural justice to minimize the risk of harm is closely associated with the condition of trust. Expectations within such relationships take the form of psychological contracts, which are tested periodically, followed by occasional clarification or renegotiation to assure that all parties understand and live up to their obligations. Relational trust may well develop in this context, but the vertical relationship tends to be stable over time. In situations of shallow interdependence, parties in ongoing horizontal relationships must engage in active discovery through exploratory dialogue, often facilitated by contiguity (such as the colocation of parts suppliers and assemblers) and electronic communication linkages. This is the equivalent of prisoners confronting the dilemma of whether to cooperate by opening a communication channel to explore ways to cope with uncertainties in their relationship. Such exploratory exchanges tend to forge the affective bonds of relational trust, which facilitate coordination and cooperation within an open-ended, emergent relationship. In the context of deep interdependence, identity-based trust is produced when parties in an ongoing relationship have internalized each other's values and preferences to a point where the risk of mistaking each other's intentions is controlled by discursive construction of a shared meaning.

CONCLUSION

The above analytical and developmental framework has powerful implications for the role of ethical governance processes in building and sustaining trust. In situations of shallow dependence, rational calculations of the risk of unreliable or incompetent behavior, backed by institutional mechanisms for deterring distrust, leave a relatively modest scope for ethics as an auxiliary tool for minimizing transaction costs in short-term exchanges. Ethical considerations have a larger role in reinforcing the normative obligations associated with deep dependency in more lasting vertical relationships. Ethics has a critical role to play in generating affective and identity-based trust within learning processes that govern interdependent relationships, particularly at the meso level of intra- and interorganizational alliances. To the extent that capability building (especially knowledge creation) supplants cost reduction as a rationale for cooperation, the production of relational trust via dialogic interactions is essentially an investment in social capital, from which increased cooperation in the production of new knowledge flows. While deep dependence obligations can be embedded within hierarchical relationships, sustaining both shallow and deep interdependence requires a collaborative, consultative style and open communication for managing near-horizontal relationships among network partners. To the extent that knowledge creation in interdependent networks supplants transaction-cost reduction in hierarchies, the scope for ethical interactions among managers and stakeholders of value-creating networks will grow. When value is defined more broadly, to encompass social and environmental as well as economic measures, the management of complex stakeholder networks must take into account more fully the role of trust and ethical obligations of fairness and justice to govern cooperative efforts to realize the promise of the good life.

—Jerry M. Calton

Further Readings

Axelrod, R. (1984). *The evolution of cooperation.* New York: Basic Books.

Hosmer, L. T. (1995). Trust: The connecting link between organizational theory and philosophical ethics. *Academy of Management Review, 20,* 379–403.

Jensen, M. C., & Meckling, W. M. (1976). Theory of the firm: Managerial behavior, agency costs, and ownership structure. *Journal of Financial Economics, 3,* 305–360.

Kramer, R. M., & Tyler, T. R. (Eds.). (1996). *Trust in organizations: Frontiers of theory and research.* Thousand Oaks, CA: Sage.

Nahapiet, J., & Ghoshal, S. (1998). Social capital, intellectual capital, and the organizational advantage. *Academy of Management Review, 23,* 242–266.

Rousseau, D. M., Sitkin, S. B., Burt, R. S., & Camerer, C. (1998). Not so different after all: A cross-discipline view of trust. *Academy of Management Review, 23,* 393–404.

Sheppard, B. H., & Sherman, D. M. (1998). The grammars of trust: A model and general implications. *Academy of Management Review, 23,* 422–437.

Williamson, O. E. (1985). *The economic institutions of capitalism.* New York: Free Press.

Trust

INTEGRITY

Integrity can be defined as the quality of being honest and morally upright. Integrity is a crucial foundation for all trustworthy stakeholder relations in business. More specifically, integrity is both a personal and a social capacity to coherently process moral awareness, deliberation, character, and conduct, to regularly render balanced and inclusive judgments regarding moral results, rules, character, and context, to routinely demonstrate mature moral reasoning and relationship development, and to design and/or sustain morally supportive intraorganizational and extraorganizational systems. The four dimensions of integrity are process, judgment, development, and system capacities; they both enable and reflect moral coherence, moral wholeness, moral maturity, and moral environment.

PROCESS INTEGRITY AND MORAL COHERENCE

Process integrity capacity is the coherent alignment of individual and collective moral awareness, deliberation, character, and conduct. The need to address lapses in process integrity capacity is evident by the frequent disconnect between business moral rhetoric and actual behavior that provokes stakeholder criticism of moral hypocrisy, for example, multinational corporations that tout their public relations images of being responsible corporate citizens while engaging in morally objectionable practices that pollute the natural environment and exploit indigenous workers.

Ordinary language definitions of personal integrity as embodying cohesive and sincere adherence to moral principles and commitments refer to process integrity capacity. A person of integrity is commonly understood to be one who is morally aware (i.e., perceives, discerns, and is sensitive to moral issues), demonstrates both autonomous reflection and interdependent moral deliberation in the analysis and resolution of moral problems, is ready to act ethically (i.e., exercises intellectual, social, moral, emotional, and political virtues that build strong character and motivation to act ethically), and engages in responsible, aligned, and sustainable conduct (i.e., takes action that is consistent with personal moral resolutions on a regular basis, even at great personal sacrifice, and can publicly applaud the moral justifications for doing so). Moral coherence between belief and expression, awareness and deliberation, word and deed, and among moral judgments, commitments, and actions is a hallmark of authentic personal integrity.

Moral coherence also entails social process integrity. Teams, firms, cities, and institutions, for example, with high process integrity capacity are more likely than competitors to be aware of and rapidly respond to multiple stakeholder moral concerns, arrive at balanced decisions that form sound policies, and build supportive moral systems that sustain business and social excellence. They exhibit a coherent unity of purpose and action in the face of moral complexity rather than succumb to collective inertia or biased decision making.

JUDGMENT INTEGRITY AND MORAL WHOLENESS

Integrity also entails moral wholeness that is enabled by and reflected in judgment integrity capacity. Judgment integrity capacity is the balanced and inclusive use of key ethics theories and dialogic resources in multiple stakeholder relationships to analyze and resolve individual and/or collective moral issues. Ethics theories can be organized into four categories: teleological ethics theories (emphasizing moral results/purposes), deontological ethics theories (emphasizing moral rules), virtue ethics theories (emphasizing moral character), and system development ethics theories (emphasizing moral contexts). Personal moral wholeness is determined by the degree to which an individual in interaction with multiple stakeholder relations achieves good results, follows the right rules, cultivates virtuous character, and sustains morally supportive contexts throughout life without underemphasizing or overemphasizing any of these factors. On the other hand, ruthless individuals who overemphasize the achievement of good short-term financial results while violating moral and legal rules, forging vicious character traits such as callous insensitivity to others and destroying morally supportive contexts, demonstrate a lack of moral wholeness and dishonor the diversity of stakeholder relationships.

At the social level, exhibiting moral wholeness and judgment integrity capacity for teams, organizations, cities, and institutions means optimally achieving good results (profits in the private sector, votes in the public sector, and donations in the nonprofit sector) by adhering to standards of right conduct and following the right rules, while habitually developing virtuous character traits in moral work climates and creating or sustaining morally supportive intraorganizational and extraorganizational contexts. All four theories and their arguments communicated in a dialogic relationship, with appropriate emphases for each issue, are necessary for inclusive and balanced analysis and resolution of moral issues. Business leaders who refuse to engage in the moral dialogue process and unilaterally insist on overemphasizing or underemphasizing good results, right means, virtuous character, and/or morally supportive contexts incur the same adverse consequences as business leaders who cannot handle behavioral complexity, that is, offended individuals, neglected opportunities, eroded trust, and corrupted environments.

The moral wholeness of social judgment integrity capacity is also demonstrated by the extent to which specific moral principles guide role relationship decisions in the private, public, nonprofit, and corporate domains. In the private domain of shared interests, for example, role relationships between doctor and patient, producer and consumer, or teacher and student, moral wholeness is demonstrated by the extent to which the moral principles of equality, decency, reciprocity, and honesty are included in and guide transactional and participatory ethics decisions. In the private domain of conflicting interests, moral wholeness is demonstrated by the extent to which the moral principles of justice, honoring diversity, and beneficence are included in and guide recognitional ethics decisions. At times morally whole persons give precedence to the rights of others over their own interests out of respect for retributive justice, the inherent value of relationship diversity, and beneficence, that is, avoid doing harm, repair or compensate the harm you did, prevent harm being done by others, avoid bringing about conditions that generate harm, and do good wherever and whenever you can to sustain trustworthy relationships.

In the public domain, for example, role relationships between elected officials and citizens, public employees and government authorities, and public administrators and natural resources, moral wholeness is demonstrated by the extent to which the moral principles of public deliberation, fairness, civic cooperation, concern for the common good and public trust, secure civic reciprocity, and responsible natural stewardship are included in and guide representative and ecological ethics decisions. In the nonprofit domain, for example, role relationships between donors and recipients, volunteers and NGO administrators, and needy populations and international aid agencies, moral wholeness is demonstrated by the extent to which moral principles of cultural openness, transparency, respecting resource boundaries, compassionate sensitivity, accountable generosity, planetary citizenship, and emancipation are included in and guide civil society and philanthropic ethics decisions. In the corporate domain, for example, in role relationships between employees and employers, suppliers and distributors, and investors and managers, moral wholeness is demonstrated by the extent to which the moral principles of meritocratic justice, respect for ownership rights and multiple stakeholder interests, legal growth and responsible property management, corporate citizenship, and triple bottom line accountability are included in and guide market ethics decisions.

DEVELOPMENTAL INTEGRITY AND MORAL MATURITY

Developmental integrity capacity is the cognitive and affective final improvement stage of individual and collective moral reasoning and caring relationship formation capabilities from an initial stage of preconventional self-interested concern (morally immature, selfish connivance) through a stage of conforming to external conventional standards (partially morally mature, external-governing compliance) to a final stage of postconventional commitment to universal ethical principles and responsive caring relationships (morally mature, self-governing civic integrity). Postconventional principled moral reasoning and caring relationship prioritization demonstrate moral maturity. Morally mature leaders are living examples of developmental integrity capacity who have internalized their identity-conferring commitment to universal principles such as justice and responsive caring relationships, are emotionally attuned to their stakeholders, and elevate the moral expectations and performance of stakeholders to the level of social integrity. Erik Erikson, for example, regarded integrity as the highest stage of personal ethical and psychological development.

Individual and collective connivance is the lowest stage of moral development, characterized by the use of direct force and/or indirect manipulation to determine moral standards. Business leaders and work climates that sustain this stage of moral immaturity are either issuing threats of force (e.g., "Get it done now or else") or developing exclusively exploitative relationships based on mutual manipulation (e.g., "I'll lie for you if you lie for me") to enact a moral jungle. Firms and societies that abuse their members perpetuate this moral immaturity.

Individual and collective compliance is the intermediate stage of moral development, characterized by either conforming to popular work norms or adherence to externally imposed standards. Business leaders and work climates that sustain this stage of partial moral maturity abandon the moral jungle and are either admonishing employees to secure peer approval (e.g., "Everyone in your work group must follow these traditional standard operating procedures") or commanding them to comply with organizational hierarchy and/or externally imposed regulations (e.g., "You must conform to government regulatory standards or you will be imprisoned"). Corporate external compliance efforts prevent criminal misconduct and limit corporate legal liability, but they do not enable responsible internally governed moral behavior. Compliant business leaders whose highest moral aspirations are to stay out of jail are not operating at the level of commitment to developmental integrity.

Individual and collective commitment to integrity is the highest stage of moral development, characterized by the use of substantive democratic participation and/or internalized respect for universal moral principles and caring stakeholder relationships as a basis for determining moral standards. Business leaders and work climates that sustain this stage of moral maturity are either identifying and satisfying the wishes of the majority (e.g., "Everyone should participate in public deliberations and vote, but the majority opinion will prevail in policy formation") or eliciting commitment to universal moral standards (e.g., "Whatever policies we adopt by consensus must meet universal standards of justice, care, and global citizenship"). Firms and societies committed to developmental integrity standards act like morally mature citizens on behalf of other internal and external stakeholders—domestically and globally.

SYSTEM INTEGRITY CAPACITY AND MORAL ENVIRONMENT

System integrity capacity is the demonstrable capability to design or sustain organizational moral infrastructures and extraorganizational relationships that provide a supportive moral environment for ethical conduct. The system contexts within an organization and outside it can either support or inhibit ethical action; for example, the morally impoverished environment of a corrupt organization located in a crime-infested city in a bribery-riddled nation on a heavily polluted planet inhibits viable institutionalization of system integrity capacity. Individuals and collectives that design or sustain supportive moral environments at the intraorganizational and extraorganizational levels demonstrate system integrity capacity.

At the intraorganizational level, system integrity leaders design or sustain purposes, policies, processes, and procedures that not only meet legal compliance standards, for example, conformity to the revised U.S. Federal Sentencing Guidelines and the Sarbanes-Oxley Act, but also support relational integrity, for example, individual respect for employees as citizens; secure trustworthy, reciprocal interpersonal work relations; empowered, justly compensated, and collaborative teams; use of organizational ethics needs assessments and system moral performance improvement measurements; and reward/reporting systems that hold all employees accountable to ethical standards.

At the extraorganizational level, subnational entities such as cities, states, or regions, national sociopolitical cultures, and international human and nonhuman standards create moral environments that enhance or inhibit process, judgment, and developmental integrity capacities. For example, since business leaders and firms are a part of the system of domestic civil society, the extent to which they form cooperative partnerships with city, state, regional, and national sociopolitical leaders to cosponsor projects that mutually support human flourishing and intergenerational coprosperity indicates their capacity for designing and sustaining domestic system integrity. In addition, since business leaders and firms are a part of the system of global civil society, the extent to which they promote responsible industry standards globally, support international laws, treaties, and standards for free and fair trade, endorse global human and natural sustainability standards, for example, the Global Compact principles of respect for human rights, fair labor standards, natural environment stewardship, and anticorruption and the Earth Charter provisions of caring for the community of life, ecological system integrity, socioeconomic justice, and democracy, nonviolence, and peace, indicates their capacity for designing and sustaining global system integrity.

—Joseph A. Petrick

Further Readings

Brown, M. T. (2005). *Corporate integrity.* New York: Cambridge University Press.
Carter, S. L. (1996). *Integrity.* New York: Basic Books.
Petrick, J. A., & Quinn, J. F. (1997). *Management ethics: Integrity at work.* Thousand Oaks, CA: Sage.
Petrick, J. A., & Quinn, J. F. (2000). The integrity capacity construct and moral progress in business. *Journal of Business Ethics, 23*(1), 3–18.

Integrity

ETHICAL DECISION MAKING

E thical decision making is a cognitive process that considers various ethical principles, rules, and virtues or the maintenance of relationships to guide or judge individual or group decisions or intended actions. It helps one determine the right course of action or the right thing to do and also enables one to analyze whether another's decisions or actions are right or good. It seeks to answer questions about how one is supposed to act or live.

ETHICAL DECISION-MAKING PROCESS

Many ethics scholars have developed models of ethical decision making or provided us with specific procedural steps enabling one to reach an ethically supported decision or course of action. In the abstract, this process is a fairly rational and logical course. In reality, ethical decision making is filled with abstractness, illogic, and even whim. Nonetheless, the following is a synthesis of these models and procedures.

Step 1: Identify the Ethical Dimensions Embedded in the Problem

In the first step of the ethical decision-making process, the decision maker must be able to determine if an ethical analysis is required. The decision maker must determine if there is a possible violation of an important ethical principle, societal law, or organizational standard or policy or if there are potential consequences that should be sought or avoided that emanate from an action being considered to resolve the problem.

Step 2: Collect Relevant Information

The decision maker must collect the relevant facts to continue in the ethical decision-making process. Related to Step 1, if an ethical principle, such as an individual's right, is in jeopardy of being violated, the decision maker should seek to gather as much information as possible about which rights are being forsaken and to what degree. A consequential focus would prompt the decision maker to attempt to measure the type, degree, and amount of harm being inflicted or that will be inflicted on others.

Step 3: Evaluate the Information According to Ethical Guidelines

Once the information has been collected, the decision maker must apply some type of standard or assessment criterion to evaluate the situation. As described below, the decision maker might use one of the predominant ethics theories—utilitarianism, rights, or justice. Adherence to a societal law or organizational policy may be an appropriate evaluation criterion. Others may consider assessing the relevant information based on a value system where various ethical principles or beliefs are held in varying degrees of importance.

Step 4: Consider Possible Action Alternatives

The decision maker needs to generate a set of possible action alternatives, such as confronting another person's actions, seeking a higher authority, or stepping in and changing the direction of what is happening. This step is important since it is helpful to limit the number of actions that it may realistically be possible to respond to or that may be required to resolve the ethical situation.

Step 5: Make a Decision

In Step 5, the decision maker should seek the action alternative that is supported by the evaluation criteria used in Step 3. Sometimes there may be a conflict between the right courses of action indicated by different ethics theories, as shown later in the illustration provided. It might not be possible in all cases for a decision maker to select a course of action that is supported by all the ethics theories or other evaluation criteria used in the decision-making process.

Step 6: Act or Implement

Ethical decision making is not purely an intellectual exercise. The decision maker, if truly seeking to resolve the problem being considered, must take action. Therefore, once the action alternatives have been identified in Step 4 and the optimal response is selected in Step 5, the action is taken in Step 6.

Step 7: Review the Action, Modify if Necessary

Finally, once the action has been taken and the results are known, the decision maker should review the consequences of the action and whether the action upheld the ethical principles sought by the decision maker. If the optimal resolution to the problem is not achieved, the decision maker may need to modify the actions being taken or return to the beginning of the decision-making process to reevaluate the analysis of the facts leading to the action alternative selected.

APPLYING ETHICS THEORIES

The following is an illustration of Step 3 of the ethical decision-making process that applies three predominant ethics theories—utilitarianism, rights, and justice—to a common business problem: Should a company close an operating plant and lay off its workers?

When using a *utilitarian perspective*—where the decision maker considers the consequences or outcomes of an action and seeks to maximize the greatest good for the greatest number of those affected by the decision—it is critical for the decision maker to determine to the greatest extent possible who will be affected by the decision. In the example used here, those affected may include the company itself (since closing the plant may improve its bottom line by dramatically reducing plant overhead and employee payroll expenses); the company's investors, if a publicly held business (who may receive a greater return on their investment if the plant closes and employees are laid off); the company's employees (who will suffer if the plant closes and they are laid off from their jobs); and the local community where the plant is located (who will suffer a reduction in the municipal tax base as well as a loss of economic activity for businesses that relied on the plant and its employees).

One might argue that the greater good is served if some workers are immediately laid off and the plant is closed, ensuring the immediate financial viability of the company. Yet others might reason to an ethical solution that requests all employees to take a slight pay cut so that no workers are laid off and the plant remains open, thus achieving the greatest good for the greatest number of people affected.

A decision maker who considers a *rights perspective* would consider the entitlements of those affected by the decision. There are economic rights affecting the displaced employees and the community surrounding the plant in question, as well as the rights of the laid-off employees to be informed of the potential plant closing. These rights may be in opposition to the managers' right to act freely in a way that could be understood as acting responsibly, by closing the plant and thus benefiting the remaining employees of the company and the company's investors.

A rights reasoner might provide ample notice to the workers of the layoffs so that they could seek other employment. Or the rights reasoner might consider the economic rights of the community and actively seek a buyer for the plant in the hope that it would remain open and continue to employ the workers. Finally, the rights of the company and its investors could persuade the decision maker to conclude that closing the plant and firing the workers is the right thing to do.

Finally, one who considers a *justice perspective* may focus on either the equitable distribution of the benefits and costs resulting from the plant closing and employee layoffs (distributive justice) or the maintenance of rules and standards (procedural justice). For the distributive justice reasoner, the ethical decision process would focus not only on the benefits incurred by the company and its investors through the plant closure and layoffs but also on the significant harms or costs imposed on those employees laid off from work and the local community and businesses negatively affected by the plant closing.

The procedural justice reasoner would focus on the preservation of the social contract that exists between the employer and employees or would seek to minimize the harm imposed on the powerless (the employees and the local community) by the powerful (the employer and investors). The procedural justice reasoner would argue that the employees, community officials, and local business leaders should have a voice in this decision since they are significantly affected by the decision.

The decision maker may decide that a more just action would require the company to assume greater financial responsibility by providing job training and outplacement services for the displaced employees. The company could consider making some type of economic contribution to the local community to soften the blow of a reduction in the tax base or economic activity in the area. Or the company could involve the employees and local community leaders in developing a system that results in the plant closure occurring over a longer period of time to spread out the eventual costs endured by the community.

CONCLUSION

People during their daily routine at work or in society are called on to make ethical decisions. Therefore, their ethical decision-making process may be a frequent, yet subconscious, cognitive process. Do you drive the speed limit or come to a complete stop at the intersection where a stop sign is posted? An individual can decide to act in the right way almost without thinking about it, but the decision maker is implicitly considering and processing the steps delineated above to reach the ethically supported decision to obey the speed limit or stop at the intersection in the road.

—James Weber

Further Readings

Beauchamp, T. L., & Bowie, N. E. (Eds.). (2004). *Ethical theory and business* (7th ed.). Upper Saddle River, NJ: Prentice Hall.

Darwall, S. (Ed.). (2003). *Virtue ethics.* Malden, MA: Blackwell.

Hartman, L. P. (1998). *Perspectives in business ethics.* Chicago: Irwin/McGraw-Hill.

Held, V. (Ed.). (1995). *Justice and care: Essential readings in feminist ethics.* Boulder, CO: Westview Press.

Velasquez, M. G. (2002). *Business ethics: Concepts and cases* (5th ed.). Upper Saddle River, NJ: Prentice Hall.

PART III

Theories of Ethics

THEORIES OF ETHICS: OVERVIEW

Ethics is the branch of philosophy that deals with morality. Ethicists are concerned with a wide range of topics, such as human nature; the meaning of life; the nature of value; how judgments are made; how judgments can be improved; how moral attitudes arise and change; and the workings of morally significant mental states such as love, hate, greed, envy, indifference, pity, desire, aversion, pleasure, and pain. Moral or ethical theories offer the means of understanding significant elements in these and other areas of inquiry.

Ethical theories tend either toward merely describing or toward both describing and judging. As a result, some moral theories seem to belong to anthropology, psychology, or sociology, while others look like instances of what ethics purports to study—that is, like moral doctrines or judgments. For this reason, a major distinction employed by moral theorists distinguishes descriptive from prescriptive, or normative, theories, or elements of theories.

Moral judgments tend to state that something is either good or bad or that something agrees or conflicts with our obligations. Consequently, a major division in moral theories is between theories of value (axiology) and theories of obligation (deontology). In each area, ethicists want to determine the meaning of moral judgments, their truth or falsity, their objectivity or subjectivity, how judgments are made, how they can be tested, how they can be justified, and the possibility of organizing judgments under first principles. A third major distinction places theories about the meaning of moral judgments in a category of their own called metaethics. Obviously, metaethical questions arise in all areas of ethics.

Prescriptive or normative moral thinking recommends at least one moral evaluation, or else it attempts the same for at least one moral obligation. Plato, Aristotle, the Stoics, the Epicureans, and the Cynics sought both to find the best kind of life and to strongly recommend the judgment that it was in fact the best. Others, such as Immanuel Kant, theorized about the nature of obligation and also provided grounds for justifying or recommending certain obligations. The theories of David Hume, Arthur Schopenhauer, Darwinism, and Logical Positivism exemplify the tendency to separate the task of description from that of prescription, or to eschew prescription altogether, in order to describe and organize moral judgments for the sake of understanding alone.

The unwavering pursuit of the metaethical question of the meaning of moral judgments brought many recent philosophers to the conclusion that moral judgments are not the sort of statements that can be true or false but instead express resolutions, preferences, feelings, demands, or other states of mind. Hume thought that they reported subjective feelings, so that a judgment such as "Insider trading is immoral" would not be understood as ascribing a predicate to insider trading but as saying something like "I disapprove of that act." A. J. Ayer, a Logical Positivist, believed that moral judgments did not report feelings but merely expressed them. For him, the statement "Insider trading is immoral" merely expresses a negative emotional reaction to stealing—along the lines of "Boo insider trading!" Such expressions are neither true nor false because they do not describe anything. Hume and Ayer represent the school known as Emotivism. A neighboring school, Prescriptivism, interprets "Insider trading is immoral" as an imperative, "Do not engage in insider trading," which is neither true nor false because it is a command rather than a description.

In value theory, the primary questions are first about the meaning of value terms, then about the status of value. With regard to meaning, the first question is whether value or goodness can be defined and, if so, how. For Plato and W. D. Ross, the good is indefinable, yet it names an intrinsic property of things, making it objective. For the Intuitionists, such as G. E. Moore, value is indefinable, objective, and absolute. Many ethicists believe that value can be defined so as to name something that is both objective and absolute, as did Aristotle, who defined the good as that at which all things aim. For others, the good has its seat in subjectivity and will be different for different persons or groups.

After the meaning and status of value, the chief concern in value theory has been the question of which things are of the highest value. The main answers have been a state of feeling, such as pleasure or satisfaction (Epicurus; Thomas Hobbes, John Stuart Mill); a state of the will, such as virtue (Epictetus) or power (Friedrich Nietzsche); or a state of the intellect, such as knowledge (Plato) or good intentions (Kant).

In the theory of obligation, similar questions have been posed. With regard to questions about the meaning and status of "right" and "wrong," Intuitionists hold that they name an indefinable, objective quality. Emotivists believe that right can have only an emotive, subjective meaning. Psychological and social thinkers typically hold that judgments of right and wrong indicate the attitudes of some person or group toward an act.

Theories of Ethics: Overview

53

In response to the question of which things are right in the sense of their being morally obligatory, there are both teleological and nonteleological answers. For the teleologist, an act is right according to how much good it brings, or will probably bring, into the world. For the egoist, the amount of good brought to the agent is decisive (Epicurus, Hobbes), while for the universalist, it is the amount brought to the world as a whole (utilitarianism). Meanwhile, Thomas Aquinas and others have argued that an act is right according to its intent, so that an act with a comparatively better intent is a comparatively more righteous act. All these answers to the question of what is obligatory rely on a theory of value and, thus, make deontology dependent on axiology.

A fully deontological theory is supposed to hold that an act is obligatory regardless of its consequences for human happiness, ends, or other values. Deontologists, such as Kant, hold that right conduct can be determined by considering a priori principles, such as rights and laws. Kant's view was that objectively right conduct could arise from many sources, such as benevolence, prudence, or habit. However, the highest and the only morally significant motive for right action was respect for the moral law. If a course of action suggested by benevolence, pity, sentiment, or any other motive conflicted with the course indicated by moral law, respect for moral law ought to win out. The good will, the will truly searching for its duties so as to fulfill them, is supremely good for Kant, and the moral worth of an act is always guaranteed by the agent's intent to follow the moral law, regardless of any other motive or consequence.

Deontology is squarely opposed to teleological approaches to obligation because it holds that the end can never justify the means. Hence, violating another's rights cannot be justified by its serving a praiseworthy goal. Consequentialist theories, such as utilitarianism, hinge the goodness of conduct to its consequences and, hence, seem prepared to overlook a violation of rights as long as the consequences of the violation are highly valuable. In contrast, it has been said that the deontologist's motto appears to be "Let justice be done though the heavens fall." Kant argued that one must not lie even to save the life of an innocent man and that one must not commit suicide even when life has no further meaning or purpose. For Kant there can be no exceptions to moral laws because if they are to count as moral laws, they must at a minimum be universalizable. Hence, if suicide is immoral when life has purpose, it must also be immoral when it does not, and if lying to obtain a loan is immoral, lying must also be immoral in life-and-death situations.

Another version of deontology comes from theology, in which our moral duties are given by a deity. Divine command theories hold that regardless of any consequences for life or limb, we must do what the deity commands.

Virtue ethics is often described as an alternative to normative deontology because its normative elements concern the qualities of persons rather than the qualities of acts. Plato, Aristotle, and many Eastern systems of thought focus on what kind of person one ought to try to be rather than on which actions one ought to take or avoid. For Aristotle, who understood ethics as the branch of learning concerned with achieving the good life, the virtues are precisely those characteristics that make the character good and that lead to the good life. These include courage, prudence, wit, truthfulness, temperance, and justice, among others. Its detractors often say that virtue ethics is dependent on prescriptive moral judgments yet offers no insight into them.

Beyond theories of value and obligation, ethicists examine moral reasoning in their efforts to understand how our conduct is chosen and how moral judgments are or ought to be made. According to the Emotivists, a moral judgment comes about when one looks at an act or policy, consults one's sentiment, and pronounces morally about it. For teleologists, moral judgments are or ought to be made by considering the comparative amount of good or bad that an action can or does bring about. For Kantians, moral judgments ought to be made by considering the one obligation that determines all others—namely, to act so that you can at the same time honestly will that all others would act as you do. For divine command theorists, the will of the deity must be consulted in making accurate moral judgments.

One of the greatest challenges to all normative ethical theories lies in the problem of free will. We generally consider acts praiseworthy or blameworthy only if their agent could have acted otherwise. If we lack free will, we are apparently never able to do otherwise and, hence, our acts do not deserve either praise or blame. The school known as Compatibilism argues that belief in the moral status of human acts is compatible with an absence of free will. Incompatibilists, such as Nietzsche, argue that if we lack free will, statements about the moral status of human acts perpetuate a cruel myth.

A second, more contemporary challenge to normative ethics arises from the question of whether there are moral facts in the world and, if there are, whether moral judgments describe them. Moral realism answers that there are moral facts and that our judgments can describe them, and thus affirms at least three things: (1) that moral judgments are propositional, meaning that they can be either true or false because they attempt to describe features of the world; (2) that there are moral facts to be described; and (3) that moral facts are objectively present in the world, independent of our thoughts and feelings. Noncognitivism in ethics holds that moral judgments do not describe, and so are nonpropositional, and thus can be neither true nor false.

—Bryan Finken

Further Readings

Aristotle. (1984). *Nicomachean ethics* (*The Complete Works of Aristotle*, J. Barnes, Ed.). Princeton, NJ: Princeton University Press.

Ayer, A. J. (1952). *Language, truth and logic.* New York: Dover.

Hobbes, T. (1994). *Leviathan* (E. Curley, Ed.). Chicago: Hackett.

Hume, D. (2000). *A treatise of human nature* (D. F. Norton & M. J. Norton, Eds.). Oxford, UK: Oxford University Press.

Joyce, R. (2006). *The evolution of morality.* Cambridge: MIT Press.

Kant, Immanuel. (1985). *Grounding for the metaphysics of morals* (J. W. Ellington, Trans.). Indianapolis, IN: Hackett.

Mill, J. S. (1991). *Utilitarianism* (Collected Works of John Stuart Mill, J. M. Robson, Ed.). Toronto, Ontario, Canada: University of Toronto Press.

Moore, G. E. (1903). *Principia ethica.* Cambridge, UK: Cambridge University Press.

PART III: Theories of Ethics

VIRTUE ETHICS

V irtue is a condition of a person's character. Having virtue makes doing the right thing the obvious choice among options. Having virtue means that immoral courses of action are ruled out, and this quickens decision making. Virtuous persons would have already determined that they ought to do only whatever is right in a situation. If a person has virtue, this means that he or she does not merely have good intentions but has the ability to act on them. People who manage to be consistently ethical are likely to have virtue to some degree. Those who knowingly act immorally lack virtue. And those who cannot tell the difference between wrong and right lack virtue.

Whether virtue is a set of qualities or just one; whether virtue is a permanent state of character or a temporary condition; whether virtue is the result of a conscious or unconscious process of development, inborn or merely a matter of culture—these are matters for the various authors of virtue ethics to determine. Authors must also decide how virtue relates to an account of right action. Either a description of virtue serves as an addendum to other ethical approaches, and the moral psychology required for virtue is not invoked in a determination of right and wrong, or the requirements of virtue alone determine what right action is. Virtue ethics may be more or less theoretical. The more theoretical accounts revise our commonsense opinions on good character. The less theoretical accounts endorse commonsense notions. Though every contemporary account of virtue derives some inspiration from the ancient accounts, most contemporary accounts are less theoretical than these and more dependent on the criteria of ethics and justice offered by alternative approaches.

There are particular challenges to determining the morality of business decisions and policies with an account of virtue. The description of a virtuous businessperson has utility, of course. The qualities that contribute to a company's success are not always recognized or well understood. Companies may be encouraged to foster or better reward these traits. Yet specific guidelines for business decisions and policies have not, thus far, been traced back to compatibility with a recommended moral psychology. This means that most often virtue serves only as an addendum to other determinations of what is ethical in business. Whatever the role of virtue in ethical theory, further empirical research into the connections between institutional practice and good behavior is sure to be a boon to the study of virtue.

ANCIENT ACCOUNTS OF VIRTUE

The ancient tradition in ethics was committed to an understanding of happiness (*eudaimonia*) as our highest good. Today, we tend to think of happiness as something fleeting, as something we can experience in an afternoon. The ancients meant, by *eudaimonia,* something more like the subjective experience of leading a good life. We are, the ancients explained, tempted to organize our lives around goals that seem immediately good to us: power, pleasure, wealth, and fame. There is, of course, some good in all these, but to pursue them all is problematic since they involve contradictory requirements. To attain great power, you may need to sacrifice pleasure. This may not seem to be a practical impediment, and indeed the ancients would not argue that it was. Many unvirtuous people attain great power. We all trade off various goals for others at any time. The common temptation, warned the ancients, was to pursue these goals in a single-minded or unreflective fashion. In either case, we are failing to reflect on why we pursue what we do. Such reflection, according to the ancients, can be fruitful. Our psychology, the ancients argued, will not find itself satisfied until we come to understand and implement an understanding of the ultimate point of our lives. And the ultimate point of our lives will not be to accumulate goods or accomplishments that can easily be taken away. It will not be to possess things whose care can so easily consume us with worry and attention. The ultimate point of our lives will not, once understood, leave us feeling that we have not had enough no matter how much we have got. The ancients argued that the ultimate goal in our lives would have to be of a different sort of nature than the goods and goals we tend to think make us happy.

The most likely candidate for an ultimate goal would be psychological in nature, since the above requirements would be met only by a change within one's self. Pursuing this goal would transform our pursuit of less long-term goods in our lives. Professional goals, for example, would be put into their proper context within a life. This would make them less likely to disappoint and more likely to be pursued responsibly. Once we discover for ourselves this most final end, we will come to understand what true happiness is, and commonsense accounts of happiness can be abandoned, recognized to be poorly developed. What remains to be explained is how morality fits into this description of an ultimate goal capable of organizing our lives.

Morality

The ancients determined that all our immoral impulses were the result of having goals other than the sort of long-term happiness just described. Whether we lie to our boss, steal from the company, or betray colleagues, we have often calculated the benefits of doing these things from a less than comprehensive perspective on our lives.

The major schools of ancient ethics came to the conclusion that a life lived for the sake of being moral was the best candidate for our most comprehensive and long-term goal, happiness. This is, of course, a striking and bold claim. Some contemporary ethicists reject it as ridiculous on its face. A virtue ethicist will not recognize, for example, that a corrupt businessperson can be happy or that a deceitful person can actually benefit from deceitful practice. The assumptions that underlie these claims are as follows. True value is not as obvious as we think it is (it is not reducible, e.g., to a promotion or a raise). Our psychologies are of such a nature that they can function unimpeded only when moral precepts have been internalized. The consequence of committing one's self to such a life would be the development of the virtues.

It is not helpful to describe ancient descriptions of virtue by listing the terms we use for moral qualities we admire. The ancients, after all, developed the theory described above. Their proposal that we focus on some ultimate, final end is hardly what we would expect to find confirmed by our common-sense judgments about people and their qualities. Commonsense judgments involve all sorts of puzzles. For example, why might a "moral" quality like courage sometimes contribute to bad action? Such puzzles do not exist when the standard for virtue is the ancient one. Clear criteria for virtue are offered by the ancients—it is the psychological condition we develop and require to make moral choices regularly, without tension or weakness of will.

To give a simple example, think of being left alone before the petty cash box in your office. Imagine that it is obvious that you could grab a handful of bills without anyone being the wiser. Many of us might consider taking the money and begin to weigh the consequences of doing so (perhaps double-checking to make sure no cameras are on, that no one is actually nearby, etc.). Others would not even consider taking the money. Those who would not consider taking the money have attained something of virtue. Evidence that considerations of virtue outweigh monetary value comes from thinking about what would happen if your reimbursement from the company for some legitimate expense was short. Even a virtuous person would then ask for the correct amount back. This shows that money has not lost value for the virtuous. Indeed, a dispute about a short reimbursement might happen in front of the very petty cash box that did not tempt the virtuous. For the virtuous, money they deserve has one sort of value; money they do not deserve does not have this same value. This is the effect of committing to a longer-term goal than the simple accumulation of money.

If we practice our commitment to our longest-term goal, we will get better at recognizing which norms apply in a moral situation. There are, of course, all sorts of norms that support not taking the money. A person who refrained from taking could easily recall any one of these ("Do not steal"). To develop virtue requires that the inappropriate and irrelevant norms are not regarded as applicable. ("Jane took from petty cash last month, so I can too.") Think of how common it is for the cost of taxi fares to be misrepresented on an expense report. Those who engage in this practice know, at a very conscious level, that this behavior is wrong, dishonest, and inappropriate. But some other norm encourages the behavior. Likely, it is something like "Everyone else does this" or "Don't be a sucker" or, perhaps, "Do what you can get away with."

In addition, the process of becoming good gets easier as a person's motivation set gets less complicated. To develop virtue requires that your motivations not include contradictions that you may not even be aware of, for example. Those who struggle not to steal, though they desperately want to avoid doing so, have an overly complicated set of motivations with which to contend. Virtue is not assisted by such a condition. To function as a virtuous person, you have to figure out which motivations interfere with doing what you have been able to determine you should do ("Am I too much of a people pleaser? Is that why I gave in to the pressure?").

According to the ancient account, virtue has an intellectual, a dispositional, and an affective component. When these components are described separately, virtue can seem an abstract and theoretical ideal, but we can recognize the effect of the conjunction of these components in the example the author has just given. The intellectual component of virtue is a matter of knowing the money is not yours, that you do not yourself expect to be taken advantage of, and perhaps that the economic system as it exists tends to function well enough for all involved, warranting your endorsement. You would, in other words, be able to explain why stealing is wrong. Virtue ethics does not require that your explanation be technical. Instead, it could be just as the author has described it.

The dispositional component of virtue is a matter of how this propensity not to steal has become second nature to you. You tend not to steal. If you steal in other contexts, and not taking the money in this case was an exception, then your character is not virtuous. To develop a virtuous disposition, you must work on developing the intellectual and affective components of virtue. You must attempt to relate your beliefs about theft, for example, to your understanding of ethics. To find yourself no longer attracted to bad behavior, you must work at internalizing, and truly coming to accept, the coherent account you develop on the topic.

The affective component of virtue is a matter of experiencing pleasure in acting right. People who have made themselves good do not regret money they have not stolen, for example, and they do not see vicious people as having made choices of which they could be envious. This condition comes about only because when we pursue virtue, we become transformed. It is this element that is most frequently left out of contemporary accounts of virtue, even those that hark back to the theory of the ancients.

Virtue Transforms Us

The process of becoming virtuous is much like getting used to being healthy. You must begin by garnering an understanding of what weight loss and health require. If you are misled about this, you are bound to fail. As you start out, you may likely have to reckon with having a taste for donuts and potato chips. This may seem insurmountable, as the donuts and potato chips taste so good and have always proven irresistible in the past. But, perhaps to your surprise, after forcing yourself to exercise for months, you find that not only the exercise itself has gotten easier to do and to include in your day, but eating healthier has gotten easier as well. You no longer even have the taste for junk food and now wonder how anyone could. You have begun to associate junk food with its bad effects: sluggishness and extra weight. Exercise has begun to pay off, and the rewards of it now seem obvious.

This description matches much of how virtue is supposed to work to integrate all our ends: by making what satisfies us fit what is actually good. A junk food fan is not getting optimal feedback from his or her body, and happily, we can transform our tastes. When we act immorally, we are not getting optimal feedback either, and happily, there is, according to virtue ethics, a way to stop ourselves from acting in such an undisciplined fashion. Once we become acclimated to good behavior, perhaps to our surprise, we will recognize that we have come to enjoy and prefer moral to immoral behavior. The temptations of immoral behavior no longer have their allure because the long-term negative consequences of it can be seen as part and parcel of the seeming gains it brings.

Of the ancients, only the Stoics understand our ethical transformation as going so far that we can come to care about virtue to the exclusion of any particular commonsense goods. If we cannot conceivably do this (if even an idealized conception of the human cannot do this) then the Stoics will be wrong about virtue being sufficient for happiness. Other ancient ethicists, such as Aristotle and the Epicureans, are reconciled to the idea that some commonsense goods need only be understood in relation to virtue in order to be properly pursued. To continue the analogy, some ice cream, at some times, might still be perfectly acceptable to the healthy person's system, given that the healthy person is aware of the amount he or she may have and the effects on his or her health.

In contrast to contemporary virtue ethics, however, what matters is that ancient virtue ethics recognizes that virtue involves transformation, and this transformation results from our committing to an accurate understanding of our most final end. This, among other things, makes a eudaimonist account of virtue differ vastly from most modern-day accounts of virtue. Ancient-based accounts of virtue are kept, by their theoretical structure, from having to rely on (or recommend that we follow) a commonsense understanding of the virtues. This is not to say that common sense does not already itself endorse some of ancient virtue theory's insights. We do not, after all, count it as generous when someone gives a gift merely for the sake of impressing someone. Many of the problems associated with the use of virtue ethics come from the invocation of common sense to settle matters that may be better handled by a theoretical standard.

CONTEMPORARY VARIANTS OF VIRTUE ETHICS

Contemporary accounts of virtue ethics always refer back to ancient accounts, and careful authors highlight both the similarities and differences. Three modifications of the traditional approach are most common in contemporary virtue ethics. The first is that ancient theory is replaced with more commonsense notions about virtue. The second is that the notion of a final end is dropped. The third is, as mentioned, that right and wrong are determined in other ways than through a description of virtue.

Common Sense and Virtue

Often, contemporary accounts of virtue are updated by inserting a common-sense conception of virtue in place of the theoretically defined one. What bravery is, for example, is taken to be obvious, and descriptions of bravery are culled from literature and life experience and used to describe the virtue. Rather than looking to what common sense takes to be virtue, the traditional virtue theories determine what virtue is by seeing what will result from a commitment to morality.

Contemporary accounts of virtue are most often more modest about the effects of attaining virtue. According to traditional accounts of virtue, aspects of ourselves under our conscious control (our emotions, our desires) will be transformed as we become virtuous. Contemporary descriptions of virtue are not this spectacular. Very rarely is a virtuous life described as one that has been transformed.

Contemporary accounts of virtue are also more likely to describe virtue as something some people just have. Role models are often given credit. The ancient schools were, in contrast, convinced that the process of developing virtue would have to be active and acutely conscious. This means that the ancient theories of virtue would not recognize as virtues character traits one attains without effort. According to ancient virtue theory, no one is surprised by the sudden discovery that they are virtuous. It is not the sort of thing you could attain without being aware that doing so was your primary agenda.

There are two possible unanticipated consequences to these modifications of traditional virtue theory in contemporary accounts. One is that virtue may be described in a fashion that is not realistic because of the self-sacrifice required. The other is that virtue may be regarded as something that cannot be attained because it is always fleeting and competing with other types of good qualities.

If common sense is our guide to what is a virtue, feelings such as "compassion" will be considered virtues. This, when associated with the traditional recommendation that one should always act out of virtue, brings us the expectation that one be compassionate all the time. And such a thing, of course, is not possible. Something like compassion could not be a virtue on the traditional account precisely because it could not be something one exhibited all the time. The modernized account leads to a pessimistic take on our natures.

Virtue Ethics

63

The second possible unintended result of invoking common sense in an account of virtue is that virtue is not associated with a lasting transformation of one's character but with certain habits one could give up or start at will. The problem with this is that virtue talk may become nearly meaningless. Helping someone once might make you "kind," at least that day, and speaking this way will be possible despite how mean you may be most of the time. The traditional accounts can explain why someone may display courage yet be dangerous or be honest yet be untrustworthy. If we are all considered to have a profusion of virtue, we are afforded no clarity when it comes to the nature of good qualities.

No Final End

A second common modification is that the intellectual component of virtue is dropped. This allows us to recognize that we can be inadvertently compassionate and that this counts toward our goodness. The traditional requirement is that one be perfectly conscious of why and that one is acting well. Far more behavior is counted as virtuous, and new standards for such behavior (even consequentialist ones) can be used to assess virtue if the traditional requirement is dropped. The notion that virtue must be developed through a focus on one's final end is abandoned. Sometimes, there is talk of the need to be habituated to virtue, but this is usually taken to be the result of practice encouraged through external incentives, or, if self-directed, the practice is a matter of discipline rather than philosophical exploration of the point of one's life.

The Supplement of Other Criteria for Right Action

A final common change from traditional accounts comes from regarding considerations of virtue to be a sort of addition or supplement to other means of establishing what is right and wrong (e.g., the invocation of a theory such as Rawls's or consequentialism). This is, of course, only to consider character in relation to other ethical approaches. Though such considerations can be referred to as a virtue-based approach and even at times as virtue ethics, there is no serious connection between this focus on character and the ancient accounts of virtue.

CRITICISMS OF VIRTUE ETHICS

Criticisms of virtue ethics abound. All too often criticisms of virtue ethics are made secondhand and without reference to either the ancient texts or the contemporary works of theory. Frequently, a commonsense conception of the virtues is inserted into an interpretation of a theorist's proposals, and as a result, the proposal seems unsound. For example, ancient accounts of the unity of the virtues are frequently dismissed as implausible because it is difficult to imagine our commonsense conception of virtue requiring that to be brave we must also be kind. But given the brief description just offered, it is clear that being naturally brave, or doing some brave action, is not the same as having consciously committed one's self to morality. On the ancient account, bravery requires awareness of the point of your activity. Without this, your actions (which may, of course, in many ways be laudable) are still not virtuous, as they do not meet the intellectual criteria for this type of behavior. And to meet these criteria in the case of courage (you understand why and when it is appropriate) means that you will surely also have an understanding of when, for example, kindness would be required.

Virtue Ethics Is Not Applicable

One objection is that virtue ethics can offer only extremely general advice and role models but no objective guidelines. (Indeed, at times this is claimed of virtue ethics to argue for imprecision in ethics.) This may be the result of Aristotle being more widely known than the other ancient ethicists who shared the structure of his ethical theory. Yet even Aristotle, in Book 9 of the Nicomachean Ethics, uses his ethical theory to assess very particular guidelines for behavior. We have evidence of the Stoics doing this far more commonly, however, as they worried very much about the justification of particular prohibitions. Cicero records debates about the type of information one must reveal before a sale. Stoics disagreed, for example, on whether you could profit as much as possible from bringing the first ship of grain to a famine-torn island (the issue concerning whether you should reveal that more ships are imminent), but they were not seeking to recommend only to "be virtuous." The two sides argued over whether it was necessary to endorse the proposition "reveal information about other sellers when the buyer's situation is dire," given a good person's overriding commitment to morality.

One reason critics assert that virtue ethics is applicable in the way an ethical theory needs to be is that virtue ethics provides a different type of standard for rightness than that to which most contemporary ethicists are accustomed. In the traditional accounts, for example, what determines whether an action is right or not is whether the actor is capable of justifying it. We, of course, function as the judges of whether the justification stands or not. But virtue ethics neither offers an abstract and rationalistic justification for a list of right actions nor recommends a set of principles that, if applied, are supposed to clarify which courses of action are right. The criteria of rightness offered by traditional virtue ethics can frustrate philosophers and applied ethicists who are used to handier means of assessing right and wrong. But what is handy to writers is not always what can be invoked by the public at large, and the assessments virtue ethics makes are clearly a refinement of the type of judgments we make in our personal lives all the time. We are not impressed, for example, by a generous gift if it comes from a person giving it just to seek favor.

The Empirical Challenge to Virtue

The most recent challenge to virtue ethics has been leveled by philosophers looking to research in social psychology that suggests human behavior is far more variable than we commonly assume. Gilbert Harman and John Doris are leaders of a movement in philosophy known as situationism or, more generally, empirical ethics. This movement looks to verify the claims of ethical theorists through surveys and experimentation. Past experiments by social psychologists have been used by these philosophers to challenge the moral psychology assumed by any account of virtue. Several of these experiments have found that a large percentage of subjects can be found to be kept from small acts of kindness by minor and irrelevant changes in their environment (their "situation"). A memorable example is that of an experiment that found certain smells can encourage or discourage minor altruistic behavior. The current reasoning of the situationists goes like this: The moral psychology required for virtue is unrealistic since experiments have shown that the majority of us act in ways that are susceptible to small changes in environment. People cannot, they argue, be assumed capable of acting morally regardless of the situation.

The difficulty in accepting this criticism of virtue ethics may be obvious. Virtue ethics of any sort is unlikely to regard the majority of the population as virtuous. Even when virtue is not described as the result of the taxing and lengthy process the ancients describe, it is considered a rare and unique condition. The experiments situationists cite give evidence of some people acting morally, regardless of situational input. This may indeed be a sign of these subjects having virtue. A final obstacle to the situationist critique of virtue is that right action is something virtue ethicists define for themselves. It is difficult to test an ethical theory by using a standard for right action other than the one the theory itself offers. The behaviors social psychologists count as minimally moral (e.g., helping a person to pick up papers) are not necessarily required by virtue. Aristotle's "great man" is described as concerning himself with serious and not trivial moral matters, for example. The conclusions of the psychologists who conduct the experiments are far more limited than the philosophers reporting on these experiments suggest. Social psychologists do not regard themselves as targeting character traits and are certainly not taking aim at an Aristotelian conception of virtue. Experiments would have to be designed around these proposals for them to be tested.

To the extent situationists are requesting empirical verification of the moral psychology associated with a virtue ethic, their influence can be a positive one. Virtue ethics has always been dependent on an accurate description of our moral psychology for its recommendations. It happens to be the case that the results of experiments in social psychology, as the psychologists themselves describe them, can be welcomed by virtue ethics. Indeed, some of the conclusions (e.g., that some of us can be easily swayed by others to change our stated opinion) are what the ancient texts would lead one to suspect is the case. Research could help us settle not only what moral psychology ought to be associated with virtue but also what business environments, policies, and decisions are compatible with virtue. Empirical methods may someday reveal to us both what the virtuous person in business would be capable of recommending and what recommendations would promote virtue.

Other criticisms about the approach are likely to be outdated. It can no longer be said, for example, that virtue ethics cannot be said to describe only right agency and not right action. It cannot be said that virtue ethics involves an opposition to rule-based thinking, to the recommendation of principles, or to more than very general advice about how to live. And it is also no longer considered helpful to merely oppose virtue ethics to two other dominant approaches in the field of ethics: consequentialism and Kantianism. Virtue ethics has had such an impact on the field of ethics that distinctions that had been assumed to be obvious are now difficult to find. Kantians now emphasize Kant's account of virtue, and consequentialists do not shy from discussions of agency.

A FUTURE ROLE FOR VIRTUE IN BUSINESS ETHICS

Virtue ethics has received a great deal of attention in the field of business ethics, though the promises that its entry would transform the field have not been fulfilled. There are two reasons why those interested in virtue still have cause for hope that business ethics can be further refined (and not merely broadened) by discussion of virtue. One is because a traditionally styled virtue ethic has not yet been developed for use in the field of business ethics. Articles have, of course, suggested that such a thing could be valuable, and some article authors have begun work in this direction. The possibility of being able to assess the output of a company according to a virtue ethic's value scheme ought to be attractive to those business ethicists looking to capture the public's imagination and attention. A second reason is due to the possibilities of empirical research supporting some of the ancient claims of virtue ethicists. If social scientists begin to test for the account of moral psychology required for virtue, they may find that certain classes of policies are more conducive to the encouragement of virtue and that certain institutional designs attract the virtuous.

—Jennifer A. Baker

RATIONALITY

Many things have been called rational, or irrational as the case may be, including beliefs, actions, desires, and persons. Of these, perhaps the two that have received the most attention are belief and action. Discussions about the rationality of belief fall under the domain of theoretical rationality; those concerning the rationality of action fall under practical rationality.

THEORETICAL RATIONALITY

Theoretical rationality is often called "epistemic" rationality, since it is concerned with the question of obtaining knowledge. An agent can be said to know that p only if, apart from believing that p and p being true, he or she is able to give reasons for his or her belief that p. Theoretical rationality, hence, can be understood as that capacity of cognitive agents that allows them to adopt beliefs about the world on the basis of reasons. This raises at least two problems. First, what are the grounds on which a rational agent may adopt such beliefs? Second, what are the rational procedures or rules that allow her to invoke those grounds to support her belief?

The first question concerns the notion of evidence. If Jane has evidence for a belief that p, then this serves as a reason for her both to adopt and to defend that belief. Maybe the most obvious candidate for evidence is perceptual information—information that the agent receives about the world by means of her sensory faculties. Furthermore, in some cases Jane will be able to justify her belief that p long after she has obtained immediate perceptual information about p. In this case, she is no longer relying directly on perceptual information but on her memory thereof. The capacity to store information and access it later is of prime importance for an agent's ability to adopt and justify beliefs. Last, Jane may come to adopt a belief because she has been told that p: In this case, she is relying on testimonial evidence.

Perception, memory, and testimony all constitute *defeasible* grounds of evidence: The correctness of information received from any of these sources depends on the adequacy of the agent's sensory faculties, her cognitive capacities, and the external circumstances under which the information is acquired. Awareness of the contestability of evidence based on such information and the capacity to assess its quality are important aspects of an agent's rationality.

Not all evidence is concerned with the outside world, however, and evidence that is not external in this sense may not always be falsifiable. For example, rational agents can have information about their own inner states, such as being in pain, that is not subject to reasonable doubt. And some writers believe that intuitive, noninferential knowledge may be available about abstract objects, such as numbers and concepts forming the basis of mathematics and logic, which is not defeasible.

The second question—the question of the rules or rational procedures that allow a rational agent to adopt a belief on the grounds of information obtained via the above-mentioned channels—falls into the domain of logic and concerns the nature of arguments. Any logical argument consists of two or more statements, at least one of which serves as a premise that supports (or, we may also say, offers evidence for) a conclusion. There are two ways in which a conclusion can follow from a premise. If the conclusion follows with a degree of probability from the premise, then the argument is *inductive.* If the conclusion follows necessarily from the premise, it is a *deductive* argument. Most arguments, including scientific ones, rely on inductive inference. On the other hand, according to the traditional view, logic and mathematics proceed deductively. The foundationalist would argue about mathematics that mathematical reasoning is based on intuitively obvious axioms from which theorems can be deduced that are true once and for all. This conception has come under threat in the 20th century from an argument by Kurt Gödel. In his famous incompleteness theorems, he shows that for a large class of important axiomatic theories, such as number theory, mathematical reasoning cannot deduce all mathematical statements that are true relative to that system and cannot even show that the system is internally consistent. Furthermore, according to the "quasi empiricism" of Hilary Putnam and Imre Lakatos, mathematical knowledge is similar to empirical knowledge in possessing a hypothetical status. Mathematical theories are then fallible, and they are arrived at not by means of formal proofs but in accordance with inductive methods of inquiry similar to those employed in the empirical sciences.

In his *Enquiry Concerning Human Understanding,* David Hume pointed out a problem with inductive knowledge. He argued that any inductive inference from true premises to a general conclusion relies on a further hidden premise—namely, that the world in the future will be relevantly similar to the world as it is when the inference is made (that nature is uniform). But the uniformity of nature cannot be presupposed and hence must be justified. The problem is that any such justification can only proceed inductively itself. Hence, Hume concluded that inductive inferences are circular. It follows that one cannot inductively obtain knowledge of those parts of the external world about which one does not have perceptual information.

The problem does not end here. Hume argued that since the idea of necessity cannot be derived from the observation of individual sequences of events, it turns out not to be possible to justify causal necessity on empirical grounds. Yet it is not possible to justify causal judgments a priori (i.e., prior to any experience) either, for it is impossible to tell how objects have behaved prior to having observed them. Hence, causal necessity can only be explained reductively in terms of constant conjunction—a relation between two events in which one invariably accompanies the other.

Immanuel Kant thought that Hume's argument, if sound, undermined not only natural science (and thus a core domain of theoretical reason) but also metaphysics, the philosophical discipline that investigates the general structure of reality. He responded by trying to show that there is a class of judgments that can be made a priori but that are nevertheless "synthetic" (i.e., revealing genuinely new information). Examples of such judgments can be found, for example, in geometry: "The angles of a triangle always add up to 180 degrees" is a judgment that is known a priori yet cannot be deduced from an analysis of the concept of triangle (judgments that can be deduced from the analysis of a concept are called "analytic"). Kant's project in the *Critique of Pure Reason* is to explain the possibility of this kind of judgment. He approaches it by arguing that there are features of experience that the mind bestows on objects and these are hence not supplied by the external world. Since metaphysics is concerned with the question of what these features are, it cannot proceed on the basis of empirical evidence, that is, inductively. The question whether Kant's response to Hume's empiricism is viable has been raised forcefully in the 20th century by W. V. O. Quine's argument that no distinction between analytic and synthetic judgments can be drawn.

PRACTICAL RATIONALITY

Practical rationality is concerned with an agent's capacity to choose from among different courses of action. It does not attempt to give an account of our knowledge of the world, but focuses on the reasons and ways of thinking that lead us to choose to do some actions and not others. Thus, a main task for theorists of practical rationality is to give an account of the exact role reason plays in action. There have been many such accounts, but for purposes of this entry we will divide them into two rough categories: those that maintain that reason's role is entirely or almost entirely confined to devising the means necessary to achieve the goals or ends of action and those that argue that the role of reason in action is much larger than simply devising the means to ends.

Writers who argue that reason is confined to working out means to ends typically endorse or have been heavily influenced by David Hume's understanding of practical rationality. According to Hume, the job of reason in action is to choose means to ends that are themselves neither discovered nor sanctioned by reason, but given by desires or passions, as he put it. Reason can devise means to satisfy desires, but since desires are neither true nor false, they are not subject to rational assessment. Furthermore, reason can assess neither which of our desires we should pursue nor the order in which we should pursue them. Consequently, Hume claimed, it is not contrary to reason to pursue goals that we realize are not in our best interests, and may even be detrimental to our interests. For Hume, reason is a mere instrument used to serve ends that are set by desire and only by desire.

Many contemporary theorists of practical rationality accept Hume's idea that our desires and goals are not subject to rational assessment but argue that reason has a role to play in selecting the order in which we ought to pursue them. This approach contends that the basic task of practical reason is to discover means that optimally advance an agent's ends, whatever they might be, and that an agent acts rationally to the extent that he or she undertakes such optimizing actions. The procedure for this, as developed with considerable mathematical precision in decision theory and the theory of rational choice, is first to propose a measure for agents to rank their goals from most to least desirable. This measure gives the "utility" of each goal. The utility of each goal is then multiplied by the agent's estimate of the probability that the goal will be achieved given the means contemplated to attain the goal, and the products are added together to get the expected utility of each action. The rational thing to do, then, is to select the action that has the highest expected utility. Thus, agents can use reason to determine which available actions maximize the satisfaction of desire and, hence, how desires can be pursued efficiently. Note that if the proposed measure of the utility of desires applies to all agents, it may be possible to discover which social policies have the highest expected utility and so guide social as well as individual choice.

Opposed to the Humean view are writers who argue that reason is not a mere instrument in the service of desire but has a much more complicated role in choosing action. There are two main strands of the non-Humean understanding of reason's role in action. The first is that reason is not purely instrumental since it has the dual role of identifying the objective ends of human life and guiding action to achieve those ends. For example, Aristotle argued that there is a good for man that is both knowable by reason and the proper goal of human action. Thus, for Aristotle, and for many writers since Aristotle, reason is not the servant of desire but is an instrument for achieving ends that are to a large extent revealed and endorsed by reason itself.

The second non-Humean strand of practical rationality claims that what makes an action rational is at least in part that it conforms to rules for action that are independent of the agent's ends and do not necessarily advance those ends. According to this position, a rational agent is one who, in circumstances in which the rules are applicable, chooses to act by the rules. There are different accounts of this rule-based conception of rational action depending on what one takes to be the source of the rules. One is that the rules are widely accepted social norms about what is or is not a socially acceptable action. For example, most of us stop at a red light even when the road is clear and no police are in sight because of the social norm that prohibits running the light, regardless of the immediate benefits of doing so. This sort of norm-based reasoning is a familiar part of ordinary life. However, there is a major controversy about how far it can be extended and, in particular, whether it can be extended to cover ethical reasoning.

Those who argue that it does apply to ethical reasoning often accept some type of ethical relativism. In its simplest form, ethical relativism is the view that what is good to do, or what is ethically proper or right to do, is regulated by socially accepted ethical norms. For example, in societies where there is a social norm against having multiple spouses, it is ethically wrong to have more than one spouse. In societies where there is no such norm, it is not ethically wrong. That is all there is to it, and, at its core, reasoning using social norms to guide action is all there is to ethics.

On the other hand, many writers who reject ethical relativism maintain that ethical reasoning is based on norms that are in principle available to all agents. The most influential version of this position was developed by

Immanuel Kant. Kant argued that practical reason should not be based on social norms that arise in different societies from arbitrary historical processes but on rational principles known by rational means, and thus in principle accessible to all rational agents regardless of their cultural affiliations. Kant claimed to have found such a principle, which he called the "categorical imperative." The basic idea here is that unless you can suppose that everyone in similar circumstances could wish to do what you now propose to do, you should not do it. This, Kant believed, is a requirement of reason itself, and reason dictates that it be followed by all rational beings regardless of the consequences.

It is a matter of continuing debate whether Kant's defense of the categorical imperative as a principle of pure practical reason is successful. However, Kant's views about practical reason have inspired contemporary philosophers and social theorists, such as John Rawls and Jürgen Habermas, to propose theories that make essential use of the notion that rational agreement can be based on principles that everyone can accept.

Practical Reason and Social Responsibility

It is not self-evident how the various conceptions of rationality introduced here bear on real-life ethical questions, in business environments or elsewhere. One reason is that it is not clear whether there exists a necessary connection between rationality and ethics. On Kant's account of practical rationality, it is rationally required to act morally and, thus, always irrational to act immorally. This is a consequence of his view that moral requirements flow from the universalizable principles of reason itself. However, on Hume's account, it is entirely possible to be completely rational in accomplishing goals that are immoral. For Hume, reason is confined to devising means to satisfy our desires, and there is no assurance that our desires match up with what is morally acceptable.

But even if we take it that the employment of one's rational faculties leads to morally worthy actions, it does not follow that a rational agent will always be in a position to resolve real-life ethical problems. The complexity of such problems, in business and other contexts, typically defies standardized solutions. The most that can be hoped for is that an agent's familiarity with theories of practical rationality might enable him to better understand the nature and scope of the problems at stake. Unfortunately, perhaps the most obvious difficulty here is that sometimes business interests and ethical concerns follow different such theories and may hence not always be compatible.

Empirical Issues Concerning Theoretical and Practical Reasoning

In recent times, the human capacity for both theoretical and practical reasoning has come under intense scrutiny from the natural and the social sciences. Psychologists have pointed out that intelligent agents frequently commit significant errors when making intuitive judgments about physics, arithmetic, and probabilities. Cognitive scientists have produced evidence that poses problems for the classical philosophical view of rationality as radically disjoint from an agent's emotive faculties. The ideally rational agent, according to this view, bases his or her actions on conclusions that are obtained through rational inferences alone. Any emotive interference makes the agent less than fully rational. It has been observed, however, that an impairment of an agent's emotive skills (through a brain injury, say) can result in a diminished capacity for theoretical and practical reasoning. How exactly philosophers might respond to these challenges is not currently obvious.

—Axel Seemann and Robert Frederick

Further Readings

Damasio, A. (2000). *Descartes' error: Emotion, reason, and the human brain.* New York: HarperCollins.

Habermas, J. (1990). *Moral consciousness and communicative action.* Cambridge: MIT Press.

Hume, D. (1978). *A treatise of human nature.* Oxford, UK: Oxford University Press. (Original work published 1740)

Hume, D. (1988). *An enquiry concerning human understanding.* Peru, IL: Open Court. (Original work published 1748)

Kant, I. (1998). *Critique of pure reason.* Cambridge, UK: Cambridge University Press. (Original work published 1781)

Kant, I. (1998). *Groundwork of the metaphysics of morals.* Cambridge, UK: Cambridge University Press. (Original work published 1785)

Lakatos, I. (1976). *Proofs and refutations.* Cambridge, UK: Cambridge University Press.

Myers, D. (2002). *Intuition: Its powers and perils.* New Haven, CT: Yale University Press.

Putnam, H. (1975). What is mathematical truth? In H. Putnam (Ed.), *Philosophical papers* (Vol. 1, pp. 60–79). Cambridge, UK: Cambridge University Press.

Putnam, H. (1979). Philosophy of mathematics: A report. In P. D. Asquith & H. E. Kyburg (Eds.), *Current research in philosophy of science* (pp. 386–398). East Lansing, MI: Philosophy of Science Association.

Quine, W. V. O. (1953). *From a logical point of view.* Cambridge, MA: Harvard University Press.

Rawls, J. (1971). *A theory of justice.* Cambridge, MA: Harvard University Press.

Rationality

UTILITARIANISM

U tilitarianism represents an old and distinguished tradition in moral philosophy, the influence of which extends to law, economics, public policy, and other realms and is evident in much of our everyday moral thinking. Two fundamental ideas underlie utilitarianism: first, that the results of our actions are the key to their moral evaluation and, second, that one should assess and compare those results in terms of the happiness or unhappiness they cause (or, more broadly, in terms of their impact on people's well-being). Both these ideas have been around for a long time; one can glimpse hints of them in philosophical and religious writings going back thousands of years. However, as an explicitly and self-consciously formulated ethical theory, utilitarianism is just over 200 years old.

By the 18th century, several philosophers were promulgating an essentially utilitarian approach to ethics. However, the English philosopher Jeremy Bentham (1748–1832) is generally considered the founder or at least the first systematic expounder of utilitarianism. In politics and ethics, Bentham and his followers saw themselves as fighting on behalf of reason against dogmatism, blind adherence to tradition, and conservative social and economic interests. They were social reformers who used the utilitarian standard as a yardstick for assessing and criticizing social and economic policies and the political and legal institutions of their day. Among Bentham's backers were his friends James Mill and Mill's son, John Stuart Mill (1806–1873), who went on to become the most important English philosopher of the 19th century. Ardently interested in economics and public affairs, Mill was an articulate defender of utilitarianism and used the doctrine to champion individual liberty and to urge the emancipation of women. Mill, in turn, was followed by Henry Sidgwick (1838–1900), the last of the great 19th-century utilitarians. Unlike Bentham and Mill, Sidgwick was a university professor with a strong interest in the history of ethics. His writings developed and refined utilitarianism as a moral philosophy, bringing it to its full intellectual maturity.

Today, the utilitarian tradition is as alive as ever. Although many contemporary philosophers believe that utilitarianism is profoundly flawed, over the years a number of able thinkers have expounded and defended the theory, honing and elaborating it in surprisingly subtle ways. Nevertheless, utilitarianism's guiding impulse is simple and transparent: Human well-being is what really matters and, accordingly, the promotion of well-being is what morality is, or ought to be, all about.

BASIC UTILITARIANISM

In its most basic and familiar form, utilitarianism holds that an action is right if and only if it brings about at least as much net happiness as any other action the agent could have performed; otherwise, it is wrong. Philosophers generally call this act *utilitarianism,* but the basic utilitarian standard can be used to assess not only actions but also rules, laws, policies, and institutions as well as people's motivations and character traits.

When we are deciding how to act, utilitarianism instructs us to assess the consequences not just for ourselves, but for everyone, of each of the actions we could perform at any given time. In addition to their immediate results, we must bear in mind any long-term consequences and any indirect repercussions that these alternative actions may have. Although we mustn't ignore our own happiness, neither are we to give it more weight than the happiness of anyone else. Utilitarianism, then, tells us to sum the various good and bad consequences for everyone of each possible action and to choose the action that will produce the greatest net happiness. In this way, the theory requires us to strive always to promote as much good as possible.

WELFARISM AND CONSEQUENTIALISM

Utilitarianism has two distinct philosophical components. The first of these is *welfarism,* the value thesis that welfare or well-being is all that ultimately matters. It is the sole good, the only thing that is intrinsically valuable or valuable for its own sake. Anything else that we think of as good for people—say, friendship, or individual freedom—is good only because, and to the extent that, it contributes to their well-being. Nothing is good unless it is good for individual people, and the supreme utilitarian goal is that people's lives go as well as possible.

Bentham, Mill, and Sidgwick focused on happiness, which they equated with pleasure and the absence of pain. Because of this, their utilitarianism is called *hedonistic.* But these three writers were concerned with happiness only because they identified it with well-being, that is, with what is good for people. In their view, our lives go well just to the extent that they are pleasurable or happy. Happiness, however, is not the only way to spell out the idea of well-being, and not all contemporary utilitarians understand welfare as happiness (and still fewer equate either concept with pleasure). For example, economists, who tend to be utilitarian in their outlook, typically identify well-being with the satisfaction of one's desires or preferences. In keeping with utilitarian tradition, this entry uses *happiness* interchangeably with *well-being*. But it is the latter concept that is the focus of utilitarianism, whether one understands it as happiness or in some other way.

The second philosophical component of utilitarianism is its consequentialist or teleological (goal-oriented) approach to right and wrong. *Consequentialism* is the thesis that actions are right or wrong because, and only because, of the goodness or badness of their outcomes. It is not an action's intrinsic nature or whether it is an instance of a certain type of act (e.g., the telling of a lie) that determines its rightness or wrongness, but rather its specific consequences in a given situation. Utilitarianism differs from other possible consequentialist theories by being welfarist, universalistic (because it takes everyone's interests into account equally), aggregative (because it sums the happiness or unhappiness of everyone to determine the overall value of an action's consequences), and maximizing (because it requires us to produce as much well-being as possible).

FUTURE CONSEQUENCES

In trying to produce the best outcome, an agent can be unlucky. A conscientious utilitarian might carefully choose the course of action that anyone in those circumstances would have judged conducive to the best result, and yet the outcome might turn out to be terrible. Alternatively, a malicious person might plot harm to a neighbor only to have the plan backfire and produce optimal results. Utilitarians divide about what to say about these cases.

"Actual-outcome utilitarianism" affirms that the unlucky utilitarian acted wrongly and the malicious person acted rightly. We should not, however, blame the unlucky person for acting as a reasonable and well-informed utilitarian would have acted in the circumstances, and we should criticize the malicious agent for seeking to cause harm. In contrast, "expected-outcome utilitarianism" asserts that the correct standard is not the actual consequences of our actions, but rather their probable, foreseeable, or expected results.

Hence, the unlucky utilitarian acted rightly and the malicious person wrongly. In practice, however, the difference between the two positions vanishes because, given that the future is uncertain, the most one can ever do is to act so as to produce the greatest expected well-being.

Critics of utilitarianism emphasize that we never know all the consequences of the things we do, still less the future results of every possible action we might have performed. Indeed, the causal ramifications of our actions extend indefinitely into the future. Talking in terms of probabilities does not eliminate this problem. We can rarely do more than guess at comparative likelihoods, and we are always liable to miss some possible outcomes and to overlook some alternative courses of action. Furthermore, comparing people's levels of well-being is tricky and imprecise at best. Finally, even if we were armed with all the relevant information, we would lack time to perform the necessary calculations before having to act.

Utilitarians concede these points and yet argue that they do not impugn the utilitarian goal of maximizing well-being. The correctness of that goal is not undermined by shortfalls in our knowledge of how best to attain it. Well-being is still what we should aim at, however difficult it may be to see the best way to bring it about. Utilitarians also point out that human beings are already well acquainted with the nature and typical causes of happiness and unhappiness. Based on thousands of years of collective experience, we are far from being in the dark about what promotes human well-being and what does not, and that knowledge will frequently suffice to justify our acting one way rather than another.

This response also addresses the complaint that we generally lack time, before acting, to perform the necessary utilitarian calculation. In ordinary circumstances, we can and should follow certain well-established rules or guidelines that can generally be relied on to produce good results. We can, for example, make it a practice to tell the truth and keep our promises, rather than try to calculate possible pleasures and pains in every routine case, because we know that, in general, telling the truth and keeping promises result in more happiness than lying and breaking promises. In this vein, many utilitarians have emphasized the practical necessity of following secondary moral principles. Relying on subordinate moral rules also alleviates the problem that even conscientious agents can suffer from bias or make mistakes in their calculations. In normal circumstances, one is less likely to err and more likely to promote happiness by sticking to certain settled guidelines than by trying to calculate afresh the consequences of various courses of action.

DOES UTILITARIANISM REQUIRE IMMORAL CONDUCT?

For utilitarians, rightness and wrongness turn on the specific, comparative consequences of the various courses of action available to us. Without knowing something about the particular situation, we cannot judge ahead of time whether acting in a certain way will be right or wrong. We cannot say that actions of a certain type will always be right or always wrong. Utilitarians see this flexibility as a strong point of their normative standard, but their critics view it as a fatal flaw: The utilitarian goal of maximizing welfare, they argue, can sometimes necessitate the agent's acting immorally. The critics concede that it generally conduces to total well-being for people to tell the truth, keep their promises, and refrain from killing or injuring other people, from damaging their property, or from violating their rights. But there can be exceptions, and in unusual circumstances, promoting overall welfare might call for the agent to do something normally considered perfectly immoral—for example, supporting slavery, violating someone's rights, or framing an innocent person for a crime. Many philosophers repudiate utilitarianism because of this possibility.

Utilitarians typically respond by arguing that their theory does not mandate the conduct the critic says it does. Faced with hypothetical examples of detestable actions, policies, or institutions that supposedly maximize well-being, they challenge the imagined facts, arguing, for example, that slavery will not in fact promote overall well-being or that abridging someone's right to free speech to pacify the majority or torturing suspects to obtain confessions will have negative long-term repercussions. And even if it really would maximize well-being, say, to frame an innocent person to forestall a riot, one could never judge with sufficient confidence that this is how things would play out. In response, the critic is unlikely to permit the hypothesized facts to be challenged but, rather, to insist that in the imagined circumstances we really do know that an action or policy we normally consider morally wrong will maximize total welfare. At this point, utilitarians have no choice but to concede that the apparently immoral thing really is the right course of action. But they will deny that this fact provides a compelling reason for rejecting their theory. Ordinary morality is not sacrosanct. If its rules sometimes conflict with utilitarianism, then so much the worse for ordinary morality. We should revise it, not abandon utilitarianism.

Consistent with their own standard of right, however, utilitarians can often endorse the ordinary moral sentiments to which the critic appeals. Although in the far-fetched set of circumstances hypothesized by the critic, slavery or torture maximizes well-being, these are not the circumstances real people ever encounter. In the world as it actually is, we do much better if people are dead set against doing those things we would normally consider atrocious—that is, if they instinctively reject slavery or refuse even to consider the possibility that framing an innocent person or torturing a suspect might be the right course of action. People who feel this way will do the nonutilitarian thing in the fanciful circumstances imagined by the critic. But they will act better in the world we actually live in, a world in which such dreadful actions will almost certainly diminish net happiness, than will someone who lacked these convictions. In line with this, utilitarianism can underwrite a strong commitment to respecting certain individual rights even if cases are possible in which people will fail to act in a welfare-maximizing way because of this commitment.

DEEPER INTO UTILITARIANISM

For utilitarians, whether an agent acted wrongly is distinct from the question whether the agent should be blamed or criticized for so acting (and, if so, how severely). Utilitarians apply their normative standard to questions of praise and blame just as they do to questions of right and wrong. In particular, they will ask whether it will best promote happiness to criticize someone for failing to maximize happiness. Suppose that a well-intentioned agent acted in a welfare-promoting way but that the person could have produced even more good by acting in some other way instead. Should utilitarians criticize this person? Depending on the circumstances, the answer may well be "No." Indeed, praising agents for actions that fail to fulfill the utilitarian standard can sometimes be right. This is because utilitarians applaud instances of act types they want to encourage, and they commend those motivations, dispositions, and character traits they want to reinforce.

Utilitarians take an instrumental approach to motives. Good motives are those that tend to produce right conduct whereas bad motives are those that tend to produce wrongful conduct. And they assess habits, dispositions, attitudes, behavioral patterns, and character traits in the same instrumental way: One determines which ones are good, and how good they are, by looking at the typical results of the actions they lead to. It doesn't follow from this, however, that utilitarians believe that a moral agent's only motivation or sole concern ought to be the impartial maximization of happiness. Indeed, utilitarian writers have long urged that more good may come from people acting from other, more particular motivations, commitments, and dispositions than from their acting only and always on a desire to promote the general good.

Utilitarianism thus implies that one should not always reason as a utilitarian or, at least, that one should not always reason in a fully and directly utilitarian way. Better results may come from our acting from principles, procedures, or motives other than the basic utilitarian one. This last statement may sound paradoxical, but the utilitarian standard itself determines in what circumstances we should employ that standard as our direct guide to acting. The proper criterion for assessing actions is one matter; in what ways we should deliberate, reason, or otherwise decide what to do (so as to meet that criterion as best we can) is another issue altogether.

Utilitarians will naturally want to guide their lives, make decisions, and base their actions on those principles, motives, and habits that produce the best results over the long run. Which principles, motives, and habits these are is a contingent matter, but utilitarians believe that we often do best to focus on the welfare of those relatively few people with whom our lives are intertwined and whose good we can directly affect, rather than on happiness in general. Nor should we forget that our own happiness is also part of the general good; indeed, it will usually be the part that we have the greatest power to affect, one way or another.

RULE UTILITARIANISM

Although utilitarianism rests on one fundamental principle, it also stresses the importance of following rules, guidelines, or secondary principles that can generally be relied on to produce good results. We should, for instance, make it an instinctive practice to tell the truth and keep our promises, except in very unusual circumstances, because doing so produces better results than does case-by-case calculation. As previously mentioned, relying on such secondary rules counteracts the fact that we can easily err in estimating the value and likelihood of particular results. In general and over the long haul, we are less likely to go wrong and more likely to promote good by cleaving to well-established, welfare-promoting rules—including those rules that identify certain individual rights—than by trying to maximize happiness in each and every action we perform. Moreover, when secondary rules are well known and generally followed, people know what others are going to do in routine and easily recognizable situations, and they can rely on this knowledge when acting. This improves social coordination and makes society more stable and secure.

These considerations have led some utilitarians to adopt a theory called *rule utilitarianism*. It maintains that the utilitarian standard should not be applied to individual actions at all but only to society's moral code as a whole. The rule utilitarian asks what moral code (i.e., what set of rules) a society should adopt so as to maximize well-being in the long run. The principles that make up that code then provide the basis for distinguishing right actions from wrong. An action is not necessarily wrong if it fails to maximize well-being; it is wrong only if it conflicts with the optimal moral code. What is the optimal code for a society to adopt? Rule utilitarians believe that it will not be a one-rule code, commanding us always to bring about as much happiness as we can. Rather, more happiness will come from people following a pluralistic moral code, one with a number of principles of different moral weight.

—William H. Shaw

Further Readings

Glover, J. (Ed.). (1990). *Utilitarianism and its critics*. New York: Macmillan.

Hooker, B., Mason, E., & Miller, D. E. (Eds.). (2000). *Morality, rules and consequences*. Edinburgh, UK: Edinburgh University Press.

Mill, J. S. (1998). *Utilitarianism* (R. Crisp, Ed.). New York: Oxford University Press. (Original work published 1863)

Scarre, G. (1996). *Utilitarianism*. London: Routledge.

Shaw, W. H. (1999). *Contemporary ethics: Taking account of utilitarianism*. Malden, MA: Blackwell.

Sidgwick, H. (1966). *The methods of ethics*. New York: Dover. (Original work published 1907)

Smart, J. J. C., & Williams, B. (1973). *Utilitarianism: For and against*. Cambridge, UK: Cambridge University Press.

Utilitarianism

COMMUNITARIANISM

*C*ommunitarianism designates a political theory that reminds us that persons live within a complex web of groups and associations by which they define themselves and take up responsibilities that form the bonds uniting them in common efforts. The modern world is dominated by the great institutions of the state and the market. Communitarians emphasize that in addition to those two great centers of power, there are numerous other communities and associations that people form so as to carve out together meaningful and effective lives together. Indeed, through these associations members can gain the power to influence the state and the market. Communitarianism is, in part, a sustained response to contemporary liberalism's tendency to emphasize the freedom of individuals at the expense of neglecting the role of communities. Communitarianism is best understood, then, as a critique of liberalism, especially of its excessive individualism, largely done as a corrective within—not against—liberalism itself.

Liberalism asserts two universal principles concerning human beings, *autonomy* and the *respect* due to persons because of their autonomy. Communitarians argue that contemporary liberalism holds society to be composed of individuals each of whom seeks his or her good through a political order protective of individual rights and private pursuits. Many liberals champion individuality to the neglect of the complex forms of cooperation that nurture and support all persons' lives; discount the interdependence essential for gaining knowledge and power; and forget the development of self-identity through reciprocally revealing interchanges with, and commitments to, others. Communitarians assert the interdependence of the self with others in numerous associations through which persons become unique individuals with perspectives, talents, and identities of their own with which to pursue the good as they conceive it together. Communitarians acknowledge and encourage the formation of associations, both large and small, in *civil society,* a space for civic action lying between the state and the market, where people discover themselves and their world through accepting the responsibility to act effectively and morally in solidarity with their fellows.

Alasdair MacIntyre emphasizes that communities endure through time because members hand down their beliefs and practices as traditions for newcomers to learn and perform with excellence. A practice, such as medicine, is widely respected because its practitioners are recognized as part of a tradition of education and performance of a widely recognized good upheld by the policing of the practitioners themselves. MacIntyre's emphasis on tradition and continuity through practices led him to turn away from liberalism and toward Aristotle and Thomas Aquinas, philosophers who discussed excellence through traditional practices within authoritative institutions, the *polis* and the Church, respectively.

Liberalism asserts persons' equality due to their freedom of choice. Liberalism is aptly named for it is a doctrine of autonomy, the view that persons have the freedom to *choose* to participate in society's institutions and to determine the goods whose pursuit is at the core of their own lives. *Autonomy* here means freedom as self-assertion and efficacy ranging from individual or private interests to the system of public deliberation, agency, and law. Autonomy includes persons' ability to accept moral obligations they decide they *ought* to perform due to a problematic situation they face. When people decide together the rules they agree to obey for their mutual benefit, they are expressing their freedom, not limiting it. When a person decides that a certain action is an objective moral obligation to which she or he holds herself or himself, she or he is exercising her or his moral freedom. Acting on a decision is an expression of power—the ability to realize in deed one's considered intention rather than to submit to extraneous forces. Due to their autonomy, persons deserve respect from one another, because in their freedom they reveal themselves as one another's equals before the law, engaged in articulating through their words and realizing through their deeds their vision of a common world. Respect requires that persons not use one another as mere instruments, but that they seek to form a common bond with others that opens the way to accord and solidarity in common purposes.

If all are free and equal, their polity should reflect and respect this fact about persons. As a result, numerous liberal theorists have sought through thought experiments to discern those organizational principles that will best enable free and equal persons to construct a fitting civil order for themselves. These experiments can be traced from Thomas Hobbes's and John Locke's "states of nature" and "social contracts" to John Rawls's "original position." These thought experiments all argue for rights due to all members of the imagined order as well as limitations on members' actions for the sake of the security and well-being of all. In return for the limitations on persons' actions, they are free to advance their self-interest in the market rendered secure by the state's oversight.

Liberal theorists, generally, have sought to construct political orders that provide, on the one hand, the equal opportunity to participate in the public realm of politics through the protection of civil rights and, on the other, security in the private realm needed for the pursuit of economic and other personal goods. Liberal theories retain the tradition's two realms: (1) a public realm in which discourse and decisions concerning politics, ethics, and law direct a government dispensing justice and (2) a private realm in which people attend to their own affairs, whether among intimates within the household or among others earning a living in the market. The protections provided to members of society are *rights* that can be claimed against anyone who would violate them while members pursue the *good* as they understand it.

People display *plurality* in their uniqueness, for no one is exactly like any other, and their different views on the good life arise from their singular experiences. Liberalism respects plurality among persons and, so, permits flexibility in choices made for a good life. That is, the polity should be neutral toward goods unless some good's pursuit leads to an injustice. Communitarians spy a problem here, for despite the specificity of persons evident in the goods they seek, the rights specified for them in a liberal state cannot honor that specificity, for justice demands universality—the application of the same rules and procedures to all independently of their uniqueness as persons. Justice in its liberal formulations necessarily treats persons as abstract individuals indistinguishable one from another. Communitarians complain that this liberal ideal provides only for universal justice as obedience to the laws. The good is left to private discernment while the state remains neutral toward citizens' decisions about private goods. Universality of justice and neutrality toward the good, however, is all that can be expected in a polity formed by the strangers in liberal thought experiments who draw up social contracts.

The liberal dedication to public justice and neutrality toward private goods is problematic because liberals do not agree among themselves concerning what are matters of justice and of good. John Rawls, for example, takes poverty to be a question of justice presenting an obligation that social and economic inequalities should be to everyone's advantage, especially the worst off. Rawls's position is an example of egalitarian liberalism. Robert Nozick, in contrast, argues that a just state ought only to protect persons in the security of their property and its legitimate transfer. Beneficence toward the less advantaged is a supererogatory good; that is, persons *may* address poverty on their own initiative but it ought not be required of some for the benefit of others. A requirement of beneficence is nothing short of confiscation of some persons' goods for their redistribution to others. Nozick's position is termed *libertarianism,* which holds the minimum government possible to be the best because it interferes least with the liberty of citizens to accumulate and transfer goods as they choose.

Charles Taylor proposes a communitarian response to Nozick's view that justice concerns only protection of one's property and its transactions alone, rendering assistance to others supererogatory. If we claim that persons have rights, we must presume persons or institutions also have the capacity to acknowledge those rights and act on them. That is, if we claim rights, we presume the capacity in someone or some institution to accept the responsibility to realize those rights. Furthermore, if we claim rights as something worthwhile, we must also affirm the worth of those capacities that enable us to enjoy our rights. We cannot look to ourselves for the source of the knowledge and use of our capacities; the source must initially reside in others. By ourselves we would be helpless to develop our own potential. Even libertarians have need for membership in those groups that enable growth in knowledge and practice. If libertarians take these human capacities as worthwhile, moreover, they have obligations to make them available to others. Standing idly by and allowing these goods to pass away through inaction would indicate that libertarians do not care about them enough to ensure their continuation in the world. Society is richer and fuller if we engage in all the institutions that enable us to become active and effective agents on behalf of our common human world.

The political core of liberalism is the establishment of a state that protects citizens' rights, establishes a rule of law, and enables citizens to enter into agreements with one another for the sake of whatever goods they choose. The public realm in a liberal polity is not the center of citizens' lives, however. Citizens enjoy their private lives while public officials administer the state so that it provides justice and security for all within its borders. Citizens expect their rights to be protected by the government, but there are few responsibilities expected of them in return. The scarcity of public duties enables citizens to concentrate on their private concerns alone. Attentive to public affairs

Communitarianism

primarily in terms of their own interests, citizens have little encouragement to take up the perspectives of other citizens. Intent on their own interests alone, citizens can mistake their needs for rights; sensitive to any infringement of their rights by injurious actions by others, citizens can become wary and litigious. Liberalism, despite its respect for the rights of all, offers too little encouragement for citizens to move beyond their concentration on their own interests toward the public attitude of citizens intent on comprehending the perspectives of their fellow citizens and participating in resolving political disputes in a way that fosters solidarity and support even for painful but reasonable resolutions of hard problems. Liberal polities are in danger of becoming soft tyrannies, using Alexis de Tocqueville's phrase, of benevolent administrators who oversee persons who have lost control of their government by forgetting how to think and act as citizens. The liberal state unites people as citizens concerned with rights but disperses them again as individuals seeking private goods.

Communitarians criticize liberalism's sharp division between "right" and "good" as artificial. Justice, after all, is itself a good and concerns goods. How can citizens determine what decisions are just until they discuss the goods that they will protect? How can citizens determine a just distribution of goods until they learn what human beings need for a decent life? It is only through the experience of living together that people can determine what is just and, so, good for human beings living within the context of their way of life. One of liberalism's achievements is the assertion and protection of plurality, but this good is best learned through forging familiarity and solidarity with various groups, not through separating oneself off from them. For liberal theory, the enumeration of rights enables people to reflect on what they consider essential components of justice in abstraction from any specific social context. But persons never live abstractly, *unencumbered,* using Michael J. Sandel's term, by particular social roles and expectations binding them together. Concepts of both the good and the right arise within the context of specific persons living together within a personal and group history that clarifies and justifies shared responsibilities and expectations.

To be sure, liberalism has advanced politics through its protection of minorities from oppression under a tyranny of the majority as well as of the majority from well-organized minorities. Living with pluralism and respecting those who disagree with oneself are virtues discovered and nurtured under liberalism in a way never achieved in earlier regimes. Public life in liberal democracies is diminished and precarious nonetheless. Communitarians fear that lack of public engagement presages a loss of democratic temperament that could endanger people's liberal commitment to plurality; liberal citizens are at risk of becoming isolated and self-absorbed even when surrounded by others.

Communitarians attempt to resolve liberalism's problem of citizens preoccupied with their private affairs by recognizing and building on the fact that we are all—always—members of numerous communities. Communitarians join other social theorists in referring to the many associations, whether in service to government and the market or not, that constitute civil society. These associations arise due to a public-minded interest in furthering certain ends, taking a stand with like-minded citizens, enjoying the company of others, and doing something of significance for the larger society. Members of civil society engage in professional work in universities, courtrooms, and hospitals; in civic work, in charities, or other nonprofits supporting the arts, health, and education; or in principled engagement in both domestic and international organizations dedicated to solving political and economic problems concerning human rights violations, famine, and disease. For protection against forces of the market, workers have formed unions, customers have organized boycotts, and environmentalists have presented educational programs and groups to build up political pressure. All these associations constitute and condition who their members become through their interactions within them, just as members participate in fashioning what these groups become through their membership.

Individuals in liberal society face danger because they too often stand alone—or think that they do—before vast political and economic institutions, unable to influence or confront the elites directing these institutions. Due to their isolation, citizens become estranged from a world within which they have no ties other than the abstract, thin ones of a voter or an employee; they come to consider all human interaction to be egoistic, market-like transactions driven by self-interest. Communitarians rely on organizations of civil society to resolve the problem of isolation liberalism produces along with autonomy and respect for plurality. *In so doing, communitarians resolve a liberal problem with a liberal solution.* It is the liberal character of the people that makes them adept at forming civil associations. Civil society organizations enable citizens to take direct action with one another for purposes they recognize as good. In civic action, citizens both learn political skills and put them into practice. One purpose of civic action, then, is to help persons grow as engaged citizens.

Civil society gives its members an alternative to government and the market for achieving social goods. Some purposes are not reducible to the private transactional interests of individuals or to legislated policy holding universally. Some goods, rather, are achieved best by persons acting together for a good held in common. Civic organizations need to require that their members think and act in a democratic way. Democracy requires the exchange of opinion, drawing citizens to consider problems in ways that take them beyond their own perspectives to those of others discovered through deliberation and disclosure. Citizens' commitment to action comes from agreement reached on possibilities none of which could have been reached alone. Liberalism provides the foundation for this communal achievement by instilling in citizens a realization of their right to participate equally with others and respectfully to consider others' points of view. Expositions of liberalism too often fail to clarify the democratic capacity at its heart, however, emphasizing instead individual autonomy. Communitarianism focuses on the vital core of liberal democracy—the community of citizens challenging one another to move beyond private interests for the sake of goods that can be sought together and held in common.

Members of civil organizations do not forsake their independence through participation; they learn to be critical of themselves, of their organizations, and of society and its institutions generally so as to prepare themselves to realize more fully their political freedom. Due to multiple group membership and conversation with their fellows, citizens assess society from many points of view—their interest and their capacity to understand their whole society grow apace. Civil society that makes possible civic engagement in the pursuit of common goods would be undermined were it to create reticent, incurious citizens confined within the horizons of their own groups. The activities essential to effective membership—attention, discussion, disagreement, and compromise—are crucial for good citizenship and are learned only by engaging citizens with different interests and views.

Public action is complicated, sometimes past all compromise. Communitarians seek to remind liberals that social exchange requires patience, experience, forbearance, and care. At times, at an impasse, only their respect for one another holds people together as fellow citizens. Unless citizens are awake to the commitments of community as well as stirred by the promise of rights and autonomy, they will not have the fortitude to be responsible and, as such, truly free.

—William W. Clohesy

Further Readings

Daly, M. (Ed.). (1994). *Communitarianism: A new public ethics.* Belmont, CA: Wadsworth.

Delaney, C. F. (Ed.). (1994). *The liberalism-communitarianism debate.* Lanham, MD: Rowman & Littlefield.

Etzioni, A. (1993). *The spirit of community: Rights, responsibilities, and the communitarian agenda.* New York: Crown.

Etzioni, A. (Ed.). (1995). *New communitarian thinking: Persons, virtues, institutions, and communities.* Charlottesville: University of Virginia Press.

Galston, W. A. (2000). Civil society and the "art of association." *Journal of Democracy, 11,* 64–70.

Gutmann, A. (1985). Communitarian critics of liberalism. *Philosophy and Public Affairs, 14,* 308–322.

Kymlicka, W. (1989). *Liberalism, community, and culture.* Oxford, UK: Clarendon Press.

MacIntyre, A. (1984). *After virtue: A study of moral philosophy* (2nd ed.). Notre Dame, IN: University of Notre Dame Press.

Sandel, M. J. (1998). *Liberalism and the limits of justice* (2nd ed.). Cambridge, UK: Cambridge University Press.

Taylor, C. (1985). *Philosophy and the human sciences: Philosophical papers* (2 Vols.). Cambridge, UK: Cambridge University Press.

Communitarianism

SOCIAL ETHICS

E thics is the application of normative standards to assess right action. Social ethics focuses on the ethical reflection as it pertains to social structures and communities of persons such as our government, school systems, and church organizations and refers to a set of standards around which we organize our lives and from which we define our duties and obligations. It results in a set of norms that establishes acceptable behavior patterns and is concerned with what people ought to do. Examples of social ethical dilemmas that occur in the business environment are privacy rights; sexual harassment; gender, age, and race discrimination; child labor; and environmental protection.

WHO DETERMINES WHAT IS NORMATIVE?

From a social constructionist perspective, what a society or organization considers to be "ethical" is a product of dialogue among its members. Dictionary definitions of *ethics* and *ethical* support this view. It is the members of a particular group that define what is or what is not ethical based on the meaning making done in their own processes of dialogue.

Dialogue originates in the public sphere, and those words, statements, and expressions are essentially actions performed with social consequences. Kenneth Gergen argues that dialogue is a form of coordinated action and the meaning of any utterance depends on its functioning within a relational environment. Because meaning is born in relationship, an individual's lone utterance contains no meaning. Rather, it provides the potential for meaning, a potential that can only be realized through another's contribution. This back and forth dialogue is the key building block to creating shared meaning and a shared reality. The central focus of generative dialogue is to bring realities (such as systems of social ethics) into being and bind them to particular patterns of action.

Ethical issues become a domino effect, and the logic of one is used by the culture to frame the debate on the other. One powerful example of this is bioethics. Biotechnology and genetics technology is advancing faster than any other area of our culture. The Human Genome Project, funded by the federal government, mapped the DNA strands to identify every human gene and its function. The results mean a degree of control that the human race has never had before. What will we do with this knowledge and control? Should we clone human beings? How should we think about the issue of using animal organs in human beings? Should we place animal tissue in human beings? Should we use gender selection when parents want to choose whether to have a boy or a girl? All these medical practices are currently being done or can be done.

This same logic is used in the euthanasia debate, where the focus is on the right of the person to die with dignity. Some states now sanction doctor-assisted suicide using the implied right of privacy that formerly sanctioned the practice of abortion. Based on the implied right of privacy, a person who is ill and no longer desires to live can legally receive assistance from a doctor to commit suicide. With the baby boomers getting older, the pressure for wide-spread euthanasia will grow.

THE IMPACT OF BUSINESS ON SOCIETY

This notion of ethics as a product of dialogue is particularly important in a business environment that is increasingly global and cross-cultural. Globalization represents an enormous intensification of ethical conflict; as organizations expand into foreign locales, there is a tendency for the reality within the organization to deviate from the surrounding community. The import of alien constructions of the real and the good may come into sharp conflict with local understandings. Particularly in developing nations, businesspeople face cultures, customs, and norms that may conflict with their own ethical standards. Examples of ethical issues that global managers face, which may be completely new to them, include corruption and money laundering, human rights under totalitarian regimes, workplace conditions, and environmental issues.

Ethical and legal concepts are contextual and culture specific. There is general disagreement on what behaviors or practices are considered appropriate, legal, ethical, or moral across cultures. What is commonly practiced and socially acceptable in one culture is repudiated in another. Ethics and morals differ not only among various countries but also among individuals in the same country. To contribute to the shared sense of what is good in the local community, organizations must discuss and integrate the values of the local community in their business practices. Notions of right and wrong or justice and injustice are validated by the values and attitudes of a given culture.

Social Ethics

Large corporations are capable of influencing mainstream societal events. Their power is not only economic but also social and political. A notable example of a corporation weighing legal, financial, and ethical points of view is the case of Johnson & Johnson's response to the Tylenol crisis in 1982. Under the leadership of CEO James Burke, the company made the decision to clear all store shelves in the Chicago area of extrastrength Tylenol after several deaths had been linked to their product. In addition, the company recalled 31 million unsold bottles and was completely candid with the medical community, the media, and the public about the situation.

Privacy has become a major issue in recent years for both government and business. The vast amount of personal information that is collected and the need to protect this information became especially sensitive after the passage of the Freedom of Information Act in 1966. This act was intended by Congress to make the government more accountable for its actions but had the inadvertent consequence of compromising the confidentiality of information about private individuals. With the proliferation of new technologies, some businesses insist that workplace monitoring is necessary.

Supervisors can eavesdrop on the telephone conversations of employees and, for example, call up on their own computer screens the input and output of the computers of their employees. In addition to collecting records of telephone calls such as the number of calls, duration, and destination, some companies are collecting medical data from employee assistance plans, which help in handling personal problems and drug addictions. These data can be used to terminate employees or defend against workplace injury claims. In some cases, hidden cameras and microphones are used to observe workers without their knowledge.

Electronic mail (e-mail) is another area in which the right to read employees' e-mail has been debated. To avoid misuse of the company communication system or to investigate misconduct, some employers claim a right to monitor employees' messages. E-mail stored on company fileservers is often backed up on magnetic tape and can be easily restored, leaving a trail of information. In the event of employee misconduct, e-mail messages as well as voice mail messages have been used to strengthen a case to reprimand or even terminate an employee. Some argue that the evidence left in e-mail messages reveal the true nature of behavioral issues and provide useful insight into an employee's conduct. One recent example is of an employee manifesting erratic behavior including frequent unexplained absences and significant performance issues.

On reading this employee's e-mail, it was discovered that she was running a drug dealing operation—selling prescription drugs to other employees as well as outside contacts.

The growth in database marketing has also been facilitated by computer technology, which is able to combine data from many sources and assemble them in usable form. Consumer privacy can become an issue when health information such as prescription data from pharmacies and patient records is shared and used to target a market for direct mailings. Internet users often find data mining "cookies" stored on their hard drives after visiting online stores, which recognize repeat users of their Web site from past visits. Cookies benefit users by eliminating the need to enter information each time, but they can also provide the site owner with data about what pages are visited; how much time is spent on each one; and demographic data such as age, gender, and zip code without the owner's consent.

Another example of social ethical issues facing business organizations is discrimination that may occur in a variety of situations such as age, religion, race, gender, and sexual orientation discrimination. Discrimination is an ethical issue beyond any legal protections because it is at the core of fairness in the workplace. Discrimination can be a subtle or not-so-subtle factor in hiring, promotions, and layoff decisions. People who do not fit the "corporate profile" may be passed over for advancement for a variety of reasons that are not covered in legislation. Some employers create job requirements that could automatically eliminate certain employees, not because of their qualification but because of personal circumstances. An example of this is age discrimination resulting from the benefits that employers perceive in marginalizing or shunting older employees aside to make room for younger employees who may be considered to have more up-to-date skills and innovative ideas. Younger employees are less expensive to employ because older employees generally have higher salaries and make more use of the fringe benefits.

Religious discrimination in employment involves conflicts between the religious beliefs and practices of employees and workplace rules and routines. Employees sometimes request revised work schedules for time off to observe religious holidays or Sabbath observance. Members of some religious groups have special dress or grooming requirements, such as a yarmulke for Jewish men and a turban and a beard for Sikh men. Some employees have religious objections to performing certain kinds of work or to submitting to medical examinations; others request prayer breaks and special foods in the company cafeteria.

Several large corporations such as Intel and IBM have created GBLT (gay, lesbian, bisexual, transgender) business units that work directly with GLBT business units in other organizations. One idea behind the creation of these business units is to provide a safe, nonhostile, open, and inclusive working environment for GBLT employees. Managers within these corporations realize the effectiveness and work productivity that is created when individuals share a social identity.

Increased attention to the problem of sexual harassment and developments in the law has made employers more aware of their responsibilities. Some employers struggle to define sexual harassment as well as determine how serious the problem may be and who is responsible for preventing it. In 1980, the Equal Employment Opportunity Commission (EEOC) issued guidelines on sexual harassment that made a distinction between two kinds of harassment. One is *quid pro quo* harassment, in which a superior uses his or her power to grant or deny employment benefits to exact sexual favors from a subordinate. The other kind is *hostile working environment* harassment, in which the sexual nature of the conduct of coworkers and others causes an individual to be very uncomfortable. Whether a work environment is hostile or offensive is not easily determined, and much depends on the attitudes of the employees involved and the response of management to employee concerns.

Social ethical issues engage our deepest values and beliefs. The ideal of a nondiscriminatory and just society is clear, and finding the proper solutions to such challenging social ethical dilemmas requires an ongoing dialogue. It is imperative that an open and honest dialogue continue where beliefs, values, and opinions about social ethical issues are respectfully considered.

—Anne Kohnke Meda

Further Readings

Desjardins, J. (2003). *An introduction to business ethics.* Boston: McGraw-Hill.

Donaldson, T., Werhane, P. H., & Cording. M. (2002). *Ethical issues in business: A philosophical approach* (7th ed.). Upper Saddle River, NJ: Prentice Hall.

Gergen, K. J. (2001). *Social construction in context.* London: Sage.

Hinman, L. M. (1998). *Ethics: A pluralistic approach to moral theory* (2nd ed.). Fort Worth, TX: Harcourt Brace College.

Newton, L. H., & Ford, M. M. (2004). *Taking sides: Clashing views on controversial issues in business ethics and society* (8th ed.). Guilford, CT: McGraw-Hill.

Treviño, L. K., & Nelson, K. A. (2004). *Managing business ethics: Straight talk about how to do it right* (3rd ed.). Hoboken, NJ: Wiley.

NORMATIVE ETHICS

Normative ethics comprises the study of those actions that moral agents *ought* to perform. In emphasizing moral obligation, normative ethics is distinguished from more descriptive ethical theories that view ethics primarily as illuminating the way in which moral agents actually do act. While normative ethics may use the tools of descriptive ethics, it seeks to articulate a set of standards that are binding on all moral agents.

Normative ethical theories are commonly divided into three broad categories described as "deontological," "teleological," and "ethological." However, useful as this typology may be, in practice, moral action may make use of elements of all three.

DEONTOLOGICAL ETHICAL THEORIES

The term *deontology* comes from the Greek word *deon* or duty. Deontological theories are primarily based on appeals to duty or some kind of unconditional obligation on the part of the moral agent. Different theories offer a variety of possible sources for this obligation. For some, it is rooted in the will of God or some other divine mandate, while for others it is rooted in the dictates of nature or reason.

Divine command theories of morality are common in theistic religious traditions, which assert some form of a personal God or gods. According to these theories, the nature of morality is prescribed by what God or the gods will to be done. Something is thus good if it accords with God's will and evil if it contradicts God's will. This idea was given a classic treatment in Plato's *Euthyphro,* where he seeks to demonstrate that the Good must be something independent of the will of God. However, this tradition has persisted and been given particularly vigorous defense in the reformed tradition of Christianity—for example, in the work of John Calvin and Karl Barth. Versions of divine command theories can be found in Judaism and Islam as well.

Kantian ethics, in contrast, seeks to root moral principles not in the external authority of a divine being, but in the autonomous exercise of human reason. Kant's theory is encapsulated in his Categorical Imperative. The first version of this theory states that one should always act in a way in which one thinks people should always act. By rooting his theory in the moral and logical consistency of the individual human will, Kant seeks an unassailable foundation from which to provide moral guidance. If the human will can consistently will a moral principle as universally binding, then it can be trusted to be a reliable principle for action.

Kant's second formulation of the Categorical Imperative puts its emphasis not on the universal validity of human reason but on the inviolability of the human person. The third formulation puts its emphasis on the autonomy of the human reason as a *legislating* will, calling on moral agents to act as autonomous legislators in a universal kingdom of ends.

The force of these three formulations, as Kant proposes them, is to offer a comprehensive conception of the nature of morality as rooted in human freedom and reason. Yet he believes that the moral law arrived at in this fashion is universally binding since all rational beings are capable of reaching the same conclusions. However, Kant's moral stringency is such that he does not allow for the possibility of contradictions among different moral principles. On the contrary, he believes that all duties are equally binding on moral agents and none can override another.

Other philosophers have sought to overcome some of the difficulties that Kant's inflexibility on this issue has produced. W. D. Ross offers perhaps one of the best examples in his theory of prima facie moral duties. Ross argues that there are moral duties that are properly described as "basic," in the sense that they cannot be reduced to other, prior duties. This includes, but is not limited to, duties such as fidelity, beneficence, nonmalificence, gratitude, and justice. Ross acknowledges that conflicts among these duties may exist and argues that it is only through a careful examination of the situation in question that one can arrive at a conditional determination of what one's "duty proper" must be in a given situation.

Another approach, which is more akin to Kant's second formulation of the Categorical Imperative, involves appeals to the idea of individual rights as constitutive of one's moral obligations. Of particular concern for business ethics is Robert Nozick's "Theory of Entitlement," which posits a natural right to the possession of certain entitlements of which one may not be deprived without one's consent. John Rawls, alternatively, offers a rights-based theory rooted in the idea of justice as fairness. This theory differs from Nozick's in a number of key respects, but most notably in that it offers a vigorous defense of a theory, rejected by Nozick, of distributive justice.

Deontological moral systems are appealing from a normative standpoint due to their clarity with regard to the nature of moral action and the source of moral authority. Most deontological moral theories are nonconsequentialist in the sense that one's duty is considered to be binding regardless of the results. This is easiest to understand in those cases where the consequences fall directly on the moral agent (e.g., if one accepts jail rather than lie or betray a confidence). Obedience to duty in such cases is seen to be a higher obligation than personal advantage. Such approaches become more problematic, however, when the consequences fall not on oneself but on others (e.g., letting an innocent person be harmed rather than lie or betray a confidence).

Deontological theories are often criticized precisely for being universal in those circumstances where they should allow for contingency. It's not immediately obvious that obedience to duty is of a higher moral value than protecting innocent life or preventing other negative consequences.

TELEOLOGICAL MORAL THEORIES

The major theoretical alternative to deontological ethics is found in teleological, or ends-based, moral theories. These theories find normative guidance in the pursuit of particular goals or outcomes, though they often differ with regard to the nature of the goals to be pursued.

Catholic moral theology is based on a teleological conception of the moral life. Although, due to its reliance on a theory of natural law it is often taken to be deontological, the natural law is itself teleologically oriented toward the fulfillment of particular human and divine ends. Unlike a divine command theory, in which the moral good is solely defined by the will of God (irrespective of other concerns), Catholic moral theology understands the good in terms of that which fulfills the purpose for which it was created. This perspective was given its classic formulation in the work of St. Thomas Aquinas. Human beings, in this theory, are created as creatures to fulfill certain ends; for example, within society, humans have the goal of bringing about justice. In sexual relationships, the goal is to create further life. The interference with the specified goals of human activity represents a disruption or perversion of their created purposes. The consequences of actions are important in this approach insofar as those consequences correspond to the desired ends of human life.

Consequentialism, on the other hand, analyzes the morality of action in terms of whether it harms or benefits morally relevant subjects. Various consequentialist moral theories exist, differing both in terms of what is considered to be harm or benefit and in terms of who constitutes a morally relevant subject.

In Jeremy Bentham's version of utilitarianism, he advocates what he calls the greatest happiness principle. Happiness in this case is defined strictly in terms of pleasure. Those actions that produce the greater pleasure are good and those that produce greater pain are harmful. Similar theories were developed by James Mill and John Stuart Mill. Bentham offers a number of criteria to enable one to evaluate whether any particular action would produce a greater net amount of pleasure over pain, such as whether one pleasure is more intense than another or whether it is likely to be followed by similar pleasure in the future. Using these criteria, he developed a "hedonic calculus" on which one could calculate the likely morality of a particular course of action.

Others have criticized this analysis by arguing that defining utility in terms of pleasure leads to morally undesirable conclusions. These thinkers have offered alternative theories of utility, some arguing that utility should be understood in terms of, for example, one's interests and some arguing that utility should be defined not in terms of what individuals believe to be good for them but according to external moral criteria of what actually can be shown to be good for them.

The other key question for consequentialist theories has to do with who or what constitutes a relevant moral subject—one to whom consideration is owed in determining one's actions. The two major alternatives within consequentialist theory are identified with utilitarianism and egoism, respectively.

Utilitarianism, as noted above, is based on some version of the greatest happiness principle, which states that what is moral is that which produces the greatest amount of net happiness (however defined). This is often described as seeking the greatest good for the greatest number. According to this theory, one's own happiness is not of greater value than anyone else's, and therefore, when calculating the morality of one's action, one should not weight one's own good higher than the good of others. Egoistic theories, on the other hand, argue that one's own interest is morally paramount in deciding what action to take. That which is good for oneself takes predominance over the good of others. Some egoists would argue that one's own good should be considered *primary* and the good of others *secondary,* while others would argue that we have no moral obligations to others and each individual is solely responsible for achieving one's own good. Note that this is a *normative* egoistic ethical theory. Some thinkers, for example Adam Smith, have argued *descriptively* that human beings by nature place their own interests above others, but they do not endorse this as an ethical good. Normative egoism argues that human beings *ought* to act in their own self-interest and, at their most radical, that taking the interests of others into account is immoral. This perspective was most prominently advocated in the 20th century by Ayn Rand, who, in both her novels and her philosophical treatises, defended the virtue of selfishness.

There are a number of attractive features to teleological ethical systems from a normative point of view, particularly its consequentialist forms. It seems to conform to our ordinary moral sensibilities that the consequences of our actions ought to matter. At the same time, certain interpretations of teleological ethics, particularly utilitarianism, seem to lead to conclusions that shock the moral conscience. For example, does the principle of the greatest good for the greatest number imply that we may sacrifice the good of a minority for the sake of the rest of the population? It is difficult to derive such an interpretation from John Stuart Mill, whose own writing emphasized individual liberty in addition to the greatest happiness principle. However, other utilitarians have been less circumspect. These problems are only magnified in egoistic theories. More generally, it is not always clear that there can be said to be a moral *telos,* whether God or Good, toward which human beings are oriented.

ACT-BASED AND RULE-BASED ETHICAL SYSTEMS

A further distinction to be made among these theories is between those that are "rule-based" and those that are "act-based." Rule-based moral systems claim that moral norms must be understood in terms of rules that, once determined, are morally binding, while act-based systems claim that morality must be understood in terms of whether particular acts in particular circumstances correspond to relevant norms.

Deontological and consequentialist moral systems each have act and rule variants. Rule deontology claims that one's moral duty corresponds to the articulation of universally mandatory rules. Act-based deontology, on the contrary, claims that one's duty can only be discerned in light of particular circumstances.

Rule utilitarianism interprets the greatest happiness principle to be that set of general principles under which the greatest good for the greatest number is generally attained. Rule utilitarianism, unlike Kantian ethics, is not absolutist and allows for exceptions. Act utilitarianism claims that moral agents must decide, on a case-by-case basis, whether their actions will bring about a greater amount of good over harm, and act accordingly.

ETHOLOGICAL ETHICAL THEORIES

Ethology is a term that applies to those moral theories that are rooted in an evaluation of the appropriateness of particular actions or sensibilities in light of contexts or circumstances. Most prominent among ethologically oriented moral systems is virtue ethics. Virtue ethics is based on the pursuit of human excellence through the cultivation of good moral character. Most theories of virtue identify the cardinal virtues as wisdom, temperance, fortitude or courage, and justice. Although not all descriptions of these virtues are ethologically oriented (e.g., Plato), in large measure they describe these virtues as the product of an education in circumstance-appropriate behavior. Thus, no one is born knowing how to act courageously. Rather, one learns bravery as a result of being exposed to circumstances that require bravery and, through practice, learning the proper response. Moral education is thus experiential and circumstantial.

The classic expression of virtue ethics is found in Aristotle's *Nicomachean Ethics*. In this work, Aristotle describes morality as doing the right thing, at the right time, in the right way. That which is ethical is that which is appropriate to the circumstance, but only the well-cultivated character can properly identify and react to the circumstances. Virtue in Aristotle's *Ethics* is identified as the mean between two extremes: one of excess and one of deficiency. Thus, courage is not fearlessness; rather it is the proper degree of fear depending on circumstances. Thus, the brave man is one who has neither an excess of fear, that is, cowardice, nor a deficit, that is, foolhardiness.

In contemporary moral theory, virtue ethics has seen resurgence, in large measure as a result of Alasdair MacIntyre's seminal work *After Virtue*. MacIntyre argues that modern normative ethical theory, as understood primarily through the tradition that culminates with Kantian ethics, on one hand, and utilitarianism, on the other, is intellectually bankrupt largely because it has lost track of its own origins. The logical end product of modern ethics is the moral nihilism of Friedrich Nietzsche. It is as though a catastrophe has taken place in which we now possess nothing but the fragments of moral knowledge out of which we must cobble together partial and incoherent moral systems. In contrast to this modern day moral confusion, the tradition of the virtues offers a complete and coherent theory.

According to MacIntyre's interpretation, a virtue is an excellence in a particular practice that is cultivated within a community that is based on a particular tradition. Thus, to be excellent means to be excellent in the context of a particular understanding of human nature. In MacIntyre's framework, in contrast to that of Kant or Mill, there are no moral principles that can be detached from the history of a particular community.

Another approach to contextually based normative ethics is existentialism, particularly as articulated by Jean-Paul Sartre. The key element of this approach to morality is its emphasis on human freedom. Sartre writes that man has no nature. Rather, we are born free and as free individuals must choose how we will respond to the world in which we are "thrown." There are no universal and binding moral norms on which human beings can rely for moral guidance. Neither the Categorical Imperative nor the greatest happiness principle can absolve individuals from the obligation to choose their actions and the resultant consequences. There is no god to whom one can appeal either for guidance or for forgiveness. One must, therefore, take the entire weight of one's actions solely on oneself. However, rather than seeing this as a morally hopeless situation in which all paths are equally meaningless and, therefore, all choices equally pointless, Sartre argues that in the *act of choosing* we create a morality and by that act lend meaning to our existence.

In some ways similar to this are various pragmatic approaches to ethics— for example, those advocated by Richard Rorty and Jeffrey Stout. Pragmatic theories of morality differ markedly from one another, but what they share in common with existentialism as well as with one another is their rejection of a *foundationalist* approach to ethical normativity. Morality is rooted in social convention rather than in either a metaphysical system or a calculus of pleasure and pain. It is because we have agreed to value certain things that they have been rendered valuable, not because they have intrinsic value themselves.

CONCLUSION

The attempt to develop a coherent philosophical basis for normative moral action has been a preoccupation of ethical theory since its inception, and yet the conversation continues. One's normative framework often says as much about one's own ethical outlook as it does about the nature of moral action itself. It is not clear that any one moral theory is solely capable of accounting for the complexity of moral action, and so it may be necessary to abandon the search for one complete normative theory and seek to develop a mixture of different theories, which perhaps would not offer anything by way of completeness but would nevertheless satisfy our need for moral guidance in the particular times and places at which we find ourselves in need of moral guidance.

This is not a rejection of the idea that there may be such things as binding deontological principles or genuine human ends, nor is it a rejection of the importance of considering consequences in evaluating morality. It is to say, however, that our apparatus effectively determining which of these has precedence over the others is severely limited. Such a melding of different theories may rely to some degree on intuition but must also be based on the careful examination of the strengths and weaknesses of the variety of theories available and a recognition of when they do, and do not, give us an adequate picture of what is right, what is good, and what is fitting.

—Scott R. Paeth

Further Readings

Aquinas, T. (1987). *St. Thomas Aquinas on politics and ethics* (P. Sigmund, Ed.). New York: W. W. Norton.

Aristotle. (2000). *Nicomachean ethics.* Cambridge, UK: Cambridge University Press.

Barth, K. (1936–1952). *Church dogmatics* (14 vols.). Edinburgh, UK: T&T Clark.

Bentham, J. (1988). *The principles of morals and legislation.* New York: Prometheus Books.

Calvin, J. (1960). *Institutes of the Christian religion* (J. T. McNeill, Ed.). Philadelphia: Westminster Press.

Frankena, W. (1973). *Ethics* (2nd ed.). Englewood Cliffs, NJ: Prentice Hall.

Kant, I. (1993). *Critique of practical reason* (3rd ed.). (L. W. Beck, Trans.). New York: Macmillan.

Kant, I. (2002). *Groundwork for the metaphysics of morals* (A. Zweig & T. E. Hill, Jr., Eds.). Oxford, UK: Oxford University Press.

MacIntyre, A. (1984). *After virtue: A study in moral theory* (2nd ed.). Notre Dame, IN: University of Notre Dame Press.

Mill, J. S. (1989). *On liberty and other writings* (S. Collini, Ed.). Cambridge, UK: Cambridge University Press.

Mill, J. S. (2002). *Utilitarianism* (2nd ed.). Indianapolis, IN: Hackett.

Nozick, R. (1975). *Anarchy, state, and utopia.* Oxford, UK: Blackwell.

Rand, A. (1992). *Atlas shrugged.* New York: Dutton.

Rand, A., & Branden, N. (1965). *The virtue of selfishness: A new concept of egoism.* New York: New American Library.

Rawls, J. (1999). *Theory of justice.* Cambridge, MA: Harvard University Press.

Rorty, R. (1981). *Philosophy and the mirror of nature.* Princeton, NJ: Princeton University Press.

Rorty, R. (1989). *Contingency, irony, and solidarity.* Cambridge, UK: Cambridge University Press.

Ross, W. D. (2002). *Right and the good* (P. Stratton-Lake, Ed.). Oxford, UK: Clarendon Press.

Sartre, J. P. (1984). *Existentialism and human emotions.* New York: Citadel Press.

Stout, J. (2001). *Ethics after Babel: The languages of morals and their discontents.* Princeton, NJ: Princeton University Press.

Normative Ethics

PLURALISM

Pluralism generally is defined as the quality or state of being plural. Often, pluralism is used in the context of political science, particularly related to modern democracy. David Truman and Robert Dahl are two important exponents of political pluralism, which typically has competed with elitism and majoritarianism as a view of modern democratic societies. In its essence, political pluralism is the idea that individuals form interest groups that then compete with each other for favorable government policies. No group has more inherent power than another, and public officials (after lobbying by the interest groups) decide on policy based on their views of the public interest. An important feature of political pluralism is the understanding that competing groups' values are equally valid—that is, the claims made by interest groups cannot be ranked generically, allowing public officials to exercise their judgment in making policy decisions.

Applied to moral philosophy, the above definition typically translates to the idea that more than one moral principle, or more than one intrinsic good, are equally and universally valid. This definition places moral pluralism in contrast both with monism (the idea that one and only one principle is always and everywhere valid) and with subjectivism (the idea that no principle is universally valid).

Isaiah Berlin, perhaps the most well-known pluralist thinker of the 20th century, worked in both political and moral philosophy. Berlin emphasized objective pluralism (*objective* meaning that human values are part of the essence of humanity), which he wished to contrast with subjectivism. For Berlin, there were many different and irreducible values (also called ends or intrinsic goods) that men could seek. Although humans can understand others' values, and perhaps even admire them, because of their irreducible plurality, those values will at times be incompatible, and there is no common yardstick by which to judge which value is more important. In a political context, Berlin infers from this that people should be allowed as much freedom as possible, compatible with freedom for all; in a moral context, he infers that people with different values should respect each other. He does, of course, allow for the

PART III: Theories of Ethics

106

possibility of people, groups, and societies being wrong and of the necessity to fight those who are.

An example of a pluralistic theory that includes principles is that of Sir David Ross, a British academic like Berlin. Ross's theory is deontological in nature as well as pluralistic. He gives seven types of duties, none of which are seen to be more basic than any of the others, and three or four intrinsic goods. The duties include fidelity (keeping an explicit or implicit promise), reparation (making up for a previous wrong), gratitude (paying someone back for a good deed), justice (ensuring that people get what they deserve), beneficence (helping people in certain ways when we can), self-improvement (trying to improve our own condition in terms of virtue or knowledge), and nonmaleficence (not harming others). The intrinsic goods Ross lists are virtue, knowledge, justice (pleasure in proportion to virtue), and (at times) pleasure. When duties or intrinsic goods conflict, Ross calls on us to use our moral judgment to decide, all things considered, what is the proper action in the specific situation.

Mark Timmons argues that the most plausible versions of most moral theories are pluralistic in nature—what he calls "limited moral pluralism" in that there is a plurality of principles or goods, and the theory cannot give a final answer regarding the right action in specific situations without resort to moral judgment. For example, utilitarianism or natural law theory could each allow for a plurality of intrinsic goods and give limited guidance on how to resolve conflicts among those goods.

Other major theories can be seen in the same light. For example, Kant's theory could be seen as containing a collection of rules that specify duties but not containing any overarching principle from which the rules themselves would be derived (admittedly, it is not often interpreted in this manner). Virtue theory under this prism actually would contain many virtues, several of which would be central to the individual as a virtuous agent but none of which would be more important in that characterization than any of the others, and such a theory would contain no principle from which to derive rules on which virtue is more important in any given situation. American pragmatism also can be seen as a pluralist theory. However, it is different from the above examples in that the pluralism results from a plurality of individual ideas, not of principles or intrinsic goods.

Pluralism often is argued for because it seems to represent the reality of moral decision making better than the alternatives. A related argument in favor of pluralism concerns its treatment of moral judgment. Such judgment can be seen to be used by nearly all people in many situations. Judgment cannot be captured in a single principle, so a pluralistic account of morality fits better with our observations of people making decisions.

Two arguments against pluralism are that it is inconsistent and that it is indeterminate. That is, people who use moral pluralism privilege different principles or goods in different situations. Also, pluralistic theories give no easily identifiable rule for people to use in making decisions. Pluralists argue in return that inconsistency is important because situations and people are different and that indeterminacy is unimportant because the real world is complex and moral judgment is needed to navigate it.

Most of the moral decision frameworks put forward in the business and society fields are pluralistic in one form or another. For example, most theories arguing for consideration of multiple stakeholder interests are pluralistic to the extent that they do not rank stakeholders, thus putting the onus on managers to balance competing and valid stakeholder interests.

—Brian K. Burton

Further Readings

Ross, D. (1930). *The right and the good.* Oxford, UK: Oxford University Press.
Timmons, M. (2002). *Moral theory: An introduction.* Lanham, MD: Rowman & Littlefield.

PART III: Theories of Ethics

RECIPROCITY

Reciprocity is a pattern of mutually contingent exchange of gratifications, or tit for tat. Reciprocity can be shown to be one of the universal aspects of moral codes all around the world and has been argued to be the key for social stability. Reciprocal social mores range from mutual gift exchange to rules of hospitality. As a normative concept, reciprocity typically focuses on an individual's or an organization's return of fitting and proportional benefits for benefits bestowed by others. The return of harm for harm (which we usually call "retribution") tends to be a more controversial aspect of reciprocity. In addition, it is important to note that, because its core element is an exchange, reciprocity is not synonymous with the Golden Rule: Do unto others as you would have them do unto you.

Sociologists, game theorists, and evolutionary psychologists have provided evidence of the evolutionary advantages of tit-for-tat strategies in difficult-to-resolve situations, such as the prisoner's dilemma. Norms of reciprocity, grounded in enlightened self-interest, do not require the invocation of benevolence, or an active concern for the welfare of others, to justify virtues such as truth telling or cooperation. What is more controversial than the cultural universality of the norm of reciprocity and its importance for the evolution of cooperation is the moral question of whether one owes favors in return for involuntary prior favors. For this reason and a few other problems (e.g., the concrete meaning of "fitting," "proportional," or "equivalent" returns of favors), reciprocity has been endorsed a bit more warily by ethicists than by social scientists.

As for organizational behavior and theory, Bowie's and a few other ethicists' formulations of corporate social responsibility have shown it to be grounded in norms of reciprocity as well. According to this conceptualization, a company is a moral community in which stakeholders both create and are bound by the rules that govern their social relations. In turn, these relationships are reciprocal; that is, when one party in business dealings infuses the relationship with moral capital, it creates reciprocal duties on the other stakeholders. The definition of corporate responsibility would be too narrow if it focused only on the obligations of the firm. Other stakeholders also have rights and duties. For example, a company may owe its employees loyalty and fair employment practices, but a similar obligation (of loyalty) falls on employees in return. Similarly, we cannot stop environmental pollution by focusing on the emissions reduction of companies exclusively; customers must also do their part to create a demand for environmentally safe or conscious products. According to Bowie, what is needed is a comprehensive theory for determining the appropriate reciprocal duties that exist among corporate stakeholders. Because of the fact of moral pluralism, such a theory will most likely have to be quite complex and sophisticated.

—Marc Orlitzky

Further Readings

Axelrod, R. (1984). *The evolution of cooperation.* New York: Basic Books.

Becker, L. C. (1986). *Reciprocity.* Boston: Routledge.

Bowie, N. (1991). New directions in corporate social responsibility. *Business Horizons, 34*(4), 56–65.

Ekeh, P. P. (1974). *Social exchange theory: The two traditions.* Cambridge, MA: Harvard University Press.

Gouldner, A. (1960). The norm of reciprocity: A preliminary statement. *American Sociological Review, 25,* 161–178.

Singer, M. G. (1963). The golden rule. *Philosophy, 38,* 293–314.

ETHICS OF CARE

The term *ethics of care* refers to ideas concerning both the nature of morality and normative ethical theory. Over the past two decades or more, a discussion has arisen regarding these ideas. The caring perspective is distinctive in that it uses a relational and context-bound approach toward morality and decision making. In doing so, this perspective stands in stark contrast to ethical theories that rely on principles to highlight moral actions—such as Kantian deontology, utilitarianism, and justice theory. Importantly, such principles are meant to be absolute and incontrovertible.

Nel Noddings has provided one of the first comprehensive theories of care. Arguing that caring is the foundation of morality, she sees the dyadic relationship as ontologically basic to our very humanity. Identity is defined by the set of relationships individuals have with other humans, and as such without relationships we would not be human. In suggesting that caring is a universal human attribute, caring relation (a relationship in which people act in a caring manner) is seen to be ethically basic to humans. Since the impulse to care (in a specific way) is universal, caring ethics is freed from the charge of moral relativism to the same degree as is virtue theory.

The particularity of relations is fundamental to the ethics of care. Each relation consists of at least two people, the one-caring and the cared-for. Such a relation can certainly be more than merely dyadic as the one-caring and the cared-for come to exhibit reciprocal commitment to each other's well-being. However, what is distinctive in all such relations is that the one-caring acts in response to a perceived need on the part of the cared-for. The act is motivated by an apprehension of the cared-for's reality, a receiving of the cared-for into the one-caring such that the one-caring feels and senses what the cared-for is experiencing. The one-caring responds to the well-being of the cared-for by initiating a commitment to help the cared-for. Authentic care provides the motivation for such assistance. This does not mean that the one-caring does exactly what the cared-for desires in all situations. Rather, the one-caring considers the cared-for's point of view, assessment of need, and expectations of the one-caring in formulating a response that provides the best opportunity for helping the cared-for. This response might be irrational, since caring involves the commitment to do something, however remote the possibilities of success, to improve the cared-for's condition. In the ideal situation, however, the reason(s) the one-caring gives for his or her actions would be sufficient to convince a disinterested observer that he or she indeed acted in a way to promote the cared-for's well-being. Caring thus involves sentiment but is not necessarily emotional in nature.

Within the ethics of care the one-caring receives the cared-for without evaluation. However, in deciding how to respond, the one-caring works in what Nel Noddings calls a "problem-solving" mode—keeping in mind the particular relationship and context to avoid slipping into the abstract, impartial, impersonal reasoning of the deontologist, the utilitarian, or the justice theorist. Ultimately, there is a defining imperative to act that is a critical function of what it means to care.

These ideals apply to both natural caring, or caring born of inclination and love for those close to the one-caring, and ethical caring, which is the feeling response of "I must" to a person's predicament. Ethical caring is a natural outgrowth of natural caring, but unlike Kant's ranking of duty as primary and inclination as secondary, in the ethics of care the inclination to care is primary. Even with regard to those with whom one has no caring relationship—complete strangers—memories of natural caring arise, generating a feeling of "I must do something." This impulse is obligatory in anyone who aspires to what Noddings calls the "ethical ideal," the sense of self as a moral, caring person. However, within the ethics of care, this obligation to the stranger is limited. Two criteria must be met for such a duty to have force: (1) The relationship with the other person must exist (or have the potential to exist), and (2) the relationship must have the potential to grow into a mutually caring relationship. One does not have either the capacity or the duty to care for everyone; however, one does hold an obligation to be prepared to care at all times for particular others—for "the proximate stranger."

ETHICS OF CARE AND FEMINISM

It would be easy to confuse the ethics of care with feminist ethics. Feminist philosophers have argued that the deontological, utilitarian, and justice moral theories are grounded in the masculine experience. More specifically, these theories are seen to emerge in concert with the traditionally masculine forum of economic activity. Within this perspective, the values of competition and domination are seen to undergird both the activities of the marketplace and the rational moral theories. Virginia Held argues for adopting more compassionate bases for our human interaction(s).

Feminist moral theory at its heart has tended to mirror the differing gender experiences of women and men, particularly as these affect the development of understanding with respect to the ways the ethical life is conducted. However, it has been noted by Robbin Derry and others that *feminist* moral theory is not *feminine* moral theory, as feminist perspectives are not fully determined by gendered points of view. Nevertheless, the suggestion that gender matters, particularly as gender relates to one's ethical predispositions, calls into question the inherent "objectivity" of ethical theories, which are advanced in part due to their universal merit and application. Feminine moral theory thereby deals a blow to the exclusively rational systems of thought, which have as their grounding an inherent disregard for the inherently personal—and sometimes gender biased—nature of knowledge construction.

It was not necessary that feminine moral theory be aligned with the ethics of care. It so happens that those writing in the feminine tradition, such as Carol Gilligan, came to associate care and responsibility to others with a female-gendered approach to ethics and individual rights and justice with a male-gendered approach to ethics. Gilligan in particular made the argument that, historically, philosophers have seen women as morally inferior to men, when in fact they are simply different in emphasizing care over justice. However, central to the feminist perspective is not the content of the gender-specific approaches but rather the more fundamental observation that gender—and by extension a host of other demographic factors and interpersonal predispositions as well—contributes substantially to an individual's moral insight and development. This being the case, there is no reason to privilege masculine-rational approaches to ethics above feminine-caring approaches to ethics.

ETHICS OF CARE WITHIN THE BUSINESS CONTEXT

The caring approach avoids the problem that many approaches to ethical management face: deciding whose rights, among people with roughly equal rights, will be respected. While all have the duty to treat others in a caring way, in cases of conflicts of duty, the responsibility of the one-caring includes deciding who is most appropriately the beneficiary of care and then acting on that judgment. It is the concrete, particular individual with whom one has a caring relationship whose well-being must take priority in each inherently unique circumstance.

If caring is regarded as a natural inclination that serves as the base for the development of specific character traits, then one can begin to understand what caring business praxis might mean. Gilligan discusses three levels of a caring morality—one where the self is cared for to the exclusion of the other, one where the other is cared for to the exclusion of the self, and a third where the needs of both self and other are understood. This third level is the one Gilligan sees as moral maturity. While stopping short of equating feminist ethics with virtue ethics, Brian Burton and Craig Dunn suggest that this portrayal sounds very much like the description of an Aristotelian virtue. Not opposed to a legitimate place for emotion in ethical discourse, Aristotle outlines the importance of feeling at the proper times, about important things, concerning the right people, and for good reasons. Aristotle further sees the moral person as possessing various character traits and describes a virtue as behavior regarding a particular trait that is a mean between two extremes of behavior, with one showing an excess of that trait and the other showing deficiency of the trait. Applying this depiction to caring, the virtue would be caring (understanding the needs of self and other), the vice of excess might be codependence (caring for others to the exclusion of self), and the vice of deficiency might be selfishness (caring for self to the exclusion of others).

To achieve the goal of the caring approach to management, the manager needs to understand what the mean of caring is, what this implies for different situations, and what specific virtues are associated with the base of caring. The manager can then care for the particular individuals involved in a specific situation by apprehending their reality, considering their well-being, and acting in a manner that is in their best interest(s) or explain, in cases of conflict, why the action taken might not readily be seen as in the best interest of the cared-for.

ETHICS OF CARE AND STAKEHOLDER THEORY

Much of the discussion regarding the relevance to management of the ethics of care has taken place within the bounds, or in attempting to expand the bounds, of stakeholder theory. Efforts have been made to use the language of stakeholder theory to describe the caring perspective or use the ethics of care to normatively justify stakeholder theory. In some instances, the ethics of care—or, more accurately, feminine ethics—have even been advanced as the grounding for a new theory of the firm.

Just as the most often discussed forms of moral theory focus on masculine principles, however, most discussions of stakeholder theory give decision rules for how to interact with stakeholders. In categorizing stakeholders and in giving generic principles for interacting with the stakeholder categories thus formed, theorists have moved away from the essence of the ethics of care—understanding the particular context and fashioning a response to that context. But caring cannot be captured in decision rules and universalizable principles. Rather, discussions of caring by their nature center on how we live or, in a business context, how we manage relationships (not contractual obligations), which, after all, form the whole of managerial behavior. Caring focuses on particular cases, with the understanding that each situation is unique. Caring elicits intuitive responses at first, with rational analysis coming later. Caring has an underlying context of moral sensitivity instead of detachment.

Numerous writers maintain that the ethics of care provide a better way of describing the environment in which a manager operates and the manager's response to that environment than principle-based approaches. The primary difficulty with stakeholder theory in the latter instance is that it imagines stakeholders not as individuals but rather as members of homogeneous groups. Although they are members of stakeholder groups, however, when approaching the manager, stakeholders do so as individuals. Each stakeholder naturally holds unique—and in some instances caring—relations to the manager. Each stakeholder holds perceived needs that he or she is trying to convince the manager to satisfy, and such needs will vary from context to context.

The moral impulse of managers is to respond to each stakeholder with understanding, concern, and the desire to do something to help the stakeholder. Such impulses cannot in all instances be explained through the perspectives of the more rational systems of ethical decision making. In fact, Noddings and Gilligan both argue that training in these systems may well extinguish the caring impulse. Furthermore, that impulse decreases as the relationship with the stakeholder becomes more distant—the "I must" response becomes less of an imperative because other stakeholders with closer relationships with the manager also bring forth the "I must" response and the manager can only react to a limited number of stakeholders.

ETHICS OF CARE AND MANAGEMENT THEORY

There is a great opportunity to apply the ethics of care to organizational research and praxis. It is not too difficult to imagine how the crafting of an organization's statement of purpose and mission might be informed by this perspective. Policies supporting work-family balance are easily seen as a matter of ethics of care. Recruiting and hiring practices might take into account the well-being of the cared-for—the prospective employee. A variety of employment practices, from job sharing to telecommuting to job rotation, could reflect caring impulses that not only explicitly acknowledge the particularity of intra-office relations but serve to honor interoffice relationships as well. Vacation and sick leave policies, termination guidelines, employee assistance programs, profit participation plans, performance appraisal, and so on— the litany of organizational practices that might prove to be natural extensions of the moral impulse to care seems limitless.

—Craig P. Dunn and Brian K. Burton

Further Readings

Aristotle. (1985). *Nicomachean ethics* (T. Irwin, Trans.). Indianapolis, IN: Hackett.

Burton, B. K., & Dunn, C. P. (1996). Feminist ethics as moral grounding for stakeholder theory. *Business Ethics Quarterly, 6,* 133–147.

Derry, R. (1996). Toward a feminist firm: Comments on John Dobson and Judith White. *Business Ethics Quarterly, 6,* 101–109.

Dobson, J. (1996). The feminine firm: A comment. *Business Ethics Quarterly, 6,* 227–232.

Dobson, J., & White, J. (1995). Toward the feminine firm: An extension to Thomas White. *Business Ethics Quarterly, 5,* 463–478.

Freeman, R. E. (1984). *Strategic management: A stakeholder approach.* Boston: Pitman.

Gilligan, C. (1982). *In a different voice: Psychological theory and women's development.* Cambridge, MA: Harvard University Press.

Held, V. (2005). *The ethics of care: Personal, political, global.* New York: Oxford University Press.

Noddings, N. (1984). *Caring: A feminine approach to ethics and moral education.* Berkeley: University of California Press.

Rawls, J. (1971). *A theory of justice.* Cambridge, MA: Belknap Press.

Wicks, A. C. (1996). Reflections on the practical relevance of feminist thought to business. *Business Ethics Quarterly, 6,* 523–531.

Wicks, A. C., Gilbert, D. R., Jr., & Freeman, R. E. (1994). A feminist reinterpretation of the stakeholder concept. *Business Ethics Quarterly, 4,* 475–497.

PART IV

Ethics of Business and Management

ETHICS OF MANAGEMENT

When discussing management ethics, it is natural to focus on the management of business as many schools of management have done. However, nearly all organizations need managers—universities, not-for-profits, sports teams, and government agencies. Thus, management ethics covers a wider terrain than business ethics. Although the emphasis in this entry will be on the ethical management of a business, many of the comments here are generalizable to ethical management in general.

MANAGING FOR SHAREHOLDER WEALTH

The starting point for ethical management should be role morality. Role morality is the morality of one's station and its duties. The duties of one's station are determined by the purpose of the organization. Suppose we take the traditional starting point for the purpose of a corporation. Milton Friedman's position is the standard: that business has only one responsibility, which is to use its resources to increase its profits, engaging in free and open competition without deception or fraud. Under this view the manager is the agent of the stockholders who are the owners of the firm. As an agent of the stockholders the ethical obligation of the manager is to do the bidding of the stockholders, which normally is to make as much money as possible while following the basic rules of society, according to both the law and ethical custom. Many people do not see making money for stockholders as a *moral* obligation, and professors of finance seldom teach it as a moral obligation, but Friedman's position is a moral position nonetheless.

It should also be pointed out that violation of this simple moral requirement is behind many of the scandals that have afflicted business and behind many of the criticisms of business with respect to corporate governance. Excessive executive compensation and lavish executive perks are a violation of the ethical obligation of managers to increase the profits of stockholders. Many of the accounting scandals of the 1990s and 2000s were the result of managers manipulating earnings so that they could get their stock options or bonuses. These managers were not working for the stockholders and violating the law and ethics on behalf of the stockholders. Rather they were violating the law and ethical custom for their own selfish gain.

The qualifications that Friedman makes to the obligation of managers to increase shareholder wealth are significant, however. Even if the manager is the agent of the stockholders, he or she cannot be asked to make profits in a way that the law deems illegal or that violates ethical custom. The term *ethical custom* can have narrow or a broad application. Friedman specifically rules out anticompetitive practices and deception and fraud. However, some in Friedman's camp do allow bluffing. Albert Carr pointed out that the ethics of business is more like the ethics of poker than the ethics of ordinary morality. There is still no consensus as to what should be included under Friedman's term *ethical custom*.

One item that is not included in ethical custom for Friedman is philanthropic giving from profits or the use of profits to help solve social problems: that is, using profits for social responsibility. If a manager uses the profits for philanthropy or social responsibility, he or she is taking the money that belongs to the stockholders and using it for other purposes without their permission. Friedman characterizes this as a kind of taxation without representation. However, Friedman is assuming that the stockholders do not want corporations to engage in philanthropy or help solve social problems. However, the stance of individual corporations with respect to philanthropy and social responsibility is well known. For example, the stockholders of the Target Corporation are well aware or reasonably should be aware of the fact that Target is one of the more generous companies with respect to corporate giving. Target stockholders either are willing to sacrifice some of their profits for the public good or, more likely, believe that Target's record of charitable giving will result in a competitive advantage that yields even more profit in the long run.

AN ALTERNATIVE TO THE STOCKHOLDER VIEW: SUSTAINABLE MANAGEMENT PRACTICE

It is important to realize that Friedman's view of the obligations of managers has a particularly American flavor to it. There is a consensus in capitalist countries that increasing shareholder or owner wealth is a moral obligation of managers; however, American managers focus on that one obligation while the consensus in other capitalist countries is that there is more to the purpose of a corporation than lawfully and ethically making money. The European

Union has as its official policy that the corporation must practice sustainable management. (A term that is often used synonymously with "sustainable management" is Corporate Social Responsibility Europe or CSR Europe. This latter terminology seems to be giving way to the former, however.) Sustainable management or management in accord with Corporate Social Responsibility broadens the duties of the manager. On the European view, sustainable management requires financial success but it also requires obligations to protect the environment and to be socially responsible. In Europe, "social responsibility" is not understood in terms of philanthropy but rather is understood in terms of respecting human rights. The Europeans have even come up with the notion of triple bottom line accounting that broadens the traditional accounting determination of financial success to include measurements of environmental responsibility and social responsibility. Triple bottom line accounting is still in its early stages of development, and it is unclear how successfully quantitative triple bottom line accounting can become.

The position of the European Union on the ethical responsibilities of managers is similar to that taken by the United Nations in its United Nations Global Compact. An international effort affiliated with the United Nations Global Compact is the Global Reporting Initiative that is designed to present common international principles for bottom line accounting.

The philosophy that will govern capitalist countries in Asia is still evolving. The Japanese are moving away from a more collective and paternalistic set of management practices, but in doing so, they seem to prefer the model of sustainability rather than Friedman's maximization of profit model. Academicians in China are working with a notion of corporate social responsibility for their society.

There is now a debate regarding the eventual financial viability of the two models. Many Americans believe that the more narrowly focused emphasis on stockholder wealth is ultimately the more successful model. Much of the rest of the world seems to disagree. One implication of this debate is that when one specifies the ethical obligations of managers one must be clear what one takes the primary function or purpose of the firm to be.

STAKEHOLDER MANAGEMENT

Whether one is an adherent of Friedman's increase shareholder wealth philosophy or an adherent of the sustainability philosophy, one will hear many references to stakeholder management. To fully understand management ethics, we need to be clear about the obligations that managers have to corporate stakeholders. In the U.S. academic literature, stakeholder management is often positioned as an alternative to Friedman's stockholder theory. As an alternative to Friedman, the theory requires that the moral obligation of the manager is to balance the interests of the legitimate stakeholders of the business. (It should be noted that any organization such as a university or charity can use stakeholder analysis.) On a narrow definition of stakeholder, a stakeholder, or more accurately stakeholder group, is defined as a group that can affect the firm's survival. On a broader definition, a stakeholder is a group or individual that is affected by the behavior of the firm. On the narrow definition, the traditional stakeholders are stockholders, customers, employees, suppliers, managers, and the local community. Some add government, media, and nongovernmental organizations (NGOs) to the list.

Stakeholder theory is still a work in progress. It is not a moral theory in its own right. The range of legitimate stakeholders is still a matter of controversy, and there is no acceptable methodology for balancing the interests of stakeholders. However, when taken as an alternative to Friedman's stockholder view, each legitimate stakeholder has the right to have its interests taken into account, and it is the obligation of the manager to do so.

It is not enough to consider the interests of the stakeholders simply to increase the wealth of the stockholders. To do so would simply use a stakeholder as a means to the wealth of another. Each stakeholder has legitimate interests of its own, which deserve ethical treatment in their own right.

It should be noted that nearly all companies, including American ones, use stakeholder language. In Europe, the discussion centers on stakeholder dialogues. Such dialogues are a device that managers use to achieve sustainability. Despite the difficulty faced in determining stakeholder interests and in balancing them, a number of the largest companies in the world, such as BP and Shell, use a rather broad definition of stakeholder analysis to guide management practice.

Stakeholder theory has important heuristic uses as one considers management ethics. Every organization has stakeholders, and one effective way of looking at the ethical obligations of managers is to do a stakeholder analysis. In this way, there is a generic principle of management ethics that applies to all types of management. That is, management has an obligation to consider the interests of legitimate stakeholders and to achieve a balance in honoring those interests.

At that point, management ethics becomes specific to the organization. A major research university has a different function and a different set of stakeholders than that of a major corporation. Thus, the obligations of a university president are different from the obligations of a typical business CEO. Even within business, management ethics may require different obligations depending on the kind of business one is engaged in. For example, an entrepreneurial firm that is dependent on venture capital has a broader range and perhaps a more stringent set of obligations to the provider of venture capital than a manager has to stockholders in a Fortune 500 company. Both the amount of risk to capital and the magnitude of the risk to the venture capitalist are usually sufficient to distinguish the venture capitalist from the ordinary stockholder.

Of course, some stakeholders are common to almost any organization. Nearly all organizations have employees as well as clients. In the university, the clients are students and in business the clients are customers. All but self-sufficient organizations have suppliers. Universities, corporations, and not-for-profit medical facilities all depend on suppliers. And all organizations exist in the natural environment and in a local community. Organizations also have different stakeholders, that is, stakeholders of one organization may not be stakeholders for another organization. Public companies are unique from both partnerships and single proprietorships and from other nonbusiness organizations in the fact that public companies have stockholders as stakeholders. Discussion of the obligations of business managers to these basic stakeholders follow.

THE ETHICAL GROUNDING OF A MANAGER'S ROLE OBLIGATIONS

The fact the stakeholder theory is a theory of management and not an ethical theory should be emphasized. Even our general principle of ethical stakeholder management described above needs to be justified. In other words, it is not enough to limit management ethics to my station and its duties. Role obligations need to be consistent with and justified by higher-order or more universal moral concepts. Otherwise, the role obligations of a mafia don becomes an example of management ethics. Effectiveness in carrying out one's role is not sufficient to establish the morality of one's carrying it out.

Organizations are made up of persons. Respect for persons is a central moral principle both in the world at large and in moral theory. Management ethics requires that those managed are treated with respect. Given this universal, the moral task of the managers is to implement respect for persons in the organizational setting in which they find themselves.

Since organizations are collectivities, ethical managers must consider the good of the entire organization. This requires that the individuals within an organization function as a team. One of the great challenges to ethical managers results when he or she needs to sacrifice the need of an individual for the good of the organization. Coaches of athletic teams often face this dilemma. But corporate CEOs do as well. Sometimes the survival of the business requires layoffs. Ethical management requires that when an individual interest is sacrificed for the organizational good, the individual must be treated with respect. Even when layoffs are justified and necessary, there is a right way (respectful way) and a wrong way (disrespectful way) of laying someone off.

Ethical management also involves certain attitudes and dispositions. Let us refer to these as the virtues of ethical management. What is to count as the appropriate virtues of the ethical manager is a matter of great controversy. Some managers believe that employees are basically self-motivated and trustworthy and thus should be mentored rather than bossed. Others believe that employees present agency problems, that is, they will always loaf and take other actions to advance their own interests rather than the interest of the organization. Such managers think that free riding on the part of employees is a serious problem. In the context of employee conduct in the real world, it is hard to say which attitude toward managing employees is the correct one. It may be that a mentoring relationship is morally appropriate in some business contexts and that a monitoring relationship is the morally appropriate attitude to take in other contexts.

At this point we can say that management ethics involves respecting the persons whom one manages, taking into account the good of the collective entity that one manages for and cultivating those managerial virtues that increase the likelihood that the manager will indeed respect persons and promote the good of the organization. A general ethical principle for ethical management is that managers consider the interests of legitimate stakeholders in management decisions.

THE ETHICAL TREATMENT OF EMPLOYEES

Respect for persons is the fundamental moral principle for managing people. What does that entail in the typical business? Many would argue that respect for persons requires some participation and voice on the part of the employee.

Certain laws and managerial norms stand in the way of employee participation and voice. One is the legal doctrine of employment at will. Employment at will indicates that in the absence of a contract and in the absence of illegal discrimination, both the employer and the employee are free to sever the employment relationship at any time for any reason—good reason, bad reason, or reason immoral. Some defenders of employment at will point out that since both the employer and the employee can exercise employment at will, any ethical issues are eliminated or at least greatly lessened. Critics of employment at will point out that it is easier for the manager to find another employee than for the employee to find another job. As a legal matter, the relationship may be symmetrical, but as a matter of fact it is not symmetrical. Critics also point out that severing a relationship for a bad reason or reason immoral is always prima facie wrong. Even the courts have gone part way to recognizing the critics' point by allowing a public good exception to the employment at will doctrine.

Another danger to the ethical treatment of employees is created by paying excessive attention to hierarchies within the organization. Hierarchies are often represented in organization flowcharts that show who reports to whom. As devices to show reporting relationships they may raise no ethical red flags. However, when they reflect how decisions are made in the organization, they can become morally problematic. If one is lower in the hierarchy, that should not mean that he or she should simply follow orders and have no voice in the decisionmaking process. There is also a danger that those at a higher position will hoard information and keep subordinates in the dark. Indeed not only will subordinates be kept in the dark, but they will be deceived as well.

There are a number of management practices that counteract these dangers. Labor unions and employment contracts serve as an antidote to employment at will. It should be noted in passing that the United States is fairly unique among industrialized countries in subscribing to employment at will. With respect to hierarchies, a number of enlightened management practices are designed to undermine hierarchies. Quality circles, team building, and participative management all represent steps in the direction of participation and voice for employees. One of the more comprehensive practices is open book management. Open book management eliminates information asymmetry by providing all financial information to all employees. In so doing, each employee will see how the business runs; in other words, the employees will think like owners. And from the perspective of management ethics, they will take more responsibility and thus exercise participation and voice.

Employees have a right to be concerned with an important change in the marketplace. By the mid-20th century, employees believed that they had a social contract with management that, when honored, justified loyalty to management and the business firm. Even within the doctrine of employment at will, it was assumed that a good worker would continue with the firm until retirement. In some industries, as many as three generations within the same family would have worked in the firm. As well as a living wage employees would receive health insurance and a pension. In other words, an element of corporate paternalism was expected even though the United States had nothing like the Japanese system of guaranteed lifetime employment. As the 20th century came to an end, there had been massive upheaval in labor markets in part caused by global competition. Downsizing became all the rage. Others lost their jobs due to outsourcing. Some layoffs were also caused by efforts to please the short-term traders on Wall Street. Too often, employees were seen simply as a cost rather than human capital. Where layoffs from the impacts of globalization are probably morally justified, layoffs to please Wall Street are ethically suspect. These layoffs are simply using some as a means for the financial ends of others. In some industries, the layoffs were in the tens of thousands. In addition, the paternalism disappeared. Early into the 21st century, employees were asked to contribute much more to their health insurance if they were fortunate enough to receive employer subsidized insurance at all. Defined pensions were dropped and workers had to save for their retirement from their salaries. The fortunate ones received a percentage of their salaries as a benefit although the individual employee was responsible for investing the funds. The size of the pension a worker was to receive was not guaranteed. Employers referred to this change as the "New Social Contract." It was hardly a contract since the employees had no say in its terms. The terms of the contract are also perceived by many to be unfair.

As a result of these changes employees need to change their expectations. Employees should not expect lifetime employment or paternalistic benefits; they need to manage their careers and make their own financial decisions. They also need to take more responsibility for managing their health care and their retirement. However, as a result of these changed expectations, the old notion of loyalty has practically disappeared. To many it seems that market considerations are now the only determinant of what employees receive in terms of salary and benefits. Ethical notions such as past promises, fair distribution from the gains of productivity, and loyalty seem far less relevant than they were a few years ago. Many ethicists believe that this change in expectations is patently unfair to employees.

MANAGING ETHICAL OBLIGATIONS TO CUSTOMERS

Since customers are so essential to the success of a business enterprise, you might think that managers would consider their obligations to customers to be paramount. On occasion a company, especially in advertisements, will talk that way, such as proclaiming that "the customer is number one." For instance, the Johnson & Johnson Credo ranks the customer first among its stakeholders. Despite this endorsement of the importance of the customer, there are a number of important issues regarding the treatment of customers that deserve the attention of the ethical manager.

Customers are often in a situation of high information asymmetry with respect to the products they buy. That is, the seller of the product knows much more about the product than the customer. In such situations, there is always a temptation for the salesperson to sell the customer something more expensive than is needed. This temptation is especially acute when the sales staff is on commission. What are the obligations of the sales manager with respect to how his or her sales staff should deal with situations of high information asymmetry?

One might argue that the customer has the obligation to search out the information that will close the information gap. In its most extreme form, this is the philosophy of "Let the buyer beware." That philosophy is neither legally nor ethically suited to a world where the products are so complex. On the other hand, a moral requirement that sales managers operate under a principle that provides the customer with whatever information he or she would want is much too broad. There is no obligation for a sales manager to tell a customer that a competitor has the same product on sale at a lower price. Some middle ground is the ethically appropriate answer here.

Surely sales people should not lie or deceive. If a customer asks if a 32" flat panel TV will work in an apartment, the sales person should not try to sell him a 58" TV on the grounds that the 32" one is too small.

To help define the ethically appropriate line in providing information to customers, two things need to be considered. First, how are salespeople compensated? An overemphasis on commissions will tempt salespeople to sell the most expensive product even if it is not needed. Second, would finding the ethical solution to this dilemma be more likely if salespeople thought of themselves as professionals rather than traditional salespeople? Putting salespeople exclusively on salary and expecting them to behave like professionals might go far in overcoming the problem of customer information asymmetry.

Vulnerable consumers ethically require more help in overcoming information asymmetry. Unfortunately, this ethical obligation is breached by the unscrupulous, who play on the information asymmetry you find in the elderly and in the uneducated. It is common to find senior citizens paying for sealed driveways or roofs they do not need. However, the ethical issues here involve more than deception. Target marketing is an accepted and even essential way of doing business. However, when a vulnerable population is targeted, ethical issues arise. The beer industry was rightly criticized for targeting inner city blacks with ads for malt liquor. Marketing managers need to be especially sensitive when their customers might be considered vulnerable and thus harmed by the product being marketed.

Other ethical issues in the treatment of customers concern fairness. Does being a good customer permit special treatment? Often it does. We seem to accept the fact that frequent flyers are entitled to special perks. However, it is alleged that good customers get special treatment when they call a credit card company or a bank regarding a problem. That is, these customers get a live person quickly or have a shorter wait time. Is that fair? Indeed, the whole system of automated phone answering devices is highly unpopular with customers. It seems to take forever to get to the option that applies to you and even when you get there you might not be able to resolve the problem. Automated check-out lines in grocery stores and discount stores as well as automatic check-in lines that the airlines have introduced shift the transaction costs from the seller to the buyer. What is the fair burden for dividing the transaction costs? These and similar issues deserve the attention of the ethical sales and marketing manager.

THE ETHICAL MANAGEMENT OF THE SUPPLY CHAIN

Managers have always had ethical obligations to their suppliers. However, recently there have been demands in some industries that managers have an ethical responsibility for their suppliers. This distinction can be illustrated by some examples.

With respect to ethical obligations to suppliers, it seems as if managers have an obligation to keep their word, for example, by honoring their contracts. Many would argue that faithful suppliers with a long history of supplying high-quality products at a reasonable price deserve loyalty and should not be instantly dropped when the manager can get a competitive product for a slightly lower price. Unfortunately, the real world is departing rather sharply from the ethical ideal. Suppliers are always being pressured to lower their price and to "renegotiate" contracts in order to keep the business. Loyalty to suppliers seems to be a thing of the past as long-term suppliers are instantly dropped if a competitor comes in at a slightly lower price. The ethical manager has a difficult balancing act to perform— on the one hand, responding to the demands of the market and on the other being fair to faithful suppliers with a long and good track record with the company.

Recently, the ethical manager has been required to take responsibility for ensuring that their suppliers behave ethically. This has been particularly true in the apparel and sportswear industry where the distributors of these products such as Nike and the Gap were criticized because of the sweatshop conditions that had existed at a number of their suppliers. Activists and nongovernmental agencies have demanded that the distributors of these products require their suppliers to provide safe working conditions and a living wage. They have demanded that distributors provide the names of their suppliers so that those suppliers could be subjected to independent inspections.

This demand that managers police their suppliers and require certain forms of behavior is controversial. There is no question that working conditions in the sweatshops are bad—indeed very bad—when compared with manufacturing facilities in industrialized countries. On the other hand, some economists have argued that sweatshops are a necessary step in economic development and that well-intentioned steps to improve sweatshops only make the economic situation worse. Beyond the debate about economics, there is also an ethical issue about responsibility. Normally, we are only held responsible for our conduct; we are not held responsible for the conduct of others. But this is not always the case. In theory, the managers of bars and taverns are required by law and ethics not to serve or continue to serve obviously drunk customers. Indeed, on occasion these managers have been sued when a drunk customer has driven away only to be involved in an accident that injures or kills another. Some states and munici- palities have passed laws holding gun manufacturers responsible in certain cases when gun owners commit a crime, especially a crime in which the victim is killed by a gun. Opponents of extending responsibility in this way are trying to pass a national law that would invalidate such attempts by states and municipalities to hold gun manufacturers liable.

Despite the controversy surrounding these cases, the public has accepted without much debate a moral requirement on sportswear and apparel distributors to take responsibility for their suppliers. Perhaps part of the reason for the willingness to extend responsibility here is because the sweatshop issue has been construed as a human rights issue; the sweatshop manufacturers are seen to be violating internationally accepted human rights. If that allegation is correct, then a serious moral wrong is taking place because the violation of human rights is a serious moral wrong. The argument then goes that major international corporations in the apparel and sportswear industry should not take advantage of the victims of human rights violations to make a profit. Indeed, under the European Union model of corporate social responsibility, managing a business consistent with human rights and in a way that supports human rights is a moral requirement. When framed in that way, the leap to taking responsibility for your suppliers does not seem like such a great leap.

MANAGEMENT'S OBLIGATIONS TO
THE COMMUNITY AND THE ENVIRONMENT

Business does not take place in a vacuum. It is contextually located in a community or communities, which in turn are located in the natural environment. There are those who say that a business provides jobs—the very lifeblood of a community. It also usually pays taxes to the community just as individuals do. As a result, there is no further obligation to the community—in the form of charitable giving or in the form of helping to resolve social problems. Indeed, those who follow the view of Milton Friedman believe that it is morally wrong for managers to assist in these ways.

Despite the view of the Friedmanites, some form of corporate social responsibility is accepted as an obligation—at least on the part of the large companies. But is such an obligation justified? Some have argued for such an obligation on the basis of the great financial resources that these large companies possess. Others have made an argument on the great power that large corporations have. With great power and great resources goes great responsibility, and part of that responsibility involves philanthropy and other activities that benefit the public good.

Another way to establish a managerial obligation to the community is to challenge the "we provide jobs and pay taxes" argument. The "pay taxes" piece is especially vulnerable since many companies get states or localities to compete for the business and the most common way that states and localities compete is to give tax breaks. Even the "create jobs" piece of the argument has been recently challenged. Wal-Mart, for example, has been criticized for paying such low wages and providing so few benefits that many of its employees need Medicaid or other forms of public assistance. The business press has taken notice and now refers to the pushing of health and pension costs on the public as another form of corporate outsourcing. To the extent that these arguments are correct, the firm has an obligation to the community on grounds of fairness.

However the theoretical arguments play out, most companies at least make gestures to a responsibility to the community. Small businesses support charitable events in their communities and large companies have foundations or designated programs for charitable giving and community service.

Concern with the effects of business activity on the environment is now a focus of managerial ethics. The first step in environmental stewardship occurred when businesses realized that there were huge cost savings in waste and energy reduction. Although great progress has been made here, the international traveler cannot help but notice that the United States is behind other industrialized countries in taking easy steps to reduce stress on the environment. In Europe and Japan, for example, sheets in hotels are not changed every day unless requested, escalators do not run day and night even when no one is using them, and lights in hallways and elevators turn off automatically when no one is there. Also when you leave your hotel room and take your key, the lights go out.

The real challenge for managerial ethics involves business decisions that help the environment and perhaps even profits in the long run but that hurt profits in the short run. The most acute example here is in the automobile industry. Car makers, especially GM and Ford, make the best profit margins on SUVs and have marketed these cars very successfully. However, these vehicles have low gas mileage and other problems. Should GM have even produced the Hummer—a monster gas guzzler? Do the automobile companies have a duty to educate consumers about the cost to the environment when purchasing SUVs? One of the great challenges for managerial ethics is in developing a business strategy that is both profitable and environmentally responsible.

Ethical Leadership

One of the tests of management ethics is whether one is both an effective manager and an ethical manager. Management ethics is more than effective management. This moral fact has important consequences in any discussion of leadership. Ethical leadership is more than effective leadership and thus not everyone who manages a company successfully can be considered a moral leader. Just what that something else besides effectiveness entails is a matter of great controversy in leadership study and practice.

Honoring the role obligations that fall on all managers such as putting the good of the organization above their own interests as well as honoring the obligations of managers to the various stakeholders are key parts of management ethics. So is moral imagination. Moral imagination involves looking at business decisions and strategy from different points of view. It involves creative attempts to be profitable and ethical. This is the challenge that faces the automobile industry as well as many other industries. In the long run being effective is not sufficient; being effective while being ethical is what successful management is all about.

—Norman E. Bowie

Further Readings

Bowie, N. E. (1999). *Business ethics: A Kantian perspective.* Oxford, UK: Blackwell.

Bowie, N. E. (2005). *Management ethics.* Malden, MA: Blackwell.

Freeman, R. E. (1984). *Strategic management: A stakeholder approach.* Boston: Pitman.

Freeman, R. E. (2004). A stakeholder theory of the modern corporation. In T. L. Beauchamp, ed. & N. E. Bowie (Eds.), *Ethical theory and business (7th ed).* Upper Saddle River, NJ: Prentice Hall.

Friedman, M. (1970, September 13). The social responsibility of business is to increase its profits. *New York Times.*

Harrison, J. and Freeman, E. Stakeholders, social responsibility and performance: Empirical evidence and theoretical perspectives. *Academy of Management Journal* vol. 42 (1999). pp. 479–487.

Pfeffer, J. (1998). *The human equation.* Boston: Harvard Business School Press.

Werhane, P. (1999). *Moral imagination and management decisionmaking.* Oxford, UK: Oxford University Press.

Werhane, P. H., & Radin, T. J. (2004). *Employment and employee rights.* Oxford, UK: Blackwell.

Ethics of Management

INTERNATIONAL
BUSINESS ETHICS

The question of what ethical norms, if any, should guide the conduct of business across national boundaries is the primary subject of international business ethics. We live in an era of increasing economic globalization. While trade among nations has been an important feature of the global economy for centuries, recent years have seen a rapid increase in international trade. Multinational corporations (MNCs) are powerful actors on this global stage, and their influence is increasing. Outsourcing of the production of consumer goods to developing nations is a standard feature of nearly all MNCs that design, market, and sell apparel, footwear, electronics, toys, and household goods. In response to increased demand for natural resources, MNCs in the extractive industries have increased their exploration and extraction operations throughout the world. And, increasingly, all MNCs that market to individual consumers are targeting relatively affluent consumers across national boundaries. These are staple features of the global economy. Typically such globalizing strategies enable MNCs to meet increased demand, offer goods and services to customers at lower prices, and at the same time enhance their own profits.

MNCs operate in a multitude of political jurisdictions and so are subject to a multitude of legal frameworks. Frequently, the laws regarding matters such as the treatment of customers, the treatment of employees, and protection for the environment are significantly different in different host nations. In the case of developing economies, consumer protection, worker safety, and environmental safeguards are often poorly developed or nonexistent. Even when such laws exist in developing nations, the law enforcement and judicial apparatus necessary to ensure compliance does not exist. MNCs operating in such nations are often free to determine for themselves whether or not they will adhere to host nation laws. As a result, MNCs must determine for themselves what minimum moral standards ought to be adhered to in their global operations.

GLOBAL JUSTICE

Global justice has become a centrally important issue in moral and political philosophy in the era of economic globalization. The facts that inspire much contemporary work on global justice are increasingly well known. Nearly 1 billion people are malnourished and without access to safe drinking water. Approximately 50,000 human deaths per day are attributable to poverty-related causes. When the attention of trade economists is called to these stark facts regarding global poverty, they are wont to point to the need for economic liberalization in the interest of job creation in the world's poorest nations. They argue that the exploitation by MNCs of cheap labor supplies, abundant natural resources, and lax regulatory regimes allows developing countries to expand export activities and to improve their economies. This economic growth brings desperately needed jobs, which cause labor markets to tighten, which will eventually force MNCs to improve the treatment of workers to attract workers. As wages rise, workers spend more and local economies expand. However, the present-day costs in human health and welfare of such development schemes are frequently at odds with basic ethical norms. Workers are often treated as disposable tools, and local environments are often polluted in ways that harm human welfare and inhibit future well-being. Furthermore, critics of this strategy of alleviating global poverty point out that the global labor supply is so vast that the theoretically sound idea that tighter labor markets alone will lead to improved working conditions is, in practicality, implausible.

Most of the philosophical literature concerning global justice may be divided into two competing views. First, proponents of the *cosmopolitan* view maintain that a system of global socioeconomic justice must be grounded in core ethical norms such as respect for basic human rights. Cosmopolitans see political institutions as a means of ensuring respect for such universal norms. Nation-states that contribute to the violation of basic rights, or merely tolerate the violation of such rights, are problems that must be overcome. Typically, cosmopolitans advocate a global system of government, such as a federal system, that has both the power and legitimate authority to compensate for failed states, stabilize weak states, and successfully coerce successful states into respecting relevant ethical norms. Furthermore, some prominent cosmopolitans regard a global government as an effective means of imposing a global fair distribution of wealth via taxation of the world's affluent populations and redistribution of those resources to the world's poor.

Second, proponents of the *political* view of justice maintain that a system of global socioeconomic justice should be grounded in political systems, rather than in core ethical norms such as human rights. Essential to the legitimacy of political systems in this view is the idea that state legitimacy is grounded in the democratic origins of the political systems. Proponents of this view of global justice, such as John Rawls, maintain that justice should be understood exclusively as a political value, rather than a moral value. They see justice as a virtue of sovereign states, one that legitimately extends to the citizens of such a state as a result of the willingness of citizens to honor the laws of the state and defend it against the aggression of other states. Socioeconomic justice, in this view, is the product of shared political relationships; as such, obligations of justice do not extend to noncitizens.

Protagonists on each side of the debate over global justice focus mainly on the obligations and interrelationships of nation-states and to a lesser extent on the obligations of individual persons. However, nonstate actors such as MNCs also have a profound influence on global justice. MNCs have capacities that enable them to have a significant impact on global justice. First, MNCs and their contractors employee hundreds of millions of workers and as such have a direct impact on the welfare of those workers. Second, MNC environmental practices have a direct impact on both the local communities in which they operate and the entire global community insofar as those practices have an impact on global climate change. Third, MNCs manufacture countless products, such as pharmaceuticals, water filtrations systems, high-yield crops, and wireless global communication systems, that can be used to dramatically improve the welfare of the world's poor. Finally, MNCs wield considerable coercive influence over sovereign-state governments, local governing authorities, political elites, labor unions, contractors, and individuals. The coercive influence that modern MNCs are inherently capable of wielding is not grounded in military power but rather economic power. This influence has been used to enhance the profits of individual MNCs and their owners, but it has also been used to improve the welfare of the citizens of the nations in which MNCs operate. Stories of MNCs engaging in the unjust exploitation of workers, despoiling local environments, and illegitimately interfering in the affairs of sovereign states are commonplace. Less well known are stories of MNCs employing legions of workers at just wages and in safe and humane working conditions, engaging in sustainable environmental practices, and cooperating with the needs and demands of local governments. MNCs are capable of respecting basic ethical norms and of acting as agents of global justice, yet the global justice literature has largely ignored these important global actors.

Proponents of the political view of justice, such as John Rawls, are least well equipped to account for the role of MNCs in promoting global justice. This is because MNCs are transnational actors operating across national boundaries. While MNCs are legitimately subject to the conceptions of justice of the sovereign states in which they are based, they are normally free to ignore that system of justice when they operate outside the political boundaries of that state. Furthermore, MNCs based in democratic nations frequently operate in developing nations that lack basic democratic institutions such as equal voting rights, multiple political parties, democratic elections, politically neutral militaries, and an independent judiciary. The laws in place in these nations lack democratic legitimacy. The concern here is not merely that the laws of nondemocratic regimes lack legitimacy, but that in the absence of such legitimacy proponents of the political view of global justice can offer MNCs no guidance regarding the appropriate norms of behavior in such nations. Of course, a single world government, the political legitimacy of which is grounded in the democratic will of the global population, could provide the necessary guidance. However, such a solution is not regarded as realistic by many theorists and is regarded by others as one of the worst possible solutions to global injustice given the loss of sovereignty this would entail.

Proponents of the cosmopolitan view are better equipped to account for the role of MNCs in promoting global justice than are proponents of the political view. Since cosmopolitans maintain that there are core ethical norms that ought to be respected by different political systems, the fact that some political systems lack democratic legitimacy poses less serious challenges. The crucial step here is to recognize that MNCs, and not merely states, can act as agents of global justice. We can see this better if we imagine a democratically legitimate but weak state. Typically, weak states lack the institutional means to act as a proper agent of global justice. For example, such a state may be unable to protect the basic rights of its workers or to protect its environment against toxic pollution. An MNC that operates in such a state may be better equipped than the local government to ensure that basic ethical norms are adhered to in its operations. Similarly, MNCs that operate in states that lack democratic legitimacy are in a position to model respect for core ethical norms in their operations. In doing so, they may advance the cause of global justice in even the most transparently illegitimate nation-states.

ETHICAL NORMS

If the claim that MNCs are properly regarded as agents of global justice subject to the constraints of ethical norms can be established, it is still necessary to identify those ethical norms. One common view regarding the ethical norms that corporate managers must adhere to holds that it is the obligation of managers to maximize profits while adhering to certain side-constraints on their actions. Proponents of this view typically emphasize the positive impact corporations can have on the welfare of society and argue that managers who expend corporate resources on activities that are not focused on corporate profits are, in effect, stealing from shareholders. Typically, defenders of this view adhere to broadly libertarian attitudes toward markets, governments, and individuals. Libertarians hold that it is the obligation of publicly held corporations to maximize profits for shareholders within the bounds of certain moral side-constraints. The most well-known defender of this view is Milton Friedman, whose stockholder theory of the corporation remains influential despite having been subjected to significant criticism. In *Capitalism and Freedom,* Friedman argues that the normative function of the corporation is to use its resources and engage in activities designed to increase its profits so long as it stays within the rules of the game, which is to say, engages in open and free competition, without deception or fraud. The rules are determined by the will of the majority of citizens in democracies. Actions that do not violate these rules are permissible, whereas actions that violate them are not.

As Denis Arnold has argued, this view provides no guidance for MNC managers operating internationally. This is because, as was noted above, many nations in which corporations operate lack democratic institutions. Furthermore, he argues that even if such a democracy were found to exist, one that acted always in a manner consistent with the will of the people and never at the behest of corporate lobbyists, basic ethical norms would still need to be operative irrespective of the will of the people. For example, one's liberty right should trump a majority of citizens in a democratic society who approve of slavery.

THE UNITED NATIONS "DRAFT NORMS"

One set of ethical norms that is a prominent feature of contemporary public discourse, especially as it pertains to globalization, is that of human rights. The promulgation of the United Nations Universal Declaration of Human Rights, together with the advocacy of organizations such as Amnesty International and Human Rights Watch, has led to the widespread acceptance of human rights as a basic tool of moral evaluation by individuals of widely divergent political and religious beliefs. This increased popular attention to human rights has prompted a resurgence of interest in theorizing about human rights in recent years.

The UN Declaration of Human Rights has well-known conceptual limitations. First, it presents a list of rights that would ideally be granted to individuals (e.g., the right to paid vacation time) rather than a rigorously grounded set of core ethical obligations. Second, the U.N. Declaration does not distinguish between the ethical obligations of different global actors and instead implicitly concerns itself with the obligations of nation-states to their citizens. More recently, the U.N. Working Group on the Methods and Activities of Transnational Corporations has produced "Draft Norms on the Responsibilities of Corporations and Other Business Enterprises With Respect to Human Rights." These draft norms articulate a robust list of ethical obligations and specifically identify MNCs as responsible for their fulfillment. Furthermore, once adapted, adherence to these norms on the part of corporations is to be monitored and verified by the United Nations. The list of basic rights identified by the Working Group includes rights that enjoy relatively universal acknowledgment in a wide range of regional and international codes, and agreements such as equal opportunity, nondiscrimination, collective bargaining, and safe and healthy working environments. However, the Draft Norms go well beyond this, stipulating, for example, that corporations must

- seek to ensure that "the goods and services they provide will not be used to abuse human rights";
- contribute to "the highest attainable standard of physical and mental health; adequate housing; privacy; education; freedom of thought; conscience and religion" for all people; and
- ensure that "human rights, public health and safety, bioethics, and the precautionary principle" are respected in all their environmental practices.

Unsurprisingly, the Draft Norms have met with strenuous resistance from business interests. Part of this resistance is due to the fact that the Draft Norms attribute such a wide and imprecise range of obligations to MNCs and do so without the benefit of a conceptual scheme for distinguishing between the basic ethical obligations of MNCs on one hand and states on the other.

INTEGRATIVE SOCIAL CONTRACTS THEORY

One influential view among social scientists working in business ethics is integrative social contracts theory (ISCT). Developed by Thomas Donaldson and Thomas Dunfee, this social contracts approach for determining the ethical norms for economic ethics has three core components: hypernorms, macrosocial contracts, and microsocial contracts. At the global level, there are "hypernorms." These are the fundamental principles or norms by which lower-order norms are to be derived. The sources of these hypernorms are intentionally left unspecified by Donaldson and Dunfee. Hypernorms are divided into three distinct categories: procedural, structural, and substantive. Procedural hypernorms set the terms for contracting microsocial contracts implied in the macrosocial contracting situation. The terms specified are the right to exit the microsocial community and the right to exercise one's individual voice within the microsocial community. Structural hypernorms are described as the principles that support the core background institutions of society. These include the right to property, the right to fair treatment under the law, and necessary social efficiency. Finally, substantive hypernorms specify fundamental conceptions of the right and the good, especially with respect to economic activity. These hypernorms are derived from outside the macrosocial contracting situation. Substantive hypernorms such as prohibitions against bribery and gender discrimination are said to emerge from the convergence of religious, cultural, and philosophical beliefs around certain core principles.

Hypernorms are identified and validated by macrocontractors who are imagined to convene in a sort of parliament of humanity. These rational global contractors would, according to Donaldson and Dunfee, derive a macrosocial contract for economic ethics that gives moral free space to microsocial economic communities so long as the microsocial contracts were compatible with hypernorms and authentic local norms. By microsocial contracts, they mean the extant agreements, both formal and informal, that exist within companies, industries, and other economic groups. The hypernorms agreed to by macrosocial contractors are necessarily general and lack specific moral guidance.

As a system of international business ethics, ISCT has been criticized on two primary grounds. First, several theorists have argued that it is relativistic with respect to substantive hypernorms and thereby fails to meet the theory's own internal standards of viability. Second, critics of ISCT argue that by invoking religious and cultural norms as a basis for hypernorms, while eschewing traditional ethical theory, ISCT fails to provide reasonable grounds for businesses operating on the global stage to adhere to any one set of hypernorms. In defending ISCT against criticism, Donaldson and Dunfee deny that their theory is relativistic and point out that their theory is the first to focus on the relevance of microsocial contracts in everyday economic life.

KANTIAN RIGHTS AND DUTIES

Kant's second formulation of the categorical imperative famously holds that individuals must always "act so that you treat humanity, whether in your own person or in that of another, always as an end and never as a means only." This principle constitutes the core of the Kantian doctrine of respect for persons. Respecting people requires honoring their humanity, which is to say it requires treating them as ends in themselves and not merely as a means to an end. This means that it is impermissible to treat persons as mere tools for the accomplishment of one's own ends. Kantians believe that persons ought to be respected because persons have a unique dignity that mere objects lack. Persons have dignity because they are self-governing beings.

Kantian agents act autonomously, and when they do so the principles they act on are grounded in morality rather than in mere inclination. Considering the proper role of self-interest will help clarify this point. Kantians hold that it is wrong to act out of self-interest when doing so conflicts with certain impartially determined moral norms such as respect for other persons. For example, suppose that a supply chain manager knows that he will be rewarded with a significant bonus if he can reduce costs by 19%. In pursuit of this bonus he decides to impose a unilateral 10% cut in the amount the MNC pays a major supplier for apparel of the same quality and quantity as before. The supplier faces the same material and energy costs and is already operating with a narrow profit margin. The only way for the supplier to meet the MNC's demand is to reduce labor costs. However, for the order to be completed on time, the same number of workers is required. The only option for the supplier is to forgo health and safety maintenance in the factory and not pay all legally required wages and benefits. In this way, the supply chain manager's actions result in workers being treated as mere tools and not as ends in themselves. In this case the pursuit of self-interest is unethical because it is accomplished by harming the dignity of factory workers. However, a creative supply chain manager may be able to work with a supplier to enhance efficiency and productivity in the factory and thereby cut costs. In this way, a supplier may be able to obtain the desired cost reductions in an ethical manner, and his self-interested pursuit of the bonus would be ethically permissible.

Kantians begin with obligations or duties to respect other persons, rather than beginning with rights claims. These duties constrain the pursuit of ends, whether they are self-interested goals or projects pursued on behalf of other parties such as shareholders. Respecting persons involves negative obligations, such as refraining from using others as mere tools via physical force, coercion, or manipulation, and positive obligations such as supporting physical well-being and the development of human capacities. When they stand in the appropriate relationship to an obligation-bearer, persons have rationally justified rights-claims against them. On the Kantian account, rights take the form of side-constraints that bound the moral space in which agents may pursue ends without unjustified interference by other agents or institutions. Whereas liberty rights to be free from being constrained or assaulted hold against all who would cause such harm to others, welfare rights appear to hold only when certain relationships exist. For without such a relationship, there appear to be no bearers of obligations and so the claimed rights could not be established in any binding manner.

If the world's poor have claim-rights, who are the corresponding obligation-bearers? One answer is that in cases where relationships already exist in the global economy, rights-claims are binding on specific obligation-bearers. Wherever MNCs do business, they are in relationships with a variety of stakeholders, such as workers, customers, and local communities. In their global operations and in their global supply chains, MNCs have a duty to respect those with whom they have relationships. MNC managers, then, have obligations to ensure both that they do not illegitimately undermine the liberty of any persons and that minimal welfare rights are met.

Critics of Kantian accounts of international business ethics argue that because of its theoretical foundations, it is susceptible to all of the criticisms that have been mounted against both Kant's ethics and Kant's metaphysics. Since this is the case, they argue, Kantian international business ethics is not a viable research project. Kantians respond by arguing that the resurgence in work by Kant scholars and Kantian ethicists in recent years has reinvigorated Kantian ethics and disarmed many traditional criticisms. Furthermore, they argue that elements of Kantian ethics, such as the doctrine of respect for persons, can be assessed independent of other elements of Kant's philosophy and have been shown to merit allegiance in their own right.

LABOR PRACTICES

Arguably, the use of global "sweatshops" for the manufacture of consumer goods is the most well-known human rights issue involving U.S. businesses since the collapse of South Africa's apartheid regime. Nongovernmental organizations (NGOs) have led boycotts and waged media campaigns against companies that they believe exploit factory workers in the interest of excessive profits. Responding to such critics, MNCs have made significant efforts to eliminate the worst abuses of worker rights in their contract factories. MNCs have significant coercive economic influence over suppliers. Typically, MNCs set the price at which they will purchase goods from contractors, and as a result they have considerable influence regarding working conditions. In many cases, contract factory owners may not have the resources to improve working conditions and wages without assistance from the MNC. Given this imbalance in power, MNC managers are well positioned to help ensure that the employees of its contractors are respected. In addition, MNCs can draw on substantial economic resources, management expertise, and technical knowledge to assist their business partners in creating a respectful work environment.

An efficient mechanism for MNCs to improve working conditions is via the adoption and implementation of voluntary codes of conduct. Such codes are created voluntarily by MNCs and are not based on the laws of any one nation but are instead designed to help managers and suppliers ensure that the basic rights of workers are protected. The mere voluntary adaptation and promulgation of a code of conduct is insufficient. Instead MNCs must oversee the full-scale implementation of their codes. A firm that merely produces a code and provides it to a contractor without further action sends a message that a similar lack of attention is all that is expected from its contractors. Serious and effective integration of a code throughout an organization's culture requires that a firm hold its contractors to the same standard regarding respect for employees to which it holds itself.

However, some companies are too small to contract for the use of all of a subcontractor's capacity but must instead place orders that represent a small percentage of a supplier's capacity. In such cases, the company has little influence over the contractor. This is especially true if the subcontractor is dealing with multiple companies at the same time, each with somewhat different standards or codes for the treatment of workers. Nonetheless, companies genuinely interested in ensuring that workers in their supply chains are treated with dignity at work can collaborate with one another to ensure that uniform standards are adopted and implemented. Efforts of this kind can help ensure that smaller and medium-sized companies meet their obligations regarding the preservation of basic human rights in their global supply chains.

Some theorists of economic globalization who are concerned about the welfare of the world's poorest people contend that what are needed are not fewer sweatshops but more sweatshops. These individuals argue that improving sweatshop conditions and respecting worker rights will result in greater harm than good. They argue that a free market eventually improves both working conditions and the overall economic well-being of host nations. Because the existence of more sweatshops will facilitate this process, such theorists argue that what is needed is more sweatshops, not fewer. In reply to this view, Kantians such as Denis Arnold, Norman Bowie, and Laura Hartman argue that morally imaginative MNC managers can voluntarily choose to improve working conditions and wages in their global factories, without laying off workers, while remaining competitive within their industry. In support of this claim they cite the current respectful treatment of workers at MNCs such as Motorola, Mattel, Nike, Adidas, and other companies.

NATURAL RESOURCES

The ethical management of natural resources is an issue of increasing importance to managers of MNCs. Since the Industrial Revolution, Westerners have consumed vast quantities of resources with little attention to efficiency or conservation. More recently, growing Asian, eastern European, and Latin American populations have begun to emulate Western, consumer-orientated lifestyles. These consumption patterns place significant demands on natural resources such as oil and coal and global commons such as the oceans and the atmosphere. MNCs encourage such consumer demand via marketing and make choices regarding production and design that directly affect the global environment. Increasingly, the global environment is at risk and with it the welfare of human populations.

MNCs do not always meet minimal ethical obligations regarding the protection of the natural environment. For example, over an 18-year period, Texaco dumped hundreds of millions of gallons of toxic waste into the Ecuadorean and Peruvian Amazon. Critics correctly pointed out that in doing so Texaco ignored prevailing industry standards and put the health of the inhabitants of those regions at risk. However, it is important to keep in mind that critics of MNCs are not always correct about the moral status of MNCs' environmental actions. For example, in the late 1990s Royal Dutch Shell planned to sink the obsolete deep-sea oil rig *Brent Spar* 150 miles off the coast of Scotland at a depth of 6,000 feet. Shell engineers had determined that this was the most environmentally friendly manner of disposing of the rig. The international environmental group Greenpeace disagreed and waged a public relations campaign against Royal Dutch Shell to stop the sinking of the *Brent Spar.*

Greenpeace leaders erroneously claimed that the *Brent Spar* contained 5,500 tons of oil that would escape and contaminate the North Sea. Shell claimed that only 50 tons of oil remained on board and that this amount of oil would not have a substantial negative impact on the ocean environment. When the rig was eventually dismantled, 152 tons of oil was found to be on board. This estimate, while it was three times the amount claimed by Shell, was 36 times less than the amount claimed by Greenpeace. Despite the fact that its position was well supported by scientific evidence, Shell lost the public relations battle to Greenpeace. In the end, Shell was forced to dismantle the rig on land. Shell's total costs came to $97.6 million, as opposed to its initial estimate of $14.4 million. The environmental costs of disposing of the rig on land, as opposed to deep-sea disposal, were substantial as well. The energy spent was equivalent to 875,000 gallons of gasoline and more than 11,000 tons of atmospheric CO_2 emissions.

The *Brent Spar* case illustrates that the science matters when assessing controversies concerning corporate environmental practices. Greenpeace was able to win the public relations battle with Shell, despite vastly overestimating the environmental harm of sinking the *Brent Spar* in the North Sea, because of superior public relations management. However, Greenpeace's position was scientifically unsound, and in the end its actions appear to have led to greater environmental and economic harm than if Shell had disposed of the rig as it initially planned. All environmental issues faced by MNC managers have an important scientific component. In many of the most controversial cases, such as global climate change and the use of genetically modified organisms, many of the facts are contested. In such cases it is necessary to consult the best available scientific evidence and only then make appropriate ethical and strategic judgments regarding MNC practices. However, as illustrated in the *Brent Spar* case, it is also necessary to successfully manage one's ethical stance.

CLIMATE CHANGE

During the 1980s and 1990s there was substantial debate over the existence of global warming. Today, the scientific debate is largely over. In 2001 a consensus emerged in the global scientific community that global climate change (GCC) is occurring and that it will have a dramatic and adverse impact on ecosystems, nonhuman species populations, and human populations. Global warming is occurring primarily as a result of anthropogenic CO_2 emissions. The increase in average global temperatures is expected to alter weather patterns, resulting in droughts and floods in many different regions and a rise in the global mean sea level. Scientists predict the extinction of a huge number of plant and animal species as a result of climate change. Among human populations, the negative impacts of climate change will be disproportionately borne by the world's poor since they are least well equipped to alter their geographical and environmental circumstances.

A basic principle of justice holds that it is unfair to require others to pay for the costs of benefits one has secured for oneself without their uncoerced consent. The atmosphere is a common resource, one that the global community holds in common. U.S. industries make use of a disproportionate level of atmospheric resources on a per capita basis. At the same time, the harm caused to present generations of non-U.S. citizens will be disproportionate to their use of atmospheric resources. So too, presumably, will the harm be to future generations. Denis Arnold and Keith Bustos argue that those who enjoy the benefits resulting from burning fossil fuels, and thereby contribute to GCC, ought to pay more for such benefits than those who do not enjoy such benefits. In the United States the transportation and electricity generation sectors are the two sectors that contribute the most to the total U.S. CO_2 emissions. For example, between 1990 and 2003, the transportation sector contributed an average of about 31% of total CO_2 emissions from fossil fuel combustion in the United States. Arnold and Bustos have argued for a historic accountability for CO_2 emissions by corporations that is effective from 2001 forward. They argue that corporations that failed to take proactive measures from 2001 forward are morally blameworthy for this failure. They argue further that corporations that have not sufficiently reduced energy emissions would be justified in being penalized by governmental agencies with a carbon tax.

In response, many libertarians and others argue that corporations are merely responding to consumer demand and that it is the obligation of consumers to alter their consumption patterns to reduce CO_2 emissions. For example, consumers should choose to use public transportation or drive smaller, more fuel-efficient cars rather than to drive large, energy-inefficient sport-utility vehicles. In this view, the obligation to reduce carbon emissions, if any, falls on individuals and their elected representatives.

LOOKING FORWARD

International business ethicists are beginning to confront a range of new issues tied to rapid increases in economic globalization. First, some companies, such as Royal Dutch Shell, Adidas, Mattel, Merck, and BHB Billiton, have taken on roles as ethical leaders within their sectors of the global economy. It remains to be determined whether such companies will be rewarded for such leadership with competitive advantages so that ethically challenged MNCs will feel pressure to act more consistently with basic ethical norms. Second, MNCs based in recently industrialized nations such as South Korea, Brazil, China, and India are beginning to take a more prominent role on the global stage. These MNCs have the opportunity to "leapfrog" into the forefront of the ethical conduct of global business by following the examples set by the most ethically forward-thinking global corporations. Some companies, for example India's Tata group, appear to be demonstrating such leadership in their global operations. It remains to be seen how many emerging MNCs will follow suit. Third, not all companies that operate globally are large MNCs. Small and medium-sized companies have supply chains that extend across national boundaries. They also outsource many services abroad. Typically such companies lack the resources necessary to closely monitor activities at their suppliers or global service providers. One challenging issue confronting managers at such organizations, as well as business ethicists, is how to ensure compliance with basic ethical norms by their suppliers or global service providers. Finally, the role and responsibilities of NGOs in promoting global justice is beginning to come under increased scrutiny. NGOs frequently market themselves as the ultimate defenders of human rights and global justice. However, NGOs have mixed records when it comes to accurately representing the practices of MNCs. As has been the case with the corporate world, we may expect to see ethical leaders emerge among these organizations. The emergence of a core group of NGOs with ethical integrity should allow careful observers of debates concerning the practice of business in a global economy to render more informed judgments. NGOs should be held to the same high ethical standards as the MNCs that they themselves critique.

—Denis G. Arnold

Further Readings

Arnold, D. G. (2003). Libertarian theories of the corporation and global capitalism. *Journal of Business Ethics, 48,* 155–173.

Arnold, D. G. (2008). *The ethics of global business.* Malden, MA: Blackwell.

Arnold, D. G., & Bowie, N. E. (2003). Sweatshops and respect for persons. *Business Ethics Quarterly, 13,* 221–242.

Arnold, D. G., & Bustos, K. (2005). Business, ethics, and global climate change. *Business and Professional Ethics Journal, 22,* 103–130.

Arnold, D. G., & Hartman, L. P. (2005). Beyond sweatshops: Positive deviancy and global labor practices. *Business Ethics: A European Review, 14,* 206–222.

Arnold, D. G., & Hartman, L. P. (2006). Worker rights and low wage industrialization: How to avoid sweatshops. *Human Rights Quarterly, 28,* 676–700.

Bowie, N. E. (1988). The moral obligations of multinational corporations. In S. Luper-Foy (Ed.), *Problems of international justice.* Boulder, CO: Westview Press.

De George, R. (1993). *Competing with integrity in international business.* New York: Oxford University Press.

Donaldson, T. (1989). *The ethics of international business.* New York: Oxford University Press.

Donaldson, T., & Dunfee, T. (1999). *Ties that bind: A social contracts approach to business ethics.* Cambridge, MA: Harvard Business School Press.

Freidman, M. (1982). *Capitalism and freedom.* Chicago: University of Chicago Press.

Hartman, L., Arnold, D. G., & Wokutch, R. E. (2003). *Rising above sweatshops: Innovative approaches to global labor challenges.* Westport, CT: Praeger.

Hsieh, N. (2004). The obligations of transnational corporations: Rawlsian justice and the duty of assistance. *Business Ethics Quarterly, 14,* 643–661.

Hsieh, N. (2006). Voluntary codes of conduct for multinational corporations: Coordinating duties of rescue and justice. *Business Ethics Quarterly, 16,* 119–135.

O'Neill, O. (2000). Agents of justice. *Metaphilosophy, 32,* 180–195.

Santoro, M. (2000). *Profits and principles: Global capitalism and human rights in China.* Ithaca, NY: Cornell University Press.

Sethi, S. P. (2003). *Setting global standards: Guidelines for creating codes of conduct in multinational corporations.* Hoboken, NJ: Wiley.

Werhane, P. H. (1999). *Moral imagination and management decision making.* New York: Oxford University Press.

Werhane, P. H. (2000). Exporting mental models: Global capitalism in the 21st century. *Business Ethics Quarterly, 10,* 353–362.

STRATEGY AND ETHICS

Strategy is commonly understood to be a plan of action adopted by an organization to attain its goals, while ethics can be described as a system of moral values and principles that govern the conduct of an individual or a group. In a business enterprise, strategy reflects a company's pattern of decisions, commitments, and actions undertaken by the company to improve its competitiveness and generate profits for its owners. However, earning a profit is not the only goal of a business. It must provide quality products for its consumers, continued jobs for its employees, and taxes for its government. In the process of formulating and implementing strategies, potential conflicts arise in the goals of the company's various stakeholders such as stockholders, managers, employees, suppliers, government, and society at large. It is while dealing with these conflicting goals that managers face ethical dilemmas in prioritizing the demands of various constituents that form the core of the strategy-ethics interface, which we address in the following paragraphs.

Ethics in business strategy has gained renewed focus due to the scandals that have unfolded in recent years at several major corporations in the world including Enron, Arthur Andersen, Tyco, and Adelphia in the United States; Parmalat in Italy; and Livedoor in Japan. As a consequence of these business debacles, numerous employees lost jobs, shareholders lost wealth, governments lost taxes, and society as a whole suffered. To prevent future occurrences of such widespread harm, the U.S. government enacted the Sarbanes-Oxley Act in 2002 to ensure governance mechanisms to protect the interests of shareholders and other stakeholders of the firm. The U.S. Corporate Sentencing Guidelines also provide a strong incentive for businesses to promote ethics at work. Tort laws, contract law, intellectual property law, and securities law all govern business behavior. However, while the law can regulate the basic actions of the firm, it tends to be reactive in nature and contains several ambiguities that present opportunities for unethical practices. Therefore, merging company strategy with an ethical framework can guide managers in their task of strategy formulation and implementation. We briefly describe the concepts of strategy and ethics as commonly understood and then discuss the role managers play in the interface between the two.

STRATEGY

Companies try to pursue strategies that will help them remain competitive and earn superior returns. While formulating a strategy, a company thoroughly analyzes its external and internal environment. The external environment includes general or macroenvironmental conditions such as global trends, industry conditions, and competitive environment. The internal environment includes the company's internal resources and capabilities such as knowledge, technology, physical assets, manpower, and capital. Based on the perceptions of its environmental opportunities and threats, and internal strengths and weaknesses, a firm will consider different strategies and implementation approaches. A company achieves sustained success only if it has an astute, timely strategic game plan, revises its strategies according to changes in the environment and company situation, and implements the strategies with proficiency. Competitive success requires companies to position well in the existing market space, develop and use distinctive competencies to support their strategy, and design internal systems and practices to effectively implement the strategy. The industrial organization (I/O) model suggests that companies should first assess the external environment, select industries with high potential for superior returns, and then develop strategies as called for by the industry. I/O theory suggests that internal resources and capabilities should be developed as called for by the external environment. On the other hand, the resource-based view suggests that the primary basis for strategy and sustained advantage are internal resources and capabilities of the company. Companies, thus, need to develop resources that are valuable, rare, nonimitable, and nonsubstitutable and craft strategies that will help both exploit current resources and develop new resources. Strategy formulation, therefore, involves analysis of both external and internal aspects of a company and developing an appropriate course of action or strategy. Strategy implementation involves developing internal organizational structure, systems, and processes to execute the strategy and matching them to the strategy.

In a large company, strategies exist at multiple levels and, correspondingly, ethical issues also arise at multiple levels. Corporate-level strategy relates to the decisions and priorities of corporate managers of large diversified corporations (such as General Electric), which may include the choice of the mix of different types of businesses it will have under its corporate umbrella, that is, whether to acquire, merge, or sell off individual business units. Each of these decisions will have ethical implications such as should employees be laid off, or will the merger stifle competition? Functional strategies relate to the pattern of actions and priorities of various functional areas such as production, marketing, human resources, and finance. Again, ethical issues can arise in each functional strategy. Production of defective products can injure innocent people, toxic production processes pose a threat to the environment, misleading product information and deceptive advertising can misguide buying decisions, excessive monitoring can invade employee privacy, and so on.

ETHICS

To understand ethics and its relationship to strategy, it is important to briefly consider some philosophical underpinnings. The utilitarian approach espoused by John S. Mill and Jeremy Bentham in the 18th and 19th centuries evaluates action based on the following maxim: greatest good for the greatest number of people. Many businesses adopt this approach to evaluate a course of action by using a cost-benefit analysis. However, costs are often hidden. For example, damage to the environment cannot be readily quantified. Besides, utilitarianism as a framework does not consider the rights of all parties concerned and, therefore, can be unfair to the minority. A small number of employees may be laid off to garner greater profits for many investors, so while this action may be consistent with the utilitarian approach it may be unfair to those few employees affected by job loss. The Kantian or rights approach framework advocates that people be treated as ends and not as means and that basic individual rights of all should be respected. Moral theorists argue that fundamental human rights are the base of the moral compass managers navigate by when making decisions that have an ethical impact. However, the rights approach is not useful when the basic rights of two groups of individuals are in conflict. The justice approach propounded by John Rawls evaluates a strategy based on the impartial and equitable distribution of benefits and harm among stakeholders. This framework suggests that managers should weigh a course of action behind a *veil of ignorance* of the particular characteristics of the people involved, and economic goods and services should be so distributed as to be just and advantageous to the least advantaged groups in society. The virtue approach developed by Aristotle is based on virtues such as honesty, fairness, trust, and toughness. According to this framework, moral virtues and habits enable a person to live according to reason and, thus, make ethical decisions. Moral education aimed at improving moral reasoning and debate and the ability to summon courage to take a principled stand regardless of pressure or punishment are considered very important.

Viewed as a continuum, a business strategy can range from being egoist to altruistic, drawing again on the philosophical underpinnings of ethics. Ethical egoism suggests that each person ought to pursue his or her own self-interest, and an action is considered right when it serves one's personal goal. Ethical egoism does not forbid actions that may help others when interests of the self and others coincide. In contrast, altruism is devotion to the interests of others. It is "other directed" behavior at the cost of one's own self-interest. Altruism emphasizes loyalty, devotion, and the subordination of self to a cause, a person, or an ideal. Put in the context of business ethics and strategy, egoism suggests that a business should focus on its primary goal of providing returns to its owners, the challenge being, however, to find the path that aligns the interests of a firm and its managers with those of all stakeholders. An altruist strategy, on the other hand, would have the firm forgo some of its immediate gains and profits to benefit some constituent, say employees or even society, by investing resources in providing health care or education or in mitigating poverty.

STRATEGY-ETHICS INTERFACE AND ROLE OF MANAGERS

Strategy and business ethics are inseparable from each other. While the corporation is a separate entity for legal purposes, it cannot act on its own will. The behavior of the corporation is the result of decisions made by the managers and top executives of the firm. Managers act as agents of the shareholders, who are one set of the stakeholders of the firm. Agency theory postulates that managers, instead of acting in the interests of their principals (owners of the firm), will act opportunistically in their own interests when not properly monitored. Such managers are ethical egoists who focus on self-interest and self-promotion. Indeed, the recent scandals of fraud mentioned earlier have been attributed to the failure of adequate monitoring of executives entrusted with the task of making decisions for the benefit of the corporation. The managers put their own personal welfare ahead of others' welfare. In an alternative view, managers are perceived to be stewards of the distinct stakeholders of the firm, acting altruistically to promulgate ethical strategies that create value and meeting the needs of all constituents of the firm. Stewardship theory is based on the premise that managers will act in a manner consistent with the long-term interests of all stakeholders basing their decisions not on short-term gains for themselves but on corporate principles that enable their firm to be viable through actions that promote sustainable profitability. Sustained profitability of the firm requires long-term investments that may not bear immediate returns. High emphasis on short-term economic returns may be detrimental to the interests of several stakeholders and the society at large. Yet employees are evaluated every year, and companies need to meet stock market's quarterly performance expectations—both short-term horizons. While the notion of "performance" is multidimensional and includes social, environmental, and economic performance, the economic dimension generally supersedes others. Some argue that strategy is at odds with ethics primarily because of the overriding concern of strategy with instant economic performance and the inability of managers to find the point of equilibrium between long-term investment and short-term reward.

While the notions of egoism and altruism described above are the two ends of the continuum to evaluate strategy with the perspective of ethics, a practical "middle" perspective is often used to balance the needs of multiple stakeholders. The notions of corporate social responsibility, corporate citizenship behavior, and corporate accountability are more appropriate to explain the interface of strategy and business ethics. As corporations are members of society, they should engage in socially responsible actions in a manner consistent with fundamental social, moral, philosophical, and ethical principles. The corporation should play an active role in benefiting society, even helping solve problems such as environmental degradation. Even from the extreme economic perspective of strategy, enlightened self-interest dictates that pure business interests are best served by being intertwined with social interests. A company enhances its business when various stakeholders support it. Employees are likely to be more motivated and committed when they perceive their employers to be just, transparent, and doing the right thing; customers are likely to be loyal when the company has a reputation for fair dealing and providing safe products; suppliers are likely to be consistent and reliable when they are treated with consideration; lenders are likely to extend credit readily when they have confidence in the governance and accounts of the firm. In sum, the costs of doing business will be reduced for a firm that follows an ethical strategy that is responsive to the needs of all stakeholders, which eventually leads to better economic performance ensuring greater shareholder returns.

STRATEGY AND ETHICS IN THE GLOBAL CONTEXT

Modern corporations operate in several competitive environments, national boundaries, societies, and cultures. The notion of ethical standards varies across countries and cultures, and managers are faced with many ethical dilemmas globally. Practices that are illegal and certainly unethical in the United States may be acceptable in some other countries. While gift giving is common and might be expected in the Japanese, Oriental, and Middle-Eastern cultures, it is unacceptable in the United States as it can be construed as bribery. While labor laws in developed countries ensure a minimum level of ethical behavior toward employees, absence of such laws in developing nations have led multinational corporations to adopt sweatshop labor conditions, use of child labor, and unsafe working conditions to reap cost efficiencies. Countries that do not legislate or have environment protection laws find themselves dumping grounds for toxic or hazardous waste by corporations following a strict wealth maximization strategy for shareholders to the exclusion of other objectives. Corporations, thus, are confronted with a great number of strategies and contextual conditions that contribute to their facing ethical dilemmas.

Several international organizations such as Social Accountability 8000, Global Compact, International Labour Organization, and United Nations Commission on Transnational Corporations provide uniform guidelines and codes of conduct to multinational corporations. These guidelines are not mandatory laws and cannot be enforced. However, many companies have found that when they have swerved away from following an ethical strategy, they have become a target of negative media attention leading to loss of customers, as Nike did when their sweatshop labor practices in developing countries came to light.

STRATEGIZING ETHICALLY

As noted earlier, strategy and ethics are intertwined. Higher ethical standards and practices improve a firm's image and reputation, and this intangible resource is likely to provide a sustainable advantage to the firm. While violating basic ethical norms may provide temporary benefits and short-term economic gains, long-term financial performance is likely to improve when firms consider the interests of all stakeholders, which results in a positive image of the company. Even investors and shareholders seek out companies that implement ethical strategies that ensure profits by following principles, as evidenced by the growth and popularity of social investing in portfolios such as domini social investments.

Strategizing ethically would mean that businesses should deeply embed ethical principles and standards in their mission, strategies, and day-to-day practices. Managers need to set high ethical standards, need to be cognizant of ethical principles while formulating and implementing strategies, and need to recognize and reward employees who follow ethical standards and penalize those who do not. Statements about the long-term direction and strategy can include a company's philosophy and values, key corporate values can be incorporated in the company's mission statement and then translated into the employee code of conduct, and the code of conduct could be strictly followed and reinforced. Similarly, the design of the organization and formal reporting systems can ensure enforcement of ethical standards and practices at all levels and in all functional areas of operation. Besides formal mechanisms, informal mechanisms such as organization culture, shared norms, values, and beliefs can be very useful in fostering an ethical climate within an organization. Human resource practices, such as recruitment, compensation, training, and promotion decisions, can also be geared to explicitly value and emphasize ethical standards. A well-developed whistle-blowing policy that allows benign disobedience and encourages constructive criticism can also be instrumental in cultivating an ethical climate. Many firms have trained ethics officers whose job is to monitor ethical behavior and counsel managers when the need arises. Above all, managers as leaders could set an example by their own behavior and serve as referent models to employees throughout the organization.

—Devi R. Gnyawali and Manisha Singal

Further Readings

Boatright, J. R. (2003). *Ethics and the conduct of business.* Upper Saddle River, NJ: Prentice Hall.

Donaldson, T. (1996). Values in tension: Ethics away from home. *Harvard Business Review, September/October,* 48–62.

Donaldson, T., & Dunfee, T. W. (1999). *Ties that bind: A social contracts approach to business ethics.* Boston: Harvard Business School Press.

Strategy and Ethics

Freeman, R. E. (1984). *Strategic management: A stakeholder approach.* Marshfield, MA: Pitman.

Freeman, R. E., & Gilbert, D. R. (1988). *Corporate strategy and the search for ethics.* Englewood Cliffs, NJ: Prentice Hall.

Green, R. M. (1994). *The ethical manager: A new method for business ethics.* New York: Macmillan.

Hill, C., & Jones, G. (2004). *Strategic management: An integrated approach.* Boston: Houghton Mifflin.

Lawrence, A. T., Weber, J., & Post, J. E. (2005). *Business and society: Stakeholders, ethics, public policy.* New York: McGraw-Hill.

Porter, M. (1996). What is strategy? *Harvard Business Review, November/December,* 61–78.

Rachels, M. (2003). *The elements of moral philosophy.* New York: McGraw-Hill.

Solomon, R. C. (1993). *Ethics and excellence: Cooperation and integrity in business.* New York: Oxford University Press.

Werhane, P. H. (1999). *Moral imagination and management decision-making.* New York: Oxford University Press.

CORPORATE GOVERNANCE

In its essence, corporate governance refers to the organization of the relationships between shareholders, board of directors, management, and other stakeholders in a corporation. According to the Cadbury Committee, corporate governance is concerned with the processes by which corporations are directed and controlled. Corporate governance especially deals with exercise of authority over the directions of the company, the supervision of actions of top management, the acceptance of accountability, and the compliance with legal and regulatory frameworks in which the company operates. The term *corporate governance* is not easy to define, as it can be used differently in different contexts. Several academic disciplines that study corporate governance bring their own distinctive meaning of the term. For example, economic theory emphasizes the mechanisms used by financial suppliers of corporations to assure themselves of getting returns on their investment. The study of law examines the power and duties of various corporate governance actors and discusses the legal instruments by which property rights are organized. The authors from the management and business administration focus on internal governance mechanisms that enhance decision making and improve performance.

Definitions of corporate governance have also changed over time to reflect the shift of the purpose and roles of corporations in modern society. In the 1960s, the main purpose of corporate governance was control of business power and authority. Therefore, corporate governance was dominated by investor predisposed definitions supported by agency theory. The corporate discussion was primarily about the control of managerial self-interest and a board of directors' monitoring role. More recent definitions adopt a much broader view, contemplating the whole complexity of corporate life. Margaret M. Blair offers one such definition, according to which corporate governance refers to the whole set of legal, cultural, and institutional arrangements that determine what publicly traded corporations can do, who controls them, how that control is exercised, and how the risks and returns from the activities they undertake are located.

Corporate Governance

155

NATIONAL GOVERNANCE SYSTEMS

Although the conceptualization of national differences in corporate governance is often debated, most comparisons categorize countries into three groups: Anglo-American, continental European, and Japanese–East Asian models. The Anglo-American model is characterized in terms of dispersed ownership and corporate financing through equity or short-term debt markets and active markets for corporate control. It is shareholder oriented and perceives the firm as the private property of its owners. This model is prevalent in the United States and the United Kingdom. The continental European model is stylized by concentrated ownership (usually by large blockholders, such as banks and families), long-term debt finance, and underdeveloped market for corporate control. Although it primarily emphasizes the interests of shareholders, it also takes into account the interests of employees. This model is widely adopted in Germany and to a smaller extent in Continental Europe. Japan and East Asian countries follow a model that emphasizes development of long-term relationships among various stakeholders—the main bank, major suppliers, distributors, owners, and employees. In this pluralist framework, employees' interests take priority. Such an inward-oriented and employee-centered environment of strong and long-term internal relationships, which dominates the firm's governance structure, also diminishes most chances for hostile takeover.

Differences in national patterns of corporate governance are shaped by a plethora of historical, political, institutional, economic, and social influences and determinants. A large number of studies have shown how historical conditions and political institutions influence certain features of property rights and financial markets and, consequently, ownership concentration and company's access to external finance in different countries. Furthermore, some authors argue that one of the main political and social factors relevant to understanding corporate governance is the conflict between owners, managers, and workers. For example, where owners and managers have more power, corporate governance institutions tend to favor shareholders over stakeholders. Property rights, financial systems, and network structures are among the major factors accounting for these national differences.

Property rights define mechanisms through which different groups of shareholders exercise their control and how this control corresponds to managerial discretion. Shareholders rights vary internationally. The outcomes of such a divergence are complex legal and economic arrangements that shape the different mechanisms of corporate control. The Anglo-American system incorporates a liberal market approach. Here, market-oriented mechanisms of control are used to reinforce shareholder rights. Liberal property rights, which postulate relatively high disclosure of company information and establish a one-share–one-vote norm, provide strong protection of minority shareholders. Therefore, this system discourages disproportional control through blocks and favors different dominant interests within corporate governance. The continental European system exemplifies a constitutional model of shareholder control. In this model, shareholders delegate substantial control rights from the general shareholder meeting to a supervisory board. This approach tends to contribute to disproportionate power effects by large blockholders (families, banks, or other corporations). Given the ability of blockholders to secure greater control, they are able to pursue their strategic interests within corporate governance. Empirical research has supported the idea that concentrated ownership increases the external influence over management, whereas in the case of dispersed ownership the shareholders are largely separated from the firm. The Japanese system conforms to a shareholder authority model in which large shareholders hold broad powers. Cross-corporate shareholdings and weak information disclosure predominately protect property rights of majority shareholders and disable minority shareholders from having any influence over the firm.

The second major determinant of governance patterns is the type of financial system on the supply side of the capital market. Financial systems are usually divided into market-based and bank-based systems. The former has greater importance in the United States and the United Kingdom (Anglo-American model). This system promotes equity finance through active capital markets, where suppliers of capital (individuals or institutions) directly or indirectly invest in equity (shares) that is publicly issued by companies. Individual shareholders have little direct influence on management. If dissatisfied with management decision, shareholders have the ability to sell their equity holdings in the firm. In the United States and the United Kingdom, banks typically do not hold company equity and their representatives do not sit as bank representatives on the board, although bank directors as individuals are represented. The bank-based financial system is found to be a dominant investment pattern in Continental Europe and Japan. Banks are the key financial institutions and are closely involved in ownership of the corporate sector. Banks hold shares either in their own right or collect deposits and invest them

Corporate Governance

into companies for others. Their double role as lenders and important share-holders has often been stressed. It has been a historical tradition for this financial system to mobilize capital to the industry. In doing so, it has contributed to the growth of strong relationships between banks, industrial corporations, and other business partners. Dominance of debt finance, through the bank-based financial system, has caused in Germany, for example, the equity market to be relatively undeveloped when compared with equity markets within the Anglo-American system. The German banks have a mechanism for evaluating companies that is not practiced in the banks of the Anglo-American system. In Japan, the same function is covered by large and powerful planning departments of the *keiretsu's* main bank and trading company. The differences between these two financial systems are evident in several measures—share market capitalization, the distribution of financial assets, and firm debt/equity ratios. Even though a large number of countries occupy a position between the two opposing models, financial systems have significant impact on corporate governance. This grip is based on their ability to provide different sources of finance and via their capacity to influence relationships between different shareholders.

Variations in governance systems are also a consequence of interorganizational arrangements or network structures. A network structure refers to the quality and quantity of direct and indirect relationships between companies. Research on social networks has shown that the company's position within the network determines its access to critical resources, diffusion of practices across the companies, and overall power of the company within the network. Interorganizational arrangements of firms that belong to the Anglo-American system of corporate governance are characterized by loosely coupled connections. Their network structure is usually not based on ownership arrangements. Such weak ownership ties, fostered by financial interests of companies, facilitate market-like behavior in their mutual relations. Corporate networks in countries of the continental European system of corporate governance often involve vertical ownership arrangements with various suppliers and the board, thereby interlocking directorates among critical shareholders and creditors. These interorganizational networks are characterized by a high degree of inter-corporate cooperation, which strategically promotes long-term relationships between various stakeholders. Codetermination policies in the German model of corporate governance, for example, see large companies as informal partnerships between labor and capital. At the center of the Japanese corporate grouping is a powerful bank or a financially strong company that can provide the other members of the group with capital at low cost. Reciprocal cross-shareholding in the Japanese system strengthens the commitments of organizations within the corporate network/group and weakens the influence of outside entities. This is why hostile takeovers in Japan are virtually unknown. Companies are acquired by other companies only through mutual consent.

THE SHAREHOLDER WEALTH MAXIMIZATION MODEL OF CORPORATE GOVERNANCE

Given an assumed separation of ownership and control in the modern corporation, the shareholder wealth maximization model regards the firm as a nexus of contracts through which various participants arrange their transactions. This theoretical perspective received the strongest support from the "Chicago School" of law and economics. Relationships between shareholders and managers are seen as classical principal-agent relationships with all the difficulties of enforcement associated with such contractual arrangements. The primary responsibility of management is to maximize the value of shareholders' investment via dividends and market prices of the company's shares. Thus, according to this model, the major concern of good corporate governance is how to control the behavior of top management and get them to run the company in the interest of shareholders.

There are at least four mechanisms by which shareholders can induce management to adopt an orientation toward shareholder value: (1) a relatively large ownership position, (2) compensation linked to shareholder return performance, (3) threat of takeover by another company, and (4) competitive labor markets for corporate executives. It is expected that a management share ownership option will motivate managers to identify more closely with the shareholders' economic interest. Though many top executives own a relatively large percentage of shares in their companies, their perspective on risk may differ from that of shareholders. It can be expected that managers have a lower acceptance of risk than shareholders. Where a company makes risky investments, shareholders can always balance this risk against other risks in their portfolio. Managers, however, can only balance an investment failure against the other activities of the company and are, therefore, more affected by investment risk.

The second mechanism that aligns managers' with shareholders' interests refers to compensation tied to shareholder return performance. This is the most direct means of influencing management behavior. Here, a variable portion of managers' compensation is linked to the shareholders' realized market returns. However, this mechanism is not without limitations. For example, an increase in the price of market share may be the consequence of factors beyond management control, regardless of whether they have worked hard or made good decisions.

The third mechanism is the threat of takeover by another company. Any extensive exploitation of shareholders' or maximization of managers' self-interest should be reflected in low share prices. A lower share price provides a takeover opportunity for another company or investors. The new owners will usually replace existing management. Where such a circumstance is plausible, an active market for corporate control proves to be both an external and ultimate mechanism that has the ability to create a convergence of interests between managers and shareholders.

The fourth and last mechanism of aligning managers' self-interest with those of shareholders is the competitive labor market for corporate executives. Managers compete for positions within and outside the company. Within this market they are evaluated on corporate performance, both in terms of accounting-based and share market–based measures. As a result, executives leading poorly performing companies will be offered fewer top executive positions within and outside the company.

The shareholder value perspective was dominant both in U.S. and U.K. companies in the 1970s and 1980s. An emphasis on sustaining share price and dividend payments at all costs encouraged the use of mergers and takeovers as mechanisms of corporate control to punish managers who were unsuccessful in improving shareholder value. Such an approach created economic instability and insecurity and was widely criticized by various economic and strategic analysts.

Throughout the years proponents of the shareholder value perspective have become more tolerant toward the interests of other stakeholders. Nevertheless, the main principles, which claim the supremacy of the ultimate owner, have remained the same. Consequently, the focus on shareholder value and stakeholder interests has become a foundation of good corporate governance.

THE STAKEHOLDER VALUE PERSPECTIVE
ON CORPORATE GOVERNANCE

The stakeholder view of corporate governance argues that all groups and/or individuals with legitimate interests in the company have the right to participate in the company's activities and gain a share of its economic success. There is no distinct priority of one set of interests and benefits over another. Therefore, a company should be seen as an organizational coalition between numerous and heterogeneous groups who provide their resources (i.e., capital, labor, management, loans, expertise, material, and service) to accomplish multiple, and not always congruent, goals through the company's activities.

Primary stakeholders are considered to be those with a legitimate claim to participate in the company's affairs, that is, those who directly participate in the economic-value-creation process and who are directly affected by the company's policies (e.g., employees, specific customer segments, key suppliers, certain financial institutions, and key governmental agencies). Other interest groups such as local communities, trade associations, and consumer groups, which are indirectly affected by the company's actions, are regarded as the secondary stakeholders.

According to the stakeholder perspective, the major concern of corporate governance is how to balance the interests of different stakeholders. Shareholders' legitimate emphasis on share prices and dividends must be balanced against the legitimate demands of other groups. However, these demands are not only financial. Different groups have different values. For example, employees might highly regard education and training support, suppliers of materials might prefer secure demand, and the local community might appreciate minimal air pollution. The balancing of these interests requires constant negotiation and compromise between inside and outside stakeholders and between directors and managers.

The trend toward the stakeholder perspective of the corporate governance is reflected in existing and emerging regulations of many developed countries. The codetermination laws in Germany, which require employee representation on the supervisory board; harmonization of the rules relating to company law and corporate governance in the European Union, which will take into account interests of employees, creditors, and customers; the Japanese well-known legal and customary model of corporations with its interrelated stakeholders including customers, suppliers, financial institutions, and other business partners; and the campaign toward stakeholder law in the United States all demonstrate demand for formal instruments to democratize the governance of corporations.

BOARD OF DIRECTORS

The board of directors is a governing body elected by shareholders to direct and supervise the management of the company. The board establishes the strategic direction and objectives of the company and sets the policy framework within which the company operates.

Different countries have different governance practices in terms of the board composition and its functioning. However, in general, members of the board of directors can be grouped into two main categories: (1) executive directors, who also have a management function in the company; and (2) nonexecutive (outside) directors, who have no managerial responsibilities. Nevertheless, they can have executive functions in other companies. Nonexecutive directors are selected to ensure that a broad range of skills and experience is available. In addition, a nonexecutive director can be formally classified as "independent." An "independent director" has no direct or indirect, current or previous, professional or personal interest or relationship in the company. It is believed that independent directors will empower the board with their ability to exercise independent judgment and effectively monitor management. Increasingly, the corporate governance practice of some countries has required or encouraged representation of formally independent directors on the board.

Within the tradition of the companies that originate in the Anglo-American system of corporate governance, boards can delegate some of their functions to various committees of the board. The purpose of a committee is to address certain issues in a more detailed manner than is possible at board meetings. The board as a whole, however, retains full responsibility. It is a standard practice for nonexecutive directors to establish the audit committee and remuneration committee. The audit committee oversees compliance with statutory responsibilities, thus ensuring that adequate internal controls are in place, advises the board regarding accounting policies and practices, and reviews the scope and outcome of the external audit. The remuneration committee deals with remuneration packages of the executive and nonexecutive directors and other groups of key executive managers. It may also consider succession issues.

Roles of the Board

Board roles can be generally categorized into three groups—control, service, and resource provision roles. The control roles involve the directors' fiduciary duties of monitoring management on behalf of shareholders. Directors' responsibilities in this role include appointing and dismissing the chief executive officer (CEO)/president and other top executives, deciding executive remuneration, and monitoring managers to ensure that shareholders' interests are protected. The services roles consider directors' advisory functions in formulating strategy and providing guidance to the CEO and top managers in other managerial and administrative issues. The resource roles refer to directors' assistance in the acquisition of critical resources for the company.

From a legal perspective, the control role is the primary purpose of the board of directors. Directors owe fiduciary responsibility to the corporation and shareholders. Fiduciary duties include the duty of care and duty of loyalty. Essentially, fiduciary duties call on directors to make every attempt to be well-informed before they make decisions, to act in good faith and the best interest of the shareholders, and to be independent in their decisions. From a financial perspective, directors' control role is primarily grounded in agency theory. That is, directors' source of power is derived from shareholders. Board members are selected by principals (shareholders) to monitor managerial behavior (agents). By actively monitoring management actions and firm performance, the board can reduce agency costs and maximize shareholder value.

One of the most prevalent roles of the board is its service role, that is, provision of advice and support to the CEO. It is argued that this role is most visible in organizations that experience external monitoring mechanisms, such as product and managerial labor markets. The service role is also stressed in the companies with major institutional shareholders, which decrease the need for active board control. Directors' involvement in the determination of corporate strategy is an important aspect of their advisory role. A number of studies have shown that directors engage in various stages of the strategic planning process, from the review of strategic initiatives to active involvement in strategy formulation.

The board is often seen as a key organizational body that could provide critical resources for the company, protect the company from environmental uncertainties, and reduce transaction costs in managing external relationships. Nonexecutive, outside directors, in particular, play an important role in providing (1) specific resources otherwise unavailable to management (e.g., financial funds, information), (2) access to external institutions and influential organizations (e.g., regulatory bodies, consulting firms, and international organizations), and (3) legitimacy. Resource scarcity prompts corporate boards to engage in interorganizational relationships in an attempt to moderate influences of external pressures on their companies. As capital is one of the key resources, companies often use interlocking directorates with financial institutions as a tool to facilitate access to cash. Contextual factors may moderate the importance of the resource role of the board. For example, small and entrepreneurial companies in which access to critical resources is problematic will benefit from the appointment of a reputable and influential director on their board.

Different Board Structures

In the Anglo-American system, boards of directors are usually unified bodies dominated by management. In a great number of large corporations in the United States and the United Kingdom, the CEO is also the chairperson of the board of directors. CEO duality is often criticized as an undesirable feature of this system, as it may limit the board's independent decision making. A typical board has between 9 and 15 members, most of whom are nonexecutive, outside directors. All directors are elected by shareholders in a general annual meeting. It is common for many individual shareholders not to attend these meetings. Most shareholders will vote on the election of directors and important policy proposals by "proxy," that is, by mailing election forms. There is no legal requirement for any specific stakeholder or interest group to be represented on the board. To achieve a greater accountability of directors to shareholders, an attempt is made to restructure the traditional board composition and introduce a majority of nonexecutive directors (i.e., directors not employed by the firm).

The continental European system of corporate governance functions on a two-tier board structure. This model is practiced in Germany, Austria, Holland, France, and Finland. The functions of the board are performed and split between a supervisory board or council and a management or executive board. The supervisory board has three core roles. First, it approves and evaluates the company's strategy and policies proposed by the management board. Second, it monitors the company's performance and accounts. Third, it appoints and dismisses members of the management board and monitors and evaluates the performance of the board itself. All members of the supervisory board are nonexecutives and no common membership is allowed between the boards. The supervisory board is headed by a chairperson, whereas the management board is headed by the CEO. The members of the supervisory council are elected at the general shareholders meeting. The management board is responsible for the day-to-day operations and running of the company. A two-tier board structure may work better where shareholdings are not as diversified as in the Anglo-American system and where there is a strong stakeholder concept, as in Germany.

In the German model, which is the most distinctive in this system, the supervisory council (*Aufsichtsrat*) consists of both employee representatives, appointed through trade unions, and capital representatives, appointed by shareholders. Members of the management board (*Vorstand*) are professional managers. Although all directors in the supervisory council are nonexecutives, they are seldom truly independent of the company. In enterprises with more than 500 employees, employees are represented in the supervisory council. In such cases, the council can have up to one third of employee representatives.

In the Japanese system, the formal corporate structure is that of a unitary board. Japanese boards are usually very large, with sometimes more than 30 members. Some researchers consider the *keiretsu* of cross-shareholdings as an informal governing body. It is a common practice that corporate governance takes place behind the scenes, between the corporate executives and representatives of major institutional shareholders. In general, the board of directors does not have external representatives of shareholders (outside directors). The only external person on the board may be a representative of the main bank. The board is composed of the corporation's own executives and former executives. The majority of directors within Japanese corporations are promoted from within the company and the rest are appointed from parent or affiliated companies. This internal promotion practice is an important component of the lifetime employment policies in Japanese corporations. The advancement to board membership is awarded to employees at the end of their working career for excellent performance during their professional employment. In this way, the boards of Japanese corporations represent the collective interests of the company and its employees rather than its shareholders.

Relations Between the Board and Management

The quality of board-management relationships is an ongoing issue for every board, regardless of the national setting. Both management and the board are

Corporate Governance

responsible for the well-being of a corporation. The main question is how do the board and corporate management strike a balance for sharing these responsibilities?

The CEO is responsible for the day-to-day company operations and is expected to be the best-informed individual and most committed to the company. The directors are usually not involved in the operational affairs of the company and rely on the information provided by the CEO. In general, the directors should give an overall direction to the company, approve strategic decisions, and propose structural changes. It is believed that the separation of the role of the CEO from that of the chairperson enables a greater balance in board functioning, by way of limiting the power of the CEO to dominate the board.

However, many scholars and corporate governance experts also believe that effective functioning of the board depends on the quality of individuals and their ability to interact among themselves, and with the CEO and other managers, rather than only on the structural composition of the board. The fact that shareholders, management, and other stakeholders have changing expectations about the directors' knowledge and contribution to and involvement in the company's strategic affairs have led boards around the world to redesign themselves and their relationships within and outside corporations. Boards are expected to be more proactive in seeking information, in challenging the CEO in a constructive manner, in working together as a team, and in getting a deeper understanding of the company's business.

Some proponents of board redesign emphasize the importance of the dynamic balance between control and collaboration approaches in the board-management relationship. According to this view, a control approach protects a corporation from self-serving behavior and reduces goal conflict, whereas a collaborative approach encourages cooperation between the board and management and fosters trust and goal alignment. Acceptance, understanding, and management of control-collaboration tensions promote learning and improve governance. Other authors stress the role of the CEO and called to attention the evolution of the CEO-board relationship. Following the evolutionary perspective, these authors argue how the advisory role of board has a relatively higher significance in the early period of CEO tenure while the control-focused approach is emphasized more in the later CEO tenure.

THE CHANGING WORLD OF CORPORATE GOVERNANCE

The emerging research on corporate governance has extensively considered new developments in national corporate governance systems, the increase of institutional shareholders activism, and the changing role of boards in knowledge-based organizations.

Changes in National Governance Systems

The Asian financial crises in the late 1990s and the U.S. corporate scandals at the beginning of this century have fuelled debate concerning the current models of corporate governance. Market failures and corporate collapses have urged the need for radical reforms in corporate governance and regulation. In the last decade, corporate governance transformation has become a major concern of national governments, stock exchanges, international organizations, and corporations themselves. More than 40 countries published corporate governance codes; the OECD has issued the principles and World Bank and IMF released the guidelines. In the United Kingdom, Sir Adrian Cadbury's final report on "The Financial Aspects of Corporate Governance" in 1992 and the final Hampel Report in 1998 were influential in setting in motion corporate governance reforms in the United States and in the United Kingdom. The Cadbury Code became a framework for international standards of governance. The main recommendations related to (1) the clear separation of responsibility at the corporate level, (2) involvement of nonexecutive directors, (3) the role of committees formed by nonexecutive directors, and (4) the formation and functions of audit and remuneration committees.

The most current major initiative to radically improve the corporate governance system in the United States came in the form of the Sarbanes-Oxley Act of 2002. The act was formed in response to a series of corporate collapses, including the Enron, WorldCom, and Tyco International financial scandals. It is designed to protect shareholder value and the general public from corporate wrongdoing. The Sarbanes-Oxley Act dealt with four major issues in corporate governance of public corporations. First, the act created an oversight board to set and enforce auditing standards and discipline public company auditors. Second, the act intended to foster auditor independence. For example, the corporate members with a financial reporting supervision role should not be employed by the external auditor. Third, the act increased corporate responsibility, by requiring that CEOs and CFOs certify all periodic reports containing the company's financial results. Having knowledge of the certification of false statements is subject to criminal liability. Finally, the act enhanced financial disclosure with regard to the off-balance-sheet transactions and obligations with consolidated entities and individuals. These key provisions of the Sarbanes-Oxley Act have significantly strengthened the role of the board of directors and have made managements more accountable.

The cooperative, inward-oriented and employee-centered model of the Japanese corporate governance system was usually portrayed as a source of competitive strength for the Japanese economy. However, since the beginning of the Japanese recession in the 1990s, many studies have shown that some of the reasons for the economic downturn in large Japanese companies originated due to a lack of effective monitoring of managers by shareholders and weak accurate disclosure of companies' financial conditions and business performance. To improve the state of the economy, Japan has embarked on the modernization of the corporate governance system emphasizing better protection of shareholders rights, increased responsibilities of directors, and regular disclosure of information. In 2003, the Corporate Governance Forum in Japan established guidelines and defined best-practice corporate governance principles. The forum proposed the adoption of specific elements of the Anglo-American system. These included appointment of nonexecutive directors on the board, introduction of an executive officer system, and enforcement of auditor power.

The German model of corporate governance has also been pressured to undertake reformative changes. The publication of the official "German Corporate Governance Code" in early 2002 marked a milestone in the development of good governance in Germany. The code addresses all major criticisms, especially from international investors, that point against German corporate governance—namely, inadequate focus on shareholder interests, insufficient independence of supervisory boards, the two-tier board structure, the limited independence of financial statement auditors, and inadequate transparency of the German corporate governance system. The main purpose of the code is to make Germany's corporate governance rules transparent for both national and international investors.

In Europe, the EU Commission's role in corporate governance has increased in recent years but is limited due to major differences in national and company laws. In May 2003, the EU Action Plan was set up to define minimum governance standards for European companies. The idea of the EU Action Plan is not to legislate for all EU member states but to achieve convergence of the many different governance regimes within a well-defined timeframe.

The Rise of Power of Institutional Shareholders

In the 1970s, individual shareholders held almost 80% of the equity in the United States. By the end of the 1990s, however, their holdings had decreased below 45% while institutional shareholding had increased to 53%. In 2002, individual ownership declined further to just over 37% while institutional ownership reached over 55%. Corporate governance is highly affected by changes in power of different categories of shareholders. Controlling shareholders, such as families, individuals, or other corporations, can have significant influence over corporate strategic behavior. Small individual shareholders, on the other hand, do not exercise governance rights as they usually do not have knowledge, power, and incentive to control corporations. However, they are concerned about fair treatment from majority shareholders and management. Institutional shareholders have emerged as a distinctive and demanding voice in corporate governance within the Anglo-American system. Institutional investors, such as large pension and mutual funds, have the power to directly influence managerial decisions in many corporations. Their activism has led to a greater emphasis on shareholder value and directed management to place greater priority on their interests rather than those of stakeholders. The board of directors meets regularly with representatives of institutional and large investor groups to actively communicate corporate developmental strategies. It is expected that such groups have higher knowledge and long-term interest in the company. In this situation, management interests are more likely to be aligned with those of shareholders. Some observers of institutional investor activism assume that this development is bringing the Anglo-American model of corporate governance closer to those of the continental European and Japanese models.

Corporate Governance in Knowledge-Intensive Firms

The context of increasing technological intensity creates additional challenges for corporate governance. A board's legal and moral authority has always been derived from their representation of shareholders of the firm. This authority, legally translated into accountability for the key strategic assets of the firm, guides deployment of these assets toward the most productive and shareholder-approved uses. However, the nature of strategic assets that needs to be accounted for in a knowledge- or technology-intensive company is significantly different. It is not only that these assets are intangible but also there is difficulty in agreement over who owns them and who is responsible for them. Specific assets, such as human capital, producer's tacit learning, or complex networks of interorganizational interactions, create a governance problem that standard models of control in corporations do not explicitly address. Due to lack of knowledge and inability to evaluate information, a traditional board of directors, for example, may be an ineffective governance mechanism.

The competitive advantage of knowledge-intensive firms comes mainly from nonphysical and nonfinancial assets, which can include employee know-what and know-how, training and development processes, and intellectual property. These companies offer different organizational cultures that thrive on ambiguity and offer an antithesis to control approaches that are more amenable to traditional industries. Such cultures reflect changes in power relations between financial and human capital. In these organizational environments, greater attention is paid to human resource issues because of an increased importance of technical and scientific personnel. As some authors suggest, human capital—the assets that each day go home and which are readily moveable—should be treated with care. Therefore, corporate governors should more explicitly affirm the rights of nonshareholders by allowing them formal involvement in governance processes. This formalization may be initiated through special compensation schemes or other arrangements that align the employees' interests with those of shareholders. Thus, if knowledge is the immanent resource and a critical asset of new companies, are individual employees becoming residual claimants in the changing world of corporate governance?

CONCLUSION

The topic of corporate governance has attracted a lot of attention and has become a subject of enormous debates in the recent years. Corporate scandals and collapses taking place in most countries have prompted regulatory reforms in all national governance systems. The issues of corporate governance are complex and deeply embedded in specific historical conditions and economic and political circumstances. Corporate governance researchers and professionals all agree that there is no one best way to design a governance system. In the modern world, an emerging perspective on corporate governance goes beyond the conventional emphasis on financial aspects of corporate control and takes into account interests, constraints, actions, resources, and influences of all constituencies in the corporate governance system. This entry has attempted to present some of the key building blocks, major perspectives, and the most recent developments and challenges of corporate governance.

—Ljiljana Erakovic

Further Readings

Aguilera, R. V., & Jackson, G. (2002). The cross-national diversity of corporate governance: Dimensions and determinants. *Academy of Management Review, 28*(3), 447–465.

Berle, A. A., & Means, G. C. (1932). *The modern corporation and private property.* New York: Macmillan.

Blair, M. M. (1995). *Ownership and control: Rethinking corporate governance for the twenty-first century.* Washington, DC: Brookings Institute.

Cadbury Committee. (1992). *Report of the committee on the financial aspects of corporate governance.* London: GEE.

Carpenter, M. A., & Westphal, J. D. (2001). The strategic context of external network ties: Examining the impact of director appointments on board involvement in strategic decision making. *Academy of Management Journal, 44,* 639–661.

Clarke, T., & Clegg, S. (1998). *Changing paradigms: The transformation of management knowledge for the 21st century.* London: HarperCollins Business.

Demb, A., & Neubauer, F. F. (1992). *The corporate board: Confronting the paradoxes.* New York: Oxford University Press.

Donaldson, T., & Preston, L. E. (1995). The stakeholder theory of the corporation: Concepts, evidence, and implications. *Academy of Management Review, 20*(1), 65–91.

Fama, E., & Jensen, M. C. (1983). Separation of ownership and control. *Journal of Law and Economics, 26,* 301–326.

Fligstein, N., & Choo, J. (2005). Law and corporate governance. *Annual Review of Law and Social Science, 1,* 61–84.

Fligstein, N., & Freeland, R. (1995). Theoretical and comparative perspectives on corporate organization. *Annual Review of Sociology, 21,* 21–43.

Government Commission. (2002, February 26). *German corporate governance code.* Retrieved March 22, 2006, from www.corporate-governance-code.de/eng/kodex

Hampel, R. (1998). *Committee on corporate governance: Final report.* London: GEE.

Hansmann, H. (1996). *The ownership of enterprise.* Cambridge, MA: Belknap.

Hillman, A. J., Cannella, A. A., & Paetzold, R. L. (2000). The resource dependence role of corporate directors: Strategic adaptation of board composition in response to environmental change. *Journal of Management Studies, 37,* 235–255.

Japan Corporate Governance Forum. (2001). *Revised corporate governance principles.* Retrieved March 22, 2006, from www.jcgf.org/en

Johnson, J. L., Daily, C. M., & Ellstrand, A. E. (1996). Boards of directors: A review and research agenda. *Journal of Management, 22,* 409–438.

Keenan, J., & Aggestam, M. (2001). Corporate governance and intellectual capital: Some conceptualizations. *Corporate Governance, 9*(4), 259–275.

Organisation for Economic Co-operation and Development. (2004). *OECD principles of corporate governance.* Paris: Author.

Pfeffer, J., & Salanick, G. R. (1978). *The external control of organizations: A resource dependence perspective.* New York: Harper & Row.

Rappaport, A. (1986). *Creating shareholder value: The new standard for business performance.* New York: Free Press.

Shleifer, A., & Vishny, R. W. (1997). A survey of corporate governance. *Journal of Finance, 52*(2), 737–783.

Sundaramurthy, C., & Lewis, M. (2003). Control and collaboration: Paradoxes of governance. *Academy of Management Review, 28*(3), 397–415.

Yoshimori, M. (1995). Whose company is it? The concept of the corporation in Japan and the West. *Long Range Planning, 28*(4), 33–44.

Zahra, S. A., & Pearce, J. A. (1989). Boards of directors and corporate financial performance: A review and integrative model. *Journal of Management, 15,* 291–334.

STAKEHOLDER THEORY

E very company exists in a network of relationships with social actors that affect and are affected by the company's efforts to achieve its objectives. Taken together, these actors are the company's *stakeholders,* implying that they hold a stake in its conduct. Typically, stakeholders of a for-profit company include its customers, employees, stockholders, suppliers, the local community, and many others groups.

Stakeholder theory is the term used to describe broadly the systematic study of these relationships, their origins, and their implications for how companies behave. As used in this context, the word *theory* raises serious problems. Social scientists who study stakeholder relations are interested in many empirical questions, such as why companies and stakeholders behave as they do and why companies succeed or fail. They use the word *theory* to refer to a specific set of cause-and-effect relationships used to answer such questions. The controversy (as explained below) is whether stakeholder theory, as a social science theory, points toward a unique set of causal statements about why organizations behave as they do that no other theory identifies. On the other hand, ethicists use the term *stakeholder theory* to describe a coherent and original answer to the central philosophical question in organizational ethics, How should organizations behave? There is less controversy about whether stakeholder theory is a form of ethical theory, though this does not mean that the theory's content is uncontroversial among ethicists. This entry discusses the development of stakeholder theory in both these contexts (social science and philosophy) and details its answers to both empirical and ethical questions.

HISTORICAL BACKGROUND

The term *stakeholder* is not a new one. It dates back at least as far as the early 18th century, where it sometimes appeared in British legal cases to describe a party holding a stake in a financial transaction. In the narrowest sense, a stakeholder was a neutral party to a transaction or wager who held the money in trust—literally holding the stakes. However, by the early 19th century—as detailed in the *Oxford English Dictionary*—the term had acquired a more expansive definition in two ways. First, its meaning expanded to include all parties to a financial interest, and second, it broadened to describe those parties holding an interest in the broader political system or commonwealth. In some sense, this more expansive use of the term would set the stage for its emergence as a term in the study of business and society.

While the term did not appear explicitly in writing about management for much of the 20th century, the notion that executives must pay attention to the demands of an organization's multiple constituencies has a long history in the early-20th-century precursors to the modern field of organization theory. Mary Parker Follett, an early American management thinker, portrayed the organization as nested in an environment of other actors, each mutually influencing and defining each other. To Follett, the manager's job was to integrate the conflicting interests held by these constituencies, and the success of the company depended, in no small part, on managers recognizing the need to (a) manage all relationships with as much attention as they traditionally paid to personal matters and (b) achieve some degree of creativity in how they dealt with conflicting demands.

Likewise, in his classic book *The Functions of the Executive,* Chester Barnard foreshadowed the eventual emergence of stakeholder thinking. For Barnard, an organization is a cooperative scheme, the result of a conscious effort by many people to work together. As such, an organization's survival depends on its relationship to its environment and its ability to satisfy those individuals interacting with it. The central role, in Barnard's thinking, of executive responsibility—the suppression of personal interest in service of the cooperative scheme—also heralds the eventual exploration of the moral side of stakeholder theory. Barnard introduces notions of balance and touches on questions of whether subordinates should be treated as having intrinsic value (valued for their own sake) or should be treated instrumentally (valued only for what they can do for the executive or the company). These are questions that, today, arise frequently in writing about companies and their stakeholders.

The early works of Follett and Barnard, though often neglected today, played some role in the emergence of the open systems view of organizations in postwar organization theory and, in turn, these authors laid much of the intellectual groundwork for theorizing about stakeholders. Efforts by Peter Blau, W. Richard Scott, William R. Dill, and James Thompson all centered on the nature of the external environment in which organizations existed, paying particular attention to the nature of the *organization set*—the immediate relationships surrounding an organization. In the ensuing decades, the attention of most organization theorists would shift from the study of organization sets to organization fields, a higher level of analysis at which all organizations and their constituents interact to create institutional norms and rules. Yet the initial insight that a company plays multiple roles within a bounded set of actors would lay the groundwork for the advancement of stakeholder theory as a continuing effort to explore the nature of organization set interactions.

The term *stakeholder* emerged in the study of organizations and management in the early 1960s through the work of the Stanford Research Institute, in the work of Albert Humphreys and others. There, efforts to map program management processes and improve long-range planning techniques led to greater attention on the parties to a management process—that is, its stakeholders—and their role in determining the success of a change program. Both Kenneth Andrews and Igor Ansoff, early advocates of the study of corporate strategy, used the term explicitly and suggested that stakeholders might have something to do with the overall strategy formulation process in a company. However, the term did not attract much attention until the early 1980s with the publication of two books, Ian Mitroff's *Stakeholders of the Organizational Mind* of 1983 and R. Edward Freeman's *Strategic Management: A Stakeholder Approach* of 1984. Of the two, Freeman's has made the more lasting contribution to stakeholder theory.

FREEMAN'S SEMINAL CONTRIBUTION

R. Edward Freeman's book *Strategic Management: A Stakeholder Approach* (1984) is widely recognized as the first major work in stakeholder theory, though misunderstandings about its contents abound. It is, therefore, worth devoting some attention to the nature of Freeman's argument and its implications for the subsequent development of stakeholder theory.

The starting point for Freeman's book is to trace those previous schools of thought that lay a groundwork for thinking about a company's strategy in stakeholder terms. There are four primary schools—the corporate planning literature, open systems theory, the study of corporate social responsibility, and organization theory. For each, Freeman discusses the contributions made to the stakeholder concept. Chief among these contributors are the organization set theorists cited above, systems theorists such as Russell Ackoff,

Stakeholder Theory

corporate strategists such as Ansoff, and business and society scholars such as Lee Preston and James Post. This section can, in some ways, be read both as a history of the stakeholder concept and as an intellectual genealogy indicative of the various circles in which Freeman was moving at the time that he was conceiving of and developing his approach to stakeholder management.

Freeman's definition of the term *stakeholder* remains the most commonly used (and is the basis for the definition provided above), despite frequent criticisms of its breadth. He writes, "A stakeholder in an organization is (by definition) any group or individual who can affect or is affected by the achievement of an organization's objectives" (p. 46). This definition also lays the groundwork for the visual figure, a hub-and-spoke diagram with the company at the center and stakeholders ranged around in a circle, most commonly associated with stakeholder thinking. Most subsequent writers, however, ignore Freeman's warning that if stakeholder thinking remains at such a generic level—ignoring the specific groups and complex interrelations that characterize actual company-stakeholder interactions—it would have little practical value.

The most obvious and lasting contribution of Freeman's book is the emergence of what has come, more recently, to be called instrumental stakeholder theory—the idea that companies that manage their stakeholder relationships effectively will survive longer and perform better than those companies that do not manage stakeholders well. (This entry will discuss more recent contributions to this stream of research.) In developing this argument, Freeman also offers what remains the most in-depth description of the actual practices and processes by which a company might be said to manage these relationships well. He suggests that stakeholder management "competence" includes a commitment to monitoring stakeholder interests, an ability to formulate strategies for dealing with stakeholders, sophistication in segmenting stakeholder needs, and the alignment of specific business functions (e.g., public affairs, marketing) to dealing with stakeholder needs. In essence, Freeman's book remains one of the most thorough "recipe books" for managers interested in stakeholder management, and far more than its contribution to theory, this remains its greatest strength.

As for Freeman's role in the emergence of an ethical literature on company-stakeholder relations, the genealogy is slightly more complicated. After all, Freeman's book contains little reference to the question of how companies should treat stakeholders, at least insofar as the question goes beyond merely prudential matters of survival or profit. The book contains only one passing reference to ethical and political theory (a stray citation of the writing of the philosopher John Rawls), and it would be a few years before Freeman would acknowledge that, only in later conversations, did he begin to explore seriously the question of stakeholders as moral agents. Yet Freeman's own training as a philosopher and his relationship to the burgeoning scholarly community of business ethicists probably created the conditions by which the 1984 book serves as a foundational work in ethics-based stakeholder theory, despite the fact that it contains little explicitly intended to kindle such discussion.

STAKEHOLDER THEORY IN ORGANIZATIONAL ETHICS

As stated above, stakeholder theory can be looked at as a marriage of two somewhat different theoretical enterprises—ethical and empirical. The first is the search for an ethics-based stakeholder theory. From its onset, in the early 1990s, this project started with several attempts by Freeman and other like-minded philosophers to formulate a so-called normative core from which to deduce the moral obligations of the company in dealing with its stakeholders. Many scholars thus sought to establish a clear philosophical foundation on which to ground statements about how companies *should* treat their stakeholders. Almost every major ethical theory—utilitarianism, property rights, feminist ethics, and Kantian deontology—offered some basis for relevant arguments.

At its heart, the quest for a normative core for stakeholder theory has clear roots in the more long-standing debate over the purpose of the corporation in a capitalist society. Ethicists tend to draw a sharp distinction between stockholder and stakeholder models of capitalism—the central question being "For whose benefit should the corporation be run?" The stockholder model, which received its most ardent defense from Nobel laureate Milton Friedman, holds that the corporation must strive to maximize returns for its shareholders. The property rights of its shareholders, the nature of fiduciary duties, the legal mandates surrounding corporate governance, and public policy considerations all offer some support for the stockholder model.

Set in opposition to this model, however, the stakeholder model holds that a corporation owes obligations to more than just the stockholders. For example, Thomas Donaldson and Lee Preston (in a widely cited article) argue that a more expansive notion of property rights allowed stakeholder groups to make legitimate claims on the value produced by the corporation. Each of the attempts to derive a normative core from some established school of ethical theory arrived at similar conclusions, though often from very different starting points. The object of the corporation, they argue, is to maximize stakeholder wealth—which includes but is not limited to stockholders.

With time, the pursuit of a normative, or ethics-based, stakeholder theory has gone beyond the simple pursuit of a normative core. Today, three major problems occupy ethicists interested in how companies should treat their stakeholders—identification, distribution, and procedure. Each has received attention in existing research but each demands further elaboration.

Identification

The problem of identification seems simple enough: Who should managers of a particular company identify as its stakeholders? Given the potentially vast number of actors claiming a stake in the company's operations, identification involves determining which actors truly have enough moral standing to be considered stakeholders. This is a moral problem rather than merely a question of description. A local business may well pay protection money to a local crime boss, and this person may affect and be affected by a company's actions. However, few ethicists would argue that crime bosses have moral standing vis-à-vis a company. Indeed, companies may well treat any number of social actors as salient (i.e., requiring attention) without considering them to have the moral standing afforded by ethics-based stakeholder theory.

From the earliest days of stakeholder theory, the identification problem has produced a great number of distinctions. Early stakeholder theorists spoke of stakeholders as either primary or secondary, indicating that some groups may have greater or lesser claims to stakeholder status. In a frequently cited article, Mitchell, Agle, and Wood suggest that the characteristics of power, legitimacy, and urgency not only determine who the company is likely to consider salient (an empirical question) but which groups merit this attention (a normative one).

It is, however, Robert Phillips's book *Stakeholder Theory and Organizational Ethics* that offers the most coherent and complete answer to the identification problem. Drawing on a principle of justice as fairness first articulated by John Rawls, Phillips contends that a company should consider as stakeholders all those parties that participate in the cooperative scheme surrounding it. In other words, a company has an obligation to attend to the claims of parties insofar as it willingly receives benefits from them. Based on this notion of fairness, Phillips distinguishes between legitimate stakeholders (i.e., those that possess moral standing based on claims of fairness or reciprocity) and derivative stakeholders (i.e., those parties whose claims on a company are indirect, deriving from their relationship to a legitimate stakeholder). Thus, a company must recognize employees as a legitimate stakeholder because the company willingly accepts benefits from the employees' efforts; however, the company need not consider the labor union acting on behalf of employees a legitimate stakeholder, except insofar as their claims derive from their relationship to employees. In sum, Phillips grounds the debate over identification more firmly in the realm of ethical theory and offers one possible solution.

Distribution

The second and arguably greater ethical question in stakeholder theory is the problem of distribution, "How should a company distribute the value that it creates?" Of course, this is a highly simplified way to express the problem, as businesses tend to generate very different types of value (many of which are incommensurate with each other), operate over long time frames in which seeming trade-offs can worsen or resolve themselves, and generate enormous costs that may well be treated as morally different from the value the company creates. If a company damages the natural environment, for example, it deprives community members of certain intangible goods (peace of mind, quality of life) for which monetary value does not fully compensate. Many of the costs involved manifest over long periods of time, during which the immediate benefits to the company of polluting may place the company in better (or worse) position to remedy the environmental problems that arise. Finally, if the damage leads to deaths in the community, these costs are unlikely to fit naturally into a cost-benefit calculation along with returns to stockholders and employee salaries enjoyed by other stakeholders.

Despite the complexities, stakeholder theorists have continued to wrestle with the distribution problem. To a great degree, solutions to the distribution problem are set in contradistinction to the notion that companies (particularly corporations owned by stockholders) owe all their residual value to their owners. Alexei Marcoux, in an important article in the *Business Ethics Quarterly,* mounts a vigorous defense of this principle. He contends that the notion that a company owes a fiduciary duty to shareholders—a duty to act first and foremost in the interests of shareholders—is the natural moral analog to other situations where fiduciary duties apply. Information asymmetries, the

Stakeholder Theory

degree of possible harm, and the need for trust all create conditions where the company should acknowledge a fiduciary duty to it stockholders similar to that of doctor to patient or lawyer to client. Of course, this idea—equally present in Friedman's justification based on the property rights of owners—actually offers only an incomplete response to the distribution problem. After all, we may agree that shareholders, as owners of the company, deserve special consideration and still have few answers about the right way to distribute value and costs. Many of the decisions companies make and the trade-offs they address have only incidental impact on stockholder value.

In most such cases, the causal relationships are so tenuous as to make considerations of fiduciary duty and residual wealth not useful, if not altogether irrelevant, for solving the practical moral problems involved. Consider a simple example of an airline deciding how much airline baggage to allow on the airplane. Insofar as a company (rather than regulators) still gets to make this choice, managers must decide between passenger convenience and the well-being of employees—flight attendants are often injured trying to help passengers with oversized carry-on baggage. To say "the company should do whatever is best for the shareholder" is to say very little indeed. There is no evidence that baggage policies are a major determinant of customer preference and little more evidence that employee morale translates directly into financial returns in this industry. Indeed, fuel costs (a very important driver of profit in the industry) are not affected either way, as the baggage will end up somewhere on the airplane regardless of whether it is checked or carried aboard. The company is still left to decide how to distribute the good among two conflicting stakeholder claims. Though this is a trivial example, it may be more representative of the problems faced by management on a daily basis.

The general principle often attributed to stakeholder theory is that companies should distribute value broadly, that the company should be managed so as to create value for all its stakeholders. In specific terms, Phillips offers the clearest interpretation of this general principle. He argues that a company owes obligations proportional to the relative contribution that the stakeholder makes to the success of the cooperative scheme. Of course, by marking out such a specific position, Phillips exposes himself to critiques that the resulting allocations are still too narrow to be morally justifiable. After all, some groups (e.g., local communities) may offer few tangible benefits to a company, contributing little to the cooperative scheme, but still deserve some consideration if, for example, the company decides to erect a particularly ugly building that will destroy property values for miles around. Still, the distribution question awaits a more persuasive argument.

Procedure

The problem of procedure concerns the proper role of stakeholders in the formulation of strategies and policies that affect them: Does a company have an obligation to engage with stakeholders and invite their input into policy decisions? Regardless of the moral issues involved, many companies do offer ways for particular stakeholder groups to express their viewpoints. However, given that companies, especially very large corporations, can exercise a great deal of power (often on a par with governmental power) over customers, employees, and local communities, the question of whether managers owe an obligation to provide due process (e.g., via grievance processes, consultations, etc.) remains an important moral question.

Arguments in this vein tend to find their roots in one of two traditions. On the one hand, ethicists may choose to draw on the work of German philosopher Jürgen Habermas. Habermasian, or discourse, ethics hold that morally right decisions in a political context are only possible insofar as they are created through open public discussion and deliberation. The only way to honor man's nature as a reasoning being is to respect reason's role in the act of communication and deliberation. Applying this principle of communicative reason, Jeffrey Smith has argued that a company has an obligation to consult with its stakeholders so that the resulting decisions will not only be better but more ethically legitimate than those created in a vacuum.

A second perspective on the moral problem of procedure is the emerging discussion of multistakeholder dialogue. Though not necessarily rooted in any particular ethical theory, authors such as Jerry Calton and Stephen Payne, drawing on insights from William Isaacs and David Bohm, argue that dialogue is a natural and important facet of all human relationships and that suppressing dialogue in stakeholder relationships is both imprudent and unnatural. It is not clear, of course, what the extent of this dialogue must be—who should be involved, how long it should last—but Calton and Payne seem to suggest that these considerations should flow organically from the dialogue itself rather than according to any external constraints.

STAKEHOLDER THEORY AS SOCIAL SCIENCE

If stakeholder theory is (as suggested above) a marriage between two somewhat different theoretical enterprises—the ethical and social science traditions—the latter has been the more fickle partner. Many social scientists researching these interactions have done so while, more or less, accepting the notion that the normative project remains an essential part of stakeholder research. For these theorists, accepting that stakeholders have intrinsic value is a shared premise for stakeholder theorizing. In other words, the social scientist must accept a fundamental ethical principle and then embark on research that advances understanding either the empirical or the ethical implications of this premise. The ideal outcome, then, is some *convergent stakeholder theory,* a phrase coined by Thomas Jones and Andrew Wicks, in which both efforts combine in a hybrid that includes both a sophisticated morally grounded concept of how companies should treat stakeholders and an empirically robust causal chain linking such moral behavior to desirable outcomes.

A minority of social scientists doing research on stakeholders tend to reject this desire for convergence and see it as a threat to traditional assumptions about how to do proper social science. From this perspective, stakeholder research is merely one domain of scholarly activity that studies how companies and their stakeholders interact, and the relationship between the ethics- and social science–based traditions is, at best, at arm's length. There is, they might argue, no reason to privilege the ethics-based element of stakeholder research (as both ethicists and those seeking convergence have tended to do). Indeed, within this second camp, there is even considerable controversy as to whether there is such a thing as "stakeholder theory," if the term *theory* is interpreted solely in social scientific terms. They ask, Does stakeholder theory refer to some unique set of causal factors that theories of power, resource dependence, networks, and institutions do not encompass?

The interplay between these two camps serves as an intellectual backdrop against which good social scientific investigation of these interactions continues unabated. This section discusses the three main areas of investigation covered to date.

What Are the Effects of Stakeholder Management?

Building on the foundation laid by Freeman's (1984) book, one of the most popular subjects for study in the stakeholder research tradition has been the question of whether it matters (financially) how a company manages its stakeholder relationships. In other words, does stakeholder management actually correlate with widely valued outcomes such as profit or stock price?

In this realm, Jones's influential *Academy of Management Review* article from 1995 on instrumental stakeholder theory remains the central work. Jones argues there that the most important characteristic of a company's behavior toward its stakeholders is its moral quality, the presence or absence of dishonesty and/or opportunism. (It is worth noting, here, that this emphasis on morality as the distinguishing feature of good stakeholder management constitutes a departure from Freeman's original model of stakeholder management as largely concerning the procedures undertaken by the company.) Jones proceeds to argue that opportunism and dishonesty will tend to make stakeholders unhappy and lead to increased contracting costs, whereby stakeholders exact higher costs from the company up-front as a way of safeguarding against future opportunism. These costs translate into lower financial performance for the company. In contrast, companies that are honest and trustworthy in their dealings with stakeholders have more efficient contracting and achieve a competitive advantage. Jones then offers an extended list of specific practices (e.g., disproportionate executive compensation, poison pills, and greenmail) that qualify as opportunism and should, thus, correlate with lower financial performance.

A great deal of empirical research has been done to substantiate, either directly or indirectly, the claims of instrumental stakeholder theory. Much of this research has followed not from the theoretical claims of authors such as Freeman and Jones but from the corporate social responsibility literature that Freeman acknowledged as one of his intellectual antecedents.

Much research, of varying levels of scholarly rigor, has been conducted on the subject of the relationship between corporate social performance and financial performance. They address the rather simplistic question, Does "doing good" lead to "doing well"? Insofar as social responsibility can be taken as a rough proxy for stakeholder management, much research hints at the fact that stakeholder management can have some measurable effect on financial performance.

More persuasive, perhaps, is that genre of empirical research designed to test the specific theoretical propositions advanced by instrumental stakeholder theory. Berman's 1998 study of executive compensation, for example, suggests that companies with abnormally high levels of executive compensation do, indeed, underperform those that do not. Subsequent examinations of similar data also suggest that companies that attend to some important stakeholder issues (e.g., product safety and employee well-being) perform better than those that do not. But there is no evidence to suggest that this relationship occurs because the companies value stakeholders intrinsically; rather, it could occur because of the interaction between business strategy and the treatment of stakeholders.

Of course, it is worth noting that financial performance is not the only outcome variable of interest in stakeholder research. Broader questions of societal welfare may also arise from the ways that companies interact with their immediate stakeholders; however, these remain waters uncharted by stakeholder researchers.

What Are the Sources of Stakeholder Management?

A second interesting area for social science inquiry is the question of why companies adopt certain approaches to stakeholder management. Often branded "descriptive" stakeholder research, this research represents the least promising area of research for those interested in advancing convergent stakeholder theory and the most promising area for those seeking to study company-stakeholder interactions on their own terms. After all, to study how a company manages its stakeholders requires that theorists appeal not to "stakeholder theory" but to more established organization theories to account for a phenomenon (stakeholder management) that is interesting in its own right.

Two contributions to this genre stand out in particular; ironically, both were published in the same issue of the *Academy of Management Review* in 1997. Timothy Rowley's network theory–based account of stakeholder management posits that a company's approach to managing its stakeholders will depend, in no small part, on the company's structural position relative to its stakeholder set. Companies existing in dense networks of stakeholders or who are more central will behave different from those in less dense networks or who have less central positions. Rowley's efforts represent a groundbreaking attempt to conceive of the stakeholder set not as a traditional hub-and-spoke system evoked by simplistic readings of Freeman but rather as a web of interrelated groups tied both to the company and to each other. Yet, as network theoretical accounts of organizational phenomena grow more sophisticated, Rowley's effort seems only a simple first step in what must become a more elaborate model of company behavior.

Ronald Mitchell, Bradley Agle, and Donna Wood's article on stakeholder salience is the second important contribution to the descriptive genre. Mitchell, Agle, and Wood posit that stakeholders possess varying levels of three important characteristics—power, legitimacy, and urgency. Insofar as stakeholders possess more of each characteristic, they will be more salient in managers' thinking, receiving priority in decisions about how to allocate value. This model is a useful integration of important insights from various schools of organization theory (i.e., resource dependence, institutional theory, and social cognitive theories), and the ability to categorize stakeholders using these characteristics is a useful managerial heuristic. However, this account also raises stumbling blocks for those who would seek to build further stakeholder theory based on it. Subsequent researchers have (a) offered various interpretations (and misinterpretations) of the term urgency; (b) overlooked the article's emphasis on managerial perception (it is, after all, not how powerful and legitimate the stakeholder is but how powerful and legitimate managers perceive them to be that determines salience); and (c) ignored the extremely simplistic notion of salience, which serves as a vague proxy for the complexities inherent in classifying approaches to stakeholder management.

Indeed, these two contributions, though exemplary, offer two caveats to those who would understand why companies adopt certain approaches to stakeholder management. First, their appeal to existing schools of organization theory, though well-conceived, exposes the stakeholder research domain to the popular critique that stakeholder research has no theory of its own. Second, their emphasis on the causal factors involved (networks, stakeholder characteristics) rather than on the outcome (stakeholder management) does little to remedy the confusion (which must, by now, be apparent to the reader) surrounding how we conceive of stakeholder management. The practices cited by Freeman, the moral qualities of Jones, and the general orientations envisioned by Rowley, Mitchell, Agle, and Wood are all elements of a many-headed beast, and we have little reason to prefer one to the other, scattering the continued efforts of stakeholder researchers.

Why Do Stakeholder Groups Behave as They Do?

From a practical standpoint, a more interesting question for the manager is the issue of how to predict stakeholder behavior. This question forms the basis of the third and, at present, the most rapidly growing stream of stakeholder literature, asking "Why do stakeholder groups behave as they do?" Marshalling theories of collective action, resource dependence, game theory, and social identity, stakeholder researchers have explored this question in several steps, starting first with the question of why stakeholder groups mobilize and then advancing to the

185

question of why, when they do mobilize, they choose the influence strategies that they do. A final step, as yet relatively unexplored, is what conditions determine whether or not these influence strategies actually succeed.

The question of stakeholder mobilization would, at first glance, seem simple enough. Stakeholders act when their interests are threatened. For many years, students of business and society argued some variant of this thesis, contending that stakeholder action resulted from some violation (real or perceived) of the stakeholder group's expectations. When they did not receive what they expected, they tended to strike, boycott, protest, or otherwise mobilize against the company. This was both an intuitive and, in many cases, entirely adequate explanation, but in many important cases, stakeholders mobilized around relatively small violations of their interests, and in many more instances, groups with clear interest did not mobilize or, at least, did not manage to do so in sufficient numbers to have much impact.

Efforts by Timothy Rowley and Mihnea Moldoveanu represent one attempt, premised on an identity-based account, to explain these phenomena. They argue that interests do play an important role in mobilization; so, too, does the collective identity of stakeholder group members. Groups (e.g., certain activist groups) that see protest as a fundamental piece of their group identity are more likely to mobilize. Moreover, structural conditions can strengthen or undermine a common sense of identity. People who are, for example, both parents and churchgoers may be much more likely to mobilize against television violence than those who occupy only one of those groups. Likewise, some groups will possess more or less of the resources necessary to overcome the considerable barriers to collective action for stakeholder groups. Here, again, previous experience with protest and overlapping identities play an important role. In sum, companies must attend to the constellation of interests and identity that surround them, lest they inaccurately assess the likelihood of stakeholder group mobilization.

A second important step in this stream of literature involves the study of why stakeholder groups, once mobilized, choose the strategies that they do to influence the company. Here, the work of Jeff Frooman, extending resource dependence theory to a stakeholder context, sheds some insight. Frooman maintains that a stakeholder's choice of influence strategy depends on just how dependent the stakeholder group is on the focal company for resources and on how dependent the company is on the stakeholder. Depending on how these conditions combine, stakeholders will choose to act either directly or indirectly and will choose either to coerce or compromise with the company.

Subsequent empirical research on the subject suggests that there is much to these insights, though other institutional factors may be at play as well.

The final step in this area remains relatively unexplored: When do these influence strategies succeed or fail to change company policy? Here, as Rowley has argued in his earlier piece, a link can be forged back to the question of antecedents of stakeholder management, yet much works remain to make this connection explicit.

CONCLUSION

Stakeholder theory remains a high growth field of research in the study of business and society, with numerous articles and books being published each year. With students of business strategy and organization theory now showing renewed interest in studying this subject, this is likely to continue. This entry has only hinted at the complexities of this literature, yet it is hoped that it has shown important steps in our evolving understanding of the empirical and normative dimensions of company-stakeholder interaction.

—Michael E. Johnson-Cramer

Further Readings

Donaldson, T., & Preston, L. (1995). The stakeholder theory of the corporation: Concepts, evidence, and implications. *Academy of Management Review, 20*(1), 65–91.

Evan, W., & Freeman, R. E. (1993). A stakeholder theory of the modern corporation: Kantian capitalism. In T. Beauchamp & N. Bowie (Eds.), *Ethical theory and business* (pp. 97–106). Englewood Cliffs, NJ: Prentice Hall.

Freeman, R. E. (1984). *Strategic management: A stakeholder approach.* Boston: Pitman.

Johnson-Cramer, M., Berman, S. L., & Post, J. E. (2003). Reexamining the concept of "stakeholder management." In J. Andriof, S. Waddock, S. Rahman, & B. Husted (Eds.), *Unfolding stakeholder thinking* (Vol. 2., pp. 145–161). London: Greenleaf.

Jones, T. (1995). Instrumental stakeholder theory: A synthesis of ethics and economics. *Academy of Management Review, 20*(2), 404–437.

Phillips, R. (2003). *Stakeholder theory and organizational ethics.* San Francisco: Berrett-Koehler.

Rowley, T., & Moldoveanu, M. (2003). When do stakeholders act? An interest and identity-based model of stakeholder mobilization. *Academy of Management Review, 28*(2), 204–219.

Schilling, M. (2000). Decades ahead of her time: Advancing stakeholder theory through the ideas of Mary Parker Follett. *Journal of Management History, 6*(5), 224–243.

ETHICS OF FINANCE

F inance is concerned broadly with the generation, allocation, and management of monetary resources for any purpose. It includes *personal finance,*
whereby individuals save, invest, and borrow money to conduct their lives;
corporate finance, whereby business organizations raise capital, mainly through
the issue of stocks and bonds, and manage it to engage in economic production;
and *public finance,* whereby governments raise revenue by means of taxation
and borrowing and spend it to provide services for their citizens. This financial
activity is facilitated by *financial markets,* in which money and financial instruments are traded, and by *financial intermediaries,* such as banks and other
financial service providers, which facilitate financial transactions.

Ethics in finance consists of the moral norms that apply to financial activity broadly conceived. That finance be conducted according to moral norms is
of great importance, not only because of the crucial role that financial activity
plays in the personal, economic, political, and social realms but also because
of the opportunities for large financial gains that may tempt people to act
unethically. Many of the ethical norms in finance are embodied in laws and
government regulation and enforced by the courts and regulatory bodies.
Ethics plays a vital role, however, first, by guiding the formation of laws and
regulations and, second, by guiding conduct in areas not governed by laws and
regulations. In general, moral norms reflect the conduct in financial activity
that follows from fundamental ethical principles.

A FRAMEWORK FOR FINANCE ETHICS

Most financial activity takes the form of *financial contracting,* in which two
parties come to some mutual agreement. For example, bank loans and stock
trades are each kinds of contracts. Because so much financial activity consists
of contracting, the ethical norms that apply in finance can be groups under two
main heads: *fairness in making contracts* and the *observance of contractual
obligations.* Virtually the whole of ethics in finance can be reduced to two

simple rules: "Be fair (in making contracts)!" and "Keep your promises (made in contracts)!"

Although the ethical issues that arise in finance are numerous, they, too, can be grouped under a few main heads. These heads are as follows: financial markets, financial services, and financial management. The main ethical concern in financial markets, such as stock markets, is that they be *fair*, especially in cases of *asymmetry*, which occur when parties have unequal information or power. Ethical issues in the financial services industry and in the financial management of corporations mainly involve *agents*, who have an obligation to act in the interests of other parties, called *principals*, and *fiduciaries*, who have a *fiduciary duty* to act in the interest of *beneficiaries*. When agents and fiduciaries have a personal interest that interferes with their ability to serve others, they are said to have a *conflict of interest*.

FINANCIAL MARKETS

In financial markets, money and financial instruments, such as stocks, bonds, futures, options, and derivatives, are issued or traded. Generally, this activity is conducted in organized markets or exchanges, such as stock or bond markets or foreign exchange markets. However, many financial transactions, including the purchase of financial products, such as mutual funds or insurance policies, and private exchanges between two parties can be viewed as taking place in a market.

Market activity of any kind may be criticized as unfair. Unfairness in financial markets is commonly ascribed to unfair *trading practices* (most notably, fraud and manipulation), the *conditions* under which a trade is made (which are often described as an *unlevel playing field*), and difficulties in the *contracting process* (that is, in forming, interpreting, and enforcing contracts). Fairness or unfairness in financial markets may be further classified as *substantive* or *procedural*. A stock trade, for example, is fair in substance when the price reflects the actual value of the shares. It is fair in procedure when the trading parties have sufficient opportunity to accurately determine the value of the shares. Thus, "blue-sky laws," which require expert evaluation of securities offered for sale, aim at substantive fairness, whereas regulations that merely require disclosure of relevant information aims at procedural fairness.

Ethics of Finance

189

Trading Practices

Fraud in a financial trade or transaction is committed when one party makes a material misstatement or omission that the other party reasonably relies on to his or her detriment. Fraud thus has three elements: a false statement about or the concealment of a significant fact; reliance by the victim of the fraud on the information provided; and some harm to the victim. Fraud is an unfair trading practice because the perpetrator uses dishonest means to induce the victim to make a trade that he or she would not otherwise make. Whereas fraud creates a false impression by means of a false statement (or an omission), manipulation deceives others by creating a false impression. In a so-called pump and dump scheme, for example, a trader buys a thinly traded stock to drive up the price (pumps) and then sells at the artificially created high price (dumps). Some large institutional investors have been accused of manipulating markets by creating volatility that they can exploit with sophisticated trading strategies.

Fair Conditions

A fair market, like a fair sports contest, requires a level playing field in which no one has an unfair advantage. A financial market may be unfair or unlevel because of inequalities in information, bargaining power, resources, and processing ability or because of special vulnerabilities. Unequal information, or information asymmetry, results when two parties either do not possess the same information or do not have the same access to information. Neither kind of information asymmetry is necessarily unfair; market participants inevitably differ in their possession of and access to information. However, it is wrong under some conditions to take advantage of another's ignorance or weakness. Thus, the law requires that issuers of securities (stocks and bonds) or financial products (a mutual fund, for example) provide a prospectus that offers sufficient information for buyers to make informed decisions. Insider trading—which is trading by a person inside a publicly held corporation on the basis of material, nonpublic information—is illegal, in part, because the parties on the other side of the transaction, being outsiders, cannot obtain the same information. The insider is thus taking unfair advantage of a privileged position.

In general, it is unfair to take advantage of different conditions when doing so violates some right or obligation. Thus, a prospectus is required for the issuance of securities because the buyers have a right to make an informed decision. In cases of insider trading, the insider is usually violating a fiduciary duty to the corporation not to use confidential information for personal gain. Laws that impose a "cooling off" period during which a buyer can cancel a large purchase or loan may be justified on the ground that it is wrong to take advantage of people's impulsiveness or inexperience. In other words, people have a right not to be taken advantage of in certain ways.

Financial Contracting

Contracts are often vague, ambiguous, and incomplete, with the result that disagreements arise about what is ethically and legally required. Implied contracts, which are unlike express contracts in that not every detail is put into writing, can usually be violated without any legal consequences. Most contracts are imperfect or incomplete either because it is not worthwhile to specify every detail or because it is impossible to do so given uncertainty about the situations that might arise. These "gaps" in imperfect contracts are commonly "filled" by relying on good faith efforts or fiduciary duties, both of which may be unreliable. Finally, contracts often fail to specify what constitutes a breach or how a breach should be remedied. In all such cases, ethical issues arise over the obligations of the parties to the contracts they have made. Because contracting by means of perfect, express contracts may be difficult, some parties rely instead on relational contracting, which involves building good working relationships.

FINANCIAL SERVICES

Financial service firms—which include banks, brokerage firms, mutual and pension funds, and financial planners—act primarily as financial *intermediaries* by enabling their clients to consummate transactions rather than by engaging in transactions themselves. In acting as intermediaries, these firms become *agents* or *fiduciaries* with certain obligations or duties. In addition to the ethical issues that arise for agents and fiduciaries, financial service firms are engaged in selling various services and products to their customers or clients and thus encounter ethical issues in their sales practices and other operations.

Agents and Fiduciaries

In an agency relationship, one party (the agent) is engaged to act on behalf of another (the principal) and to serve that other party's interest. For example, a homeowner may hire a real estate agent to handle the sale of a house because the real estate has knowledge and skills that the homeowner lacks. In selling the house, the real estate agent is duty bound to act as the homeowner-principal would if that person possessed the agent's knowledge and skills. In this relationship, the agent has agreed—for a fee, of course—to forgo any personal interest and to act solely in the interest of the homeowner in all matters connected with the sale of the house. Thus, an agent owes a duty of loyalty to a principal in all matters within the scope of the engagement.

A fiduciary is a person who has been entrusted with the care of another's property or other valuables and who has a responsibility to exercise discretionary judgment in this capacity solely in the interest of the intended beneficiaries. Common examples of fiduciaries are trustees, guardians, executors, and, in business, directors and executives of corporations. Fiduciaries provide a valuable service for individuals who are unable for some reason to exercise control over their own property or assets. Thus, the pension funds of retirees are commonly controlled by trustees, who, like agents, have a duty of loyalty. Fiduciary duty is especially valuable in situations like those of directors and executives of corporations in which it would be difficult, if not impossible, for the intended beneficiaries—the stockholder, in this case—to specify precisely what should be done. As a result, considerable discretion must be allowed a fiduciary.

Although fiduciary relationships are similar to agency relationships, they are also characterized by a stronger duty to act in the interests of others as well as more latitude or discretion in serving the beneficiaries' interests. Whereas agents are generally engaged by a contract to perform specific tasks, fiduciaries assume positions of trust to exercise judgment about a broader range of matters. The duty of loyalty of a fiduciary is thus more open-ended and comprehensive than that of an agent. In addition, fiduciaries are specifically barred from gaining any material benefit from the relationship without the knowledge and consent of those the fiduciary serves.

Financial service professionals are almost always agents and frequently fiduciaries in their relations with customers and clients. For example, a stockbroker is an agent, but not a fiduciary, when he or she agrees to execute a stock trade for a client. Such a broker is acting merely as an intermediary in a particular transaction. However, a broker who manages a client's portfolio by offering financial advice and especially a broker who has the authority to trade on the client's behalf become a fiduciary as well. In contrast, a broker who merely recommends a stock to a client is acting as a salesperson and not as an agent or fiduciary, although the broker still has the moral obligations of any salesperson to avoid deception and offer only suitable products.

Opportunism

Agency and fiduciary relationships are subject to two well-known problems: opportunism and conflict of interest. Opportunism or shirking refers to the tendency of agents or fiduciaries to slack off and not expend the full amount of expected effort. This phenomenon, which is central to agency theory, occurs when principals are not able or willing to monitor the behavior of their agents. A client cannot easily monitor a stockbroker, for example, and the cost of doing so, even if it could be done, might exceed the benefit. As a result, the stockbroker might take advantage of the opportunity to increase his or her compensation by engaging in excessive trading of a client's portfolio, a practice known as churning. Similarly, a CEO might seek to acquire other companies, not because doing so benefits shareholders but because it expands the CEO's compensation and power, a practice called empire building.

Opportunism can be reduced by a number of measures besides closer monitoring. One of these involves changes in the incentives of the agent or fiduciary. For example, the self-interested incentives of brokers to churn client accounts can be countered by basing compensation on the performance of clients' portfolios rather than the volume of trades. Similarly, compensating CEOs with stock options aligns their interests more closely with those of shareholders and thus reduces the incentives to engage in empire building. Other means are to increase the sense of professionalism of agents and fiduciaries, which may involve the adoption of codes of ethics, and to use moral suasion to emphasize their ethical and legal responsibilities.

Conflict of Interest

A conflict of interest is a situation in which a person has an interest that interferes with that person's ability to act in the interest of another when that person has an obligation to act in that other person's interest. Agents and fiduciaries are called on to exercise judgment on behalf of others, and their judgment can be compromised if they stand to gain personally from a decision. Unlike opportunism, which involves merely the natural human tendency to act self-interestedly, conflict of interest arises when a person acquires an interest that competes with the interests an agent or fiduciary is pledged to serve.

A conflict of interest is created, for example, when brokers are offered a higher commission for selling a firm's own in-house mutual funds than for selling the funds of other firms. A conflict of interest is present in such cases because the broker, who has a duty to serve the clients' interests, has a countervailing incentive to sell a fund that may not represent the best value for clients. Mutual fund managers who also trade for their own account face a conflict of interest since they can direct especially attractive trades to their own account instead of the funds they manage. Analysts for an investment bank may also have a conflict of interest if they are involved in the bank's deals because the analysts' recommendations, which should be objective, might be influenced by a desire to attract and retain clients for the bank.

Conflict of interest can be managed by many means, including avoidance, that is, not acquiring any conflicting interests. Thus, a brokerage firm can avoid conflict of interest by not offering higher commissions for in-house mutual funds; a mutual fund can also avoid conflicts by not allowing fund managers to trade for their own account; and an investment bank can prohibit analysts from participating in its deal-making business. When avoidance is not practical, conflict of interest can also be managed by requiring disclosure on the assumption that when a conflicting interest is disclosed, other parties can take steps to protect themselves. A conflict of interest may also be managed by requiring a person with a conflict to recuse and not take part in a decision. Conflicts of interest can also be managed by fostering a greater sense of professionalism so that agents and fiduciaries appreciate the importance of exercising objective and independent judgment.

The Financial Services Industry

Financial services firms operate as businesses, and like any business, they have an obligation to observe the accepted standards of ethical business conduct. Thus, in their sales practices, firms should avoid deception and provide adequate information about products and services. Some advertising for mutual funds, for example, has been criticized for exaggerating a fund's past performance, omitting sales charges, and downplaying the level of risk. The generally accepted standard for disclosure is materiality, which refers to information that a reasonable or prudent investor would consider important in making a decision. Financial service professionals also have an obligation to recommend securities and products that are suitable for the client. This suitability requirement is violated by abusive practices such as twisting and flipping. Twisting occurs when an insurance agent persuades a client to replace an existing policy with a new one merely to generate a commission, and flipping is the practice in banking of inducing a customer to replace one loan with another to generate additional fees.

In the financial services industry, it is common for firms to require both customers and employees to sign a predispute arbitration agreement (PDAA) that commits them to submit all disputes to binding arbitration. Although arbitration has many benefits over litigation (that is, bringing suit in court), some critics consider mandatory arbitration to be unfair because it may deny customers and employees adequate protection. This is especially true if arbitration panels, as is sometimes alleged, have an industry bias. In addition, customers such as credit card and insurance policy holders generally have no choice when signing a PDAA as a condition for making an application. Mandatory arbitration for employees denies them the right that other employees have to sue in court over matters such as harassment or discrimination.

Bank lending practices have many impacts that raise ethical concerns. If banks refuse to issue mortgage loans for homes in distressed areas of a city, a practice known as *redlining,* then they contribute to further urban decay. Redlining has been addressed in the United States by the Community Reinvestment Act of 1977 and subsequent legislation that require banks to meet the credit needs of people in their service area. Large banks that finance massive infrastructure projects such as dams and pipelines in less developed countries have been criticized for failing to evaluate the impact of these projects on the local people. Cases in which banks have financed the fraudulent transactions of companies such as Enron raise questions about their responsibilities. Do banks have an obligation to act as "gatekeepers" when they have the ability to detect and prevent fraud by their clients?

Mutual and pension funds have an opportunity to enable investors to satisfy their desires to do good with their investments or at least to avoid profiting from businesses of which they disapprove. So-called ethical or socially responsible investment (SRI) funds use negative screens to avoid the stocks of companies with certain products, most commonly tobacco, alcohol, gambling, nuclear energy, and military weapons, or that have an objectionable record of social responsibility. In some cases, SRI funds also use positive screens to seek out companies that exhibit notable social responsibility. Some SRI investors hope, through their investments, to influence the behavior of corporations; others seek merely to avoid being complicit in certain kinds of activities. However, it is questionable whether SRI, in fact, has any impact on corporate behavior or whether profits from the makers of certain products really are morally tainted. In any event, it is morally permissible for investors to seek out SRI funds and for firms to offer such funds as long as there is full disclosure.

Some critics contend, though, that the screening done by SRI funds is arbitrary, inconsistent, and largely ineffectual, with the result that SRI investors may be misled.

FINANCIAL MANAGEMENT

Financial managers, especially the chief financial officer (CFO) of a firm, have the task of raising capital for a corporation and determining how that capital is to be deployed. In a sense, a CFO is making investment decisions and developing a portfolio, but these decisions are not about which securities to hold but about what business opportunities to pursue. A corporation can be understood, then, as a portfolio of lines of business that can be bought and sold. Capital budgeting is making decisions about which businesses to invest in and how much to invest. Every firm must also have a financial structure in which its capital is divided between equity, debt, and other types of obligations. All these decisions are guided by a single corporate objective: to maximize shareholder wealth.

Ethical issues in financial management fall into two broad categories: the ethical obligations or duties of a financial manager of a corporation, and the ethics of organizing a corporation with shareholder control and the objective of shareholder wealth maximization. The former category bears on decisions made by financial managers, whereas the latter is a matter largely for government in establishing the laws of corporate governance.

Duties of Financial Managers

Financial managers are agents and fiduciaries who have a duty to manage the assets of a corporation prudently, avoiding the use of these assets for personal benefit and acting in all matters in the interest of the corporation and its shareholders. Specifically, this duty prohibits unauthorized self-dealing and conflict of interest, as well as fraud and manipulation in connection with a company's financial reporting and securities transactions.

It may be noted in this regard that the CFO of Enron allegedly committed all these offenses by personally benefiting from partnerships that he created to do business with Enron, serving as a principal of these partnerships while acting as CFO (although this conflict was approved by Enron's directors), hiding debts in these partnerships, which properly belonged on Enron's balance sheets, and preparing false reports that misrepresented Enron's financial condition. Although Enron is an exceptional case, the use of financial engineering through the use of off-balance-sheet partnerships and complex derivative transactions, not only to manipulate earnings but also to avoid government regulations, is a common practice that raises significant ethical and legal questions for financial managers. Even when accounting rules are satisfied, financial engineering may facilitate a lack of transparency that prevents investors from being fully aware of a firm's true financial condition.

To meet these possible failings in financial management, Section 406 of the Sarbanes-Oxley Act, passed in 2002 in response to the scandals at Enron and other companies, requires publicly held companies to adopt a code of ethics for senior financial officers that includes, among other elements, standards for honest and ethical conduct, including the ethical handling of conflicts of interest, full, fair, accurate, timely, and understandable disclosure, and compliance with applicable governmental rules and regulations.

In addition to a financial manager's duties as an agent and a fiduciary, there are other areas in which ethical judgment is called on, most notably in determining a level of risk, declaring bankruptcy, and responding to takeover offers. Although these matters involve financial management, the responsibility for decision making generally rests with the CEO and the board of directors.

Risk

Any business firm must determine an appropriate level of risk, and generally greater rewards require greater risk. Usually, shareholders, whose wealth is not tied closely to any one firm, prefer that corporations in their portfolio assume a higher level of risk than is favored by managers and employees, whose wealth is heavily dependent on one firm. Finance theory also suggests that for properly diversified shareholders, the level of risk for any given firm, called unique risk, is irrelevant and that only market or systemic risk is important. Shareholders might even support a strategy that courts bankruptcy if the returns are high enough. For these reasons, financial managers serving only shareholder interests might be led to pursue a very high-risk strategy. However, such a strategy poses dangers for employees and suppliers, as well as bondholders and managers themselves, who place a high value on the continued operation of the corporation as an ongoing entity. At issue, then, is the question, "Is it ethical for financial managers to increase risk in a firm so as to benefit shareholders at the expense of other parties?"

Bankruptcy

If a firm is truly insolvent, then bankruptcy may be forced on it, but entering bankruptcy can also be a means for achieving strategic ends. The bankruptcy code in the United States has been used by companies to avoid or reduce the payment of heavy legal judgments and to void or renegotiate collective bargaining agreements and other onerous contracts. Some solvent but unprofitable corporations enter bankruptcy to gain additional leverage with employees, creditors, and other groups as part of a reorganization. In such situations, bankruptcy is a strategic choice rather than an unavoidable condition. Although such strategic bankruptcy may save companies (think of some American airlines), critics have charged that such strategic bankruptcies are an abuse of the Bankruptcy Code.

Takeovers

Corporate takeovers often affect many groups, including employees who may lose jobs and local communities, their economic base. Bondholders often suffer when the debt incurred in the takeover, especially a highly leveraged buyout, lowers bond ratings. Some critics argue that directors, who generally have a fiduciary duty to act solely in the shareholders' interest, ought to be able to consider the interests of all affected parties. Some states have antitakeover laws and so-called other constituency statutes that permit consideration of a wider range of interests. Moreover, incumbent management has many defenses, including poison pills, golden parachutes, and greenmail, which may also be criticized on ethical grounds. Insofar as takeovers are conducted in a market through the buying and selling of shares, there is a market for corporate control. Broadly speaking, the rules for this market should be fair to all parties and provide a level playing field, but some critics of hostile takeovers question whether such important decisions as corporate control should be made in the marketplace.

The Corporate Objective

That a corporation should have the objective of maximizing shareholder wealth has been questioned by some critics, who hold that an exclusive pursuit of shareholder interests unjustly neglects the interests of other corporate constituencies. The argument for this objective of shareholder wealth maximization, as well as for the fiduciary duty of management to serve shareholder interests, is, in brief, that shareholders, who provide equity capital to a firm in return for the residual income or profits, ought to have control because this is the best means for securing their return. Other constituencies—employees who are compensated with wages, suppliers whose bills are paid, and bondholders, who receive principal and interest payments, to mention three of these constituencies—have little need for control. Shareholder control also benefits other constituencies automatically because only residual risk bearers have an incentive to operate the firm for maximum profitability and because their assumption of residual risk insures the return of all other stakeholder groups.

This argument is open to criticism, first, by those who reject the economic view of the firm that underlies it and adopt a communitarian view of the firm. Whereas the economic view considers the firm to be like a market, the communitarian position is that the firm is more like a community. Stakeholder theory, which maintains that a corporation ought to serve the interests of all those with a stake in the firm, also rejects the economic view. Second, the pursuit of shareholder wealth maximization may lead to social costs, such as pollution and urban blight, and also to an unequal distribution of wealth. Advocates of shareholder wealth maximization do not deny these consequences but hold that these problems are better addressed by means other than changes in the corporate objective.

—John R. Boatright

Further Readings

Boatright, J. R. (1999). *Ethics in finance.* Malden, MA: Blackwell.

Boatright, J. R. (2000). Conflicts of interest in financial services. *Business and Society Review, 105,* 201–219.

Dobson, J. (1997). *Finance ethics: The rationality of virtue.* Lanham, MD: Rowman Littlefield.

Hoffman, W. M., Kamm, J. B., & Frederick, R. E. (Eds.). (1996). *The ethics of accounting and finance: Trust, responsibility, and control.* Westport, CT: Quorum Books.

Shefrin, H., & Statman, M. (1993, November/December). Ethics, fairness and efficiency in financial markets. *Financial Analysts Journal, 49*(6), 21–29.

Williams, O. F., Reilly, F. K., & Houck, J. W. (Eds.). (1989). *Ethics and the investment industry.* Savage, MD: Rowman Littlefield.

Ethics of Finance

ETHICAL ISSUES IN PRICING

Pricing, one of the four functions of marketing (along with product, place, and promotion), is a dynamic process by which buyers and sellers determine what, and how many, units of wealth should be exchanged for a needed product or service. Buyers and sellers have differing goals in this exchange process. Usually, buyers are interested in obtaining needed products and services at the lowest possible price, while sellers tend to concern themselves with maximizing their profits.

Price affects both the supply of, and the demand for, a particular item. Generally, higher prices encourage sellers to produce more of an item but discourage buyers from purchasing large quantities of the item. Contrariwise, low prices tend to whet buyer demand for an item while discouraging sellers from producing. There is a price point, called *price equilibrium,* at which the supply of and demand for an item are equal. At price equilibrium, buyers purchase as many units of production as sellers make available.

The ethical issues in pricing are similar to those governing other aspects of business and deal primarily with fairness—fair competition and fair treatment of buyers and sellers. Generally, any pricing practice that maintains the competitive nature of the market and is fair to market players is ethical; practices that hamper free competition or unfairly treat specific constituencies of buyers or sellers are likely to be unethical.

ANTICOMPETITIVE PRICING

Anticompetitive pricing practices impede the natural dynamism of a free market. Some anticompetitive pricing practices are illegal, in addition to being unethical. In *price discrimination,* the seller offers identical products or services at different prices. There are three types of price discrimination. Price may vary by customer, when the value of the product or service is subjective or demand is highly elastic. Price may vary by quantity sold, which allows the buyer to enjoy scale economies on large purchases. Price may vary by location or customer segment, which allows both the seller and the buyer to enjoy economies of location. From the seller's perspective, perfect price discrimination would allow the seller to charge each buyer the maximum price the buyer is willing to pay; this form of price discrimination would create an infinite number of points along the demand curve at which the maximum price could be attained from various buyers, each involving a different quantity sold. In theory, perfect price discrimination could be attained at any level of seller output at which there is at least one buyer willing to pay the asking price for the good.

Many forms of price discrimination are ethical. For example, many restaurants offer a children's or senior citizen's menu. Supermarkets offer discounts to customers who use coupons or become price club members. Cinemas may have lower-priced tickets for matinees or for children. Price discrimination may occur even when the seller does not have a monopoly. In this instance, sellers operate in competitive markets but enjoy some degree of discretion in pricing due to brand loyalty, special product characteristics, or market segmentation.

Price discrimination may be predatory in nature, such as when prices are set below cost for certain preferred customers or with the intention of driving smaller competitors out of the market. *Predatory price discrimination* may violate specific laws, such as the Robinson-Patman Act, antitrust legislation, and Federal Trade Commission regulations. Determination of the legality or ethicality of pricing discrimination must be done on a case-by-case basis.

Price-fixing is the process by which a number of sellers agree to sell their commodity for a specified price in a specific market. While all sellers in a market may indeed sell their wares for the same price, this situation is price-fixing only when the sellers agree to do so in advance. In most states, seller collusion to set prices at a certain level is illegal. There is often tacit collusion to fix prices when some sellers' pricing strategy is to match, but not exceed, the price of an industry leader. The Federal Trade Commission has decided in many instances of tacit collusion that the circumstances did not meet the definition of price-fixing because the sellers did not agree among themselves in advance to charge the same price. Tacit collusion can only be considered price-fixing as defined by the Federal Trade Commission when the sellers have advance knowledge of each other's pricing actions and agree to behave similarly. Many states also have "below-sales-costs" laws, which make it illegal to sell goods or services below costs if the purpose of such a strategy is to force competitors out of the market to create a monopoly. Price-fixing is sometimes a form of *predatory pricing* and may be determined as such on a case-by-case basis.

Another anticompetitive pricing practice, *resale price maintenance,* occurs when producers make rules that govern the pricing behaviors of wholesalers or retailers of their products. This is done to limit free competition among sellers and keep all sellers reasonably profitable. Resale price maintenance also helps maintain a premium image for some products and might be used to support after-sales customer service. While resale price maintenance is not strictly illegal, it does inhibit free trade.

UNFAIR PRICING

Unfair pricing practices are also unethical. Unfair pricing techniques are those that involve fraud or manipulation or violate the requirement that fair market exchanges be informed and voluntary. Unfair pricing also exploits buyers in cases of significant time pressure beyond the buyer's control, emotional distress, and lack of information or experience or where the buyer's normal bargaining power is diluted in a situation of emergent need. *Price-gouging* is a form of unfair pricing that is often considered unethical and is sometimes illegal. It occurs when sellers raise the price of scarce goods to the highest price the market will bear regardless of the cost associated with the production of the goods being sold. Price-gouging is often targeted in areas where substitute goods are not readily available. Frequently, price-gouging is also practiced for items in temporary shortage, such as ice during a power outage or temporary lodging after a natural disaster. Generally, sellers who are able to price-gouge enjoy at least temporary monopoly status in the market in which the price-gouging takes place. Many communities have outlawed price increases during emergency situations unless the seller can show demonstrable cause for the price increase.

Deceptive pricing is another form of unethical pricing and occurs when a seller intentionally misrepresents the total cost of an item, makes incorrect comparisons between the seller's price and the prices offered by competitors, or significantly and artificially inflates the asking price of a product or service with the intention of offering a deep discount for the item. In such a case, the bargain received by the purchaser is a false one, unless the original price is one at which the product was offered for a reasonably substantial period of time or a significant number of items were sold for the original price. In another form of deceptive pricing, products or services are sold as a set; buyers are not given an opportunity to purchase each item independently or decline those items for which they have no desire. The buyer ends up paying for items not needed or wanted.

Hidden costs are another type of deceptive pricing, in which the costs of the item are not readily apparent on examination of the item or the accompanying documentation. Undisclosed shipping or handling costs, finance charges, or maintenance fees are some examples of hidden costs. Failure to disclose such costs is illegal in many states and may violate some Federal Trade Commission regulations. In short, deceptive pricing occurs anytime the price of a product or service is misrepresented, is incorrectly compared with the price of a competitor's product, or includes items the buyer does want but is not given the right to refuse or when all costs are not revealed and made explicit to the buyer at the time of purchase.

Manipulative pricing is another form of unethical pricing, in which price points are set to make buyers think the actual price of an item is lower than it really is. Odd-even pricing is one kind of manipulative pricing, wherein an item is priced in such a way that buyers think the item costs less than it really does. For example, a seller might price an item at $9.99 to lead buyers to believe that the price of the item is significantly less than $10.00. In another form of manipulative pricing, sellers allow buyers to purchase goods and make payments over time, in an attempt to make buyers believe the item costs less than it would if paid for in one lump sum. For example, an item might be sold for $50.00, or for five payments of $9.99. The five-payment scheme might confuse buyers into believing that paying for the item in increments is a significant savings over making just one payment. Another form of manipulative pricing involves setting the price of an item and then offering a seeming discount for volume purchases. The seller might price a particular item for $5.00 or two for $9.99. Again, this form of pricing may confuse buyers into thinking purchasing two of the item results in savings, when it really does not.

THE CONCEPT OF A "JUST PRICE"

Many discussions of the ethics of pricing decisions stem from the idea of the *just price,* an economic concept originated in the 16th century by Dominican theologians at the School of Salamanca. The theory of just price uses concepts of natural law philosophy as the foundation of economic thinking. The just price of an item is the sum of material costs necessary to produce the item plus a reasonable wage that would allow the seller to maintain a lifestyle appropriate

Ethical Issues in Pricing

to his or her station in life. The just price, therefore, represents the inherent value of the good or service. Just price theory predates capitalist economic thought. Its origins in Spain in the 1500s mean that just price theory is based on certain assumptions about culture and commerce that do not hold true in a free market economy.

First, just price theory assumes that the household, rather than the firm, is the owner of the tools of production and that human labor is the chief source of wealth. Therefore, a just price must compensate the seller for the cost of materials and labor expended in the production of goods. Fair exchange is based on the value of the labor of the seller, which may increase only if the seller's station in life improves. Since this was unlikely in medieval times, the established price for an item rarely changed.

Second, just price theory assumes that people in similar occupations do not trade goods or services with each other and that the value of labor and raw materials does not change due to factors external to the naturally established price.

Third, profit is not a factor in the computation of a just price; in circumstances where production or labor costs decrease, sellers are expected to pass those savings along to buyers.

Finally, the theory of just price has as an underlying principle the assumption that virtuous human conduct is characterized by restraint from extreme action. Thus, a merchant's most virtuous conduct would be to take a moderate stance by holding to the naturally established price for an item.

The four assumptions underlying the just price theory create the following practical implications for its implementation:

1. Sellers may not sell their wares for more than the naturally established exchange price.

2. Sellers may not raise prices to recoup losses due to business downturn or inventory shrinkage.

3. Sellers may not raise prices in times of natural disaster.

4. Sellers may not raise their price for a commodity once it has been established.

While just price theory may have worked in medieval Europe, the degree to which it would be successful in a secular, capitalist economy is unclear. The limitations on seller behavior imposed by just price theory are incongruent with the demands of a free market and would probably impede the efficient allocation of goods. In addition, the inability to earn a reasonable profit would most likely retard long-term economic growth as it would hinder expansion and discourage new competitors from entering the market.

The question of ethics in pricing is best answered by considering the seller's motivation for choosing a particular strategy and the impact the strategy has on stakeholder constituencies. If it is a seller's intention to use pricing as a means of profit maximization regardless of its impact on those who need the product or service, if the intention is to use price to limit the availability of products needed to sustain life, or if pricing is used as a means of forcing competitors out of the market, such motives are likely to be unethical. If, however, the seller's intention is to make needed products and services available to all who need them, and to make a fair living in the process, this would likely be an ethical approach in pricing. Thus, it is not the strategy itself that is ethical or unethical; it is the reasons for choosing a particular strategy and its impact on the market that determine the ethics of the particular pricing approach.

—Cheryl Crozier Garcia

Further Readings

Baldwin, J. (1959). The medieval theories of the just price: Romanists, canonists, and theologians in the twelfth and thirteenth centuries. In *The evolution of capitalism: Pre-capitalist economic thought*. Philadelphia: American Philosophical Society.

Berry, L. (2001). The old pillars of new retailing. *Harvard Business Review, 79*, 4 [Electronic version]. Retrieved May 18, 2006, from http://hgswk.edu/item.jhtml?id=2282&t=marketing

Boatright, J. (2007). *Ethics and the conduct of business* (5th ed.). Upper Saddle River, NJ: Prentice Hall.

Federal Trade Commission. (1997). *FTC guides against deceptive pricing*. Retrieved May 18, 2006, from www.ftc.gov/bcp/guides/deceptprc.htm

Federal Trade Commission, Division of Special Projects, Bureau of Consumer Protection. (1975). *Funeral industry practices: Proposed trade regulation rule and staff memorandum*. Retrieved May 18, 2006, from www.ftc.gov/bcp/fulemaking/funeral/proprule.pdf

Gilbert, M. (1968). *The gold-dollar system: Conditions of equilibrium and the price of gold*. Princeton, NJ: Princeton University, Department of Economics, International Finance Section.

How to price a product. (n.d.). Retrieved March 21, 2005, from www.ineed2know.org/ProductPricing.htm

Lustgarten, S. (1984). *Productivity and prices: The consequences of industrial concentration*. Washington, DC: American Enterprise Institute for Public Policy Research.

Ethical Issues in Pricing

Mandy, D. (2003). *Dynamic pricing and investment from static pricing models.* Washington, DC: Federal Communications Commission, Office of Strategic Planning and Policy Analysis. Retrieved May 4, 2006, from http://hraunfoss.fcc .gov/edocs% SFpublic/attachmatch/DOC-238934A2.pdf

Norman, G., & La Manna, M. (1992). *The new industrial economics: Recent developments in industrial organization, oligopoly, and game theory.* Aldershot, UK: Edward Elgar.

Phlips, L. (1983). *The economics of price discrimination.* New York: Cambridge University Press.

Price discrimination. (n.d.). Retrieved May 3, 2006, from www.ftc.gov/bc/compguide/ discrim.htm

Seeley, R. (1986). *Equilibrium price solution of net trade models using elasticities.* Washington, DC: U.S. Department of Agriculture, Economic Research Service, International Economics Division.

U.S. Congress, House Committee on the Judiciary, Subcommittee on Monopolies and Commercial Law. (1987). *Clarification of the evidentiary and substantive antitrust rules governing resale price maintenance: Hearing before the Subcommittee on Monopolies and Commercial Law of the Committee on the Judiciary.* In One-Hundredth Congress, first session, on HR 585, Freedom From Vertical Price Fixing Act of 1987, April 2, 1987. Washington, DC: Government Printing Office.

CORPORATE CITIZENSHIP

Corporate citizenship, sometimes called corporate responsibility, can be defined as the ways in which a company's strategies and operating practices affect its stakeholders, the natural environment, and the societies where the business operates. In this definition, corporate citizenship encompasses the concept of corporate social responsibility (CSR), which involves companies' explicit and mainly discretionary efforts to improve society in some way, but is also directly linked to the company's business model in that it requires companies to pay attention to all their impacts on stakeholders, nature, and society. Corporate citizenship is, in this definition, integrally linked to the social, ecological, political, and economic impacts that derive from the company's business model; how the company actually does business in the societies where it operates; and how it handles its responsibilities to stakeholders and the natural environment. Corporate citizenship is also associated with the rights and responsibilities granted to a company or organization by governments where the enterprise operates; just as individual citizenship carries rights and responsibilities, however, companies have considerably more resources and power than do most individuals and do not have the right to vote.

While CSR has historically referred to a company's economic, legal, ethical, and discretionary responsibilities, corporate citizenship emphasizes the integral responsibilities attendant to a company's strategies and practices. There are other definitions of corporate citizenship, but they are generally consistent with the theme of integrating social, ecological, and stakeholder responsibilities into the companies' business strategies and practices. For example, the United Nations' definition states that corporate citizenship is the integration of social and environmental concerns into business policies and operations. The U.S. association Business for Social Responsibility defines it as operating a business in a manner that meets or exceeds the legal, ethical, commercial, and public expectations that society has of business. The definition of the Center for Corporate Citizenship at Boston College requires that a good corporate citizen integrate basic social values with everyday business practices, operations, and policies so that these values influence daily decision making across all aspects of the business and takes into account its impact on all stakeholders, including employees, customers, communities, suppliers, and the natural environment.

The definition of the Corporate Citizenship Unit at Great Britain's University of Warwick Business School indicates that corporate citizenship involves the study of a broad range of issues, including community investment, human rights, corporate governance, environmental policy and practice, social and environmental reporting, social auditing, stakeholder consultation, and responsible supply chain management. Australia's Deakin University's Corporate Citizenship Research claims that corporate citizenship recognizes business's social, cultural, and environmental responsibilities to the community in which the business seeks a license to operate and recognizes economic and financial obligations to shareholders and stakeholders.

BACKGROUND

The term *corporate citizenship* as applied to companies' core business practices, strategies, and impacts became popular particularly in the European Union in the mid-1990s but has been in use at least since the 1950s. The terminology evolved from earlier conceptions of business in society, particularly from the concept of CSR, which connotes doing explicit good for society mainly through philanthropy and is considered voluntary on the part of companies. Although some scholars and practicing managers do define corporate citizenship more narrowly than the definitions above, believing that discretionary activities on the part of companies to deliberately improve societies constitute corporate citizenship initiatives, most of the business associations and centers in academic environments have developed the more broad-based conception accepted here.

Typical manifestations of CSR occur through philanthropic programs, volunteer activities, in-kind giving, and community relations. In contrast, the dominant conception of corporate citizenship applies to the ways a company operates, that is, its fundamental business model, and the stakeholder, societal, and nature-related impacts that derive from the way the company does business. Although some definitions of corporate citizenship do focus more narrowly on social good activities of companies, the more business model-based definition related to overall corporate responsibilities is widely accepted, as the definitions given above indicate.

In the 1960s, U.S. legal scholar Dow Votaw noted that companies needed to be understood not just as economic actors in society but also as political actors.

Votaw focused on specific issues related to a company's corporate citizenship that retain currency today, particularly in light of the vast size and economic clout of many large multinational corporations. The issues that concerned Votaw included companies' influence and power, which are derived from a company's size and control of economic and other resources; questions about the legitimacy of firms in society and how they are to be made accountable to broader societal interests; and how companies could be sanctioned when wrongdoing occurs. Thus, deeply embedded in the notion of corporate citizenship is the idea that companies gain legitimacy through a form of social contract granted by societies typically in the form of incorporation papers. With legitimacy comes a set of rights and also responsibilities. Corporate citizenship highlights the specific arenas in which those responsibilities apply, encompassing relationships with stakeholders and impacts on the natural environment and societies.

The reach, scope, and size of many large companies have created significant pressures from different groups in society for better corporate citizenship and greater attention to the ethical values that underpin it. These pressures are highlighted by the fact that, by 2002, 51 of the world's largest economies were said not to be countries but companies. In part, it is this spectacular size and attendant power that have created much of the attention to corporate citizenship, fueled further by concerns about globalization's impacts; management practices of outsourcing key functions to developing nations to reduce costs; ethical and accounting scandals; and corporate influence on governments, communities, and whole societies.

Corporate leaders began paying significant attention to issues of corporate citizenship during the late 1990s and early 2000s, following waves of antiglobalization protests; critiques of corporate outsourcing practices; fears about climate change and other serious environmental problems said to be at least partially created by businesses; and the rise of anticorporate activism sometimes directed at specific companies and sometimes at policies of powerful global institutions such as the World Trade Organization, the World Bank, and the International Monetary Fund. Advanced communication technologies fueled the ability of activists and other critics to question corporate activities and create increasing demands for responsibility, transparency, and accountability by companies.

On the business side, numerous new activities and organizations designed to highlight good corporate citizenship emerged during the 1990s and early 2000s. At least partially in response to vocal activism about supply chain practices, many multinational corporations developed and implemented internal codes of conduct during the 1990s. Some of these companies also asked their supply chain partners to implement the codes in their operations as well. In addition to internal codes, a number of codes and sets of principles, frequently generated by multisector coalitions that included companies, governmental representatives, activists, and nongovernmental organizations (NGOs), also emerged. These codes represent what their developers consider to be a base-line or floor of ethical conduct that serves as the foundation of corporate citizenship. Prominent business ethicists Thomas Donaldson and Thomas Dunfee have labeled such foundational values hypernorms. Although still somewhat controversial as to whether they exist, hypernorms identified by Donaldson and Dunfee include basics such as respect for human dignity, basic rights, good citizenship, and, similarly, fundamental values. Such hypernorms serve as a foundation for all human values and also as a basis for good corporate citizenship. They are built on three principles, including the respect for core human values that determine a floor of practice and behavior below which it is ethically problematic, respect for local traditions, and respect for the context in which decisions are made.

During the 1990s and into the 2000s, there was a great deal of activism against certain corporate practices such as outsourcing, which frequently involved contracting with manufacturers in developing nations whose workers were subjected to abusive conditions, ecological deterioration, and poor labor standards, as well as the impact of globalization. This activism generated a flurry of development of codes of conduct that attempted to codify how such basic principles could be put into practice in companies. As the codes developed, many companies, particularly large multinational firms with brand names to protect, began demanding that their suppliers live up to the standards articulated in the codes.

Many companies developed their own codes of conduct; in addition, a number of codes emerged that were developed by multisector coalitions working from internationally agreed documents or core ethical standards. Among the most prominent, although not without its critics, was the United Nations' Global Compact's set of 10 (originally nine) principles, which were drawn from internationally agreed declarations and treaties. The Global Compact, which had nearly 2,000 members by 2005, was established in 1999 by UN Secretary-General Kofi Annan to "initiate a global compact of shared values and principles, which will give a human face to the global market." In signing onto the Global Compact, companies agree to uphold 10 fundamental principles on human rights, labor rights, environment, and anticorruption.

The Global Compact's 10 principles focus on core or foundational principles and are drawn from major UN declarations and documents that have been signed by most of the countries of the world. Documents from which the principles are drawn include the Universal Declaration of Human Rights, the International Labour Organization's Declaration on Fundamental Principles and Rights at Work, the Rio Declaration on Environment and Development, and the United Nations Convention Against Corruption. The two human rights principles require companies to support and respect the protection of internationally proclaimed human rights and make sure that they are not complicit in any human rights abuses. The four labor standards require companies to uphold the freedom of association and the effective recognition of the right to collective bargaining, eliminate all forms of forced and compulsory labor, effectively abolish child labor, and eliminate discrimination in employment. The three environmental principles require companies to support a precautionary approach to environmental challenges, undertake initiatives to promote greater environmental responsibility, and encourage the development and diffusion of environmentally friendly technologies. The corruption principle, added in 2004, requires companies to work against all forms of corruption, including bribery and extortion.

There are other important codes and principles aimed at putting corporate citizenship efforts into operating practices and strategies. These codes include the Guidelines for Multinational Enterprises of the Organisation for Economic Co-operation and Development, the Global Sullivan Principles of Corporate Social Responsibility, the Marine Stewardship Council's Principles and Guidelines for Sustainable Fishing, the Natural Step's Sustainability Principles, the UN's Norms on the Responsibilities of Transnational Corporations and Other Enterprises with regard to Human Rights, the Equator Principles (for the financial services industry), the Sustainable Forestry Principles, the Caux Principles, the Business Principles for Countering Bribery, the CERES (Coalition for Environmentally Responsible Economies) Principles, the Clean Clothes Campaign model code, the Workplace Code of Conduct of the Fair Labor Association, the Keidanren Charter for Good Corporate Behavior and the Keidanren Environment Charter, the Canadian Business for Social Responsibility Guidelines, the World Federation of the Sporting Goods Industry Model Code, and numerous others. One observer at the International Labour Organization, a division of the United Nations, counted more than 400 such principles and codes including individual company codes. Many, although certainly not all, of the core issues embedded in these codes are similar, despite differences in wording and specific focus.

Corporate Citizenship

These codes and principles evolved, in part, because of societal concerns about corporate practices and impacts. For example, the practice of outsourcing operations including manufacturing and production of many goods and services to low-wage developing nations became very popular among large companies starting in the 1990s and continuing to the present. This practice drew attention to the companies' corporate citizenship because many of the facilities in the developing nations were exposed in media reports as having sweatshop working conditions, abusing the human rights of workers, having poor safety standards, or employing weak environmental management. The practice of outsourcing continued into the 2000s and expanded to call and support centers, programming, and other technologically sophisticated services, which shifted from the developed nations to the developing nations. Concerns about domestic job loss for communities where the outsourcing company had facilities combined with low wages and poor conditions in some developing nations created a public focus on the implications of this type of practice for different groups of stakeholders.

Other factors fueling attention to corporate citizenship include the array of ethical scandals, accounting misrepresentations, and frauds that were uncovered in the United States in the early 2000s, as well as in Europe and elsewhere. Accompanied by accusations of corruption and undue influence in the political affairs of nations, and participation by companies in abusive regimes in certain countries, these scandals drew attention to corporate citizenship or what some believed to be lack thereof. Chief executive compensation, estimated to be on the order of 450 times that of the average worker in the early 2000s, and a wave of consolidations through mergers and acquisitions that created huge oligopolies and even near monopolies in many industries, further fanned the desire for better corporate citizenship and also fanned the flames of attention to corporate citizenship.

Pressures for ever-increasing short-term financial performance from financial markets beginning in the 1980s and continuing to the present have focused many corporate leaders' attention on short-term share prices. The attention to share price caused some observers and critics to believe that companies were failing to pay sufficient attention to other stakeholders, that is, those affected by and able to affect the company's activities. Corporate citizenship thus evolved during the 1990s and 2000s in part as a voluntary effort by many large, and therefore highly visible, transnational corporations as well as numerous smaller ones, to demonstrate their goodwill in the face of concerns about their size, shortterm decisionmaking orientation, their power accrued through control of financial and other resources, and not always positive impacts on stakeholders, societies, and the natural environment.

CRITICISMS OF CORPORATE CITIZENSHIP AND RESPONSES

Criticism of a company's corporate citizenship can come from many sources, including activists, the media, local communities affected by company activities, customers, and sometimes nations. Some activists set up Web sites that attempt to foster action against a company, such as a boycott. Wal-Mart, for example, has faced significant problems in some communities because of the company's impact on local shopping districts, low wages, and discrimination against women. Some investors are also concerned about corporate responsibility or citizenship and choose their investments at least in part on the basis of how they perceive the company's corporate citizenship through what is called socially responsible investing. The Social Investment Forum in the United States estimated in 2003 that some $2.16 trillion or more than one of every nine equity investment dollars in the United States was invested in assets that employed at least one of the three main responsible investment strategies—screening investments, shareholder advocacy, and community investment. Screening investments means paying attention to particular negative practices, including poor supply chain management practices such as child labor or abusive working conditions, poor environmental practices, or harmful products such as cigarettes, which some investors wish to avoid. Some investors look for positive practices that they wish to encourage. Returns for investments in screened funds as compared with traditional funds are roughly comparable.

Shareholder advocates focus on changing corporate practices by submitting shareholder resolutions. Shareholder resolutions are aimed at changing matters of concern to activist investors and are directed to the board of directors through the annual meeting process. Shareholder resolutions can focus on a wide range of issues of concern, including environmental policies and practices, labor standards, wages, harmful products, and excessive executive compensation, to name a few areas of criticism. Some chief executives engage in dialogue with the shareholder activists and promise changes, resulting in the resolutions being withdrawn, while others come to a vote during the annual meeting process. Community investors sometimes put their money into projects that are aimed specifically at helping to improve communities, such as housing developments, retail establishments, and similar projects. They may carry a somewhat lower rate of return than traditional investments, but social investors are willing to make that trade-off when necessary.

Defining corporate citizenship as the contributions of businesses to society through the combination of core business activities, social investment and philanthropy, and participation in the public policy process, the World Economic Forum created a framework for action signed by 40 multinational companies' CEOs in 2002. This framework for action focuses on three key elements that help flesh out what corporate citizenship means in practice: the companies' commitment to being global corporate citizens as part of the way that they operate their businesses; the relationships that companies have with key stakeholders, which are fundamental to the company's success internally and externally; and the need for leadership on issues of corporate citizenship by the CEOs and boards of directors of those companies. This statement also points out the array of terminology used to signify corporate citizenship activities: triple bottom line or sustainable development, ethics, corporate responsibility, and corporate social responsibility. The statement also emphasizes key elements of managing responsibility: leadership that defines what corporate citizenship means to a company, integration into corporate strategies and practices, implementation, and transparency.

Evidence of growing interest on the part of companies in corporate citizenship can be found not only in their joining organizations such as the UN Global Compact, the World Business Council for Sustainable Development (WBCSD), and similar organizations but also in a growing acceptance of the need to manage their responsibilities explicitly. The WBCSD focuses on three pillars of corporate citizenship that have come to be called the triple bottom line—economic growth, ecological balance, and social progress through the lens of sustainable development. For example, many transnational firms with long supply chains have been exposed to criticisms by activists that practices in supply chain companies, which may not actually belong to the multinational company, are problematic, with poor labor standards, working conditions, and environmental standards.

Some companies have actively begun to manage their supply chain relationships by asking suppliers to live up to the multinational's own code of conduct and standards of practice, as well as ensuring that conditions in their own operations are managed responsibly. Such responsibility management approaches are aimed at helping companies protect their reputations for good citizenship by establishing global standards throughout their supply chain.

They are supplemented by an emerging institutional framework aimed at assuring that stated and implicit corporate responsibilities are actually met.

STAKEHOLDERS AND CORPORATE CITIZENSHIP

The definition of corporate citizenship as having to do with the impacts of corporate practices and strategies on stakeholders, nature, and the natural environment links corporate citizenship integrally to the relationships that companies develop with their stakeholders. In the classic definition offered by R. Edward Freeman, stakeholders are said to be those who are affected by or who can affect a company. Stakeholders can be classified into two categories—primary and secondary. Primary stakeholders are those groups and individuals without whom the company cannot exist and typically are said to include owners or shareholders, employees, customers, and suppliers, particularly in companies with extended supply chain. Secondary stakeholders are those affected by or can affect the company's practices and strategies, but who are not essential to its existence. Secondary stakeholders typically include governments, communities where the company has facilities and operations, and activists interested in the company's activities, among numerous others. Sometimes governments or communities can be considered primary stakeholders, as when a company is in a regulated industry or when its business directly serves a given community. The environment is not a person but because all companies and indeed all of human civilization depend on its resources, it is frequently treated as if it were a stakeholder; hence, environmental management and related issues of ecological sustainability are tightly linked to concepts of corporate citizenship.

Each stakeholder group either takes some sort of risk with respect to the company, makes an investment of some sort in it, or is tied through some sort of emotional, reputational, or other means into the company's performance. Shareholders or owners, for example, invest their money in the company's shares and rightfully expect a fair return on that investment. Employees invest their knowledge, physical strength and abilities, skills, intellectual resources, and frequently also some of their emotions in the firm, and the firm invests in training and developing employees. Employees are repaid through their salaries and wages. A significant body of research exists that suggests that when employees are treated well by a company through progressive employee practices that are representative of good corporate citizenship, their productivity will be better and the company will benefit financially and in other ways. Customers trust that the products or services that they purchase will serve the purposes for which they are designed and add appropriate value. Good corporate citizenship with respect to customers, therefore, involves the creation of value-adding products and services. Problems with suppliers can result in numerous issues for companies relating to product quality, delivery, and customer service, not to mention the fact that if the supplier itself uses problematic practices, such as sweatshops or poor labor standards, the company purchasing its products will suffer from a degraded reputation. Hence, it is important for companies to manage their relationships with suppliers and distributors well, particularly because many external observers fail to differentiate between the corporate citizenship of the main company and its supply and distribution chain.

Communities are important to companies because they create local infrastructure, such as sewers, communications connections, roadways, building permits, and the like that companies need. Many companies that view themselves as good corporate citizens have extensive corporate community relations programs, including philanthropic programs, volunteer initiatives, and community-based events intended to enhance their local reputation as a neighbor of choice and sustain what is called their license to operate. Governments are important stakeholders, too, and most large companies have developed significant public affairs functions to deal with governmental relations. They also participate in the political processes of countries where they are located to the extent permissible locally, including contributing to campaigns and working through lobbyists to influence legislation.

Environmental management and sustainability have become important elements of good corporate citizenship as worries about the long-term sustainability of human civilization in nature have become more common. Many large companies have implemented environmental management programs in which they attempt to monitor and control the ways in which environmental resources are used so that they are not wasted through programs that encompass resource reduction, reuse, and recycling. A few progressive firms have begun to focus on issues of long-term ecological sustainability as well.

RESPONSIBILITY MANAGEMENT AND ASSURANCE

Most large corporations today have developed specific functions to deal with these different stakeholder groups in what are called boundary-spanning functions. Because the quality of the relationship between a company and its stakeholders is an important manifestation of the company's corporate citizenship, these boundaryspanning functions, which include position titles such as employee relations, community relations, public affairs, shareholder relations, supplier relations, customer relations, are increasingly important.

In most large companies today there is still no one particular job title or function in which all the corporate citizenship activities reside, though some corporate community relations officers have assumed a great many of these responsibilities. A few companies have appointed individuals to positions with titles such as corporate social responsibility officer, vice president of corporate responsibility, or director of corporate citizenship. These jobs, however, are still far from common as of 2005.

In response to criticisms about their negative impacts on society, stakeholders, and nature, and questions about the credibility of their corporate citizenship, many large companies have developed corporate citizenship statements and strategies; some have even appointed managers to positions with titles such as corporate citizenship, corporate social responsibility, or corporate responsibility officer. By the early 2000s, many large corporations voluntarily began to issue social, ecological, or so-called triple-bottom-line reports, which encompass all three elements of corporate citizenship, aimed at economic, social, and ecological impacts.

Responsibility Management

Responsibility management and reporting in the early 2000s consisted of voluntary efforts on the part of companies to be more transparent about some of their practices and impacts. Because companies were able to report how, when, and what they wanted to, however, many critics still found problems with their corporate citizenship. In response, what can be called a responsibility assurance system, consisting of principles and codes of conduct, credible monitoring, verification, and certification systems to ensure that those principles were being met, and consistent reporting mechanisms began to evolve in the early 2000s.

A given company's corporate citizenship is guided by the company's vision and underpinned by its values. Responsibility management approaches begin with vision and values and are reinforced by stakeholder engagement, which helps companies to determine the concerns and interests of both internal and external stakeholders and make appropriate changes. Unlike CSR, which focuses on discretionary activities, corporate citizenship in its broadest sense represents a more integrated approach to the broad responsibilities of companies that is increasingly being accepted by leaders of global enterprises. When a company adopts a responsibility management approach as part of its corporate citizenship agenda, it also focuses on integrating the vision and values into the operating practices and strategies of the firm, typically by focusing on human resource practices and the array of management systems, corporate culture, and strategic decisions that constitute the firm. Another important aspect of responsibility management, which can be compared in its major elements to quality management, is developing an appropriate measurement and feedback system so that improvements can be made as necessary. A final element is that of transparency, as many companies managing corporate citizenship explicitly publish some sort of report that focuses on their social, ecological, and economic performance. Such reports have come to be called triple-bottom-line reports.

Responsibility Assurance

Skeptical stakeholders need reassurance that companies actually manage their stakeholder, societal, and ecological responsibilities well and were unsatisfied with voluntary internal responsibility management approaches, particularly since such approaches were still mostly in use by large branded companies concerned about their reputation, leaving most business-to-business companies and small and medium-sized enterprises to their own devices. Such critics need reassurance that stated standards are actually being met and that statements about corporate citizenship made by companies are accurate. As a result, in addition to internal and voluntary responsibility management approaches, during the early 2000s some large multinational companies began participating in an emerging and still voluntary responsibility assurance system. Responsibility assurance attempted to provide some external credibility to what companies were doing internally to manage their corporate citizenship. Responsibility assurance involves three major elements: principles and foundational values; credible monitoring, verification, and certification systems that help ensure that a company is living up to its stated values; and globally accepted standards for transparently reporting on corporate citizenship and responsibility activities.

Principles and Foundation Values

Principles and foundation values can be found in documents such as the UN Global Compact, OECD Guidelines for Multinational Corporations, and similar codes of conduct as discussed above. They provide guidance to companies about a floor of practice below which it is morally problematic to go and typically rest on core ethical principles or, as noted above, internationally agreed documents and treaties.

Credible Monitoring, Certification, and Verification Approaches

The second aspect of responsibility assurance encompasses credible monitoring, certification, and verification approaches. Because there is a great deal of skepticism about companies' actual corporate citizenship practice, many critics are unwilling to believe companies when they state that they are ensuring that their codes of conduct are actually being implemented. This skepticism increases in long global supply chains, where companies outsource manufacturing, assembly, and related low-skill work to facilities in developing nations; the outsourced work is granted to suppliers who are not actually owned by the customer or sourcing company. Although the supplier facilities are not actually part of the sourcing company, some multinationals' reputations have nonetheless been tainted when activists have uncovered problems in the suppliers' operations related to human and labor rights, environment, safety, working conditions, abuses that involve poor pay even by local standards or failure to pay overtime, and related problems. Child labor is another serious concern for some activists. It turned out that the media, activists, and ultimately the general public did not make a distinction between the supplying company manufacturing in developing nations and the customer company that was purchasing those goods—both were blamed for the use of child labor, but the multinationals were the nearer and more familiar target, so they bore the brunt of the blame. Even when the multinationals implemented their codes of conduct and asked their suppliers to live up to those codes, problems persisted.

As a result, some footwear, clothing, toy, and sports equipment multinationals and some large retailers, who were among the first companies targeted by activists for poor sourcing practices, not only asked their suppliers to implement a code of conduct but began hiring external verifiers to go into those companies and ensure that standards were actually being met. These verifiers are mostly independent agents; they include both NGOs and sometimes accounting firms attempting to develop an expertise in social, labor, and ecological monitoring. The verifiers perform three main functions in supplying companies, wherever they are found: verification that the standards of the sourcing firm are being met; monitoring of working conditions, pay, labor standards, and health, safety, and environmental standards; and certification to the external world that conditions are what the company says they are. Major companies such as Nike, Reebok, Levi Strauss, The Gap, Disney, and Mattel, and numerous others who have been spotlighted in the past, now employ external verifiers in addition to having their own codes of conduct and internal management systems.

Among the many organizations involved in the verification or social audit process are the Fair Labor Association; SAI International, which offers a set of standards called SA 8000; and the British firm AccountAbility, which offers a set of standards called AA 1000. Others include the Clean Clothes Campaign, the Worldwide Responsible Apparel Production program, the Ethical Trading Initiative, Verité, the Fairwear Foundation of the Netherlands, and the Worker Rights Consortium. Many of these independent monitoring and verification organizations are NGOs, while some social auditors are for-profit enterprises. In addition, some represent women's rights groups, some are focused on labor and human rights, and others are backed by religious groups. Some are local in scope and use local parties to actually conduct the monitoring, while the larger ones are international in scope. Concerns about this type of monitoring or responsibility audit, according to the U.S. association Business for Social Responsibility (BSR), range from issues about the effectiveness of monitors in actually uncovering abuses; lack of resolution of issues uncovered in reports by corporate headquarters; and opinions that other means of reducing poverty, corruption, and related systemic problems will be more effective than verification processes. BSR also suggests several positive reasons why companies wish to employ social auditors and verifiers, including cost reduction by using local monitors rather than in-house monitors especially when facilities are globally distributed, benefits to corporate reputation, better compliance both with the code and legal requirements, enhanced productivity and quality brought about by better working conditions, and greater transparency and related credibility with the public.

Globally Accepted Reporting Standards

The third important element of responsibility assurance is having globally accepted reporting standards that ensure that real transparency exists about corporate practices and impacts. Here, the analogy needs to be made to financial auditing and reporting. The auditing and accounting industry, at least within each nation, has long established standard practices, formats, and criteria for reporting corporate financial performance. Such standardization is important so that investors can compare one company's performance against others in the same industry or across different industries. Currently, the same cannot be said for corporate reporting about social and ecological matters, yet there are increasing demands on companies for greater transparency about their practices and impacts.

Although many companies issue triple- or multiple-bottom-line reports that focus not only on economic and financial matters but also on social and environmental ones, there is still no fully accepted reporting procedure that details what, how, and when different aspects of performance are to be reported. As a result, comparing the social or ecological performance of one company with that of others even within the same industry can be problematic. Restoring public trust in corporate citizenship ultimately will require standardization of social reports and even potentially some legal requirements that all companies issue such reports.

There are a number of initiatives aimed at developing globally accepted reporting standards that ensure social and ecological transparency, including a major initiative by the European Union to standardize CSR reporting. Indeed, the ISO organization, which sets quality and environmental standards, began to develop a set of corporate responsibility standards in 2004, which will be voluntary for companies once completed. A company called One Report helps multinationals and other companies gather and report on issues related to sustainability, which include both social and ecological elements, in a standardized format. Perhaps the most prominent of the initiatives around standardized triple-bottom-line reporting, sometimes called sustainability, reporting is that of the Global Reporting Initiative or GRI.

The GRI began in 1997 as an initiative of the CERES and became independent in 2002. Its mission is to develop globally standardized guidelines for sustainability reporting. Formed by a multistakeholder coalition, the GRI regularly gets input from businesses, accounting firms, and investment, environmental, research, human rights, and labor organizations to ensure that its standards are comprehensive, correct, and appropriate to the situation of different businesses. Linked cooperatively with the UN Global Compact, the GRI has developed specific reporting guidelines, principles for determining what to report and how, and content indicators that guide organizations in developing their own reports. In addition, because industries differ dramatically in the characteristics of what needs to be reported, the GRI also has begun developing industryspecific standards.

The GRI attempts to help companies integrate a number of complex attributes related to their corporate citizenship. These include their code of conduct, international conventions and performance standards, management systems standards, accounting for intangibles, assurance standards, and specific standards related to the company's industry. Sometimes criticized for its complexity, the GRI represents the most recognized approach to date of standardized triple-bottom-line or sustainability reporting.

Criticisms of Corporate Citizenship

Some observers believe that corporate citizenship merely represents an effort on the part of companies to create a positive public image rather than substantive change within the corporation. Particularly when corporate citizenship is treated as discretionary or voluntary activities designed to improve aspects of society, critics believe that it does not go deep enough. Others point out that while the United Nations estimates that there are approximately 70,000 multinational corporations in the world with hundreds of thousands of subsidiaries, only a few highly visible, mostly brand-name companies are actively engaged in explicitly forwarding themselves as good corporate citizens. For example, as of 2005, about 2,000 companies had joined the UN Global Compact, while about 350, many of which had joined the Global Compact, had completed triple-bottom-line audits following the procedures of the GRI.

Another criticism of the concept of corporate citizenship focuses on the fact that citizenship is an individual responsibility involving a corresponding set of rights that relate to membership in a political entity, typically a nation-state, that involve civil, social, and political rights and responsibilities, while companies are not people. Companies, however, do bear responsibilities for their societal and ecological impacts, because they command significantly more resources than do most individuals, because they can influence the public policy process in many nations, and because when they participate in civil society or the political process, they carry more weight than do most individual citizens.

—Sandra Waddock

SUSTAINABILITY

Sustainability is an evolving concept that expresses holistic thinking integrating society, economy, and ecology. This concept has been advanced to guide actions within present society to ensure continued existence and prosperity into the foreseeable future. Therefore, *sustainability* can be defined as an integrated understanding of the interconnectedness of human activity with all related man-made and naturally occurring systems. The goal of sustainability is often conflated with the approach needed to attain the goal—*sustainable development.* Understanding these two terms is an essential first step for addressing a set of global challenges embodied by sustainability. To that end, the Brundtland Commission, created through the United Nations, published a report in 1987 in which *sustainable development* is defined as seeking to meet the needs and aspirations of present society without compromising the ability to meet those of future generations.

Because of profound changes to our shared ecological systems, the question of sustainability is being considered around the world. From advancing ozone depletion, which leads to progressively higher levels of life-damaging radiation, to accelerating greenhouse gas emissions, which contribute to complex climate change, to habitat destruction, which results in decreased biodiversity, shared ecosystem resources are being depleted or damaged. Among the consequence of ecosystem damage and loss are that it can threaten and create social unrest in the future, while at the same time drive numerous species toward extinction. Abject poverty that attends the growing gaps between the rich and the poor is a proven driver of environmental degradation and fuels resource, trade, and policy disputes. This type of economic unrest has provided a source of motivation to address sustainability issues not only in organizations such as the United Nations but also at the World Bank and the World Trade Organization.

As our society wrestles with the meaning and actions implied by sustainability, it is helpful to consider that more than 400 years ago the Haudenosaunee (also known as the Iroquois) had their "Great Law," which, in part, requires that leaders consider the impact of their decisions on the seventh generation following that decision. There are other such examples of statements regarding sustainability from the past that very clearly define our collective responsibility to protect and plan for the future. Understanding the recurrence of this theme in human society helps us to understand the centrality of sustainability. It is also instructive to note that thinking about sustainability is not the same as achieving a sustainable outcome. Many civilizations have risen only to prove unsustainable, the Haudenosaunee being among them. What is very different today is the accumulating metrics and resulting data that confirm the impact of human activity on global ecosystem services, such as water cycles, carbon cycles, and resource renewal cycles to name a few. Climate scientists are in general agreement that global warming is real, and it is the product of human activity. The main questions now are as follows: How bad will the consequences be? How fast will they manifest? What can be done to mitigate some of the damage already done?

Sustainability explores how we collectively and individually move into the future while learning to understand how global ecosystem services underpin the social and economic activity on the planet. Business organizations are human society's most efficient resource concentrators, transformers, and distributors; thus, they create what might be called a "corporate ecology" and, therefore, business-oriented solutions central to any working and attainable definition of sustainability.

A few business organizations have viewed increased emphasis on sustainability as an opportunity. If environmental and social costs are included as additional performance metrics, then those firms that comply early and set new standards may be able to create a basis for competitive advantage. For instance, when the California Environmental Protection Agency found that two-stroke engines (the type often used in lawn mowers and gas-powered gardening equipment) were causing a large amount of air pollution, it began to demand more stringent emissions standards for these machines. At first, these new standards were opposed by industry, but a few innovators not only were able to meet the new standards but exceeded them and used 33% less fuel with their more efficient motors. In this case, a sustainability effort, once embraced by these companies, provided the compliant companies with a competitive advantage and achieved a social and environmental objective simultaneously. Sustainability, when pursued by businesses with creativity and purpose, can achieve financial, social, and environmental objectives in an integrated and positively reinforcing manner.

The concept of sustainability is not without its detractors. Some notable scholars, such as Julian Simon, feel that the combined mental power of more people will solve whatever environmental or social problems further human activity produces. The Cato Institute in 2002 concluded that sustainable development is a dubious solution in search of a problem or that it is simply a restatement of a commonsense position of taking care of one's own productive resources that is already well addressed by the current free market policy. It has also been argued that the cost of taking action to comply with sustainability initiatives such as the Kyoto Treaty on Climate Change would cost the U.S. economy a disproportionate amount. These arguments were central to the Bush administration's refusal to become a signatory nation to that agreement on "greenhouse gas" reduction. Some climate scientists and ecologists argue that greenhouse gas damage to ecosystems services may be irreversible and this damage has real costs now that will grow in the future. A concept as complex and far-reaching as sustainability will always present business and society with very conflicted and ambiguous trade-offs.

Because business organizations are uniquely transformative institutions in modern society, how business approaches the concept of sustainability is of primary importance. This central role of business in modern society is also discussed in such topics as corporate social responsibility, corporate citizenship, and corporate ecology. A number of management efficiency approaches have been suggested for business organizations that could make important contributions to our societal goal of sustainability. Some of these include ISO14000, triple-bottom-line accounting, the balanced scorecard approach to strategic management, natural capitalism, the natural step, industrial ecology, Zero Emissions Research Initiative (ZERI), ecological foot printing, and eco-effectiveness (cradle-to-cradle model). In the following sections, these approaches will be discussed briefly.

ISO14000

ISO stands for the International Standards Organization. It is a nongovernmental organization that has grown out of the General Agreement on Tariffs and Trade. As the World Trade Organization pursues agreements on global trade, quality standards have become increasingly important. One of the outcomes of the 1992 Rio Summit on the Environment was the creation of ISO14000 to create a comprehensive set of standards designed to address the most pressing environmental issues for organizations in a global market. As it currently stands, these standards are voluntary for organizations to abide by. However, the ISO14000 is building on up-to-date environmental health and safety standards. These are important standards and make significant contributions to our understanding of sustainability. However, the ISO does not make specific mention of sustainability and states as its primary focus the application of best practices that are geared toward helping organizations come into compliance with globally accepted standards on environmental health and safety. Depending on the application, the ISO approach to standardized reporting and efficiency measures can lead a company to improvements or to follow an industry to the lowest common denominator of acceptable practice.

TRIPLE-BOTTOM-LINE ACCOUNTING

This term and approach originated with the publication of John Elkington's 1998 book *Cannibals with Forks: Triple Bottom Line of 21st Century Business*. In it, Elkington argues that accounting practice should be expanded to include environmental and social costs as well as financial costs. Some scholars argue that corporate social responsibility, or corporate social performance, must measure the social, environmental, and economic performance of the corporation for a firm to be consistent in its approach to these commitments to good practice. There are obvious problems associated with assessing the costs to society for various corporate actions. According to Elkington, the price of a product should include the cost of the ecological services consumed in the production of the product and embodied in the use and disposal of the product. Great strides in ecological economics and research in social capital have helped create metrics to fill in these gaps. The triple-bottom-line approach would have a substantial impact on how organizations operate and may advance our understanding of sustainability. But there are many scholars and practitioners who oppose this type of approach, arguing that it confuses the division of labor and would make firms inefficient and uncompetitive.

BALANCED SCORECARD

This systematic approach to enterprise management was developed in the early 1990s, by Robert Kaplan and David Norton, as a way to remove some of the vagueness out of strategic management. This approach was not developed specifically as a tool to achieve sustainability, but it has promise as such. Like the triple bottom line, the balanced scorecard approach requires that management look beyond financial measurement; it incorporates a more holistic systems perspective into organizational management. This system uses what has been referred to as a double-loop feedback: One loop is business process focused, and one loop is strategic outcome focused. Both loops are intended to use measurements to provide managers with data on which decision making is based. The application for sustainability comes from the reliance on internal and external data collection and an inherent acceptance of a systems approach.

NATURAL CAPITALISM

In 1999, Paul Hawkins, Amory Lovins, and L. Hunter Lovins published a book proposing the redesign of industry based on biological models. They argue that the living systems of the earth are in decline and that the next industrial revolution will be driven by corporations. Natural capitalism is built around the idea that business opportunities become more abundant as entrepreneurs recognize environmental resource limitations. Those that can do more with less will prosper. The advocates of natural capitalism propose four interlinked principles to unlock and ultimately restore natural capital: (1) radically increase resource productivity; (2) adopt closed-loop systems and zero waste in industry; (3) sell services in place of selling products; and (4) recognize that natural capital is the source of future prosperity, thus that businesses will be incentivized to invest in its maintenance. This approach is not only an explicit plan for the concept of sustainability but also a vision of what sustainable business practice might look like.

THE NATURAL STEP

This approach is the outcome of a series of studies initiated by Karl-Henrik Rob, who established principles for sustainable society based on thermodynamics and natural cycles. Since 1989, the Natural Step Foundation has been refining and promoting its four-phase program. These phases are (1) aligning key decision makers and stakeholders around a common understanding of what it takes to be a sustainable society, (2) creating baseline data that detail the resources necessary for an organization to be sustainable,

Sustainability

(3) creating a vision-driven strategic plan based on the data gathered through the study of the organizational system, and (4) recognizing that success depends on step-by-step implementation and continued support. While this approach is comprehensive and holistic, an organization's implementation of this approach seems dependent on the Natural Step Foundation and may be self-limiting because of restrictive access. Here again, as in natural capitalism, the emphasis and essence of the approach to sustainability is on systems thinking, confronting natural resource and cycles dependence, and creating strategies to support the health and continuation of these processes.

INDUSTRIAL ECOLOGY

The idea of industrial ecology, which has grown rapidly over the past decade, originated in a 1989 publication by Robert Frosch, and a book by this title was published by Graedel and Allenby in 1994. Very simply, industrial ecology is the idea that an industrial system should function like an ecosystem. There is no waste product in nature; the end of one process is the beginning of another. Some scholars have defined industrial ecology as the science of sustainability. Yet others would argue that this overreliance on science is the weakness of industrial ecology. It has been said that the answer to the question of sustainability will not be engineered; society must come to an understanding of the interdependence of natural systems and their limitations. These writers advocate caution regarding industrial ecology and suggest that technological fixes help human populations extend their overconsumption of resources, whether they are renewable or fixed in quantity. However, all would agree that industrial ecology will be at least part of the solution, because it provides the engineering solutions that can teach us to do much more with less consumption and helps eliminate waste and pollution.

ZERO EMISSIONS RESEARCH INITIATIVE

ZERI is a concept and a network started by Pauli and deSouza at the United Nations University in Japan. The ZERI network has more than 50 projects worldwide that are applying the ZERI sustainability ideas regarding biodiversity, waste elimination, creativity, and efficient design. ZERI is similar to the Natural Step in that it employs systems thinking to address business, production, and consumption problems. ZERI seeks to create a global network of participants to create alternative organizations that produce goods and services in ways that alleviate poverty and reduce environmental degradation. ZERI is another holistic, systems-based approach to sustainability—one that seeks to model human organizations based on our understanding of naturally occurring systems.

ECOLOGICAL FOOTPRINT

Ecological Footprint is a tool created in 1993 by Mathis Wackernagel and William Rees to help quantify human demand on natural systems relative to the planet's ability to meet those demands. By showing that these demands are consistently in excess of the planet's ability to sustainably provide for these demands, the Global Footprint Network seeks to get business, government, and communities to adopt more sustainable behaviors. Unlike most of the other approaches presented here, the footprint concept is a tool that helps individuals and organizations get a sense of what their actions cost in terms of ecological services. This is an important place to start when considering the meaning and application of sustainability. Our current global ecological footprint overshoots ecosystem capacity by almost 20%, which can be absorbed for a time but not without damage and not indefinitely. Tools such as ecological foot printing are important for people to map our current trajectory and to be able to measure change when action is taken.

ECO-EFFECTIVENESS (CRADLE-TO-CRADLE MODEL)

This is a management consulting and sustainability model that is similar to the approach of natural capitalism. It was developed by Michael Braungart and William McDonough in 1995. The idea of eco-effectiveness is not simply doing more with less but designing products and services in ways that are systemically appropriate. Such products and services are designed to produce no waste and to support rather than disrupt natural systems. By studying the industry as a natural system, this concept seeks to design business processes that mimic metabolic systems both biological and mechanical. Like natural capitalism, this approach envisions the next industrial revolution as one where the end of a product use cycle is the beginning of the next nutrient cycle—where waste equals food and ecological intelligence drives profitability and competitive advantage.

As this brief survey of approaches for addressing sustainability illustrates, many scholars and practitioners have expressed urgency and insight about the global need for sustainability. A successful approach to sustainability will not be engineered. Simply building better, more efficient products will not on its own yield a sustainable future. Along with the efficient use of resources, sustainability requires some fundamental changes in how organizations work on all levels, from the individual action to international coordination. These are not insignificant changes. This fact alone captures the profound difficulty in even defining sustainability—sustainability will have different meanings depending on the level of analysis; ultimately they must all contain the understanding that a sustainable world cannot support irresponsible and inequitable resource use.

—David H. Saiia

Further Readings

Cyphert, D., & Saiia, D. (2004). In search of the corporate citizen: The emerging discourse of corporate ecology. *Southern Communication Journal, 69*(3), 241–256.

Doppelt, B. (2003). *Leading change toward sustainability: A change-management guide of business, government and civil society.* Sheffield, UK: Greenleaf.

Elkington, J. (1998).*Cannibals with forks: The triple bottom line of 21st century business.* Gabriola Island, British Columbia, Canada: New Society.

Frederick, W. C. (1998). Creatures, corporations, communities, chaos, complexity. *Business & Society, 37*(4), 358–390.

Hart, S. (2005). *Capitalism at the crossroads: The unlimited business opportunities in solving the world's most difficult problems.* Upper Saddle River, NJ: Wharton School Press.

Hawkins, P., Lovins, A., & Lovins, L. H. (1999). *Natural capitalism: Creating the next Industrial Revolution.* New York: Little, Brown.

Simon, J. (1996). *The ultimate resource 2.* Princeton, NJ: Princeton University Press.

CORPORATE SOCIAL RESPONSIBILITY (CSR) AND CORPORATE SOCIAL PERFORMANCE (CSP)

The concept of corporate social responsibility (CSR) refers to the general belief held by many that modern businesses have a responsibility to society that extends beyond the stockholders or investors in the firm. That responsibility, of course, is to make money or profits for the owners. These other societal stakeholders typically include consumers, employees, the community at large, government, and the natural environment. The CSR concept applies to organizations of all sizes, but discussions tend to focus on large organizations because they tend to be more visible and have more power. And, as many have observed, with power comes responsibility.

A related concept is that of corporate social performance (CSP). For the most part, CSP is an extension of the concept of CSR that focuses on actual results achieved rather than the general notion of businesses' accountability or responsibility to society. Thus, CSP is a natural consequence or follow-on to CSR. In fact, it could well be argued that if CSR does not lead to CSP then it is vacuous or powerless. Interestingly, many advocates of CSR naturally assume that an assumption of responsibility will lead to results or outcomes. Thus, the distinction between the two is often a matter of semantics that is of more interest to academics than to practitioners. Most of our discussion will be focused on CSR with the general assumption that CSP is a vital and logical consequence.

DEVELOPMENT OF THE CSR CONCEPT

The concept of CSR has a long and varied history. It is possible to trace evidences of the business community's concern for society for centuries. Formal writings on CSR, or social responsibility (SR), however, are largely a product

CSR and CSP

of the 20th century, especially the past 50 years. In addition, though it is possible to see footprints of CSR thought and practice throughout the world, mostly in developed countries, formal writings have been most evident in the United States, where a sizable body of literature has accumulated. In recent years, the continent of Europe has been captivated with CSR and has been strongly supporting the idea.

A significant challenge is to decide how far back in time we should go to begin discussing the concept of CSR. A good case could be made for about 50 years because so much has occurred during that time that has shaped theory, research, and practice. Using this as a general guideline, it should be noted that references to a concern for SR appeared earlier than this, and especially during the 1930s and 1940s. References from this earlier period worth noting included Chester Barnard's 1938 publication, *The Functions of the Executive,* J. M. Clark's *Social Control of Business* from 1939, and Theodore Kreps's *Measurement of the Social Performance of Business* from 1940, just to mention a few. From a more practical point of view, it should be noted that as far back as 1946 business executives (the literature called them businessmen in those days) were polled by *Fortune* magazine asking them about their social responsibilities.

In the early writings on CSR, the concept was referred to more often as just SR rather than CSR. This may have been because the age of the modern corporation's prominence and dominance in the business sector had not yet occurred or been noted. The 1953 publication by Howard R. Bowen of his landmark book *Social Responsibilities of the Businessman* is argued by many to mark the beginnings of the modern period of CSR. As the title of Bowen's book suggests, there apparently were no *businesswomen* during this period, or at least they were not acknowledged in formal writings.

Bowen's work proceeded from the belief that the several hundred largest businesses at that time were vital centers of power and decision making and that the actions of these firms touched the lives of citizens at many points. Among the many questions raised by Bowen, one is of special note here. Bowen asked, what responsibilities to society may businessmen reasonably be expected to assume? This question drove much subsequent thought and is still relevant today. Bowen's answer to the question was that businesspeople should assume the responsibility that is desirable in terms of the objectives and values of society. In other words, he was arguing that it is society's expectations that drive the idea of SR.

Bowen went on to argue that CSR or the "social consciousness" of managers implied that businesspeople were responsible for the consequences of their actions in a sphere somewhat wider than that covered by their profit-and-loss statements. It is fascinating to note that when Bowen referenced the *Fortune* article cited earlier, it reported that 93.5% of the businessmen agreed with this idea of a wider SR. Because of his early and seminal work, Bowen might be called the "father of corporate social responsibility."

If there was scant evidence of CSR definitions in the literature in the 1950s and before, the decade of the 1960s marked a significant growth in attempts to formalize or more accurately state what CSR means. One of the first and most prominent writers in this period to define CSR was Keith Davis, then a professor at Arizona State University, who later extensively wrote about the topic in his business and society textbook, later revisions, and articles. Davis argued that SR refers to the decisions and actions that businesspeople take for reasons that are at least partially beyond the direct economic or technical interest of the firm.

Davis argued that SR is a nebulous idea that needs to be seen in a managerial context. Furthermore, he asserted that some socially responsible business decisions can be justified by a long, complicated process of reasoning as having a good chance of bringing long-run economic gain to the firm, thus paying it back for its socially responsible outlook. This has often been referred to as the enlightened self-interest justification for CSR. This view became commonly accepted in the late 1970s and 1980s.

Davis became well known for his views on the relationship between SR and business power. He set forth his now-famous *Iron Law of Responsibility,* which held that the social responsibilities of businesspeople needed to be commensurate with their social power. Davis's contributions to early definitions of CSR were so significant that he could well be argued to be the runner-up to Bowen for the "father of CSR" designation.

The CSR concept became a favorite topic in management discussions during the 1970s. One reason for this is because the respected economist Milton Friedman came out against the concept. In a 1970 article for the *New York Times Magazine,* Friedman summarized his position well with its title—"The Social Responsibility of Business Is to Increase Its Profits." For many years since and continuing today, Friedman has maintained his position. In spite of Friedman's classic opposition, the CSR concept has continued to be accepted and has continued to grow.

CSR and CSP

233

A landmark contribution to the concept of CSR came from the Committee for Economic Development (CED) in its 1971 publication *Social Responsibilities of Business Corporations*. The CED got into this topic by observing that business functions by public consent, and its basic purpose is to serve constructively the needs of society to the satisfaction of society. The CED noted that the social contract between business and society was changing in substantial and important ways. It noted that business is being asked to assume broader responsibilities to society than ever before. Furthermore, the CED noted that business assumes a role in contributing to the quality of life and that this role is more than just providing goods and services. Noting that business, as an institution, exists to serve society, the future of business will be a direct result of how effectively managements of businesses respond to the expectations of the public, which are always changing. Public opinion polls taken during this early period by Opinion Research Corporation found that about two thirds of the respondents thought business had a moral obligation with respect to achieving social progress in society, even at the possible expense of profitability.

The CED went on to articulate a three-concentric-circles definition of SR that included an inner, an intermediate, and an outer circle. The *inner circle* focused on the basic responsibility business had for its economic function— that is, providing products, services, jobs, and economic growth. The *intermediate circle* focused on responsibilities business had to exercise its economic activities in a sensitive way by always being alert to society's changing social values and priorities. Some early arenas in which this sensitivity were to be expressed included environmental conservation; relationships with employees; and meeting the expectations of consumers for information, fair treatment, and protection from harm. The CED's *outer circle* referred to newly emerging and still ambiguous responsibilities that business should be involved in to help address problems in society, such as urban blight and poverty.

What made the CED's views on CSR especially noteworthy was that the CED was composed of businesspeople and educators and, thus, reflected an important practitioner view of the changing social contract between business and society and businesses' newly emerging social responsibilities. It is helpful to note that the CED may have been responding to the times in that the late 1960s and early 1970s was a period during which social movements with respect to the environment, worker safety, consumers, and employees were poised to transition from special interest status to government regulation. In the early 1970s, we saw the creation of the Environmental Protection Agency, the

PART IV: Ethics of
Business and Management

Consumer Product Safety Commission, and the Equal Employment Opportunity Commission. Thus, it can be seen that the major initiatives of government social regulation grew out of the changing climate with respect to CSR.

Another significant contributor to the development of CSR in the 1970s was George Steiner, then a professor at UCLA. In 1971, in the first edition of his textbook, *Business and Society,* Steiner wrote extensively on the subject. Steiner continued to emphasize that business is fundamentally an economic institution in society but that it does have responsibilities to help society achieve its basic goals. Thus, SR goes beyond just profit making. Steiner also noted that as companies became larger their social responsibilities grew as well. Steiner thought the assumption of social responsibilities was more of an attitude, of the way a manager approaches his or her decision-making task, than a great shift in the economics of decision making. He held that CSR was a philosophy that looks at the social interest and the enlightened self-interest of business over the long-run rather than just the old narrow, unrestrained short-run self-interest of the past.

Though Richard Eells and Clarence Walton addressed the CSR concept in the first edition of their book *Conceptual Foundations of Business* (1961), they elaborated on the concept at length in their third edition, which was published in 1974. In this book they dedicated a whole chapter to recent trends in corporate social responsibilities. Like Steiner, they did not focus on definitions, per se, but rather took a broader perspective on what CSR meant and how it evolved. Eels and Walton continued to argue that CSR is more concerned with the needs and goals of society and that these extend beyond the economic interest of the business firm. They believed that CSR was a concept that permits business to survive and function effectively in a free society and that the CSR movement is concerned with business's role in supporting and improving the social order.

In the 1970s, we initially found mention increasingly being made to CSP as well as CSR. One major writer to make this distinction was S. Prakash Sethi. In a classic 1975 article, Sethi identified what he called dimensions of CSP and, in the process, distinguished between corporate behavior that might be called social obligation, SR, or social responsiveness. In Sethi's schema, social obligation was corporate behavior in response to market forces or legal constraints. The criteria here were economic and legal only. SR, in contrast, went beyond social obligation. He argued that SR implied bringing corporate behavior up to a level where it is congruent with the prevailing social norms, values, and expectations of society. Sethi went on to say that while social obligation is pro-scriptive in nature, SR is prescriptive in nature. The third stage in Sethi's model was social responsiveness. He regarded this as the *adaptation* of corporate behavior to social needs. Thus, anticipatory and preventive action is implied.

Some of the earliest empirical research on CSR was published in the mid-1970s. First, in 1975, Bowman and Haire conducted a survey striving to understand CSR and to ascertain the extent to which companies were engaging in CSR. Though they never really defined CSR in the sense we have been discussing, the researchers chose to measure CSR by counting the proportion of lines devoted to SR in the annual reports of the companies they studied. While not providing a formal definition of CSR, they illustrated the kinds of topics that represented CSR as opposed to those that were strictly business in nature. The topics they used were usually subheads to sections in the annual report. Some of these subheads were as follows: corporate responsibility, SR, social action, public service, corporate citizenship, public responsibility, and social responsiveness. A review of their topical approach indicates that they had a good idea of what CSR generally meant, given the kinds of definitions we saw developing in the 1970s.

Another research study in the mid-1970s was conducted by Sandra Holmes in which she sought to determine executive perceptions of CSR. Like Bowman and Haire, Holmes had no clear definition of CSR. Rather, she chose to present executives with a set of statements about CSR, seeking to find out how many of them agreed or disagreed with the statements. Like the Bowman and Haire list of "topics," Holmes's statements addressed the issues that were generally believed to be what CSR was all about during this time period. For example, she sought executive opinions on businesses' responsibilities for making a profit, abiding by regulations, helping to solve social problems, and the short-run and long-run impacts on profits of such activities. Holmes further added to the body of knowledge about CSR by identifying the outcomes that executives expected from their firms' social involvement and the factors executives used in selecting areas of social involvement.

In 1979, Archie B. Carroll proposed a four-part definition of CSR, which was embedded in a conceptual model of CSP. Like Sethi's earlier article, Carroll sought to differentiate between CSR and CSP. His basic argument was that for managers or firms to engage in CSP they needed to have (1) a basic *definition* of CSR, (2) an understanding/enumeration of the *issues* for which a SR existed (or, in modern terms, stakeholders to whom the firm had a responsibility, relationship, or dependency), and (3) a specification of the *philosophy or pattern of responsiveness* to the issues.

At that time, Carroll noted that previous definitions had alluded to businesses' responsibility to make a profit, obey the law, and to go beyond these activities. Also, he observed that, to be complete, the concept of CSR had to embrace a full range of responsibilities of business to society. In addition, some clarification was needed regarding that component of CSR that extended beyond making a profit and obeying the law. Therefore, Carroll proposed that the SR of business encompassed the economic, legal, ethical, and discretionary expectations that society had of organizations at a given point in time.

A brief elaboration of this definition is useful. First, and foremost, Carroll argued that business has a responsibility that is *economic* in nature or kind. Before anything else, the business institution is the basic economic unit in society. As such it has a responsibility to produce goods and services that society wants and to sell them at a profit. All other business roles are predicated on this fundamental assumption. The economic component of the definition suggests that society *expects* business to produce goods and services and sell them at a profit. This is how the capitalistic economic system is designed and functions.

He also noted that just as society expects business to make a profit (as an incentive and reward) for its efficiency and effectiveness, society expects business to obey the law. The law, in its most rudimentary form, represents the basic rules of the game by which business is expected to function. Society expects business to fulfill its economic mission within the framework of legal requirements set forth by the society's legal system. Thus, the *legal* responsibility is the second part of Carroll's definition.

The next two responsibilities represented Carroll's attempt to specify the nature or character of the responsibilities that extended beyond obedience to the law. The *ethical* responsibility was claimed to represent the kinds of behaviors and ethical norms that society expected business to follow. These ethical responsibilities extended to actions, decisions, and practices that are beyond what is required by the law. Though they seem to be always expanding, they nevertheless exist as expectations over and beyond legal requirements.

Finally, he argued there are *discretionary* responsibilities. These represent voluntary roles and practices that business assumes but for which society does not provide as clear cut an expectation as in the ethical responsibility. These are left to individual managers' and corporations' judgment and choice;

therefore, they were referred to as discretionary. Regardless of their voluntary nature, the expectation that business perform these was still held by society. This expectation was driven by social norms. The specific activities were guided by businesses' desire to engage in social roles not mandated, not required by law, and not expected of businesses in an ethical sense, but which were becoming increasingly strategic. Examples of these voluntary activities, during the time in which it was written, included making philanthropic contributions, conducting in-house programs for drug abusers, training the hard-core unemployed, or providing day care centers for working mothers. These discretionary activities were analogous to the CED's third circle (helping society). Later, Carroll began calling this fourth category *philanthropic,* because the best examples of it were charitable, humanistic activities business undertook to help society along with its own interests.

Though Carroll's 1979 definition included an economic responsibility, many today still think of the economic component as what the business firm *does for itself* and the legal, ethical, and discretionary (or philanthropic) components as what business *does for others.* While this distinction represents the more commonly held view of CSR, Carroll continued to argue that economic performance is something business does for society as well, though society seldom looks at it in this way.

CORPORATE SOCIAL PERFORMANCE

As suggested earlier, the concept of CSP is an extension of the CSR concept that places more of an emphasis on *results achieved.* The development of the CSP concept has occurred somewhat in parallel with the CSR concept, but with a slightly different emphasis. The *performance* focus in CSP is intended to suggest that what really matters is what companies are able to accomplish, that is, the results or outcomes of their CSR initiatives and the adoption of a responsiveness strategy or posture. Many of the writers on CSR would argue that results were implied in their concepts and discussions of CSR, but the literature added a branch in the 1970s when writers began emphasizing the "performance" aspect rather than the "responsibility" aspect. Obviously, the two go hand in hand.

Actually, many of the earlier discussions of CSR transitioned to an emphasis on corporate social *responsiveness* before the performance focus became common. Brief mention should be made of this in the discussion on

CSP. William Frederick is often credited with best describing the difference between responsibility and responsiveness when he dubbed them CSR_1 and CSR_2. With CSR_1, he was referring to the concept of CSR that we discussed in the previous section. The emphasis there is on accountability. CSR_2, in contrast, was intended to reflect the emphasis on responsiveness, or action. In the responsiveness focus, attention turned to the mechanisms, procedures, arrangements, and patterns by which business actually responds to social expectations and pressures in society. The responsiveness focus, therefore, turned the attention from responsibility (business taking on accountability) to responsiveness (business actually responding to social expectations).

In many respects, the emphasis on performance in CSP continues to carry this line of thought forward. That is, the term implies the field has transitioned from *accountability* to *responding* to *results* achieved.

The concept of CSP began appearing in the literature in the mid-1970s. Writers such as Lee Preston, S. Prakash Sethi, and Archie Carroll were among the early authors to speak of the importance of CSP. As mentioned earlier, Carroll presented a conceptual "model" of CSP that motivated a series of improvements and refinements to the concept. Steven Wartick and Philip Cochran took Carroll's three dimensions and broadened them into more encompassing concepts. Wartick and Cochran proposed that the social issues dimension had matured into a new management field known as social issues in management. They extended the model further by proposing that the three dimensions be viewed as depicting *principles* (corporate social responsibilities, reflecting a *philosophical* orientation), *processes* (corporate social responsiveness, reflecting an *institutional* orientation), and *policies* (social issues management, reflecting an *organizational* dimension). In short, Wartick and Cochran updated and extended the three dimensions of the model.

The CSP model was further developed by Donna Wood in her reformulation of the model. Wood expanded and elaborated Carroll's model and Wartick and Cochran's extensions and set forth a reformulated model that went into further detail emphasizing the *outcomes* aspect of the model. Wood argued that CSP was a business organization's configuration of principles of SR; processes of social responsiveness; and policies, programs, and other observable outcomes related to the firm's relationship with society. More than previous conceptualizations, she emphasized the importance of the *outcomes* of corporate efforts.

Diane Swanson extended Wood's model by elaborating on the *dynamic nature* of the principles, processes, and outcomes reformulated by Wood.

Relying on research from corporate culture, Swanson's reoriented model linked CSP to the personally held values and ethics of executive managers and other employees. She proposed that the executive's sense of morality highly influences such policies and programs of environmental assessment, stakeholder management, and issues management carried out by employees. One of Swanson's major contributions, therefore, was to integrate business ethics into the implementation of the CSP focus.

Other concepts have developed in recent years that have embraced a concern for CSR and CSP. They are mentioned here but not developed because they get somewhat outside the traditional boundaries of these concepts. *Corporate citizenship* is a concept that must be mentioned because in the minds of many it is synonymous with CSR/CSP. The entire *business ethics movement* of the past 20 years has significantly overlapped these topics. The *stakeholder concept* has fully embraced and expanded on these concepts. The concept of the "triple bottom line," a concern for economic, social, and environmental performance, has embraced the CSR/CSP literature. The concept of "sustainability" has also embraced CSR/CSP thinking. Corporate sustainability is the goal of the triple-bottom-line and CSR/CSP initiatives—to create long-term shareholder value by taking advantage of opportunities and managing risks related to economic, social, and environmental developments.

BUSINESS'S INTEREST IN CSR AND CSP

To this point, we have been discussing primarily the contributions of academics to the development of the concepts of CSR and CSR. To be sure, the business community has had a parallel development of its interest in the concepts as well. The business community, however, has been less interested in academic refinements of the concept and more interested in what all this means for them, in practice. Prominent business organizations have developed specialized awards for firms' social performance. One example of this would be *Fortune* magazine's "most admired" and "least admired" categories of performance. Among *Fortune*'s eight attributes of reputation, one will find the category of performance titled "social responsibility." The Conference Board is another organization that has developed an award for corporate leadership in the CSR realm. The Conference Board annually gives an award titled the "Ron Brown Award for Corporate Leadership" that recognizes companies for outstanding achievements in community and employee relations. Among the core principles for this award are that the company be committed to corporate citizenship, express corporate citizenship as a shared value visible at all levels, and it must be integrated into the company's corporate strategy.

For several years now, *Business Ethics* magazine has published its list of Annual Business Ethics and Corporate Citizenship Awards. In these awards, the magazine has highlighted companies that have made stellar achievements in CSR/CSP. One of the important criterion used by the magazine in making this award is that the company have programs or initiatives in SR that demonstrate sincerity and ongoing vibrancy that reaches deep into the company. The award criteria also stipulate that the company honored must be a standout in at least one area of SR, though the recipients need not be exemplary in all areas.

Though one will always find individual businesspeople who might reject or fight the idea of CSR/CSP, for the most part today, large companies have accepted the idea and internalized it. One of the best examples of this acceptance was the creation in 1992 of the association titled Business for Social Responsibility (BSR). BSR is a national business association that helps companies seeking to implement policies and practices that contribute to the companies' sustainability and responsible success. In its statement of purpose, BSR claims to be a global organization that helps its member companies achieve success in ways that respect ethical values, people, communities, and the environment. A goal of BSR is to make CSR an integral part of business operations and strategies. An illustrative list of BSR's more than 1,000 members includes such well-known companies as ABB Inc., AstraZeneca Plc., Coca-Cola, Johnson & Johnson, Nike Inc., Office Max, GE, GM, UPS, Procter & Gamble, Sony, Staples Inc., and Wal-Mart.

THE BUSINESS CASE FOR CSR AND CSP

After considering the pros and cons of CSR/CSP, most businesses today embrace the idea. In recent years, the "business case" for CSR/CSP has been unfolding. Before buying in to the idea of CSR, many business executives have wanted the "business case" for it further developed. The business case is simply the arguments or rationales as to why businesspeople believe these concepts bring distinct benefits or advantages to companies, specifically, and the business community, generally. Even the astute business guru Michael Porter, who for a long time has extolled the virtues of competitive advantage, has embraced the concept that corporate and social initiatives are intertwined.

Porter has argued that companies today ought to invest in CSR as part of their business strategy to become more competitive. Of course, prior to Porter, many CSR academics had been presenting this same argument.

Simon Zadek, a European, has presented four different business rationales for being a civil corporation. These reasons form a composite justification for businesses adopting a CSR/CSP strategy. The first is the defensive approach. This approach is designed to alleviate pain. That is, companies should pursue CSR to avoid the pressures that create costs for them. The second is the cost-benefit approach. This traditional approach holds that firms will undertake those activities that yield a greater benefit than cost. The third is the strategic approach. In this approach, firms will recognize the changing environment and engage in CSR as a part of a deliberate corporate strategy. Finally, the innovation and learning approach is suggested. Here, an active engagement with CSR provides new opportunities to understand the marketplace and enhance organizational learning, which leads to competitive advantage. Most of these rationales have been around for years, but Zadek has presented them as an excellent set of business reasons for pursuing CSR.

Putting forth the business case for CSR requires a careful and comprehensive elucidation of the reasons why companies are seeing that CSR is in their best interests to pursue. Two particular studies have contributed toward building this case. One study by PricewaterhouseCoopers, presented in their 2002 Sustainability Survey Report, identifies the following top 10 reasons why companies are deciding to be more socially responsible:

1. Enhanced reputation
2. Competitive advantage
3. Cost savings
4. Industry trends
5. CEO/board commitment
6. Customer demand
7. SRI demand
8. Top-line growth
9. Shareholder demand
10. Access to capital

A survey conducted by the Aspen Institute, in their Business and Society Program, queried MBA student about attitudes regarding the question of how companies will benefit from fulfilling their social responsibilities. Their responses, in sequence of importance, included the following:

- A better public image/reputation
- Greater customer loyalty
- A more satisfied/productive workforce
- Fewer regulatory or legal problems
- Long-term viability in the marketplace
- A stronger/healthier community
- Increased revenues
- Lower cost of capital
- Easier access to foreign markets

Between these two lists, a comprehensive case for business interest in CSR/CSP is documented. It can be seen how CSR/CSP not only benefits society and stakeholders but also how it provides specific, business-related benefits for business.

EXAMPLES OF CSR IN PRACTICE

There are many ways in which companies may manifest their CSR in their communities and abroad. Most of these initiatives would fall in the category of discretionary, or philanthropic, activities, but some border on improving some ethical situation for the stakeholders with whom they come into contact. Common types of CSR initiatives include corporate contributions (or philanthropy), employee volunteerism, community relations, becoming an outstanding employer for specific employee groups (such as women, older workers, or minorities), making environmental improvements that exceed what is required by law, and so on.

Among the 100 Best Corporate Citizens identified in 2005 by *Business Ethics* magazine, a number of illuminating examples of CSR in practice are provided. Cummins, Inc., of Columbus, Indiana, has reduced diesel engine emissions by 90% and expects that within 10 years the company will be at zero or close to zero emissions. In addition, the engine maker underwrites the development of schools in China, is purchasing biodiverse forest land in

Mexico, and funds great architecture in its local community. Cummins also publishes a sustainability report that is available to the public.

Xerox Corporation, Stamford, Connecticut, is a multinational corporation that places high value on its communities. One of its most well-known community development traditions has been its Social Service Leave Program. Employees selected for the program may take a year off with full pay and work for a community nonprofit organization of their choice. The program was begun in 1971, and by 2005, more than 460 employees had been granted leave, translating into about half a million volunteer service hours for the program.

Green Mountain Coffee Roasters, Waterbury, Vermont, was a pioneer in an innovative program designed to help struggling coffee growers by paying them "fair trade" prices, which exceed regular market prices. The company has also been recognized for offering microloans to coffee-growing families and underwriting business ventures that diversify agricultural economies.

Another example of CSR in practice is the Chick-fil-A restaurant chain based in Atlanta, Georgia. Founder and CEO Truett Cathy has earned an outstanding reputation as a businessman deeply concerned with his employees and communities. Through the WinShape Centre Foundation, funded by Chick-fil-A, the company operates foster homes for more than 120 children, sponsors a summer camp, and has hosted more than 21,000 children since 1985. Chick-fil-A has also sponsored major charity golf tournaments.

In the immediate aftermath of Hurricane Katrina in 2005, judged to be the worst and most expensive ever in terms of destruction, hundreds of companies made significant contributions to the victims and to the cities of New Orleans, Biloxi, Gulfport, and the entire Gulf Coast. These CSR efforts have been noted as one of the important ways by which business can help people and communities in need.

As seen in the examples presented, there are a multitude of ways that companies have manifested their corporate social responsibilities with respect to communities, employees, consumers, competitors, and the natural environment.

CSR IN THE NEW MILLENNIUM

As we think about the importance of CSR/CSP in the new millennium, it is useful to review the results of the millennium poll on CSR that was sponsored by Environics, International, the Prince of Wales Business Leaders Forum, and the Conference Board. This poll included 1,000 persons in 23 countries on six continents. The results of the poll revealed how important citizens of the world now thought CSR really was. The poll found that in the 21st century, companies would be expected to do all the following: demonstrate their commitment to society's values on social, environmental, and economic goals through their actions; fully insulate society from the negative impacts of company actions; share the benefits of company activities with key stakeholders, as well as shareholders, and demonstrate that the company can be more profitable by doing the right thing. This "doing well by doing good" approach will reassure stakeholders that new behaviors will outlast good intentions. Finally, it was made clear that CSR/CSP is now a global expectation that now requires a comprehensive, strategic response.

—Archie B. Carroll

Further Readings

Ackerman, R. W. (1973). How companies respond to social demands. *Harvard Business Review, 51*(4), 88–98.

Ackerman, R. W., & Bauer, R. A. (1976). *Corporate social responsiveness.* Reston, VA: Reston.

Asmus, P. (2005). 100 Best corporate citizens. *Business Ethics,* Spring, 20–27.

Aupperle, K. E., Carroll, A. B., & Hatfield, J. D. (1985). An empirical investigation of the relationship between corporate social responsibility and profitability. *Academy of Management Journal, 28,* 446–463.

Backman, J. (Ed.). (1975). *Social responsibility and accountability.* New York: New York University Press.

Barnard, C. I. (1938). *The functions of the executive.* Cambridge, MA: Harvard University Press.

Bowen, H. R. (1953). *Social responsibilities of the businessman.* New York: Harper & Brothers.

Carroll, A. B. (1979). A three-dimensional conceptual model of corporate social performance. *Academy of Management Review, 4,* 497–505.

Carroll, A. B. (1991, July/August). The pyramid of corporate social responsibility: Toward the moral management of organizational stakeholders. *Business Horizons, 34,* 39–48.

Carroll, A. B. (1999). Corporate social responsibility: Evolution of a definitional construct. *Business & Society, 38*(3), 268–295.

Carroll, A. B., & Buchholtz, A. K. (2006). *Business and society: Ethics and stakeholder management* (6th ed.). Cincinnati, OH: South-Western/Thomson.

Committee for Economic Development (CED). (1971, June). *Social responsibilities of business corporations.* New York: Author.

Davis, K. (1960, Spring). Can business afford to ignore social responsibilities? *California Management Review, II,* 70–76.

Davis, K. (1973). The case for and against business assumption of social responsibilities. *Academy of Management Journal, 16,* 312–322.

Davis, K., & Blomstrom, R. L. (1966). *Business and its environment.* New York: McGraw-Hill.

Drucker, P. F. (1984). The new meaning of corporate social responsibility. *California Management Review, XXVI,* 53–63.

Eels, R., & Walton, C. (1974). *Conceptual foundations of business* (3rd ed.). Homewood, IL: Richard D. Irwin.

Epstein, E. M. (1987). The corporate social policy process: Beyond business ethics, corporate social responsibility, and corporate social responsiveness. *California Management Review, XXIX,* 99–114.

Frederick, W. C. (1960). The growing concern over business responsibility. *California Management Review, 2,* 54–61.

Frederick, W. C. (1978). *From CSR$_1$ to CSR$_2$: The maturing of business and society thought.* Working Paper No. 279, Graduate School of Business, University of Pittsburgh.

Friedman, M. (1962). *Capitalism and freedom.* Chicago: University of Chicago Press.

Griffin, J. J. (2000). Corporate social performance: Research directions for the 21st century. *Business & Society, 39*(4), 479–491.

Griffin, J. J., & Mahon, J. F. (1997). The corporate social performance and corporate financial performance debate: Twenty-five years of incomparable research. *Business & Society, 36,* 5–31.

Harrison, J. S., & Freeman, R. E. (1999, October). Stakeholders, social responsibility, and performance: Empirical evidence and theoretical perspectives. *Academy of Management Journal, 1999,* 479–485.

Husted, B. W. (2000). A contingency theory of corporate social performance. *Business & Society, 39*(1), 24–48.

Jones, T. M. (1980, Spring). Corporate social responsibility revisited, redefined. *California Management Review, 1980,* 59–67.

Manne, H. G., & Wallich, H. C. (1972). *The modern corporation and social responsibility.* Washington, DC: American Enterprise Institute for Public Policy Research.

McGuire, J. W. (1963). *Business and society.* New York: McGraw-Hill.

Parket, I. R., & Eilbirt, H. (1975, August). Social responsibility: The underlying factors. *Business Horizons, XVIII,* 5–10.

Preston, L. E. (1975). Corporation and society: The search for a paradigm. *Journal of Economic Literature, XIII,* 434–453.

Preston, L. E., & Post, J. E. (1975). *Private management and public policy: The principle of public responsibility.* Englewood Cliffs, NJ: Prentice Hall.

Rowley, T., & Berman, S. (2000). A brand new brand of corporate social performance. *Business & Society, 39*(4), 397–418.

Schwartz, M. S., & Carroll, A. B. (2003). Corporate social responsibility: A three domain approach. *Business Ethics Quarterly, 13*(4), 503–530.

Sethi, S. P. (1975, Spring). Dimensions of corporate social performance: An analytic framework. *California Management Review, XVII,* 58–64.

Steiner, G. A. (1971). *Business and society.* New York: Random House.

Swanson, D. L. (1995). Addressing a theoretical problem by reorienting the corporate social performance model. *Academy of Management Review, 20,* 43–64.

Wartick, S. L., & Cochran, P. L. (1985). The evolution of the corporate social performance model. *Academy of Management Review, 10,* 758–769.

Wood, D. J. (1991). Corporate social performance revisited. *Academy of Management Review, 16,* 691–718.

PART V

Employee and Human Resources Issues

EMPLOYEE PROTECTION AND WORKPLACE SAFETY LEGISLATION

EMPLOYEE PROTECTION IN THE WORKPLACE

Employee protection and workplace safety address the question of who is responsible for ensuring that employees have protection from various dangers on the job. While employees certainly bear some responsibility for their own protection and safety, the employer may be held responsible for not only providing protective equipment and information but also ensuring that employees properly use that protection. When the cost of workplace protections in more heavily regulated markets increases, demand for labor in less regulated, lower-cost markets may increase, resulting in potential trade-offs between cost competitiveness and worker safety.

Early Perceptions of Protection Needs

A century ago, agriculture and small-scale retail were the dominant work settings, although manufacturing was growing. Agriculture has long been a major area of inadequate worker protection, from both an economic and a social perspective. Many agricultural pursuits were small-scale and family owned. The economic pressure of having limited financial resources sometimes led to inadequate worker protection. Often equipment was not well maintained, and farmers could not afford the latest technology of the era. Poor maintenance precipitated many accidents, but few records were maintained.

As manufacturing grew, the same mind-set was transferred from the agricultural sector; thus, employees were not viewed as resources to be protected. There were plenty of able-bodied men, and the pay was better than in agriculture. The major motivation for work was regarded as financial. Manufacturing plants, especially in clothing and textiles, were not considered safe by the employees. Fire was a critical threat, given the massive cotton dust accumulated each day. No one considered that employees needed protection from the dust in the air; lung damage was not a well-understood issue in health circles. A similar unknown problem in the lumber mills of the early to mid-20th century was sawdust. The most common cause of employee fatality in the lumber, textile, and clothing mills was fire. Yet, 100 years ago, there was little effort or apparent interest in fire safety.

Employer's Role in Hazard Identification

Each workplace is unique, and different hazards are likely to be found in each. However, some common categories of hazards can be identified. Equipment hazards abound in most industrial settings: Equipment is often large, heavy, and at times dangerous. Regretfully, employers have not always taken the time to instruct their employees about the hazards, emphasizing instead the use of the machine and the need to minimize downtime. When rushed, employees act like anyone else; they become careless, and accidents occur. Lumber mills, metal-stamping plants, and firefighting situations are among the highly accident-prone job sites. Proper use of equipment must be continuously emphasized by the employer.

Numerous environmental hazards may be present, ranging from explosives to chemical leaks to malfunctioning equipment. Each work site will have its unique environmental hazards. The employer is charged with having an inventory of all potential hazards and working to reduce such hazards to the lowest levels. Protective equipment and protective clothing are crucial in some work areas. For example, persons in construction sites may be required to wear hard hats. However, a typical site visit reveals that many managers and some workers avoid wearing protective gear. The equipment may be provided, but whose responsibility is it to ensure that a worker uses the equipment? Legally, it is the employer's. Regretfully, the consequences of not assuming that burden are minor, and many employers do not even enforce their own work rules.

Unsafe Conditions and Whistle-Blower Protection

In many workplaces, employees best understand the conditions requiring management attention. Employees may be aware when conditions are dangerous and senior management is unaware of the problem. In some cases, there may be an organizational culture that communicates to employees that they are to maintain silence about the workplace. The Occupational Safety and Health Administration (OSHA) addresses this concern by offering protection from reprisals brought about by reporting hazards or other data under OSHA. If an employee is subjected to reprisals, the employee may complain to the Department of Labor for protection.

Violence in the Workplace

In the contemporary media, workplace violence has received increased attention. Employees have been attacked, in rare cases even murdered, on the job, by both fellow employees and strangers. Violence in small retail establishments has led to the installation of electronic surveillance cameras, but the electronic records are only valuable as evidence after the fact. Banks, and their large stores of cash, are also vulnerable, as are taxi drivers and other cash-carrying workers. However, employers have rarely viewed the problem as one of employee protection. In manufacturing facilities, there is often more restricted access as compared with retail and banking. Thus, the violence has tended to be more work-community related; for example, disgruntled employees have instigated violent episodes.

The National Institute for Occupational Safety and Health reports that an average of 20 workers are murdered each week in the United States. Homicide is the second leading cause of workplace deaths, second only to motor vehicle crashes. The majority of workplace homicides are robbery-related crimes, with only about 10% committed by coworkers or former coworkers.

In addition, there are 18,000 victims of nonfatal workplace assaults each week. Most nonfatal workplace assaults occur in service settings such as hospitals, nursing homes, and social service agencies. About half the nonfatal assaults in the workplace are committed by a health care patient. Nonfatal workplace assaults result in more than 800,000 lost workdays annually.

Employer Strategies for Workplace Violence Prevention

A number of strategies have been developed for reducing the occurrence of workplace violence. A few examples of prevention strategies include improving the visibility within and outside the workplace, policies for handling cash, physical separation of customers from employees, brighter lighting, security devices, escort services for employees, and an emphasis on employee training. A workplace violence prevention program should include three variables: a system for documenting incidents, well-communicated procedures to be taken in the event of incidents, and truly open communication between employers and workers. An effective employee education program is crucial to making a meaningful difference in preventing workplace violence in any type of business.

Smoking in the Workplace

Until the 1980s, it was common for a large proportion of the work population to smoke, even on the job. Some employers were in fact protective of the employee's right to smoke. By 1990, most employers were developing no-smoking policies based on OSHA standards. By 2005, a majority of work-places were nonsmoking. This is an example where research, legislation, public pressure, and potential large penalties in court have reduced the threat of a known danger. Public pressure was a major force.

Workers' Compensation

One reason employers have directed attention to employee safety and pro-tection is the potential cost incurred in not paying attention to the early warning signs. Early in the 20th century, states found that workers injured on the job became a drag on the economy. Thus, states began to develop protective legislation to protect workers' future earnings and minimize the impact on the employer. Workers' compensation laws seek to ensure that employees who are injured or disabled on the job are provided with fixed monetary awards, eliminating the need for litigation. Benefits are also pro-vided for dependents of workers who are killed because of work-related accidents or illnesses. Laws in some jurisdictions protect employers and fellow workers by limiting the amount an injured employee can recover from an employer and by eliminating the liability of coworkers in most acci-dents. State statutes establish this framework for many types of employment, from office work to metalworking to hospital employment. Federal statutes are limited to federal employees or those workers employed in some unique and significant aspect of interstate commerce, such as stevedoring. The laws in the 50 states are similar but differ greatly in the fixed-income formula and in the ease of receiving the funds.

WORKPLACE SAFETY LEGISLATION

As the U.S. workplace has evolved, both in physical and in human dimen-sions, the interest in minimizing the dangers in the workplace and encouraging safe conditions and behavior has grown, as have the number and breadth of stakeholders. Since 1902, there have been safety statutes at the state level. Each state has reacted to safety concerns within its borders and offered protective

PART V: Employee and Human Resources Issues

legislation. For example, Virginia has a safety statute relating to coal mining, whereas Arkansas does not. Critics have often been vocal about the enforcement of the state statutes, claiming that workers have no real protection. Ultimately, the subject gained sufficient support for the federal government to consider the workplace safety issue.

Union Influence on Legislation

During the 1960s, labor unions noted an increased concern among their members about poor safety conditions and increased accidents and fatalities as workplace changes took place and efforts to control costs began anew. The United Steelworkers of America used a modified nominal group technique in several of its university-cosponsored summer leadership programs and came away after 2 years with a clear notion of some major concerns: a perceived lack of concern for workers, which was growing especially in larger firms; lack of maintenance of safety equipment or lack of needed equipment; lack of training in the safety area; lack of government inspections; and discharge of workers involved in safety mishaps.

The result of an intense union lobbying effort was the (Williams-Steger) Occupational Safety and Health Act of 1970. One indication of the success of the statute is the inclusion of safety provisions in 9 out of 10 labor agreements today. Unions have been the moving force in the law's establishment and in its evolution during employer-dominated legislative sessions since its passage. The major OSHA provision is its "general duty" clause; the employer is required to provide each employee with a safe and healthy working environment. The workplace must be free of all recognized hazards that may cause illness, injury, or death to an employee. Furthermore, the employer must comply with all the occupational safety and health standards adopted by the Department of Labor. Recognizing that not all employers would receive the act in a positive manner, OSHA requires employers to provide access to federal safety inspectors and post any notices and maintain an extensive array of records on employees and on the actions taken by the employer to meet the OSHA standards.

Workplace Inspections

Workplace inspections, designed to reduce hazards to workers' health and safety, may be of two types. Random inspections usually target specific industries where hazards are known to exist. The targets are changed periodically in an attempt to alleviate the more serious problems first. While there have been very significant investments of time and money by employers and the federal and state governments, the injury rates changed little in the first 30 years. The Department of Labor has initiated a new infusion of funds for employee safety training, with an emphasis on personal hazard identification and self-protection.

OSHA responses to employee complaints under the law yield more effective enforcement. Usually, an employee complaint is made only after some effort has been made internally to have potential hazards addressed. However, the problem often becomes one of enforcement of inspector orders and the relatively small monetary penalties available under the law. The collective bargaining process and the use of joint safety and health committees have minimized the risks in major industries. Employees in smaller firms and in nonunion firms are fearful of filing complaints, although there is a whistle-blower protection clause in the act. While the act provides protection, an affected employee must file a complaint within 30 days of the alleged reprisals.

Major Impediment to Higher Priority

Employee protection can impose costs that affect global competitiveness. Employers in developing markets may not face the same level of safety and health regulation and thus face lower economic costs. In recent years, employers have lobbied heavily against increasing regulatory requirements, arguing that higher costs lead to diminishing returns.

—Jerald F. Robinson

Further Readings

Bohlander, G. W., & Snell, S. A. (2007). *Managing human resources* (14th ed.). Cincinnati, OH: Southwestern.

Denenberg, R. V., & Braverman, M. (1999). *The violence-prone workplace: A new approach to dealing with hostile, threatening, and uncivil behavior.* Ithaca, NY: Cornell University Press.

Hartnett, J. (1996). *OSHA in the real world: How to maintain workplace safety while keeping your competitive edge.* Landsdowne, PA: Silver Lake.

Kohn, S. M., Kohn, M. D., & Colapinto, D. K. (2004). *Whistleblower law: A guide to legal protections for corporate employees.* Westport, CT: Praeger.

Moran, M. M. (2005). *The OSHA answer book* (8th ed.). Walnut Creek, CA: Management Advantage.

Occupational Safety and Health Administration [Web site]. Retrieved from www.osha.gov

Workers' Compensation Service Center [Web site]. Retrieved from www.workers compensation.com

EMPLOYEE RIGHTS
MOVEMENT

E mployee rights refer to the entitlements that employees have vis-à-vis
their relationship with their employers. These rights dictate how
employers are expected to treat their existing employees. Such entitlements
are, however, contingent on the nature of the workplace environment—that is,
whether it is "public" (linked to the government) or "private." Whereas public
employees benefit from the protection afforded by the United States Bill of
Rights, private employees do not, except where explicit protection is offered
by other state or federal legislation.

PUBLIC/PRIVATE DISTINCTION

Which rights are protected depends first and foremost on the nature of the
workplace. Workplaces are distinguished as either public or private depending
on their relationship to the state. Public workplaces are those that are operated
by and for the state—that is, governmental agencies. Private workplaces, on
the other hand, are defined as those that are separate from the state—that is,
privately owned corporations. Although this distinction is often hidden and
arguably artificial, the classification of a public workplace versus a private
workplace is instrumental in determining the rights granted to employees and
the responsibilities assigned to employers.

An employee of the public workplace is protected by the Constitution and
its Bill of Rights. Many of the rights protected by the Bill of Rights are considered natural rights or fundamental rights. Even so, these rights are not
protected for employees in private workplaces. The private workplace is therefore void of many rights—that is, freedom of speech, due process, and so
on—considered fundamental outside the workplace.

The reason for this is quite simple: The original intent of the Constitution
was based on the history of the American colonies and their relationship with
England. The purpose of the Bill of Rights was to protect American citizens
from excessive encroachment by the government, not to isolate citizens from

one another. The founders of this country focused on civil society, without knowledge of the strong presence that business would have on the future United States and without anticipating in any way the significant impact this would have on the evolution of distinctly public and private workplaces. Although the operation of these workplaces is remarkably similar, the rights granted to their respective employees remain distinct.

EMPLOYMENT AT WILL

The default rule for employment in the majority of jurisdictions in the United States is employment at will (EAW). EAW operates in the absence of an employment contract and is recognized as the ability of either the employee or the employer to terminate their relationship at any time, for any reason, or for no reason at all. No justification for termination is required. The only prohibition is against reasons specifically deemed illegal (i.e., whistle-blowing, in those states where whistle-blower protection is in effect, gender or racial discrimination, and so on).

Unless otherwise specified, employees in the private sector are considered employees "at will" and can be terminated at any time. Except in cases where legislation has carved out specific exceptions or in Montana, the single "right-to-work" state, employees have no job security.

Although both employers and employees are ostensibly granted equal rights according to EAW, it can be argued that these rights are equivalent but not equal. There is a significant power imbalance often at play in that it is typically easier for employers to find new employees than vice versa. Furthermore, because no reason for termination is required, employees are stripped of their rights to due process and their prior investment in their work is ignored.

Due process is also a concern. Due process refers to the rights that individuals have not only to be notified of the charges made against them but also to respond to these charges. Due process is linked to employee rights in that whereas public employees are guaranteed due process, private employees enjoy no such protection.

LEGISLATION

With EAW as the prevailing norm, legislation has been passed to carve out rights for employees. There currently exist significant legislative and statutory exceptions to EAW. The Family and Medical Leave Act of 1993, for example, mandates that employers allow employees in both private and public workplaces to take an unpaid leave of absence due to illness, maternity, or caring for a sick family member. Employers are required to keep open the position of the employee on leave, who has a protected right to return to his or her job at the end of the leave.

There also exist several pieces of legislation regarding discrimination in the workplace. For instance, the Americans with Disabilities Act prohibits discrimination based on disabilities in the workplace. Firing an employee based on a disability is deemed inappropriate and illegal. The Civil Rights Act of 1964 forbids employers from discriminating against employees according to race, color, religion, sex, or national origin. Discrimination based on age is also prohibited by the Age Discrimination in Employment Act of 1967. Though these pieces of legislation are not without certain exceptions, they provide employees with rights not otherwise granted to them according to EAW.

PRIVACY AND TECHNOLOGY

Advances in technology have further limited the rights of employees in the private workplace. Legal systems have experienced difficulty keeping up with the fast pace of technological innovation. This has resulted in numerous challenges to privacy. In fact, employees in the private sector enjoy no reasonable expectation of privacy. Furthermore, what little privacy they previously enjoyed is slowly being eroded.

An example of this stems from e-mail in the workplace. People today communicate frequently by e-mail in both their work and their personal lives. This form of communication is very different from other forms of communication because it is more difficult to destroy and much easier to trace. Although many people consider this personal communication, in fact, it is not. Employers have the right, which many exercise, to monitor employees' e-mail. Some consider this not only a right but also a responsibility, in light of the possibility of inappropriate exchanges taking place via e-mail. Furthermore, monitoring applies not only to work-related e-mail but to any e-mail accessed by the employee in the workplace. The rationale is that the employer has the right to monitor anything that takes place at the workplace, with or without the employee's knowledge.

PRE- AND POSTEMPLOYMENT

The relationship between employees and employers is strictly defined. Job candidates (preemployees) and retirees (postemployees) have interests but few if any protected rights. Employee status differs from pre- or postemployee status in that employees have a current existing relationship with their employers. This is not the case for preemployees, since no relationship has been established. Postemployees had a previous relationship with their employer, but this relationship is no longer in existence.

This is significant in that while the rights of employees are limited, the rights of pre- and postemployees are virtually nonexistent. The rights protected for pre- and postemployees are only the fundamental civil rights—that is, the right to not be discriminated against on the basis of age, skin color, sex, disability, and so on. Job candidates are subject to any means of testing the employer deems appropriate, which can include inquiries into credit histories, driving records, medical records, and so on. Neither permission nor disclosure is required. Failure to concede to the "requests" of the potential employer constitutes a justifiable reason for not hiring a job candidate. Employers are not required to provide the reasons for not hiring potential employees, and they are permitted to test them by any means they deem acceptable.

As for retirees and other postemployees, because they no longer have a relationship with their employers, the same conditions apply. This is unfortunate in that postemployees still have a stake in their employer. They might need job references, and many have invested in pension plans and the like.

CONCLUSION

The workplace in the United States has changed drastically in the past 20 or 30 years. Employment relationships have beginning and end points in terms of rights, whereas previously, employment relationships were considered to be indefinite. Issues connected to preemployment and postemployment rights, EAW, and public versus private workplaces were not at the forefront. Today, however, long-term employee-employer relationships are becoming increasingly rare.

Although Americans tend to assume that they receive the greatest workplace protection, in fact, this is not always the case. Cultural values in many workplaces outside the United States, such as in Europe, create very different workplace standards. This is interesting, particularly as compared with other countries, where the balance of power is tilted much more in favor of employees. For example, in Canada and in many countries in Europe, women are guaranteed 1 year of paid maternity leave. This is just one example of how workplace norms differ around the world.

—Tara J. Radin and Megan E. Dayno

Further Readings

Hartman, L. P. (2001). Technology and ethics: Privacy in the workplace. *Business & Society Review, 106*(1), 1.

Radin, T. J., & Werhane, P. H. (1996). The public-private distinction and the political status of employment. *American Business Law Journal, 34*(2), 245–260.

Radin, T. J., & Werhane, P. H. (2003). Employment at will, employee rights, and future directions for employment. *Business Ethics Quarterly, 13*(2), 113–130.

Rowan, J. R. (2000). The moral foundation of employee rights. *Journal of Business Ethics, 24*(4), 355–361.

Rummler, G. A., & Rummler, M. E. (2003). Employee Bill of Rights. *T+D, 57*(4), 27.

Werhane, P. H., & Radin, T. J. (1996). Employment at will and due process. In T. Donaldson & P. H. Werhane (Eds.), *Ethical issues in business: A philosophical approach* (5th ed., pp. 364–374). Englewood Cliffs, NJ: Prentice Hall.

EQUAL OPPORTUNITY

E qual opportunity is the goal of laws, regulations, and policies attempting to ensure that similarly situated people are treated equally in
virtually all aspects of life, including jobs, education, housing, public accommodations, and so forth. The United States has a long and difficult history
regarding equality based on race, gender, ethnicity, and other characteristics.
Women, blacks, Native Americans, Asians, Jews, gays, the differently abled,
and others were variously denied the right to vote, not given equal pay for
equal work, not allowed to have certain jobs, denied access to equal education,
and denied access to public facilities and generally did not enjoy the same
rights to pursue the same quality of life as white males. In an effort to live up
to the statement in the Declaration of Independence that "we hold these truths
to be self-evident, that all men are created equal, that they are endowed by
their Creator with certain unalienable rights, that among these are life, liberty
and the pursuit of happiness," the U.S. Congress has passed laws guaranteeing
its citizens an equal opportunity to receive the basics determined to be part of
a civilized and humane democratic society: housing, education, employment,
voting, public accommodations, and receipt of federal funds. Equal opportunity encompasses a set of laws that are an attempt to rid the country of the
effects of its history of denying equality based largely on immutable characteristics such as race, gender, or ethnicity.

The primary vehicle for providing equal opportunity is the Civil Rights
Act of 1964. There are also other major laws providing equal opportunity on
the basis of age or disability. States also have equal employment laws that by
and large track those of the federal government, though some states have
added other categories, such as affinity orientation, marital status, or political
affiliation. The major equal opportunity laws are reviewed here.

FOURTEENTH AMENDMENT TO THE U.S. CONSTITUTION

Arguably, the first major equal opportunity provision, the Fourteenth
Amendment, ratified in 1868, undergirds much of the expectation that

Americans have to be treated fairly and be treated the same if they are similarly situated. The amendment states that "all persons born or naturalized in the United States, and subject to the jurisdiction thereof, are citizens of the United States and of the State wherein they reside. No State shall make or enforce any law which shall abridge the privileges or immunities of citizens of the United States; nor shall any State deprive any person of life, liberty, or property, without due process of law; nor deny to any person within its jurisdiction the equal protection of the laws."

The Fourteenth Amendment was subjected to a great deal of resistance during its passage, since it was put in place to give the newly freed slaves the same rights as U.S. citizens, something they had not heretofore enjoyed. Under the law, the federal government, generally through the U.S. Supreme Court, could nullify state laws that operated to deny blacks the rights enjoyed by white citizens.

Despite passage of the Fourteenth Amendment, several southern states still maintained, either formally or informally, ironclad "Black Codes," which subjected blacks to a different set of rules and laws than whites. Such laws were in effect for nearly 100 years after passage of the amendment, until they were outlawed by the Civil Rights Act of 1964. The Fourteenth Amendment's denial of equal protection and due process has become the primary means of challenging laws that create barriers to equal opportunity in the United States.

FIFTEENTH AMENDMENT TO THE U.S. CONSTITUTION

The right to vote was granted to blacks after the Civil War ended slavery in 1865 and Congress passed the Fifteenth Amendment to the U.S. Constitution in 1870. The Fifteenth Amendment provided that the right to vote "shall not be denied or abridged on the basis of race, color or previous condition of servitude," thus nullifying the laws passed by states to prohibit blacks from voting. The Enforcement Act of 1870, providing criminal penalties for interference with the right to vote, and the Force Act of 1871, providing for federal election oversight, allowed a brief time of Reconstruction-era voting and election to office by blacks. Since blacks outnumbered whites in five southern states and had substantial numbers in other southern states, this resulted in their election to office, and even to the governorship of Louisiana (which lasted only 1 month, due to white resistance). This period of seeming equality was, however, short-lived due to the rise of the Ku Klux Klan and its attendant violence designed to return the south to the pre–Civil War status quo. The Fourteenth

Amendment required state governments, like the federal government, to ensure that citizens have a right to due process and equal protection, while the Fifteenth Amendment granted to blacks the right to vote.

NINETEENTH AMENDMENT TO THE U.S. CONSTITUTION

This provision, ratified in 1920, granted women equal opportunity in voting by allowing them to vote in elections. Gender-based disenfranchisement had been the norm since the country's founding and was nullified only after an acrimonious decades-long fight by those believing the disenfranchisement to be totally at odds with the Declaration of Independence and the U.S. Constitution. Women's suffrage, as the movement to gain voting for women was called, included a group called the Silent Sentinels, who staged an 18-month demonstration outside the White House to gain voting rights for women.

THE CIVIL RIGHTS ACT OF 1964

This major equal opportunity law was passed largely in response to the turbulence erupting from the Civil Rights movement in response to racial discrimination and "Jim Crow" segregation in the United States, primarily in the south; it guaranteed equal opportunity for all citizens in housing, education, employment, voting, and receipt of federal funds. The Civil Rights Act, one of the most ambitious pieces of legislation in the history of civilization, is divided into titles that address the various contexts for protection.

Title I: Voting

Equal opportunity in voting was included in the Civil Rights Act of 1964 because blacks were routinely denied the right to vote, particularly in the south, despite the Fifteenth Amendment and other legislation passed after the Civil War guaranteeing them the right to vote. In the same year that the Civil War ended, the Ku Klux Klan was born. Violation and intimidation by the Klan and other such white supremacist groups increased after the federal troops left the South in 1877. The federal troops had been in the South since the end of the Civil War in 1865, during the period known as the Reconstruction. Without the presence of the federal troops, life reverted to much the way it had been during slavery.

Blacks' homes were burned down, jobs were taken away, and poll taxes were imposed, with the knowledge that blacks would not be able to pay to vote. Blacks were routinely intimidated, harassed, beaten, and lynched for attempting to register to vote. Their economic lives were also threatened, as most were employed as menial laborers for whites, and it was understood that they would lose their jobs if they voted. Those who made it inside the voting registrar's office were often asked to explain extremely difficult arcane passages from the Constitution, asked questions such as how many bubbles there are in a bar of soap or how many grains of sand there are on the beach, or asked to pay poll taxes that were far out of their financial reach. This was not done to whites, which ended in leaving the voting to them. Blacks were effectively disenfranchised for the next nearly 100 years until passage of the Civil Rights Act in 1964.

Realizing that the Civil Rights Act of 1964 was not enough to curtail the continued harassment of black voters, the next year, Congress passed the Voting Rights Act of 1965, but not before the events of March 7, 1965, and what became known as "Bloody Sunday." In the Selma-to-Montgomery March for Voting Rights, 600 nonviolent civil rights protesters attempted to walk from Selma to Montgomery, Alabama, via the Emund Pettus Bridge, to demonstrate the need for federal voting legislation. They were met with mounted police on horseback and dogs, which were set loose on the crowd. Television coverage horrified the nation, and after obtaining a court order to allow the march, 25,000 marchers from across the country and world successfully made the trek on March 21, 1965. Less than 5 months later, the Voting Rights Act of 1965 was passed. The act outlawed the kinds of impediments to voting and registering to vote that had routinely been used to disenfranchise blacks since after the Reconstruction. The U.S. Department of Justice Civil Rights Division enforces voting laws.

Titles II and III: Public Accommodation

At various times, blacks, Native Americans, the Irish, Jews, and others were not allowed into public places or to use public facilities. Libraries, theaters, restaurants, public auditoriums, swimming pools, recreational facilities, parks, hotels, stores, public transportation, and other places were all off-limits to them, especially to blacks. If blacks were allowed in, they often had to sit in a different place from whites. For instance, in theaters, blacks often had to sit in the balcony or attend on different days from whites; blacks had to board public buses and pay the full fare, then get off, go to the back of the bus, and take a seat in the rear. If a white person needed a seat, the black person would have to get up and give his or her seat to the white person, even though both had paid full fare. If blacks were allowed into restaurants at all, they generally had to go to the rear entrance and order their food to take away. Some towns had special days for blacks to shop, and fairs had special days for blacks to attend.

The Civil Rights Act prohibited these practices and required equal access to public facilities. Blacks and others were no longer denied the right to enter into or use public facilities. Private clubs and facilities such as country clubs can still discriminate, however.

Title IV: Education

Prior to passage of the Civil Rights Act, many public schools remained segregated even though the U.S. Supreme Court had outlawed them in its 1954 Brown v. Board of Education decision 10 years earlier. Black children were not permitted to go to school with whites and did not have access to the same funding, materials, facilities, and programs that were provided to white students. Black schools were generally in poor condition, with few supplies and books. Often, the first few days of school were spent taping up discarded, outdated books from white schools to be used by black schools since the white students had received new textbooks.

Such acts were outlawed by the Civil Rights Act of 1964. Equal opportunity in education is enforced by the U.S. Department of Education's Office of Civil Rights.

Title V: Housing

Prior to passage of the Civil Rights Act, segregation on the basis of race or ethnicity in housing was widespread. Restrictive covenants in property deeds were common. Such covenants dictated that the property could not be sold or rented to certain groups, such as blacks or Jews. Owners routinely refused to sell or rent their property to blacks or Jews regardless of their appearance, ability to pay, education levels, or jobs. If they did rent or sell to blacks or Jews, whites living in the area would soon move away, and the property values would decrease. Such practices relegated the groups discriminated against to enclaves exclusively peopled by those groups.

Under the provision that prohibited discrimination in programs receiving federal funds, the Civil Rights Act outlawed such practices. To further strengthen its commitment to equal opportunity in housing to ensure equal access to housing, in 1968, Congress passed the Fair Housing Act as Title VIII of the Civil Rights Act of 1968. The law prohibits discrimination in the sale, rental, and financing of dwellings and in other housing-related transactions, based on race, color, national origin, religion, sex, familial status (including children under the age of 18 living with parents or legal custodians, pregnant women, and people securing custody of children under the age of 18), or disability, and provides the structure for equal housing opportunity. Equal opportunity in housing is overseen by the U.S. Department of Housing and Urban Development's Office of Fair Housing and Equal Opportunity, which administers the federal laws and establishes national policy that ensures that everyone has equal access to housing on a nondiscriminatory basis.

Title VI: Federally Assisted Programs

From federally guaranteed school loans to welfare, from schools and universities that receive federal funding and grants to arts programs funded by government grants, no one can discriminate, and all must provide equal opportunity in their programs.

Title VII: Employment

Title VII of the Civil Rights Act of 1964 prohibits discrimination in employment on the basis of race, color, gender, religion, or national origin by employers with 15 or more employees, labor unions, and employment referral agencies. Sexual harassment and pregnancy discrimination are also prohibited as types of gender discrimination. Under Title VII, the prohibited categories cannot be used as a basis for employment decisions of any kind, including hiring, firing, discipline, promotions, raises, or any other term or condition of employment. The Equal Employment Opportunity Commission (EEOC) enforces claims of all bases for employment discrimination under Title VII, the Equal Pay Act, the Age Discrimination in Employment Act, and the Americans with Disabilities Act. By law, the EEOC must dispose of all claims filed, as appropriate, and does so through mediation, conciliation, investigation, and, if necessary, litigation. The agency's role has been strengthened over the years by Congress, and it is considered the top equal opportunity agency in the United States.

THE EQUAL PAY ACT OF 1963

Enacted into law even before the Civil Rights Act of 1964, the Equal Pay Act prohibits pay discrimination based solely on gender. Under the law, men and women must be paid the same wages for work requiring equal skill, effort, and responsibility and performed under similar working conditions. Wages can be different based on other factors, such as the quantity or quality of production, a valid seniority system, a valid merit system, or any factor other than gender.

THE AMERICANS WITH DISABILITIES ACT OF 1990

The Americans with Disabilities Act of 1990 provides equal opportunity in employment and access to facilities to those who have a physical or mental impediment that substantially affects a major life function, who have a record of such an impediment, or who are perceived to have such an impediment. If the employee with disabilities is otherwise qualified and can perform the job, with reasonable accommodation that does not cause the employer undue hardship, and the employee presents no threat to the safety of people or property, the employer cannot discriminate against the employee because of his or her disability.

THE AGE DISCRIMINATION IN EMPLOYMENT ACT OF 1967

Employees aged 40 years or older may not be discriminated against in employment and must be given an equal opportunity to work. Such employees may not be terminated and replaced with younger employees, have their job duties diminished solely because of age, be denied training, or be otherwise denied equal employment opportunity because of their age. The EEOC handles claims of age discrimination.

THE FAMILY MEDICAL LEAVE ACT OF 1991

The Family Medical Leave Act of 1991 (FMLA) provides up to 12 weeks of unpaid leave for employees who take time from work because they or their child, spouse, or parents are ill or because they have a new biological, adopted, or foster care child. Men are often denied this leave based on gender stereotypes and expectations that women will handle such matters. Historically, women were often denied such leave or were given the leave but found on their return to work that they had been demoted or terminated and their benefits, leave, and/or seniority suspended during their absence. This is illegal under the FMLA. FMLA claims are handled by the U.S. Department of Labor's Employment Standards Administration, Wage and Hour Division.

EXECUTIVE ORDER 11246

This is one of the most controversial sources of equal opportunity. The executive order, signed into law by President Lyndon B. Johnson in 1965, dictates that those who wish to provide goods and services valued at $10,000 or more to the federal government or through contracting with the federal government must agree not to discriminate on much the same bases as those mentioned in Title VII of the Civil Rights Act. If the amount involved is $50,000 or more, in addition to not discriminating, the contractor must also conduct a workplace assessment to determine the participation of women and minorities at all levels of the contractor's workplace. If there is a significant underrepresentation of women and minorities, given their availability in the area from which the contractor's employees are drawn, then the contractor must devise a plan to remedy this underrepresentation. This is generally called an affirmative action plan.

Those who feel adversely affected by the operation of an affirmative action plan have brought lawsuits on the basis of "reverse discrimination." That is, although Title VII is designed to protect everyone equally, they allege that the operation of the affirmative action plan to include those shown to have been excluded from the workplace discriminates against them and should not be allowed to be used. Affirmative action has also been used in the area of college admissions and minority set-aside programs. The theory is that unless there is a conscious effort to include groups traditionally excluded from the workplace and educational institutions, the underrepresentation will continue despite the laws prohibiting discrimination.

Affirmative action may only withstand court scrutiny if done properly. Quotas are prohibited, though the employer may set goals, setting forth appropriate numbers, to attempt to attain more representation of the underrepresented groups given their availability in the area from which employees are drawn, as well as timetables within which these goals should be accomplished. However, the plan is not cast in stone and can be adjusted as circumstances dictate. Availability only applies to those who are available for the type of job under consideration. For instance, if there are 38% females in the population, it does not mean that 38% are qualified to be doctors. Nothing in the law requires that someone who is not qualified be given a job or admission to college, and the law specifically prohibits employers from taking those presently in jobs out of them to make space for someone pursuant to an affirmative action plan.

The law provides no specifics as to what affirmative action must be taken to correct a significant underrepresentation, but certain approaches have been deemed by courts to be inappropriate. Setting quotas is not permitted. In the seminal 1987 U.S. Supreme Court case of *Johnson v. Transportation Agency, Santa Clara County, California,* the high court ruled that plans that take into account factors such as race and gender are permissible if the plan is to address a manifest imbalance that reflects underrepresentations in the workplace of traditionally excluded groups, race or gender is only one of several factors considered, the plan is made to attain rather than maintain a balanced workforce, and the plan does not unnecessarily trammel the legitimate settled rights of other employees or create an absolute bar to their advancement. If these factors are adequately addressed in the affirmative action plan used by the employer, then the plan will be able to withstand judicial scrutiny in court when the plan is challenged as reverse discrimination.

In addition to the EEOC, there are several other federal government offices whose missions are to enforce equal opportunity in various contexts, including the U.S. Department of Justice, Office of the Attorney General, Civil Rights Division; the U.S. Commission on Civil Rights; the U.S. Department of Health and Human Services, Office for Civil Rights; the U.S. Department of Agriculture, Civil Rights Office; the Federal Aviation Administration, Civil Rights Office; the U.S. Department of Transportation, Civil Rights Office; and the U.S. Department of Labor, Civil Rights Enforcement for Department of Labor Grant Recipients.

—Dawn D. Bennett-Alexander

Further Readings

Bennett-Alexander, D., & Hartman, L. (2007). *Employment law for business* (5th ed.). Burr Ridge, IL: McGraw-Hill/ Irwin.

Fox, G. E. (1997). *Hispanic nation: Culture, politics, and the construction of identity.* Tuscon: University of Arizona Press.

Frazier, I. (2000). *On the rez.* New York: Farrar, Straus & Giroux

Kay, H. H. (2002). *Sex-based discrimination* (5th ed.). St. Paul, MN: West Publishing.

Lemann, N. (1991). *The promised land: The great black migration and how it changed America.* New York: Vintage Press.

McCall, N. (1994). *Makes me wanna holler: A young black man in America.* New York: Vintage Press.

Nelson, J. (1993). *Volunteer slavery: My authentic Negro experience.* New York: Penguin.

Ross, T. (1997). *Just stories: How the law embodies racism.* Boston: Beacon Press.

Wu, F. H. (2002). *Yellow: Race in America beyond black and white.* New York: Basic Books.

AFFIRMATIVE ACTION

The origins of affirmative action lie in a 1965 executive order issued by U.S. President Lyndon Johnson that required federal contractors to develop policies to combat discrimination. Since this order, several U.S. policies and laws have encouraged or required corporations and other institutions to advertise jobs fairly and to promote the hiring and promotion of members of groups formerly discriminated, most notably women and minority ethnic groups. Implementation of both the letter and the spirit of these federal requirements has often involved employment goals and targeted employment outcomes intended to eliminate the vestiges of discrimination. These goals and policies are the core of affirmative action.

Target goals, timetables, and quotas were originally initiated to ensure more equitable opportunities by counterbalancing apparently intractable prejudice and systemic favoritism. Over the years, many policies initiated with these lofty ambitions were criticized on grounds that they establish quotas that unjustifiably elevate the opportunities of members of targeted groups, discriminate against equally qualified or even more qualified members of majorities, and perpetuate racial and sexual paternalism. The problem of affirmative action is whether such policies can be justified and, if so, under which conditions. At its roots, this problem is moral rather than legal. However, the most influential arguments have been legal ones advanced in the opinions of judges.

WHAT DOES "AFFIRMATIVE ACTION" MEAN?

The term *affirmative action* refers to positive steps to rank, admit, hire, or promote persons who are members of groups previously or presently discriminated against. It has been used to refer to everything from open advertisement of positions to quotas in employment and promotion.

The original meaning of affirmative action was minimalist. It referred to plans to safeguard equal opportunity, advertise positions openly, ensure fair recruitment, and create scholarship programs for specific groups. Few now oppose these means to the end of equal treatment, and if this were all that were meant by affirmative action, few would oppose it.

However, affirmative action has acquired broader meanings—some advanced by proponents, others by opponents. Most important, it became closely associated—especially through its opponents—with quotas and preferential policies that target specific groups, primarily women and minorities, for preferential treatment. Stern critics of affirmative action hold that affirmative action today means little more than naked preference by race. Proponents of affirmative action wholly reject this suggestion. They see affirmative action as confined to policies that favor qualified women and minority candidates over similarly qualified men or nonminority candidates, where there is an immediate objective of remedying persistent discrimination, achieving diversity, and achieving a race- and color-blind society.

Criticism of affirmative action policies has often centered on the alleged use of quotas. *Quota* here refers to fixed numbers of a group that must be admitted, hired, or promoted—even to the point of including less qualified persons if they are the only available members of a targeted group. However, the term *quota* originally was not used with this meaning. Quotas were understood as target numbers or percentages that an employer, admissions office, recruitment committee, and the like sincerely attempts to meet. In this second sense, quotas are numerically expressible goals pursued in good faith and with due diligence, but they do not require advancing unqualified or even less qualified persons.

The language of quotas seems now to be going out of fashion, most likely to be replaced with the language of "diversity." Many goals of affirmative action are today discussed as issues of "diversity in the workplace."

DIVERGENT ACCOUNTS OF DISCRIMINATION AND ITS REMEDIES

Although racism and sexism—the primary sources of discrimination in the history of affirmative action—are commonly envisioned as *intentional* forms of favoritism and exclusion, intent to discriminate is not a necessary condition of discrimination in the relevant sense. Employees are frequently hired through a network that, without design, excludes women or minority groups. For example, hiring may occur through personal connections or by word of mouth, and layoffs may be controlled by a seniority system. It has proved particularly difficult in the more camouflaged areas to shatter patterns of discrimination and reconfigure the environment through affirmative action remedies.

Empirical evidence of social discrimination is readily available, though not always easy to interpret. Data indicate that in sizable parts of American society (and many other societies) white males (or other male groups) continue to receive the highest entry-level salaries when compared with all other social groups and that women with similar credentials and experience to those of men are commonly hired at lower positions or earn lower starting salaries than men. Whether these statistics demonstrate invidious discrimination is controversial, but additional data drawn from empirical studies reinforce the judgment that racial and sexual discrimination are the best explanation of the data. For example, studies of real estate rentals, housing sales, home mortgage lending, and employment interviews show significant disparities in rejection rates, usually comparing white applicants and minority applicants. Disparities seem to exist even after statistics are adjusted for economic differences. Race appears to be as important as socioeconomic status in failing to secure both houses and loans.

Persons who believe that such apparent discrimination is detectable and correctable by recourse to legal remedies are unlikely to defend strong affirmative action measures. In contrast, anyone who believes that discrimination is securely and almost invisibly entrenched in many sectors of society will likely endorse, or at least tolerate, affirmative action policies. These policies have had their strongest appeal, and firmest justification, when discrimination that barred groups from desirable institutions persisted even though strictly forbidden by law. All parties today agree that *individuals* who have been injured by past discrimination should be made whole for the injury by some form of compensation and that when we reach the point that a color-blind, sex-blind society can be achieved by legal guarantees of equal opportunities to all, affirmative action policies should be dispatched.

Those who support affirmative action and those who oppose it both seek the best means to the end of a color-blind, sex-blind society. In this respect their ends do not differ. Nor do they entirely disagree over the means to these ends. If a color-blind, sex-blind society can be achieved and maintained by legal guarantees of equal opportunities to all, both sides agree that social policies should be restricted to this means. But here agreement ends. Those who support affirmative action do not believe that such guarantees can, at present, be fairly and efficiently achieved other than by affirmative action policies. They see the goals of affirmative action as broader than mere legal guarantees of equal opportunity—for example, diversity itself can be a warranted goal. Those who oppose affirmative action believe that this recourse is unnecessary and that affirmative action policies unjustifiably discriminate in reverse. Many also try to show that today's affirmative action policies are, on balance, more harmful than beneficial.

THE JUSTIFICATION OF AFFIRMATIVE ACTION

Presumably, affirmative action policies (in whatever form) are justified if and only if they are necessary to overcome the discriminatory effects that could not otherwise be eliminated with reasonable efficiency. Those who believe in aggressive policies of affirmative action point to the intractable, often deeply hurtful, and consequential character of racism and sexism. The history of affirmative action, from their perspective, is an impressive history of fulfilling once-failed promises, displacing disillusion, and protecting the most vulnerable members of society against demeaning abuse. They believe that affirmative action policies will likely be needed in pockets of the most vicious and visceral racism for roughly another generation, after which it can be reasonably expected that appropriate goals of fair opportunity and equal consideration have been reached. The goal to be reached at that point is not proportional representation, which has occasionally been used as a basis for fixing target numbers in affirmative action policies, but merely the end of discrimination. That is, the ultimate goal is fair opportunity and equal consideration. Once this goal has been achieved, affirmative action will no longer be needed or justified and should be abandoned.

Many supporters of affirmative action do not hold that it is needed now for *all* institutions. They believe that racial, sexual, and religious discrimination has been so substantially reduced or eliminated in some sectors of society that affirmative action no longer has a purpose in these sectors. The problem is that in other social sectors it is still common to encounter discrimination in favor of a favored group or discrimination against disliked, distrusted, unattractive, or neglected groups.

THE ROLE OF THE COURTS

The U.S. Supreme Court has upheld some affirmative action programs and found others insupportable. It is difficult to pin down exactly what, in the history of the Court's opinions, has been sustained and what has been discouraged. Both sides of the moral controversy over affirmative action have commonly appealed to the authority of the Court for support.

In two cases decided in the late 1980s, the Supreme Court supported the permissibility of specific numerical goals in affirmative action plans that are intended to combat a manifest imbalance in traditionally segregated job categories (even if the particular workers drawn from minorities were not victims of past discrimination). In *Local 28 v. Equal Employment Opportunity Commission,* otherwise known as *Sheet Metal Workers,* a minority hiring goal of 29.23% had been established. The Court held that specific numbers of this sort are justified when dealing with persistent or egregious discrimination. The Court found that the history of Local 28 was one of complete "foot-dragging resistance" to the idea of hiring without discrimination in their apprenticeship training programs from minority groups. The Court argued that "affirmative race-conscious relief" may be the only reasonable means to the end of assuring equality of employment opportunities and to eliminate deeply ingrained discriminatory practices and devices that have fostered racially stratified job environments to the disadvantage of minority citizens.

In a 1989 opinion, in contrast, the Supreme Court held in *City of Richmond v. J. A. Croson* that Richmond, Virginia, officials could not require contractors to set aside 30% of their budget for subcontractors who owned "minority business enterprises." This particular plan was not written specifically to remedy the effects of either prior or present discrimination. The Court found that *this way* of fixing a percentage based on race, in the absence of evidence of identified discrimination, denied citizens an equal opportunity to compete for subcontracts. Parts of the reasoning in *Croson* were affirmed in the 1995 case of *Adarand Constructors Inc. v. Pena.* Some writers have interpreted *Croson, Adarand,* and a 1997 decision of a three-judge panel of the 9th U.S. Circuit Court of Appeals—to the effect that a California voter-approved ban on affirmative action (Proposition 209) is constitutional—as the dismantling of affirmative action plans that use numerical goals.

This prediction could turn out to be correct, but the U.S. Supreme Court has not specifically so determined and has, with reasonable consistency, adhered to a balancing strategy. As important as its landmark cases are, no comprehensive criteria have yet been established by the Court for legally valid affirmative action plans.

IMPACT ON BUSINESS

Affirmative action programs and various attempts to achieve diversity in the workplace have affected U.S. businesses in profound ways. Some of these plans were imposed by government on business, but most plans that survive today have been voluntarily undertaken by corporations.

Nonvoluntary Plans

In the early history of affirmative action, plans were nonvoluntary. In the typical circumstance, the government announced that it found a pattern of discrimination and that diversity was noticeably lacking in a company and that affirmative action must be enforced. An early and classic case in law and business ethics is an AT&T affirmative action agreement in the 1970s. The salient facts of this case are as follows: The U.S. Equal Employment Opportunity Commission (EEOC) had investigated AT&T in the 1960s on grounds of employee-alleged discriminatory practices in hiring and promotion. In 1970, the EEOC stated that the firm engaged in "pervasive, system-wide, and blatantly unlawful discrimination in employment against women, African-Americans, Spanish-surnamed Americans, and other minorities" (U.S. Equal Employment Opportunity Commission, "Petition to Intervene," Federal Communications Commission Hearings on A.T.&T. Revised Tariff Schedule, December 10, 1970, p. 1). The EEOC argued that employment practices at AT&T violated several civil rights laws and excluded women from all job classifications except low-paying clerical and operator positions.

AT&T denied all charges and produced a massive body of statistics about women and minorities in the workforce. However, these data ultimately worked to undermine the corporation's own case. The data showed that half of the company's 700,000 employees were female and that the women were uniformly either secretaries or operators. It became apparent that the company categorized virtually all its jobs in terms of men's work and women's work. The federal government was determined to obliterate this aspect of corporate culture in the belief that no other strategy would break the grip of entrenched sexism. Eventually AT&T entered a consent decree, which was accepted by a Philadelphia court in 1973. This agreement resulted in payments of $15 million in back wages to 13,000 women and 2,000 minority-group men and $23 million in raises to 36,000 employees who had been harmed by previous policies.

Out of this settlement came a companywide "model affirmative action plan" that radically changed the character of AT&T hiring and its promotion practices. The company agreed to create an "employee profile" in its job classifications to be achieved in an accelerated manner. It established racial and gender goals and intermediate targets in 15 job categories to be met in quarterly increments. The goals were determined by statistics regarding representative numbers of workers in the relevant labor market. The decree required that under conditions of a target failure, a less qualified (but qualified) person could take precedence over a more qualified person with greater seniority. This condition applied only to promotions, not to layoffs and rehiring, where seniority continued to prevail.

Today it is no longer seriously doubted that AT&T's hiring and promotion practices did, at the time, involve unjustified discrimination and serious wrongdoing. Even basic moral principles were violated—for example, that one ought to treat persons with equal consideration and respect, that racial and sexual discrimination are impermissible, and the like. Less clear—and still unresolved today—is whether or to what degree the responsible corporate executives should be morally blamed. Several factors place limits on judgments about the blameworthiness of agents—or at least the fairness of doing so. These factors include culturally induced moral ignorance, a changing landscape in civil rights law, and indeterminacy in an organization's division of labor and designation of responsibility. All were present to some degree in the AT&T case.

Judgments of exculpation depend, at least to some extent, on whether proper moral standards were openly acknowledged in the culture in which the events transpired—for example, in the professional ethics of the period. If society generally had possessed clear standards regarding the justice of hiring and promotion in the 1950s and 1960s, it would be easier to find AT&T officials culpable. The absence of such standards is a factor in assessing culpability and exculpation, but need not be included in judgments of the wronging that occurred. Individuals and groups may be owed compensation even when parties to the wrongdoing cannot reasonably be held culpable for their actions.

However, the fact of culturally induced moral ignorance does not by itself entail exculpation or a lack of accountability for states of ignorance. A major issue in the past, and still today, is the degree to which persons are accountable for holding and even perpetuating or disseminating discriminatory beliefs when an opportunity to remedy or modify the beliefs exists. If such opportunities are unavailable, a person may have a valid excuse; but the greater the opportunity to eliminate ignorance the less is exculpation appropriate. Culturally induced moral ignorance was a mitigating factor in the 1960s and early 1970s, but history also suggests that it was mixed with a resolute failure to face moral problems that were widely appreciated to be serious, and they were problems that had been directly faced by other institutions.

Voluntary Affirmative Action Plans

Most corporate affirmative action policies are now voluntary plans, and these plans have arguably been more successful in transforming multiple corporate workplaces than have government-mandated policies. Many American corporations have welcomed these plans, on grounds that discrimination causes the institution to lose opportunities to make contact with the full range of qualified persons who might be contacted. These institutions have found that carefully controlled selection for diversity in the workforce is correlated with high-quality employees, reductions in the costs of discrimination claims, a lowering of absenteeism, less turnover, and increased customer satisfaction. Many corporations also report that they have invested heavily in eliminating managerial biases and stereotypes while training managers to hire and promote appropriately. They are concerned that without the pressure of an affirmative action plan managers will fail to recognize their own biases and stereotypes.

One moral worry about today's voluntary plans concerns a failure of truthfulness in publicly disclosing and advertising the practical commitments of the policies. Advertisements for jobs and the public statements of corporations about their affirmative action plans rarely contain detailed information about a corporation's objectives and policies, yet more information would be of material relevance to applicants and employees. The following are examples of facts or objectives that might be disclosed: a unit may have reserved its position for a woman or a minority candidate; the chances may be overwhelming that only a minority group member will be hired; the interview team may have decided in advance that only women will be interviewed; or the advertised position may be the result of a corporate policy that offers an explicit incentive (perhaps a new position) if a minority representative is appointed. Incompleteness in disclosure and advertising sometimes stems from fear of legal liability, but more often from fear of embarrassment and harm either to reputation or to future recruiting efforts.

Many corporations seem to be in the odd situation of fearing to make public what they believe to be morally commendable in their recruiting efforts.

There is something deeply unsatisfactory about a reluctance to disclose one's real moral commitments and goals. This situation is striking, because the justification for the policy is presumably that it is a morally praiseworthy endeavor. Here we have a circumstance in which the actions taken may not be wrong, but the agents may be culpable for a failure to clearly articulate the basis of their actions and to allow those bases to be openly debated so that their true merits can be assessed by all affected parties.

—Tom L. Beauchamp

Further Readings

Anderson, E. S. (2002, November). Integration, affirmative action, and strict scrutiny. *New York University Law Review, 77,* 1195–1271.

Beckwith, F., & Todd, E. J. (Eds.). (1997). *Affirmative action: Social justice or reverse discrimination?* Amherst, NY: Prometheus Books.

Bergmann, B. R. (1996). *In defense of affirmative action.* New York: Basic Books.

Cahn, S. M. (Ed.). (2002). *The affirmative action debate.* New York: Routledge.

Cohen, C., & James, P. S. (2003). *Affirmative action and racial preference.* New York: Oxford University Press.

Fullinwider, R. (2005). Affirmative action. In E. N. Zalta (Ed.), *The Stanford encyclopedia of philosophy* (Spring Edition). Retrieved from http://plato.stanford.edu/archives/spr2005/entries/affirmative-action/

Sowell, T. (2004). *Affirmative action around the world: An empirical study.* New Haven, CT: Yale University Press.

PART VI

Consumer Issues

Consumer Rights

Consumer Protection Legislation

Consumer Activism

Consumer Fraud

CONSUMER RIGHTS

T he subject of consumer rights historically covers two related areas: issues related to the actual products and services that a company sells to consumers and corporate business practices that directly affect consumers. As part of the evolution of consumer rights and concerns, a third area, spawned in large part by the growth in information processing industries and integrated computing networks, has emerged. This area concerns the use of information *about* the consumer, including privacy and security of that information. While there is little legislation establishing actual rights of consumers, there is a large body of law dealing with a range of consumer issues, which taken together are often referred to as "consumer protection."

At its core, a discussion of consumer rights implies that the interactions between consumers and corporations will naturally tend to be to the advantage of the corporation (due not only to size but also due to political, economic, and social influence) and so legal and political means should be used to equalize any imbalance of power. (More bluntly, many laws passed to protect consumers assume that the consumer is either unable or incapable of protecting himself or herself, due to the complex nature of business or products, and must be protected in the most basic sense of the word.) The key assumption of most consumer rights initiatives is that, absent any restraining influences, corporations will make decisions that ignore the welfare of consumers and maximize the assumed advantages of the supplier. A secondary assumption is that the consumer will (1) usually have less information than a business and (2) will be more easily confused by business complexities and, therefore, must be protected from businesses that will take advantage of these informational or experiential asymmetries. (Note that the advent of the Internet has greatly reduced the information disparity between consumers and suppliers, as well as offering a significant increase in resources that consumers can use to defend their rights. Consumer rights advocates believe information is power and that information transparency is critical to producing informed consumers.)

Most of the societal and legislative initiatives over the years either prohibit what is considered to be anticonsumer behavior or provide tools to consumers by which they may force companies to address individual (or sometimes group) grievances related to products or business practices. Anticonsumer behavior has historically included clear-cut examples such as price-fixing and price-gouging, deceptive marketing and sales practices, production and distribution of dangerous products (including pharmaceuticals and medical devices), and failure to deliver promised products or services. Less obvious but no less critical to the consumer are more recent developments in the consumer-business relationship, such as information privacy (especially in health care matters), unsolicited sales and marketing, and refusal to provide services or nondiscriminatory prices to a particular class of consumer.

While there is a case to be made that the Hippocratic Oath (the traditional oath that physicians take that binds them to keep the best interests of the patient uppermost in their considerations) embodied the first consumer protection principles in history, arguably the first U.S. legislation intended to protect the consumer was the Sherman Antitrust Act, signed by President Benjamin Harrison in 1890. The act declared that "Every contract, combination in the form of trust or otherwise, or conspiracy, in restraint of trade or commerce among the several States, or with foreign nations, is declared to be illegal." Often assumed to restrict monopolies, the act was targeted not at the size or form of corporations or trusts but at "restraint of trade," which would ultimately lead to artificially high prices for the consumer. Free markets were deemed better for the consumer; anything that prevented free markets was, therefore, bad and should be outlawed.

Following the enactment of the Sherman Antitrust Act, just what was allowed and forbidden by the law remained open to interpretation, as the U.S. economy evolved and the size of corporations allowed greater market control by a few companies or individuals. Such questions were debated and refined over the ensuing 24 years, particularly during President Theodore Roosevelt's administration. Roosevelt believed the solution lay in a commission that would regulate business practices and established the Bureau of Corporations in 1903. In 1914, Woodrow Wilson signed the Federal Trade Commission and Clayton acts. These acts established the Federal Trade Commission (FTC) as an investigative and enforcement body, creating the first government agency with the power to protect consumers, and explicitly outlawed monopolies, respectively. Since 1914, Congress has continued to expand the reach and powers of the FTC, allowing the FTC to address consumer issues as diverse as defining deceptive or unfair practices, establishing rules for granting credit, and regulating telemarketing practices.

The modern era of consumer rights traces to March 15, 1962, when President John F. Kennedy sent a special message to Congress containing his statement of the four basic consumer rights that the government should work to protect and promote:

1. *The right to safety:* protection against hazardous goods

2. *The right to be informed:* the right to access information the consumer needs to make an informed choice and protection against fraud and deceit

3. *The right to choose:* access to a variety of products and fair prices and protection against business practices that reduce competition

4. *The right to be heard:* the guarantee that consumer concerns will be heard and fully considered by the government

Since Kennedy's message, these rights have been added to by various groups worldwide, most notably the United Nations, to include the following:

- *The right to consumer education:* early and lifelong education about the consumer marketplace and the laws supporting consumer rights
- *The right to consumer redress:* the right to be compensated for misrepresented or unacceptable goods and services and the responsibility to actively pursue such redress
- *The right to a healthy and sustainable environment:* the right to live and work in a safe and healthy environment that supports a life of dignity
- *The right to basic needs:* access to goods and services necessary for survival throughout societies
- *The right to access:* fair and equitable distribution of goods and services throughout society

Kennedy's main point was clear and has been echoed by many others: From an ethical perspective, consumers have certain rights that exist outside of government policy and law, and it is the government's job to ensure these rights are not infringed on in the marketplace. In the ensuing years, the federal government and state legislatures worked to implement laws and policies that institutionalized those rights.

Inherent in Kennedy's message is a more subtle requirement that the consumer, and the public as a whole, have a responsibility to *proactively* use consumer information, education, and rights to not only make informed decisions but also to actively work to be sure that government and industry act in the consumer's interest. The classic example of citizen responsibility in this regard is Ralph Nader and his group of young activists known as Nader's Raiders. Arguably the beginning of the modern consumer rights movement, Nader began in 1965 by taking on the auto industry over the alleged safety problems of GM's Corvair automobile. His activities soon expanded to include waste in government, including monitoring and exposing government agencies who were failing to effectively perform their duties to protect consumers.

While there are many laws at the federal and state levels aimed at protecting consumers by legislating against harmful business practices, a few are worthy of special note as examples of the philosophy of the government's role in protecting consumers. The Truth in Lending Act was originally enacted in 1968 and revised in 1980. It requires complete disclosure to consumers of all costs involved during the life of a credit transaction, including loans and leases, and demands explicit and clear statement of the conditions under which credit is granted. In addition, the law provides legal recourse for consumers against lenders who violate the terms of the act. The act was in response to predatory lending and leasing arrangements, deceptive credit marketing, and discriminatory practices in granting credit based on nonfinancial factors.

The Fair Credit Reporting Act (FCRA) passed in 1970 regulates the way that consumer credit information is collected, distributed, and reported. Prior to the passage of this law, major credit bureaus operated largely independently of oversight or even cursory review as regards to accuracy, privacy, security, use, and dissemination of consumer's credit information. Consumers for their part had no recourse against incorrect information provided by credit unions or the resulting burdens on their financial dealings. In the most egregious cases, consumers could be denied credit based on credit reports to which they had no access and were not even aware were the basis for the denial. In response to growing evidence of incorrect credit reporting, information and privacy abuses, and pressure from consumer advocates, Congress passed the FCRA to provide tools to consumers for dealing with credit reporting issues and to legislate how credit bureaus would conduct their businesses relative to consumers. The FCRA requires credit bureaus to provide consumers with the information in their files and to take all reasonable steps to be sure the information is complete and accurate. It also requires that credit bureaus undertake "reasonable investigations" of any information disputed by a consumer and inform the consumer of the disposition of that dispute.

In 2003, the FCRA was updated through the Fair and Accurate Credit Transaction Act (FACTA). As part of the FACTA, consumers are entitled to a free credit report every 12 months, from each of the three major credit reporting agencies (Equifax, Experian, and Transunion), available through an FTC Web site established for that purpose. In addition, consumers are entitled to notification when credit is denied based on negative information in a credit report and at that point are also entitled to a free credit report. FACTA also required the FTC create a "Summary of Rights for Consumers," which would be supplied with any credit report provided to a consumer, detailing the specific consumer rights and credit bureau responsibilities provided by FACTA.

Combined with the FCRA, the Fair Debt Collection Practices Act (FDCPA) provides the major portion of consumer credit rights. Passed in 1978, the FDCPA was in response to serious abuses by the debt collection industry that included home and workplace harassment by phone, misrepresentation, threats of arrest or legal action that are outside the scope of debt collection and therefore not credible, and reporting false information to credit bureaus. The FDCPA regulates the means by which third-party debt collectors may do business, details the rights of consumers when dealing with such agencies, and provides legal recourse for consumers against abusive or non-FDCPA-compliant debt collectors.

The Telephone Consumer Protection Act of 1991 was passed to limit the number of unsolicited phone calls consumers receive at their homes. Congress recognized that as well as being a nuisance to consumers, such calls were often the vehicle by which unscrupulous business operators and fraudsters preyed on the public. The act limits the entities that may call a consumer's house to those with which the consumer has an existing business relationship (although "existing" is loosely defined) and also prohibits calls from entities with an existing business relationship whom the consumer has specifically asked to cease calling. The act also required the FTC and the Federal Communications Commission to establish a National Do-Not-Call registry, containing the numbers of all consumers who do not wish to be subject to uninvited telephone solicitations. The registry requires consumers to proactively register phone numbers and is one of the laws that provides the tools for consumers to use to protect themselves.

The Health Insurance Portability and Accountability Act of 1996 (HIPAA) is intended to do for a consumer's health information what other laws have done for financial information.

HIPAA specifies a set of "patient rights" regarding access and dissemination of medical and health information and, in many ways, parallels the protections of financial data provided by the FCRA and the FACTA. As with the other laws, it also provides for consumer redress in cases where the law is violated.

HIPAA also signaled a fundamental shift in how personal data of all kinds, not just financial data, is to be considered by businesses. HIPAA established the rights of people to control access to information about themselves and placed the burden of information security and protecting confidentiality of personal information clearly on those who store and access it. Personal information is now a "thing," associated with a person, to be protected rather than information to be collected and used for the benefit of the business.

All these laws serve to protect consumers by leveling the playing field in complementary ways. It is clearly the intent of the government to force businesses to become more transparent in their dealings with consumers, as well as allowing consumers to dictate how they will interact with businesses. In addition, the government has chosen to specify what kinds of information must be given to the consumer, how it is to be presented, and how information about the consumer may or may not be disseminated. Perhaps most critically, these laws provide specific redress for the consumer when businesses violate the laws. Again, the assumption is that information is power, if put in the hands of the consumer, and short of being forced to act in a fair manner, businesses will withhold, misuse, or misrepresent information. The new assumption in these laws, though, is that given the proper tools, consumers can protect themselves, as well as other consumers, through penalties and processes specified by these laws.

While the aforementioned laws deal with protecting consumers from harmful business practices, there is also a "right" or expectation that businesses will not sell *products* that are harmful to consumers. Toward this end, Congress established the Consumer Product Safety Commission (CPSC) by passing the Consumer Product Safety Act of 1972. Again, Congress posited a fundamental inability of the consumer to understand the implications of using a product, finding that "complexities of consumer products and the diverse nature and abilities of consumers using them frequently result in an inability of users to anticipate risks and to safeguard themselves adequately." In the language of the act, the CPSC exists

1. to protect the public against unreasonable risks of injury associated with consumer products;

2. to assist consumers in evaluating the comparative safety of consumer products;

3. to develop uniform safety standards for consumer products and to minimize conflicting state and local regulations; and

4. to promote research and investigation into the causes and prevention of product-related deaths, illnesses, and injuries.

The other laws mentioned previously are somewhat passive in their protections, establishing guidelines for businesses and providing tools for consumers. The CPSC, however, was established as an active agency, charged with "protecting the public," "assisting consumers," and "investigating causes and prevention of injuries." When commerce and business practices are concerned, the consumer is given assistance in protecting his or her "rights." When injury and death are possible, the government is expected to not only assist but also to proactively work to protect the consumer.

—Tom Bugnitz

Further Readings

Krohn, L. (1995). *Consumer protection and the law: A dictionary.* Santa Barbara, CA: ABC-CLIO.

Meier, K. J., Garman, E. T., & Keiser, L. R. (1998). *Regulation and consumer protection: Politics, bureaucracy and economics.* Houston, TX: Dame.

PART VI: Consumer Issues

CONSUMER PROTECTION LEGISLATION

Consumer protection regulation refers to government involvement in the marketplace to protect consumers in commercial transactions from potential harm caused by businesses. The potential harm may arise from the use of unreliable or unsafe products, deceptive advertising, asymmetry of knowledge of products and services, and privacy intrusion in the Internet age. In the United States, the federal and state governments took important steps in consumer protection, especially in the late 1960s and 1970s. Before this, the ancient rule of *caveat emptor,* or "let the buyer beware," generally guided consumer transactions. Although consumer protection regulation did exist (e.g., the 1906 Food and Drug Act, the creation of Federal Trade Commission [FTC] in 1914), it was limited and weakly enforced.

The surge of government protection regulation in the 1960s and 1970s derives from a strong consumer movement and the general politics of the time. The 1980s, however, saw a decrease in support for consumer protection regulation. The Reagan administration cut budgets and staffing sharply and was later forced to restore much of the cuts in support for consumer protection regulation due to regulatory failures. Although the Clinton administration was more aggressively involved in consumer regulation in the 1990s, there have been very sharp cuts during the Bush years in the 2000s. The current consumer protection regulation has addressed issues related to the digital age as well, such as consumer privacy.

Both the federal and state governments are responsible for consumer protection regulation. The key federal agencies involved in consumer regulation include cross-industry regulatory agencies, such as the FTC and the Consumer Product Safety Commission (CPSC), and industry-specific agencies, such as the Food and Drug Administration (FDA), the National Highway Traffic Safety Administration (NHTSA), and the U.S. Department of Agriculture (USDA). At the state level, regulatory responsibilities reside with the state attorney general and a number of state agencies that promulgate regulations. However, for reasons such as politics of the state and budget constraints, all states are not equally forceful in consumer regulation. In some states, the attorney general actively defends consumer interests; in others, she or he protects local industries, often accepting political contributions from them. In other words, state laws place different burdens on the state attorney general to act as a defender of consumer interests, investigating and bringing cases against firms under state consumer protection statues. In states that lack effective state enforcement of consumer laws, consumers often act as "a private attorney general" by resorting to tort laws and suing businesses for incurring harms or injuries. Although state regulation remains crucial, the focus here is on consumer protection regulation at the federal level. The following part discusses the two aspects of consumer protection regulation: the need for consumer protection and the areas of consumer protection.

THE NEED FOR CONSUMER PROTECTION

The Argument Against Government Regulation

Though consumer protection regulation is widely regarded as necessary for the well-being of consumers, some scholars take a different stance. Milton Friedman, for example, argues that government legislation on consumer protection is, in general, an intervention in the free market system and that an efficient market system without fraud, deceit, or coercion will take care of consumer interests. He maintains that government regulation on consumer protection disrupts the free market system in various ways: suppressing innovation, limiting consumer choices, and raising product prices. Such intervention, according to Friedman, can only result in market inefficiency. For example, the FDA, a government regulatory agency, Friedman maintains, does more harm than good. Friedman asserts that the FDA can make two types of errors: (1) approves a drug that has harmful effects on patients and (2) refuses or delays approving a drug that can save the lives of millions of people. While the first error, according to Friedman, is traceable and can be documented, the second worries him the most. Friedman warns that the nature of the bureaucracy is such that even the best-intentioned and most benevolent individuals are led to reject a drug that has the slightest possibility of harmful side effects.

The Argument for Government Regulation

Friedman's arguments against government regulation derive from his faith in an efficient market system. With the tremendous power that corporations hold today, critics challenge the efficiency of the marketplace. Stone, for instance, argues that although the market generally allocates resources efficiently, it does not solve all the problems in the system. Very often, the consumer does not have perfect information to determine whether she or he may be injured by a product. Elbing and Elbing, for another example, also point out that the marketplace is dominated by business; consequently, consumer power is weak, compared with the power of business. The following demonstrates some of the issues in the marketplace that call for consumer protection.

Unsafe Products

The issue of product safety involves a wide range of industries. For example, Ralph Nader's exposure of the unsafe features of the Corvair in 1965 illustrates the need for government to regulate the automobile industry for safety reasons. In addition, the extensive use of food additives and preservatives has created potential public health hazards. The risk of pesticide residues is another source of concern. Recently, biotechnological companies, such as Monsanto, have introduced genetically modified foods to developing countries before thorough knowledge of their side effects has been established. In short, the hazards that a wide range of consumer products pose to human safety and health compel government regulation.

Deceptive Advertising

A deceptive advertisement is one that includes a distortion or omission about a product or service that misleads a consumer. Deceptive advertising causes consumers to make purchasing decisions based on false beliefs about the nature of the products. It hinders the flow of information in the marketplace. For example, in the 1940s, R. J. Reynolds, a tobacco company, with the knowledge of harmful effects of smoking on health, declared to consumers that "More Doctors Smoke Camels." In the 1950s, Lorillard Tobacco Company claimed that the micronite filter in Kent Cigarettes was so safe and effective that it had been selected to help filter the air in hospital operating rooms. The deceptive advertising misled people to consume a hazardous product that often resulted in diseases and deaths.

Asymmetry of Information

In light of modern technology, many products are becoming highly complex. Some products, such as Intel processing chips, are hidden inside already complex products such as computers so that consumers cannot even see them. Consumers, no matter how technologically savvy they are, have difficulty judging the merit of some products in today's high-tech society. In other words, the complexity of products also obscures adequate information in the marketplace. This asymmetry of information can play into the hands of opportunistic sellers. In addition, the specialization of services also hinders consumers from being clearly informed about the services they receive. The specialized knowledge of professions, such as attorneys, dentists, and financial and insurance brokers, can baffle a consumer seeking services in these areas.

Privacy Intrusion

In the Internet age, consumer privacy has become more vulnerable. Whenever one uses a credit card online or surfs or shops on the Internet, one risks revealing unique personal information—credit card numbers, birth date, hobbies, and purchasing characteristics and preferences. New technology allows businesses to gather personal data about their customers; however, people, in general, are not comfortable with this information collection, especially when they do not know who is collecting the information and what they are going to do with it.

AREAS OF CONSUMER PROTECTION

Consumer protection regulation seeks to fulfill several goals. Owing to the potential existence of unsafe products, one area of consumer protection is *hazard avoidance.* The major method of regulating potential hazardous products has been the issuance of standards, which are typically used to provide necessary information to consumers. The CPSC plays a key role in protecting consumers from harms caused by unsafe products. It regulates the manufacture and sale of more than 15,000 types of products, including toys, swimming pools, and consumer electronic products. Furthermore, individual industry agencies are also responsible for setting industry-specific safety standards. For example, the NHTSA sets motor vehicle standards; the FDA sets safety standards for food, drugs, food additives, cosmetics, and medical devices; and the USDA sets guidelines regarding the labeling of genetically modified foods.

To redress harms that have been caused, consumers most often resort to product-liability torts for cases involving personal injury or death from product use. Product liability refers to burden of responsibility on the supplier side for damage caused through consumers' use of a product. Damage is attributed to any or all parties throughout the manufacturing and the distribution chain. Strict liability is sometimes at work when it comes to product liability: The manufacturer or supplier is held solely responsible for harm done to a consumer through the use of a product, even if the consumer was negligent in using the product. For example, McDonald's huge settlement with an elderly New Mexico woman in 1994, who spilled McDonald's hot coffee in her lap and was severely burned, exemplifies the extent of strict liability. In the late 1990s, about 20% of noncriminal cases in the United States were product liability cases. The average settlement in these cases was $141,000.

The second area of government regulation is *information disclosure,* addressing problems raised by deceptive advertising and information asymmetry, as mentioned in the previous section. Business can lure consumers using false advertising, bait-and-switch tactics, and breaches of warranty claims. The FTC was created, in part, to halt such practices. The Truth in Lending Act of 1968, for example, specifies conditions for advertising credit plans. In addition to creating laws against deceptive advertising, the FTC seeks remedies against violators through measures such as cease-and-desist orders, temporary restraining orders, or civil action suits, depending on how public interest is best served.

Furthermore, industry-specific agencies also set standards for information disclosure for products within a particular industry. For example, the FDA requires that food and beverage labels show more complete information. In 2003, the FDA required that all food items list the amount of trans fat, a potential contributor to heart disease. Also, manufacturers of tobacco products and alcoholic beverages are required to display health-warning labels. Automobiles are required to display a breakdown of price, and potentially hazardous home appliances and toys are required to carry a warning label. Although consumers today in some areas are far from having access to perfect information, government intervention in information disclosure has, in general, enabled consumers to make more informed purchasing decisions.

The third area of government regulation is *consumer privacy protection.* Privacy is a constitutional right protected by the Fourteenth Amendment. The FTC plays the role of enforcing privacy laws in the marketplace. Privacy laws include the Privacy Act of 1974, the Gramm-Leach-Bliley Act of 1999, the Fair Credit Reporting Act of 1970, and the Children's Online Privacy Protection Act of 1998.

The Privacy Act of 1974 prevents personal information held by the federal government from unauthorized disclosure. The Gramm-Leach-Bliley Act of 1999 (also known as Financial Modernization Act of 1999) protects consumers' personal financial information from misuse by financial institutions. The Fair Credit Reporting Act of 1970 limits access of personal financial information collected by consumer reporting agencies. A recent amendment in 2003 to the Federal Fair Credit Reporting Act has provided consumers access to a free copy of a credit report from each of the nationwide consumer reporting companies once every 12 months. Finally, The Children's Online Privacy Protection Act of 1998 places limits on information collection of children under 13 years of age. Although laws exist that protects children's privacy, online consumer privacy is generally inadequately protected. Consumer information, such as age, name, demographics, e-mail address, and financial information, can easily be collected through computer cookies.

Other privacy regulations include the national "do-not-call" registry and the Can-Spam Act of 2003. The FTC's do-not-call registry, established in 2003, was designed to put a stop to the bombardment of unsolicited telemarketing calls to households. The Can-Spam Act of 2003 (Controlling the Assault of Non-Solicited Pornography and Marketing Act) addressed the issue of unsolicited bulk e-mails. The act specified certain accountability on commercial senders. For example, it requires that the header information and the subject line cannot be misleading and that the subject line must match the content of the message. The Can-Spam Act also prescribed opt-out methods for receivers. Violators of the provisions can be fined up to $11,000 per violation. The FTC and the Department of Justice are the federal agencies that enforce this law.

In sum, consumer protection regulation is generally grounded in issues related to hazard avoidance, information disclosure, and privacy protection. Consumer protection regulation is an ongoing process and evolves over time; it adapts to the economic, technological, political, and social forces.

—Jiyun Wu

Further Readings

Elbing, A. O., & Elbing, C. J. (1976). *The value issue of business.* New York: McGraw-Hill.

Marsh, G. (1999). *Consumer protection law in a nutshell* (3rd ed.). St. Paul, MN: West Group.

Nader, R. (1965). *Unsafe at any speed: The designed-in dangers of the American automobile.* New York: Grossman.

Stone, C. (1975). *Where the law ends.* New York: Harper & Row.

CONSUMER ACTIVISM

onsumer activism is a term that describes a variety of disparate movements that seek to influence the behavior of companies through
activities ranging from providing information to boycotts, pickets, and litigation, with the aim of forcing companies to act in a way that benefits the
perceived interests of consumers. Underlying the unifying idea of consumer
activism is the belief that consumers can and should exercise their market
power to improve not only the quality of products but also the conditions
under which they are made, distributed, advertised, and sold. Consumer activism takes Adam Smith's dictate that the consumer is king to mean not only that
the market responds to consumer demand for products but also that consumers
can translate that demand into power for the sake of social transformation.

Consumer activism has played a role in debates on many important issues
in the past several decades, from environmental activism and workers rights to
antiglobalization and fair trade movements. In mobilizing consumer power on
behalf of these issues, activists have occasionally been able to effect changes
more quickly and more effectively than they would have by going through
governmental or regulatory institutions (although these institutions have also
been affected by consumer activist movements).

Early consumer activism movements included the work of the National
Consumer's league, which worked in the first half of the 20th century to
improve the labor conditions of workers through the promotion of "ethical
consumption." In using consumer power to create pressure for social change,
this organization had some success in the 1930s in bringing about better labor
standards for American workers.

The contemporary period in consumer activism may be said to have
begun with the publication of Ralph Nader's *Unsafe at Any Speed* in 1965. As
an exposé of the American automobile industry, this book revealed a number
of the hazardous practices that were common among car manufacturers. He
subsequently founded the group Public Citizen, through which he continued to
work on consumer issues.

In the 1990s and into the 21st century, consumer activism has become much
more closely involved in movements critical of the phenomenon of globalization

and the concentration of corporate power. Activists such as David Korten have written critiques of the global economy, not on anticapitalist grounds, but on the ground that an unregulated global economy creates the conditions for an unhindered expansion of corporate power, the degradation of democracy, and the inability of consumers to control key aspects of their lives as both citizens and as participants in the market. Such critiques are also often tied to environmental concerns about the effects of particular patterns of production and consumption that become more difficult to control in a global economy.

MORAL FOUNDATIONS OF CONSUMER ACTIVISM

The moral basis of consumer activism is rooted in the morality of the act of consumption itself. Capitalism rests on the premise that in a free market consumers are free to make choices with regard to what they consume and how. The market itself cannot be an arbiter of the morality of any particular transaction. Demand can produce a supply, whether the demand be for solar energy or illicit drugs. The moral character of the market is ultimately determined by the morality of the consumers who inhabit it. As such, it is the responsibility of the consumer to demand those products that most fully conform to his or her core moral convictions.

In addition, consumers may take responsibility not only for the particular products they consume but also for the manner in which those products are manufactured and supplied. Consumers as well as manufacturers are responsible for products that are produced in ways that are harmful to workers or to the environment or use unethical or illegal production methods.

The reverse side of this is the responsibility of the producer to the consumer. The producer is obliged to provide the consumer a safe and reliable product that is produced using morally acceptable methods. *Caveat Emptor* ("let the buyer beware!") does not absolve the producer or seller of a product from the need for scrupulousness in ensuring that products meet minimal standards of quality and morality.

This view rejects the idea that buyer and seller exist as isolated individuals engaged in a decontextualized commercial transaction. Rather, it recognizes both the consumer and the producer as part of a capitalist economic and social system. The consumer and producer are morally bound together as members of this system and bear moral responsibility for the results that they jointly bring about—the producer through his methods of production and the consumer through his demand for the product.

However, this moral analysis assumes that the consumer has knowledge of all the morally relevant aspects of production. Without such knowledge, the consumer cannot be held responsible. Thus, a key issue in consumer activism is that of transparency, the idea that consumers must have adequate information to make informed choices with regard to the products they purchase. In the absence of informed consent or the threat of exposure, it is argued, companies have no incentive to make safe products. Consumer activists seek to create conditions of transparency either by exposing unsafe or unethical business practices or by advocating for regulations that would either require that companies meet particular standards or inform consumers of information relevant to their purchasing decisions.

TYPES OF CONSUMER ACTIVISM

Many consumer activists are primarily concerned with protecting consumers from unethical or fraudulent business practices. Through use of legislation and litigation, as well as through raising public awareness, they attempt to identify and target particular companies or particular practices that they view as being unethical. Often, their work is aided through cooperation with state or local consumers affairs departments or with the Better Business Bureau, an organization of businesspeople that aims at holding businesses to high ethical standards.

This brand of consumer activism operates by providing a forum through which consumers can make one another aware of those businesses they should patronize and those they should avoid. By providing such forums, consumers thus cooperate in enforcing high ethical standards among competing businesses. Consumers given a choice between two companies offering the same product can be expected to prefer a company with a better reputation for good customer service and ethical behavior to one with a number of negative reports.

The moral presupposition of this brand of consumer activism is that it is in a company's self-interest to act ethically when it is held publicly accountable for its actions. Absent such public accountability, companies may lack sufficient incentive to moral behavior.

Another approach to consumer activism seeks to evaluate companies' claims about their products, comparing them to similar products on the market. This approach is typified by the magazine *Consumer Reports,* which evaluates and rates products to enable consumers to make informed choices among competing brands. This approach to consumer activism does not seek to make any direct moral claims but rather seeks simply to inform consumers of their available options.

Other approaches to consumer activism concern themselves with how companies treat their employees. These approaches seek to publicize companies that either violate labor laws or take advantages of gaps in the law that allow them to treat their workers in ways that are viewed by activists as failing to uphold an adequate moral standard. One case of consumer activism of this kind was the attempt made by consumer activists in the United States to raise awareness of the treatment by the manufacturer of Nike athletic shoes of many of its workers in Vietnam and Indonesia, where people were being paid low wages and were working in poor conditions. By raising this issue in a way that garnered a great deal of publicity, these activists succeeded in forcing Nike to address the issue of their treatment of workers and, in some cases, to improve working conditions.

Another, though similar approach, is one in which a company is targeted due to the treatment of workers by its subcontractors. This strategy is frequently used in the apparel industry, where well-known companies will often farm out much of their work to low-wage, and sometimes illegal, "sweatshops." Because of the difficulty of targeting these sweatshops individually, activists will often seek to exert pressure on their contract partners, who have more at stake in preserving a good reputation.

It is not clear how effective these strategies are. In the case of Nike, although the company launched a public relations campaign to restore its image, it is unclear that they made any substantial changes to their business practices in either of the countries in question. In addition, although activists tried to enlist the support of Nike's chief spokesperson, Michael Jordan, they failed to do so. In the end the campaign may have succeeded in raising the consciousness of U.S. consumers about the issue of low-wage foreign workers, but it is not clear that it did much to resolve the underlying issue. Similarly, although pressure on companies that employ sweatshop labor may have some limited effect, it does not appear to have done much to change the overall practices of the apparel industry.

Another approach to consumer activism relies on giving consumers a choice between products that meet certain ethical standards and those that do not. The "fair trade" movement, particularly in the coffee industry, has had some success in providing consumers alternatives to coffee that is grown on large plantations under exploitative conditions. Through certification and inspection programs, some brands of coffee have been recognized as "fair trade" coffees. Consumers can purchase these brands for the sake of supporting better conditions for workers in the coffee industry.

A variation on this theme involves the labeling of products to allow for informed consumer choices, for example, labeling genetically modified foods on the one hand, or labeling television programming content on the other. In each case, by allowing the consumer to know in advance what they are consuming allows them to make an informed decision as to whether or not to consume.

Yet another form of consumer activism can be seen in movements for socially responsible investing and shareholder activism. Both these strategies rely on the role of the stockholder as a form of consumer as well as an owner. Socially responsible investing involves choosing stocks on the basis of criteria of moral acceptability. For example, an investor might choose, either individually or through a mutual fund, to avoid investing in military contractors or tobacco companies. Alternatively, they might choose to invest in companies that promote particular social goods, for example, companies that promote sustainable agriculture or renewable energy. Either or both of these strategies may be used by a given investor, though the particular social screens might vary from investor to investor, or from mutual fund to mutual fund.

Shareholder activism could be thought of as the opposite strategy. Instead of avoiding investment in morally problematic companies, consumer activists might try to change a company's behavior from within, either by buying a relatively small number of shares to have the right to speak at shareholder meetings or by seeking to influence the attitudes of other shareholders with the objective of altering a company's policies.

By operating from within a company's structure, these approaches have the advantage of being perceived as coming from those having a vested interest in the financial good of the company. However, it is once again not clear whether this has been a particularly effective strategy in altering corporate policies.

Consumer activism, as the Nike example above may indicate, also has global implications. As markets become more flexible, and both labor and materials are increasingly able to transcend national boundaries, and thus the legal and regulatory oversight of particular nations, it becomes more difficult for consumers to know the conditions under which products are made, or to control those conditions. If national governments are unable or unwilling to institute or enforce labor or product safety laws, it becomes more and more necessary for activists to appeal directly to the companies themselves, either via moral suasion or via the use of bad publicity. If these appeals have the effect of eroding a company's consumer base, then the company becomes more likely to institute desired change. In the absence of a strong set of legal protections within a global economy, consumer activism becomes a more viable strategy to achieve desired aims.

TACTICS OF CONSUMER ACTIVISM

The various approaches to consumer activism discussed above each represent a strategic choice as to how they affect change in the behavior of companies. In addition, there are various tactics that can be brought to bear in consumer activist movements. Some of these tactics are relatively nonconfrontational, while others are more so.

Consciousness-raising is a large part of the work of consumer activism. Through raising the public's awareness of particular issues, activists have a greater likelihood of success at mobilizing consumer sentiment in a way that will affect company policies. Such consciousness-raising can take place on many different levels. Books, such as Nader's *Unsafe at Any Speed* or Rachel Carson's *Silent Spring,* can have a galvanizing effect on both movements and governments, but smaller efforts can include picketing, letter-writing campaigns, newspaper editorials, or exposés. These tactics can be particularly effective when companies are unable to mount a successful campaign to counter the bad publicity.

Beyond consciousness-raising, however, is the active effort to change corporate policy. A variety of tactics may be used with relatively open and cooperative companies to seek to create changes. For example, activists may seek to secure a meeting with corporate leaders to air their grievances and seek policy changes for the sake of consumers. This tactic tends to be very effective in those circumstances where activists can demonstrate that they represent a relatively broad constituency and where the issue in question is one that affects the consumer directly. In the case of many product safety and labeling issues, this tactic may prove to be quite effective, since companies are unlikely to take actions that risk alienating a significant portion of their customer base.

Activists can also turn to the courts in those cases where informal attempts at mediation fail. Class action suits can sometimes be an effective tool in addressing consumer grievances, particularly where it can be shown that a company or industry acted in a corrupt way. As a tactic to achieve change, such lawsuits can be effective, though as a means of compensating victims they may often produce limited results.

Legislation is another tactic that can be an effective tool for consumer activism. By convincing lawmakers of the need for some form of regulation or remedy, consumer activists can succeed in affecting corporate behavior precisely by making such behavior illegal or by regulating the behavior in question.

From a product safety perspective, regulation is an important tool of consumer activism. By creating legislation that created agencies such as the Food and Drug Administration, the Consumer Product Safety Administration, the Environmental Protection Agency, and the Occupational Health and Safety Administration, the U.S. Congress created a web of institutions the task of which was to ensure that consumers were provided information necessary to make informed decisions. The Securities and Exchange Commission can also be considered a consumer protection agency, insofar as its mandate is to ensure that stock transactions take place in a maximally fair and open manner.

A tactic associated, in particular, with shareholder activism involves the use of shareholder resolutions to affect company policies. Activists may seek to bring issues of concern to a company's shareholders, in an effort to mobilize them to vote in favor of changes in corporate policies. Although not frequently successful, this tactic does have the benefit of raising consciousness if done well.

Another very common technique in consumer activism is the boycott. Boycotts have been used in numerous situations, with mixed success, to affect the policies of particular companies or entire industries. The California grape boycott in the 1970s aided the worker of the United Farmworkers Union to secure the right to organize California's produce workers, while a boycott of Nestlé products had the effect of changing corporate policies regarding the marketing of baby formula in underdeveloped countries.

Boycotts are not always so successful however. When, in the 1990s, the Southern Baptist Convention urged Christians to avoid Disney World because of Disney's perceived toleration of homosexuality, the boycott fell flat, as have some other boycotts of supposedly gay friendly companies. The practice of boycotting itself has recently become less prevalent as well, in part perhaps because it sometimes seems to have the effect of harming workers while not noticeably altering corporate policies.

These tactics are among the most common, but the particular tactics used will depend on the circumstances in question, the goals sought by activists, and the receptivity of the company. If activists are perceived to represent a large movement, then these tactics may prove to be quite effective, while activists who are perceived to have an insignificant constituency may not be effective no matter what tactics they attempt. However, a movement is not always necessary for successful consumer activism. The advantage of litigation and legislation is that they do not necessarily rely on popular movements if it can be demonstrated that they are responses to violations of existing laws or deeply held moral or civic ideals. In any consumer activism campaign, however, it will be the abilities of the activists to effectively mobilize their constituency and properly choose tactics that will do much to determine the outcome of the campaign.

CONCLUSION

Although not all activism is consumer activism, consumer activism plays at least some part in a wide variety of movements that involve the interaction of social questions with market forces. As part of an overall strategy for social change, consumer activism has the potential to be an effective tool. By attempting to affect companies at the level of the individual purchase, consumer activism can succeed in ways that litigation or appeals to government may not. It is effective because it relies on the freedom of the consumer in a capitalist economy to buy or not buy that which he or she desires and on the ability of social movements to affect the moral sensibilities of consumers in such a way that they choose to refrain from consumption rather than lend support to an institution they deem to be acting immorally.

—Scott R. Paeth

Further Readings

Barnett, C. (2005). The political ethics of consumerism. *Consumer Policy Review, 15*(2), 45–51.

Daviss, B. (1999). Profits from principles: Five forces redefining business. *The Futurist, 33*(3), 28–33.

Elster, J. (1985). Rationality, morality, and collective action. *Ethics, 96*(1), 136–155.

Fitzgerald, N. (1997). Harnessing the potential of globalization for the consumer and citizen. *International Affairs, 73*(4), 739–746.

Glickman, L. (1994). Consumers of the world, unite. *Reviews in American History, 22*(4).

Greathead, S. (2002). Making it right: Sweatshops, ethics, and retailer responsibility. *Chain Store Age, 78*(5), 42–44.

Harrison, R. (2003). Corporate social responsibility and the consumer movement. *Consumer Policy Review, 13*(4), 127–131.

Kaplan, C. (1995, Autumn). "A world without boundaries": The body shop's trans/national geographics. *Social Text, 43,* 45–66.

Moon, E. (2004). *Examination of consumer activism and its impacts: An empirical study of the Korean consumer movement.* Unpublished Ph.D. dissertation, Oregon State University.

Nader, R. (1991). *Unsafe at any speed* (25th Anniversary Edition). New York: Knightsbridge.

Newman, K. (2004). *Radio active: Advertising and consumer activism 1935–1947.* Berkeley: University of California Press.

Noe, T., & Rebello, M. (1995). Consumer activism, producer groups and production standards. *Journal of Economic Behavior and Organization, 27*(1), 69–85.

Pandit, G. (1992). *Fostering consumer activism.* New Delhi, India: Consumers' Forum.

Storrs, L. (2000). *Civilizing capitalism: The national consumers' league, women's activism, and labor standards in the new deal era.* Chapel Hill: University of North Carolina Press.

CONSUMER FRAUD

Fraud is a purposeful, unlawful act to deceive, manipulate, or provide false statements to damage others. In general, fraud is viewed as false communication that conceals or contains a scheme to create a materially false statement or representation. Often, fraud is associated with documents that are transmitted by mail, wire, or through any type of electronic signal to a receiver. Statements that a court determines as false or fictitious or that have the intent to deceive constitute a crime and are subject to a fine or imprisonment or both. In 2005, fraud cost U.S. organizations more than $600 billion annually, and consumers lose more than $30 billion annually from fraud. The U.S. Department of Justice has identified major categories of consumer fraud including identity theft and fraud, solicitation of donations for victims of terrorist attacks, Internet fraud, telemarketing fraud, bank fraud, and mortgage scams. Mail and wire fraud is a broad category that captures many consumer and business fraudulent activities.

TYPES OF FRAUD

The *mail fraud* statute, first enacted in 1872, enabled the government to prosecute undesirable activity (e.g., securities fraud, real estate scams, etc.) years before such behavior was specifically outlawed by other laws. In 1994, Congress amended the mail fraud statute by adding the words "any private or commercial interstate carrier" to the mail fraud statute. As a result, delivering communications or merchandise via carriers such as FedEx and UPS as part of their fraudulent scheme will now violate the law.

The *wire fraud* statute was patterned after the mail fraud statute, and judicial analysis of one applies with equal force to both. When combined with wording in the mail fraud statute that prohibits fraudulent schemes involving interstate transmission of "wire, radio, or television communication . . . writings, signs, signals, pictures, or sounds," these provisions give the federal government virtually unlimited jurisdiction to regulate direct marketing activity through mail and wire fraud legislation.

Telemarketing fraud is a term that refers generally to any scheme in which the persons carrying out the scheme use false statements carried over the telephone. Most typically, fraudulent telemarketers will include current business trends or widely publicized news events as references in their attempts to solicit victims. Types of telemarketing schemes include charity schemes, credit cards, investment schemes, lottery schemes, office supply schemes, prize promotion schemes, and so on. The Federal Trade Commission (FTC) indicates that sweepstakes and lottery fraud were among the top 10 complaints filed in 2004. An AARP study, based on a survey, indicates that lottery victims are likely to be older, with an average age of 74.5 years, and more likely to be women living alone.

Internet fraud refers to any type of scheme involving the Internet, such as chat rooms, e-mail, message boards, or Web sites, to present fraudulent solicitations to perspective victims, to conduct fraudulent transactions, or to transmit proceeds of fraud to financial institutions or to others connected with the scheme. Consumers are increasingly worried about becoming victims of online fraud. Among the complaints and accusations is "shell bidding" in online auctions, which involves sellers bidding on their own items to heighten interest and competitive bidding. Another problem is sellers not delivering promised items after receiving the buyers' funds. *Phishing* is a general term for criminals' creation and use of e-mails and Web sites that are designed to look legitimate but deceive Internet users into providing personal data.

Identity theft and *identity fraud* are crimes in which someone obtains and uses another person's personal information in some way that involves fraud or deception, typically for economic gain. In 2005, more than 40 million credit card holders were susceptible to the loss of personal information and identity theft when their Visa, MasterCard, and other credit card data were compromised. In 2006, the number of identity theft complaints increased 5% over the previous year; however, the annual losses increased much more rapidly reaching $680 million. Credit card fraud loss has been slowed by corporate investment in antifraud technologies and risk management systems. Visa USA reports its fraud losses at 6 cents out of every $100 processed, down from 12 cents a decade ago. Child identity theft also increased steadily.

A growing area of identity theft is the theft of employee records. In 2006, the personal information of more than 26.5 million U.S. veterans was stolen. As the top consumer fraud complaint filed with the FTC, identity theft is becoming an increasingly important risk area for companies to manage. Often, personnel identity theft occurs as an "inside job." A disgruntled, departing, or opportunistic employee sees the revenue potential from selling personal data of employees. Companies and employees are working to control notebooks and hard drives that contain sensitive employee data. Employers who exhibit negligence in this area can be susceptible to civil lawsuits from employees who have been affected.

In response to the September 11, 2001, terrorist attacks on the United States, *terrorist attack fraud schemes* have become a major concern. Consumer groups and members of the public have reported receiving unsolicited e-mail messages that urge people to donate money to the Red Cross or to funds for victims of the attacks and their families. Some of these e-mails are sincere and reputable; others try to encourage donors to leave valuable personal and financial data, such as credit card numbers at Internet Web sites not affiliated with legitimate charitable organizations. Fraudulent telemarketers have been involved in suggesting that a portion of magazine subscriptions will be used to provide disaster recovery and relief.

Mortgage scams use taglines such as "trouble making your home mortgage," "are you facing foreclosure," and so on. Fraudulent assistance with mortgages and false mortgage rates with fees are a growing category of consumer fraud.

The FTC enters Internet, telemarketing, identify theft, and other fraud-related complaints into *Consumer Sentinel,* an online database made available to civil and criminal law enforcement agencies worldwide. In 2005, the most prevalent form of fraud, based on complaints, was identity theft (37%); Internet auctions (12%); foreign money offers (8%); shop-at-home and catalog sales (8%); prizes, sweepstakes, and lotteries (7%); Internet services and computer complaints (5%); business opportunities and work-at-home plans (2%); advance loan and credit protection (2%); and others (17%). The total consumer fraud complaints in 2005 totaled 686,683, up slightly from the previous year.

FRAUD PERPETRATED BY CONSUMERS

Consumer fraud involves intentional deception to derive an unfair economic advantage by an individual or group over an organization. Examples of fraudulent activities include shoplifting, collusion or duplicity, and guile. Collusion typically involves an employee who assists the consumer in fraud. For example, a cashier may not ring up all merchandise or may give an unwarranted discount. Duplicity may involve a consumer staging an accident in a grocery store and then seeking damages against the store for its lack of attention to safety. A consumer may purchase, wear, and then return an item of clothing for a full refund. In other situations, the consumer may ask for a refund by claiming a defect. Although some of these acts warrant legal prosecution, they can be very difficult to prove, and many companies are reluctant to accuse patrons of a crime when there is no way to verify it. Businesses that operate with the "customer is always right" philosophy have found that some consumers will take advantage of this promise and have, therefore, modified return policies to curb unfair use.

FRAUD PERPETRATED BY ORGANIZATIONS

If a consumer believes that a product is not worth the price paid for one reason or another or perhaps because he or she believes the product's benefits have been exaggerated by the seller, there may be reason to investigate the possibility of fraud. For example, although some marketers claim that their creams, pills, special massages, and other techniques can reduce or even eliminate cellulite, most medical experts and dermatologists believe that only exercise and weight loss can reduce the appearance of this undesirable condition. If consumers believe that a firm has not fulfilled its basic economic responsibilities, they may ask for a refund, tell others about their bad experience, discontinue their patronage, contact a consumer agency, and even seek legal redress. Many consumer and government agencies keep track of consumer complaints.

To protect consumers and provide businesses with guidance, a number of laws and regulations have been enacted to ensure that economic responsibility is met in accordance with institutionalized standards. The FTC works to stem unfair and deceptive trade practices through both law enforcement and consumer education. The FTC tries to alert as many consumers as possible to telltale signs of fraud. Working with a variety of partners (e.g., other federal agencies, state and local consumer protection agencies, trade associations, professional organizations, volunteer groups, corporations, the Better Business Bureau, the military, and extension agencies), the FTC's goal is to disseminate information to consumers and businesses to prevent fraud.

—O. C. Ferrell and Linda Ferrell

Further Readings

Armour, S. (2006, May 24). Worker records especially at risk. *USA Today,* p. 3b.

Conkey, C. (2006, January 26). ID theft complaints still rising, but rate of increase slows. *Wall Street Journal,* p. D1.

Consumer Sentinel. (2006, January 25). Sentinel Top Complaint Categories: January 1–December 31, 2006. Retrieved October 24, 2006, from www.consumer.gov/sentinel/Sentinel_CY-2005/CS_TopComplaint_Categories.pdf

McNeese, W. T., Ferrell, O. C., & Ferrell, L. (2005). An analysis of federal mail and wire fraud cases related to marketing. *Journal of Business Research, 58*(7), 910–918.

Swartz, N. (2006, May/June). ID theft tops FTC complaints for 2005. *Information Management Journal, 40*(3), 19.

United States Department of Justice [Web site]. Retrieved July 25, 2006, from www.usdoj.gov

PART VII

Ethics of Advertising, Marketing, and Public Relations

Ethics of Marketing

Advertising Ethics

Public Relations Ethics

ETHICS OF MARKETING

M*arketing ethics* is the systematic study of how moral standards are applied to marketing decisions, behaviors, and institutions. Because marketing is a process inherent to most organizations, marketing ethics should be viewed as a subset of business ethics; thus, much of what is written about business ethics applies to marketing ethics as well. At the outset, it is also useful to distinguish between *positive* and *normative* marketing ethics. Positive marketing ethics looks at marketing practices from the standpoint of "what is." For example, specifying the percentage of organizations that have codes of ethical marketing practice or tracking the number of violations that deal with *deceptive advertising* would be examples of positive marketing ethics. In contrast, normative marketing ethics deals with how marketing *ought* to operate according to some moral standard or theory. The sort of moral standards (or theories) applied to marketing situations involve the usual moral frameworks commonly applied when evaluating business ethics (e.g., utilitarianism, duty-based theories, virtue ethics). When the words "marketing ethics" appear in the general media or business press, the reports typically describe a marketing strategy, tactic, or policy that some constituency feels is "unfair" or "exploitive" or "deceptive." Often, the subsequent discussion turns to how marketing practices might become more consumer-friendly, socially compatible, or put in philosophical terms, how marketing might be *normatively* improved.

Normative marketing practices might be defined as those that emphasize transparent, trustworthy, and responsible personal and/or organizational marketing policies and actions, and exhibit integrity as well as fairness to consumers and other stakeholders. In the true spirit of normative ethical standards, this definition provides certain virtues and values (e.g., trust, fairness) to which marketing practitioners ought to aspire. However, the definition also raises myriad questions. What do we mean by transparent? Does that mean no trade secrets are ever allowed? What is the essential nature of integrity? Does it mostly involve keeping organizational promises to customers or is it broader than that? What is the nature of fairness, and who decides what standard of fairness is to be applied? Should it be consumers, the company at focus, regulatory agencies, or a broader cross-section of society? What stakeholder interests should be taken into consideration, and how should they be weighted? As one can see from these questions, the area of normative marketing ethics is likely to generate considerable controversy because there are differing views among various parties about what constitutes "proper" behavior in marketing.

GENERAL PERSPECTIVES

Because marketing is the organizational process focused directly on exchange, ethical issues in marketing have existed since the inception of trade. The Roman philosopher Cicero counseled merchants to avoid raising prices too high in times of shortage, lest they alienate their customers, who might shun them when supplies were more abundant. However, the analysis of marketing ethics from a more systematic and analytical standpoint has only begun to develop in the past 40 years. Since the mid-1960s, the literature on marketing ethics has grown substantially. A recent 2005 ABI/Inform literature search using the term *marketing ethics* as its search query generated a list of more than 400 citations to the literature—all of which presumably addressed marketing ethics in some scholarly form or fashion. While cynics view the term *marketing ethics* as an oxymoron, no doubt due partly to the frequent questionable activities of some used car dealers, advertising copyrighters, and telemarketers, there exist clear and articulated standards of proper behavior that are "peer endorsed" by marketing practitioners. In other words, marketing managers themselves have expressed their opinions as to the ideal obligations inherent in the honest and forthright conduct of marketing. Perhaps the best known of these codes of conduct is the American Marketing Association's (AMA's) "Statement of Ethical Norms and Values for Marketers." This document—endorsed by the largest professional organization of marketing practitioners in the world—and available for review at www.marketpower.com (search: code of ethics) specifically states that marketers serve not only their company enterprises but also act as stewards of society in creating, facilitating, and executing the efficient and effective exchange transactions that are part of a greater economy. The AMA statement recognizes the duties that marketers have to all stakeholders (e.g., customers, employees, investors, channel members, regulators, and the host community) as they discharge their job responsibilities. This document explicitly warns that marketers must not knowingly do harm in executing their selling responsibilities, that marketers have a duty to foster trust in the marketing

Ethics of Marketing

system, and that they should embrace basic marketplace values, including truth telling, genuine service to customers, avoidance of practices acclaimed to be unfair, and an adherence to honest and open communications with clients. Significantly, it states that marketing organizations have responsibilities of "citizenship" just as individuals do. Documents such as the AMA Statement represent hard evidence that there are bedrock ethical standards and values that have been agreed on by numerous marketing practitioners.

Of course, the extent of practitioner compliance with these values is another issue. Over the years, surveys of marketing managers report that the vast majority of practitioners discharge their job responsibilities in a lawful and meritorious manner. Nonetheless, every year brings its share of horrific and controversial marketing blunders. Current issues in the news involving marketing practices have to do with price-gouging when gasoline shortages occur (as they did in the wake of Hurricane Katrina) and stealth marketing techniques such as surreptitiously gathering information about consumer patterns when they surf shopping sites on the Web. In general, national opinion polls of the public suggest that marketers have plenty of room to improve their ethical performance before it conforms to public expectations. Perhaps the "truth" about marketing lies somewhere between the practitioners view that marketers are predominantly "good guys" and the public perception of marketers as suspect purveyors of sometimes dubious goods and services.

While the above-mentioned statement of AMA of "norms and values" is partly inspirational in nature, there has also been substantial effort expended by marketing academics and ethics scholars to develop pragmatic models of marketing behavior that delineate the factors that shape and affect ethical (or unethical) marketing decisions. An example of such a work (*positive* marketing ethics) would be the Hunt-Vitell model of marketing ethics—a framework that has been subjected to extensive empirical testing. This complex model takes into account various factors such as (1) environmental dimensions in industry and the organization influencing ethical actions, (2) the recognition by decision makers of an ethical problem and its likely consequences, (3) the teleological and deontological norms used by marketing decision makers that might affect their selection of various alternative choices, (4) the type of ethical judgments made in various situations, (5) the formation of any intentions attributable to the marketing practitioners at focus, and (6) a measure of the outcomes of actual behavior. The purpose of weighing the myriad factors involved in real-world marketing decisions associated with ethical questions is that it helps specify the gaps between what the actual behavior of marketing practitioners *is* versus how far managers need to go in order to be in conformance with various marketing ideals. Empirical studies, using models such as Hunt-Vitell, have suggested, for example, that the standards managers use to address ethical questions vary considerably (e.g., some are utilitarian; some derive their perspectives from religious traditions). Moreover, the response to ethical issues by managers depends on the issue being addressed. For instance, the majority of managers might be very concerned that clandestine competitive intelligence gathering is growing in their industry but most may not be bothered by "puffery" (advertising exaggeration). Yet both practices are subject to ethical debate in the public realm. It is in the conduct of such systematic *ethics research* that the positive and normative aspects of marketing come together because marketers can learn what to "fix" based on what is actually going on.

MARKETING PRACTICE

At the heart of marketing ethics are decisions that marketing practitioners make about ethical questions. Ethical questions most often arise in marketing when a stakeholder group or some segment of the public feels that the actions taken by some (or many) marketers might be judged to be morally inappropriate. Currently, for instance, many consumers feel that *spam* advertising over the Internet is far too prevalent and/or that product rebates have too often been intentionally made to be difficult to redeem. Similarly, other ethical questions occur when marketing managers believe that they might be compromising their own personal values in the quest for increased organizational profit. In such situations, marketers are often evaluating whether they should take *business* actions that they feel ought *not* to be done from the standpoint of *personal* ethics that they hold—the essence of an ethical dilemma. Most managers cannot avoid facing such tough issues because the majority of marketing professionals report confronting such ethical questions at some point in their careers. These "ethical" branch points can pertain to a host of marketing issues such as selling cigarettes to teenagers, the promotion of violence-oriented video games, pricing products at a level that exploits unsuspecting consumers, bluffing in negotiations with long-time suppliers, writing intentionally misleading ad copy, and so on. If the marketing actions that are taken happen to be in violation of the law, these are also typically characterized as unethical. However, our focus in this entry is particularly on actions that are *not* illegal but that are criticized as "improper" according to some ethical value or norm. Therefore, marketing ethics is mostly focused on marketing behaviors that are not prohibited by the law but perhaps should not be indulged due to certain moral considerations. And thus, marketing ethics is often concerned with actions that are currently legal but still might be judged improper according to some invoked moral standard. For instance, NASCAR has every legal right to have their automobiles sponsored by and festooned with the logos of brewers, distillers, and other alcoholic beverage makers. Whether it is ethical to link speeding race cars to alcohol beverages given the significant "driving while intoxicated" problem that exists in the United States is a matter for debate.

Most generic areas of marketing practice provoke substantial ethical comment and discussion. These areas include marketing segmentation, marketing research, product development, pricing, distribution, personal selling, and advertising. In the paragraphs below, a sampling of marketing issues, often suggesting ethical questions from these areas of marketing practice, is briefly reviewed to illustrate both the nature and the scope of marketing ethics in the conduct of business operations.

Market Segmentation

One of the basic strategies of marketing campaigns involves the division of the mass market into "segments" followed by the development of specific offerings to appeal to the selected "target market." Ethical questions especially surround the target marketing of segments that include potentially vulnerable populations such as children, the elderly, the impoverished, and marketing illiterates. The "ethical issue" at focus here centers on whether marketers have too much "power" over certain groups who are not prepared to independently participate in the marketplace.

For example, children are a $25+ billion market in the United States alone for products such as toys, sugared cereal, DVDs, and video games. One major ethical question involves the extent to which marketers can freely treat children as "consumers in training" (mini adults) subject to pretty much the same promotions as the rest of the (adult) market. For young children (less than 8 years old), there is the issue of whether they even understand the difference between (for instance) television advertising and the programming itself. For older kids, the ethical issues might focus more on the appropriateness of certain products (violent video games), or the degree to which young teenagers might be susceptible to particular kinds of provocative fashion or lifestyle advertising. The key issue involved in targeting children turns on whether marketers should be held to a higher standard care and caution when marketing to children. One illustration of emergent constraints when approaching children involves the passage of the Children's On-line Privacy Protection Act of 1998 that was promulgated because of significant parental concerns regarding the collection of market research information data over the Internet from children younger than 13. Essentially, this federal legislation, inspired by numerous ethical questions raised by the general public, prohibits the collection of any personal information by market researchers from "under 13s" without verifiable permission from parents allowing it.

Similar questions about vulnerability to marketing scams occur with regard to older consumers—especially those more than 80 years of age. Such seniors are living longer, and as they grow older, they become less confident in their decision-making ability and become potential targets for the fraudulent sales of financial services, vacation packages, insurance annuities, and prescription drug plans—to name only a few product categories. As the baby boomers grow older and make up a larger percentage of the population, the focus on the appropriateness of marketing practices to this senior segment will only increase in prominence. Various scams that exploit seniors (e.g., sweepstakes that promise winnings but are designed only to sell magazines) are reported in the press almost weekly.

Marketing Research

Since marketing decisions are often data driven, market research techniques and outputs are frequently used by marketing practitioners. Market researchers themselves often have considerable training in methodological and statistical techniques, and one might surmise that because of their greater education, they exhibit a higher degree of ethical professionalism than other marketing practitioners. Certainly, it is true that various professional organizations related to the practice of marketing research such as the Council for Survey Research, the Market Research Society and the European Society of Marketing and Opinion Research have developed detailed codes of ethics addressing common conflicts that occur in the execution of marketing research. These "conduct codes" of these professional organizations can be accessed at their Web sites and provide a modicum of guidance for marketing researchers when facing common situations that occur as part of the research process. These codes stress that tactics such as protecting respondent confidentiality when it

313

is promised, not misrepresenting the identity of the research sponsor, properly disclosing research procedures, and many other professional practices should be adhered to.

Additional ethical issues arise owing to the fact that marketing research often involves contact with the general public, usually through the use of surveys that are increasingly being conducted online. Because marketing research activity relies heavily on publicly submitted information, some of which is personally sensitive, marketing research is ripe for ethical abuse or misuse. As survey research has become digitized, researchers have gathered substantial records about consumer product and service usage as well as their satisfaction. As a result, the issue of *consumer privacy* is at the forefront of marketing research ethics. It is hoped that the coming decade will yield definitive answers about the extent of privacy protection that consumers can expect when shopping online. Second, most marketing research is conducted by for-profit organizations to aid decision making within corporations. As a result, the profit motive may cause researchers or their clients to compromise the objectivity and precision of the research that is undertaken. Researchers inherently want to provide support for the outcomes their sponsors hope to find. Clients basically want the research they conduct to tell the best possible story about their company and their products. It should not be surprising then that marketers sometimes fall to the temptation of misusing market research information by manipulating or exaggerating the results.

Product Management Ethics

Ethical issues surrounding the management of products are central to marketing because the marketing process generally begins with a product (broadly defined to include goods, services, or ideas). The most common ethical concerns in this area pertain to the safety of products. Earlier, in the brief discussion concerning the AMA practitioner norms and values, the notion of "never knowingly doing harm" was introduced as a central ethical percept. Certainly, this prescription directly applies to the area of products. That products are safe "for their use as intended" is a basic consumer expectation and is embodied in common law within the concept of "implied warranty." While the sale of safe products is a fundamental marketing expectation, many consumers remain skeptical as to whether they are likely to receive this protection. A 2005 Yankelovich/MONITOR poll of consumers found that 61% agreed that even long-established companies cannot be trusted to make safe, durable products without the government setting basic industry standards. Indeed, a minimal base line of consumer protection in this area is assured via regulation by the U.S. Consumer Product Safety Commission, which has the general mandate to oversee product safety in the United States. Other government agencies also oversee specialized areas of product category such as the U.S. Department of Agriculture, the Food and Drug Administration, and the U.S. Department of Justice, which has specific jurisdiction for alcohol, tobacco, and firearms.

Despite all these protections, perennial ethical questions about product safety continue to be asked: How safe should products be? How safe is safe enough? When products harm consumers in the course of normal usage, who should be held liable? Too often marketers fail the safety test. For example, each Christmas season various consumer advocacy groups identify and publicize toys that are potentially dangerous to young children unless used with extreme care and under adult supervision. And, exactly where to draw the line in automobile safety is a never-ending debate. Should SUVs, which American consumers both love and demand, roll over as often as they do? Should side air bags, which consumers generally are reluctant to pay for as "add-ons," be mandatory because they can prevent serious injuries?

Another growing area of concern is product counterfeiting. Product counterfeiting involves the unauthorized copy of patented products, inventions, and trademarks or the violation of registered copyrights (often for the purposes of making a particular product look like a more popular branded leader). Common examples of product counterfeiting include fake Rolex watches, knockoff Levi jeans, and illegally pirated video and audio tapes of popular movies and music. It is estimated that product counterfeiting costs American companies $450 billion in sales each year. Product counterfeiting is unethical and, in most markets around the world, illegal as well. Counterfeiting is unethical because it involves an attempt to unfairly capture the "goodwill" created by one company's brand equity and unfairly transfer it to a knockoff product without royalty payment to the originating party. Simply put, counterfeiting is a form of intellectual theft. Interestingly, the majority of college students in the United States find "downloading" music from the Internet without paying to be a mostly harmless and ethical practice. With the expansion of China's economy and the many knockoff products that seem to originate there, product counterfeiting will be a major ethical issue for organizations in the early part of the 21st century.

Another instance of common ethical concern involves products that create problems for the physical or natural environment. Examples would include product packaging that is not biodegradable; products that use inordinate scarce resources such as large sports utility vehicles (e.g., the Hummer) along with their unusually low fuel mileage; various chemicals and detergents that pollute the land, air, and groundwater when improperly disposed of; and medical wastes that are sometimes dumped into oceans or lakes because the proper disposal of such material is burdensome for the user. Contributing further to all this is an increasingly "disposable lifestyle" in many developed countries that generates waste-handling problems, a residue of the convenience-oriented mentality—fueled by marketing. For example, the average American generates approximately 4 pounds of garbage a day of which 30% represents product packaging. The fundamental ethical issue connecting all these ecological examples is that of *externalities.* Basically, externalities are costs that are imposed on the society as a whole that are not paid for by the original producer or consumer. To take an obvious example, when beer bottles and soft drink cans are littered in public parks or recreational areas, the cleanup of that packaging represents an "externality." As a response to all this, a "green marketing" movement has developed, which puts a premium on product marketing and programs being compatible with environmentally protective principles. To this end, some organizations have embraced the Coalition for Environmentally Responsible Economies (CERES) principles—some of which speak directly to marketing-connected issues. In general, these principles involve adhering to an environmental ethic of strong commitment to ecological excellence as well as human health and safety. The CERES principles, which can be accessed online, are yet another normative code of conduct to help guide marketing actions in particular areas of operations.

Pricing

Perhaps no area of managerial activity is more difficult to assess fairly and to prescribe normatively in terms of morality than the area of pricing. The given price of a product or service commonly results from the confluence of three factors: demand, competition, and cost. Each of these factors can be central to ethical questions about pricing fairness. For example, when high demand puts pressure on supply, such as the desperate need for construction materials after a natural disaster, there may be a temptation for sellers to price-gouge. Or in an attempt to gain dominant market share, strong competitors may use predatory pricing (below cost pricing) to drive economically challenged sellers from the marketplace. In a business-to-business setting, a vendor may simply mislead a client concerning what "actual costs" have been incurred especially if they are operating under a "cost plus" pricing contract. While there is agreement that sellers are entitled to some profit margin above their full cost, how high prices can be and still be "fair" has been debated since medieval times. According to theologians such as Thomas Aquinas, the "just price" was often conceived of as the (debatable) amount above cost that the merchant needed to charge in order to maintain his or her business and to provide for his or her family. Charging more than that was to commit the grievous sin of avarice.

There is presently considerable regulation that helps establish some minimum behaviors for "fair pricing" (e.g., *price-fixing* by sellers, sometimes called "collusion," is illegal; similarly, "price discrimination" to different distributors by sellers without economic justification is also contrary to commercial law). Nevertheless, the concept of ethical pricing seems destined for considerable future debate. One current practice in the news has to do with the pricing strategy engaged in by the so-called pay day loan stores (i.e., those lending businesses that provide instant cash advances in lieu of unpaid, but earned, wages). These operations charge extremely high interest rates mostly to the impoverished segment of the market. A second dubious pricing instance involves some forms of adjustable rate mortgages that can often trigger significantly higher repayment rates for a variety of dubious reasons. And, a third questionable pricing scheme centers on "rent-to-own" furniture/appliance stores whose cumulative rate schemes often translate to payment totals far in excess of the total cost of the items rented. In each of these instances, it is argued that the pricing is "exploitive" because the high rates take advantage of certain unwary or desperate consumers.

Distribution

The distribution element of marketing involves the entire supply chain from manufacturer through wholesalers and distributors (including retailers) on to the final consumer. At each point in the supply chain, because there are economic interactions between these various parties, the potential for ethical issues to occur is quite common. Perhaps the most overarching issue within the channel of distribution supply chain has to do with the question of power and responsibility within the channel itself. Often one organization within the channel has greater economic leverage than other channel members, and with that economic leadership comes a potential for ethical abuse. A current example of this situation might be the enormous economic power that Wal-Mart possesses over its suppliers. Due to their dependence on Wal-Mart's access to the market, suppliers must conform to Wal-Mart's various contract requests or face losing a distribution outlet that serves tens of millions of customers. One perhaps encouraging lesson of marketing history is that channel members who abuse their power eventually lose it, often through the enactment of new government regulations that restrict and constrain certain competitive practices.

Another common concern within channel relationships has to do with "gift giving" that sometimes mutates into bribery. A long-standing business custom is to entertain clients and to give modest gifts to business associates. Such practices can cement important economic relationships. The pervading ethical question, of course, is, "When does a gift become a bribe?" Historically, for example, pharmaceutical companies have offered medical doctors lavish entertainment and gifts. The drug companies have argued that these amenities are not being provided to influence physician prescription decisions, but rather simply to inform them of the availability of new branded drugs. Consumer advocates contend that such practices are forcing consumers away from less-expensive generic drug alternatives and contribute directly to escalating health care costs. Not surprisingly, one of the best ways for channel members to deal with such potential ethical questions is to develop clear guidelines that address some of the typically questioned practices that exist within their particular industry. For instance, some companies restrict their employees from giving or accepting anything worth more than $20 in a given year when dealing with a business partner. In this manner, managers are given at least minimal guidance as to what constitutes acceptable and nonacceptable gift-giving practices.

Personal Selling and Sales Management

Sales positions are among the most typical marketing jobs. Ethical conflicts and choices are inherent in the personal selling process because sales reps constantly try to balance the interests of the seller they represent with the buyers that they presumptively serve. Moreover, sales reps seldom have the luxury of thoughtfully contemplating the ethical propriety of their actions. This is because sales reps operate in relative isolation and in circumstances that are dynamic with their business transactions frequently conducted under great time pressures. Even when sales reps electronically submit real-time sales reports of their client calls, such "outcome-oriented" paper evaluations contribute to a perceived clinical distance between sales managers and their representatives. Business case history tells us that sales people seem to be most prone to acting unethically if one (or more) of the following circumstances exist: when competition is particularly intense; when economic times are difficult placing their vendor organization under revenue pressure; when sales representative compensation is based mostly on commission; when questionable dealings such as gifting or quasi-bribes are a common part of industry practice; when sales training is nonexistent or abbreviated; or when the sales rep has limited selling experience.

Sales managers in particular bear a special responsibility for questionable selling practices because they are in a position both to oversee their sales staff and to influence content and implementation of sales policies. Ethically enlightened sales managers should regularly review their sales literature before distribution to minimize the possibility that inflammatory (to competitors) material is inadvertently circulated. They should counsel their sales people not to repeat unconfirmed trade gossip. They should strive to maintain a sales environment free of sexual harassment. They ought to encourage their sales people never to make unfair or inaccurate comparisons about competitive products and avoid claiming the superiority of their own product/service offerings unless it is supported by scientific facts or statistical evidence documented or prepared by an independent research firm. Despite best efforts of marketers, the area of sales will continue to have its share of ethical controversies. Sales are the most common entry-level position into the field of marketing and also the job position in marketing about which the general public feels most suspicious.

Advertising

Advertising is a significant economic force in the world economy, with global ad spending projected to be well over $300 billion in calendar year 2005. The visibility and marketplace influence of advertising is so great that many consumers think of advertising as synonymous with marketing. Various critics charge that advertising is biased, needlessly provocative, intrusive, and often offensive. Yet most surveys suggest that the majority of consumers, on the balance, find advertising both entertaining and informative. While some types of advertising involve outright transgressions of the law (e.g., deceptive advertising containing intentional errors of fact), a great deal of advertising controversy involves practices that are perfectly legal but still raise moral questions. For example, promoting handguns in magazines with a substantial teenage readership, the featuring of bikini-clad Paris Hilton suggestively soaping down a car in an ad campaign for hamburgers, and implied health claims for products that may not be especially healthy (e.g., low-carb beer) are instances

319

of controversial (but legal) advertising approaches. Over the years, many lists of citizen concerns about the ethics of advertising have been put together. Often included on those lists are questions about the appropriateness of tobacco and alcohol advertising, the use of stereotypical images in advertising (e.g., Hispanic gardeners, hysterical housewives), the increased amount of negative (i.e., attack) political advertising, and various attempts to exploit children as buyers. The last issue is particularly sensitive to the public and, since the early 1970s, the Children's Advertising Review Unit, established by the Better Business Bureau, has monitored advertising directed to children less than 12 years and has sought the modification or discontinuance of ads that were found to be inaccurate or unfair in some fashion.

One of the more curious features of ethics in advertising is that the involvement of several parties (i.e., ad sponsor, ad agency, and the media) in the creation of advertising has probably led to a *lower* ethical standard in the practice of advertising than one might expect. The presence of multiple parties, none of whom has full responsibility, has created the default position of "leaving it to the others" to articulate and enforce an appropriate ethical standard.

IMPLEMENTING MARKETING ETHICS

Of course, at the heart of marketing ethics is the issue of how to improve the ethical behaviors of organizations as they discharge their marketing tasks and responsibilities. There are several elements of successful implementation that have been regularly articulated in the business ethics literature and successfully applied to marketing. Good ethics begins with a chief marketing officer (CMO) who must not only publicly embrace core ethical values but also live them. It is often said that the organization is but a lengthened shadow of the person at the top; this is no less true of the marketing organization. Implied also, then, is that the CMO is supported in the endeavor to maintain strong ethical values in marketing operations by the chief executive officer (CEO) of the corporation. Put another way, a key role of the leadership of any company wanting to travel the high ethical road is to keep publicly voicing the importance of ethical conduct in the discharge of their business affairs. Such ethical exhortations involve espousing the core ethical values identified in the corporate mission statement. These values should be made operational in a code of conduct that addresses the specific ethical issues that are most common to a particular company or industry sector. For instance, the Internet sellers must explicitly address privacy policies for their shoppers, vintners should comment on the question of responsible drinking, and so forth. Furthermore, it is important that any such marketing code be dynamic and periodically revised. Caterpillar Corporation, a manufacturer of heavy construction equipment, has revised its code of conduct five times since the mid-1970s. Moreover, any organizational code or statement of norms must also be communicated well enough that all employees can verbalize its essential values. It is equally important that managerial and employee behavior in the organization be monitored, including that of the CMO, so that conformance to company values is checked on in a pragmatic way. One tool for doing this is the usage of a periodic *marketing ethics audit* to systematically check company compliance with ethics policies and procedures. When ethical violations occur, proportionate punishment must be meted out. Similarly, when organizational managers perform in an ethically exemplary fashion, appropriate rewards also should be provided. This last step testifies to something beyond financial results leading to recognition in the organization. Details of executing all these steps have been exhaustively treated in the business ethics literature and modified for a marketing context. Johnson & Johnson and Ford are examples of organizations that conduct audits of their social performance that includes the evaluation of multiple marketing dimensions.

CONCLUSION

At the end of the day, the most vexing ingredient in the recipe for better ethical behavior by marketers remains the force of will to always keep ethics at the heart of a company's purpose. The pressure on individual organizations to maintain and improve their profitability and to grow revenues is incessant. The nature of marketing management is to provide needed consumer goods and services by undertaking risk that, if calculated properly, is rewarded with financial profit. Ethical operations, at least in the short run, can be detrimental to that profitability because they often include some economic cost. Keeping ethical marketing at the forefront of operations is an exceedingly difficult challenge given the constant pressures on marketing managers to remain financially successful and growing.

—Gene Laczniak

Ethics of Marketing

Further Readings

Brenkert, G. C. (1997). Marketing trust: Barriers and bridges. *Business and Professional Ethics Journal, 16*(1–3), 77–98.

Cohen, D. (1995). *Legal issues in marketing decision making.* Cincinnati, OH: South-Western College Publishing.

Davidson, K. (1996). *Selling sin: The marketing of socially unacceptable products.* Westport, CT: Quorum Books.

Ferrell, O. C., & Gresham, L. G. (1985). A contingency framework for understanding ethical decision making in marketing. *Journal of Marketing, 49,* 87–96.

Hunt, S. D., & Vitell, S. J. (1986, Spring). A general theory of marketing ethics. *Journal of Macromarketing, 6,* 5–16.

Karpatkin, R. H. (1999, Spring). Toward a fair and just marketplace for all consumers: The responsibilities of marketing professionals. *Journal of Public Policy and Marketing, 18*(1), 118–122.

Laczniak, G. R. (1983, Spring). Frameworks for analyzing marketing ethics. *Journal of Macromarketing, 3,* 7–18.

Laczniak, G. R. (1999, Fall). Distributive justice, Catholic social teaching and the morality of marketers. *Journal of Public Policy Marketing, 18*(1), 125–129.

Mascarenhas, O. A. J. (1995, April). Exonerating unethical marketing executive behaviors: A diagnostic framework. *Journal of Marketing, 59,* 43–57.

Murphy, P. E., Laczniak, G. R., Bowie, N. F., & Klein, T. A. (2005). *Ethical marketing.* Upper Saddle River, NJ: Pearson Education.

Murphy, P. E., & Pridgen, M. D. (1991). Ethical and legal issues in marketing. *Advances in Marketing and Public Policy, 2,* 185–244.

Robin, D. P., & Reidenbach, E. R. (1987, January). Social responsibility: Ethics and marketing strategy: Closing the gap between concept and application. *Journal of Marketing, 51*(1), 44–58.

Schlegelmilch, B. (1998). *Marketing ethics: An international perspective.* Boston: International Thomson Business Press.

Smith, N. C. (1995). Marketing strategies for the ethics era. *Sloan Management Review, 36*(Summer), 85–97.

Williams, O. F., & Murphy, P. E. (1990). The ethics of virtue: A moral theory for marketing. *Journal of Macromarketing, 10*(1), 19–29.

ADVERTISING ETHICS

In a modern capitalist society, ads are ubiquitous; criticisms of advertising are nearly as common. Some ethical criticisms concern advertising as a social practice, while others attack specific ads or advertising practices. Central to ethical criticisms are concerns that ads subvert rational decision making and threaten human autonomy by creating needs, by creating false needs, by developing one-sided narrowly focused needs that can only be satisfied by buying material products and services, and/or by appealing to genuine and deeply rooted human needs in a manipulative way. A second sort of criticism is that ads harm human welfare by keeping everyone dissatisfied. At a minimum, ads try to make us dissatisfied with not currently having the product, but many ads also aim at keeping us permanently dissatisfied with our social positions, our looks, our bodies, and ourselves. Advertising has been blamed for people today being neurotic, insecure, and stressed.

Business ethicists have traditionally either considered advertising in general or divided ads into information ads, which are ethical as long as they are honest, and persuasive ads, which are always problematic. However, recent literature on advertising ethics considers the division of ads into informative and persuasive to be entirely inadequate because it fails to consider separately the various persuasive techniques that ads use.

ECONOMIC CRITICISMS AND THE FUNCTION OF ADVERTISING

One economic criticism of advertising in general is that advertising is a wasteful and inefficient business tool; our standard of living would be higher without it. This criticism fails to understand that economies of scale for mass-produced goods can often more than offset advertising costs, making advertised products cheaper in the end. It is also suggested that advertising causes people to spend money they do not have and that advertising combined with credit cards creates a debt-ridden society, which causes stress and unhappiness. Furthermore, it is claimed that advertising encourages a society based on immediate gratification, which discourages savings and the accumulation of capital needed for a thriving capitalist economy. Granted that American society may currently be deeply in debt, this cannot be blamed on advertising because there are numerous societies that are inundated with ads but have positive savings rates and fiscal surpluses. Canada is one, and there are others in Europe and Asia.

There are also economic defenses of advertising. It has been argued that the creation of consumer demand is an integral part of the capitalist system; capitalism needs advertising since capitalism has an inherent tendency toward overproduction. And capitalism is an economic system that has made us the richest, longest lived, healthiest society in human history; even the poor in consumer societies are better off than most people in the Third World. Surely such well-being makes advertising ethically justified.

INFORMATION ADS

Many ads are simple information ads. Consider, for example, the flyers left on your doorstep that say that certain products are on sale at a certain price at a store in your neighborhood. Such ads are generally considered ethical provided they are honest. Problems arise if they make claims that are false, misleading, or exaggerated. Making false claims is a form of lying and, hence, clearly unethical. A claim is misleading if it is literally true, but is understood by most consumers in a way that includes a false claim. The ad is misleading whether or not the advertiser intends the misunderstanding. Generally, the honesty of ads should be judged not on their literal truth, but on how consumers understand the ad; this is because companies have, or can easily get, this understanding of the ad from focus groups and other marketing research techniques. Exaggeration, or puffery, in ads is thought acceptable by many people on the grounds that consumers can be expected to discount claims in ads. This is true except for vulnerable groups such as young children.

Normally, withholding information in advertising does not raise ethical issues. Car ads, for example, do not often print crash and repair reports; such information is readily and inexpensively available, and obtaining it is rightly viewed as the customer's responsibility. However, ethical constraints on exaggeration, withholding information, and misleading advertising become much more severe in cases where the customer cannot obtain accurate information, or cannot obtain it at reasonable cost, and the information is important to the customer's physical or financial well-being. Drug advertising by pharmaceutical companies is often criticized for failure to meet these more stringent standards, even though regulations in many countries try to control this for prescription drugs by requiring details on possible side effects, contraindications, and so on. This is a clear case of the information not being available since drug trial results are often confidential to the corporation, and the implications for the user's well-being are clear. This situation is not helped by press coverage of new drugs; such coverage tends to emphasize benefits over risks.

IMPACT OF PERSUASIVE ADS ON INDIVIDUALS

Discussion of the ethical issues surrounding persuasive advertising must consider separately various persuasive techniques such as benefit advertising, emotional manipulation, symbol creation, and so on.

Benefit ads emphasis a product's benefits to the user rather than product features. Typically, benefit ads show an enthusiastic, often exuberant, person enjoying the results of using the product; for example, a housewife is shown as jubilant that her laundry detergent got her sheets whiter than her neighbors.' In benefit ads, users tend to appear like real people and are not overly idealized; their emotions, however, are greatly exaggerated. Most benefit ads are ethically harmless if we allow for consumer discounting of exaggeration. Some critics, however, question the hidden premise that the consumer ought to want the benefit. Why should a person care if their wash is whiter, their car is faster, their hair is bouncier? Though a consumer's ability to deal with this form of persuasion may be made more difficult by the fact that a benefit ad assumes but does not state its premises, most of these ads are not a serious threat to human autonomy. However, there are some cases for concern. Consider, for example, ads placed by pharmaceutical companies for mood-changing drugs; life's little hassles become stress, sadness becomes depression, tranquility becomes listlessness, and contentment becomes apathy. Normalcy is not stated but assumed to be a medical condition requiring prescription pills. We are encouraged to be constantly dissatisfied with our most personal emotions. There are ethical problems with the intentions of the advertisers in this case, regardless of the actual effect on people's autonomy.

Ads try to manipulate many human emotions; fear ads are only one example, but they make clear the ethical issues. Fear ads tend to become more common during economic recessions, and they reached a crescendo during the 1930s. A Johnson & Johnson ad for bandages from 1936, for example, shows a boy with his right arm amputated because a cut without Johnson & Johnson bandages became infected. More recently, American Express used a print ad in eerie gold and black colors showing a distraught mother frantically phoning while her feverish daughter lies in the background. The solution offered is that American Express keeps lists of English-speaking physicians in most large cities. Critics maintain that appeals to emotions undermine rational decision-making processes and threaten our autonomy. Defenders point out that the fears portrayed (of infection before penicillin, communication problems with foreign doctors) are real even if dramatized, and the product offers a legitimate solution for the problem.

Advertising can persuade by turning a product into a symbol of something entirely different from itself. Chanel is a symbol of Parisian sophistication, Calvin Klein a symbol of sex, DeBeers diamonds symbolize love, and Mercedes Benz is a status symbol. We often do not buy products for what they are, but what they mean to us, and, just as importantly, what they mean to others. Critics claim this undermines human rationality by preventing us from assessing products based on their intrinsic worth; symbolic meaning of the product invariably biases our judgments. But, in fact, it is not irrational for people to buy a symbol if they want to express something meaningful. There is nothing irrational, for example, with buying and waving your country's flag. If you want to project high economic status, a Mercedes does indeed do so. Symbolic ads are not false or misleading for the simple reason that they do in fact work; products and logos do come to have symbolic meaning for us. To give a diamond is to give an object useless in itself, but the symbolic meaning, largely created by decades of DeBeers advertising, can give the gift life-changing significance. Symbolic meaning can add to the price you pay for a product (consider designer labels, for example), but there is nothing irrational in paying a price for a symbol that you want. Indeed, advertising provides a useful social service by creating symbols that allow consumers to communicate various meanings to those around them.

A self-identity image ad turns the product into a symbol of a particular self-image; the product then allows the buyer to express to themselves or others what sort of person they are. For example, Marlboro cigarette ads for decades featured the Marlboro man, a symbol of rugged independence and masculine individuality. Marlboros were very popular with teenage males, not because they thought the product would turn them into cowboys, but because they wanted to conceive of themselves as ruggedly masculine and because they wanted their peers to see them like that.

The more unnecessary a product type is, the more likely it will be promoted with self-identity image ads; they are a common type of ad for perfumes and colognes, cigarettes, beer, and expensive designer labels. One of the ethical objections to self-identity ads is that they manipulate our fundamental conceptions of ourselves to sell us dangerous (as in the case of Marlboro cigarettes mentioned above) or useless products. In response, it can be argued that these ads do not manipulate us without our active participation; we have to play the image game for these ads to have any affect, and experimenting with one's self-image is voluntary. Perhaps concern should only be for vulnerable groups or individuals, such as insecure teenagers under peer pressure; but then, images available through logos may help teenagers feel more secure if they can afford the product with the label. There have been stories of people who have committed violent crimes to obtain footwear with the right logo, but advertising cannot be held responsible for poverty or the resulting violence. Ads that specifically target the poor may be unethical because they target a vulnerable group; ads for "power" beer that target inner-city neighborhoods have been criticized for this.

Self-identity image ads cannot be criticized for being false or misleading because they do not work by giving information or making promises. They mostly appeal to our fantasies, and fantasies as fantasies are not false. A woman, for example, does not buy a perfume because she thinks it will transform her into the slim, beautiful, chic young woman in the ad. Consumers are not that gullible. She buys the perfume because associating herself with that image in her own mind makes her feel good about herself. The resulting self-confidence may, in fact, make her more attractive. If we actively buy into the identity images of ads, there may be an element of self-fulfillment. None of this threatens human autonomy since active participation is required and is voluntary.

Even if self-identity image advertising is considered generally an ethical technique, there may still be ethical objections to specific images. For example, the images of women in ads have raised many ethical complaints. The most serious complaints concern the unremitting presentation as beautiful of an ideal body that is excessively thin or even anorexic looking, is extremely tall and long legged, and has a poreless, wrinkleless, perfectly smooth china-like complexion. That this body image dominates ads for women's beauty and

Advertising Ethics

327

fashion products is true, though recently there has been an increase in ads using more realistic body types. The tall thin image extends to fashion models, who now average more than 6 feet in height and are generally underweight. This body type is impossible for most women to achieve even with dieting and plastic surgery. In fact, the images in ads often have their hair and complexions airbrushed and their legs stretched using computer techniques; the result is a distorted body image that no woman, not even the models in the photos, have or can ever obtain.

The purpose of this idealization and distortion is to make women dissatisfied with their own bodies; this leads them to purchase the "beauty" product in the hope of looking and feeling better. But since the ideal is so extreme and unachievable, dissatisfaction quickly returns, and the woman is ready to buy more beauty products. Constant dissatisfaction with one's own body is the objective.

Ethical objections to these beauty ads include claims that they undermine women's self-confidence; that they cause anorexia and other serious eating disorders; that they distract women from family, careers, and other serious aspects of life; that the "beauty myth" drains women of energy and locks them into a stereotype that belittles the serious contributions they make; and that all this is a male power move that oppresses women. There is much debate about how many of these criticisms are true, but the fact that many women react so strongly against body image ads seems by itself to indicate that there is at least some problem. Some advertisers have listened to women and other critics, and other more realistic body types have become more common in advertising over the past few years. The accusation that such body image ads are unfair to women is mitigated by the fact that in the past 15 years or so more and more body image ads have been targeted at men. How men will be affected by this in the long run will not be clear for a generation. This trend may mitigate the gender fairness issue, but the other ethical issues are made twice as extensive. Of course, the idealized body image is different for men, but it is nearly as hard to attain; we may soon be seeing excessive steroid use for fashion reasons as the male equivalent of anorexia.

Self-identity image ads also raise the problem of false consciousness. Image ads try to create a consumer who desires products as symbols of his or her self-image. The individual is seen by defenders of advertising as a free and autonomous self who chooses to play the image game and chooses which self-image to project. But the autonomous self may be an illusion: The reality is (according to some) that people are not defined by consumption; they are defined by their role in the system of production. That the individual can choose a self-image is an illusion that would be shattered by the consciousness of the person's true alienated relationship to themselves and others. A young male may choose Marlboros, for example, as a symbol of ruggedness and independence, but reality is earning the money for the Marlboros by working in a fast-food franchise where he humbly takes orders from both his boss and the customers, adapts his every movement to a predefined time-and-motion system, and is forced to fake a smile on cue. The real self is his role as worker; the consumer self is an illusion created by the capitalist system through advertising precisely to prevent consciousness of reality. Defenders of advertising can reply that people's consumer self-image is just as real to them as the self-image they derive from their job. Though the consumer image game is pleasant, why should we assume it blinds people to their role in production? They may be well aware of it.

IMPACT OF ADS ON SOCIETY

Besides concerns about how ads affect individuals, critics have raised ethical issues about how advertising affects society. For example, J. K. Galbraith argued that advertising creates the desires that the production of consumer goods then satisfies. This dependence effect, in which consumer desires for goods depend on the process of creating the goods, undermines the usual ethical justification of capitalism based on consumer freedom of choice and the value of supplying people with the goods that they want. Others accuse advertising of creating a materialistic society full of people who think that happiness lies in owning things and who are obsessed with buying consumer goods. These critics think we are creating a society in which private goods are plentiful but in which public goods, which are seldom advertised, are ignored—a society rich in private cars but whose highways and streets are disintegrating. Ads drive selfish consumption at the expense of friendship, community, art, and truth. Furthermore, advertising allows the system to "buy off" politically unsatisfied people with promises and consumer goods, leading to political apathy and the undermining of democracy.

However, there are many who think these sorts of criticisms exaggerate the impact of ads on society. Schudson, for example, claims that advertising does not have much impact on society because it does not increase product-type usage; it only leads to brand switching and functions primarily as reminders to people who are already heavy users of a product-type. Major social changes are not caused by advertising; ads follow social trends, they do not create them.

This debate centers on two perhaps unresolvable issues. First, there is the empirical question of how much impact advertising has on society; this is difficult to answer because the effect of ads cannot be separated from other social forces, and because it is hard to determine whether ads cause or follow social trends. Second, there is the ethical question of whether the purported effects, such as materialism, are morally objectionable. Perhaps it is more helpful to look at specific issues rather than the social impact of advertising in general.

LIFESTYLE ADS: SEX AND VIOLENCE IN ADS

Some people object to ads that encourage sex, gambling, smoking, the consumption of alcohol, and other "vices." Even people who are not much concerned about such vices are still concerned that ads encourage *underaged* sex, gambling, smoking, the consumption of alcohol, and other vices. They believe that ads present bad role models. Advertising, some critics say, contributes to the moral breakdown of society because it presents ubiquitous images of unconstrained hedonism.

Ethical concerns about ads for gambling, tobacco, and alcohol are often legitimate. Products that are harmful and sometimes addictive raise ethical issues in themselves; encouraging the use of such products is even more questionable. Many countries and states limit, control, or even ban ads for some or all these products.

Violence in advertising would be ethically objectionable if there was much of it, but it is rare. The main exceptions are ads for films and video games, but objections in these cases should be aimed at the violence in the products, not just in the ads. The exposure of unsuspecting people and children to such ads is an issue that should be, and in many jurisdictions is, controlled by regulations on the placement of the ads.

Sex in advertising is a much bigger issue because there is so much of it. The ethical issues can be best seen if we separate consideration of sex in ads for products that are connected to sex from consideration of sex in ads where it is gratuitous and has no or only a tenuous connection with the product.

Ads for condoms and sex clubs, of course, emphasize sex. Except for puritans, the only ethical issue about these ads is making sure young children are not exposed. Other products, such as fashions, jeans, underwear, perfume, and chocolate, are related to sex, and advertising is often used to associate a product or logo with sex. Calvin Klein, for example, has built his business on making his clothes and perfumes sexy. Raising ethical objections to this is difficult unless one objects ethically to current sexual mores in most developed countries. Advertising did not cause our liberal attitudes toward sex; the sexual revolution was caused by the pill, penicillin, and other social forces. Any decrease of sex in advertising would probably not change society's sexual attitudes, so there is no ethical problem with Calvin Klein jeans, underwear, and perfume being thought sexy.

Sex is also used gratuitously in ads for products that have nothing directly to do with sex. We are all familiar with scantily clad women in ads for beer, cigarettes, cars, trucks, and vacation beaches. Note that for the most part these ads are aimed at straight males and use the stereotypical sexy woman—sexy, that is, in the minds and fantasies of straight males. Consider, for example, a two-page ad from a men's magazine that shows on the first page a woman with huge breasts, clad only in a bikini and posed in a sexually suggestive fashion. The copy asks if her measurements get the reader's heart racing. Turn the page and there is a pickup truck and the reader is asked to look at the truck's measurements. Horsepower, torque, and so on are listed. How do such ads work? Their ubiquity in men's magazines certainly suggests that they do sell cars, trucks, and beer. Such ads seem to say, "If you are a straight male attracted to big breasted women, you can prove it to yourself and others by buying our 'masculine' product." This interpretation presupposes that many straight males are very insecure about their sexual orientation and need to have their masculinity constantly confirmed by buying products with a masculine image. Is this manipulation of insecurities unethical? Perhaps not; straight males are generally capable of freely choosing to buy or not buy these products.

A more serious ethical objection to such ads is the attitude toward women that they imply and encourage. Women in these ads are being used as sex objects. One does not have to be a radical feminist to be concerned about the effects that exposure to thousands of such ads might have on straight men. It does not encourage them to see women as intelligent, productive, and competent individuals. Perhaps the vast majority of straight males are not greatly affected individually, but it does set a social tone about what are acceptable attitudes toward women. And the few men who take the objectification of women as sex objects seriously sometimes commit extremely unethical actions.

ADVERTISING AND CULTURE: CLUTTER, APPROPRIATION, AND IMPERIALISM

Some critics of advertising are deeply concerned about the impact of advertising on our culture. Many of these criticisms are not so much about ethics as they are about aesthetics and taste, but some raise genuine ethical concerns.

Ads clutter our culture. Outdoor ads are unsightly, commercials interrupt television programs and sports, jingles jam the airwaves, and magazines seem to be nothing but ads. And ads are creeping everywhere. Clutter and ad creep raise two issues: general concerns about the ubiquity of ads and concerns about ads creeping into specific places such as public schools.

The ubiquity of ads certainly raises aesthetic issues, but in itself is not an ethical problem. Most ads are placed in media that people can choose to use or not. Magazines, newspapers, television, and radio can be avoided if a person wishes, and there are ad free news sources and alternatives to most media. Outdoor ads cannot be avoided, but their unsightliness is and should be a matter for local bylaws. Ad creep will not increase the impact of advertising on the consumer or society. The psychological wall we all have that blocks out ads is only made stronger by more ads. In terms of advertising impact, more is less. It is the lack of impact of advertising that is forcing advertisers to place more and more ads.

There are, however, specific places that many feel should be ad free. These include religious institutions, government buildings, and schools. The first is a private matter for the institution. Policy on placing ads on government property should be decided democratically. Ads in schools, on the other hand, raise ethical issues. School attendance is compulsory and so the audience for the ads is trapped; school pupils are children or adolescents so they may be vulnerable; the ads are shown in an educational environment so children may find it hard to discount their message; and finally, the peer pressure and groupthink inevitable in classrooms may dramatically increase the impact of ads. However, as long as schools are underfunded, schools will be tempted to accept advertising. Any solution to the ethical concerns about ads in schools will have to be enacted democratically.

Ads appropriate images from cultures and history, using them for the private gain of the advertiser. For example, perfume ads have used images of the beautiful

"Indian princes"; motorcycles and cigarettes have used the "Indian brave" with feathers or a headdress as a symbol of masculinity. Is it ethical to use cultural symbols and images such as this? If an ad does use such a symbol, do they have any obligation to historical accuracy, or are faux simulacra acceptable? The peoples who created these symbols and images in the first place are generally not able to trademark or copyright them. Asking permission is often not an option; it is frequently not possible to identify whom to ask. One possibility that would minimize the ethical concerns would be to refrain from using cultural symbols if people from the relevant culture object. Images that do not receive complaints could be used; the Scots, for example, seem to like the kilted curmudgeon who sells malt whiskey. This approach requires a certain amount of cultural sensitivity on the part of corporations and a willingness to pull ads if they offend, even if those offended are not consumers of the product advertised.

Some critics complain that advertising is a form of American cultural imperialism. It is true that American advertising images such as Ronald McDonald and Coca-Cola are a large part of globalization, but European and Japanese corporations advertise worldwide too, and Chinese, Indian, and other cultures will be playing much larger roles in the future. Also, the dominance of American images is partly caused by the desire of many people for these images; Coca-Cola is advertised in many countries because the people there are eager to buy the product. In fact, it is this local popularity of American symbols and products that make some people in other cultures feel threatened. Some Italians and French may think that liking McDonald's food shows bad taste compared with liking their traditional foods, but the fact that McDonald's offends some people does not make it unethical to promote a popular symbol or product. Interfering with people's free choice by, for example, occupying or destroying restaurants raises more ethical issues than does advertising foreign products.

ADVERTISING TO VULNERABLE GROUPS

Children and some people in the Third World are especially vulnerable to manipulation by advertising. Furthermore, we are all vulnerable to subliminal techniques if subliminal advertising works.

Children are vulnerable to advertising because they do not understand the purpose of ads; cannot tell ads from the rest of their environment; cannot separate fantasy from reality; find it difficult to control their emotions; do not understand finances, takeoffs, and deferred gratification; and do not have the psychological wall that blocks most ads in adults. Some people defend ads aimed at children by pointing out that young children cannot themselves buy most of the products advertised; they have to ask their parents who can and should make rational decisions on the child's behalf. But this defense leaves out advertising's intentional and conscious use of the "nag factor." Ads are designed (with verification using focus groups) to get children to whine and nag their parents for the advertised products. This technique tends to undermine the rationality of parental decisions, and it causes unhappiness in both parents and children, which is unethical on utilitarian grounds.

Some jurisdictions, such as Quebec and some European countries, ban altogether television or other advertising aimed at children. Many others ban only images that might be traumatic to children, such as sex and violence, or try to control the use of fantasy by insisting ads be realistic. Some people advocate also banning ads for products that might harm a child, calling, for example, for bans on junk food ads during children's programs. Ethically, corporations ought at least to stay within the law, but should also consider the impact of their ads on children's happiness and welfare.

Advertising to people in those Third World countries in which advertising is not a traditional part of their culture and who are not used to advertising yet can raise special ethical issues. These issues can be aggravated if the population targeted by the ads is illiterate, uneducated, and lacking in freedom and empowerment. A good example is the advertising campaigns Nestlé used in Africa that featured images of Caucasian "doctors" and "nurses" advocating the use of Nestlé baby formula in place of breast-feeding. The ads exploited the target market's illiteracy and lack of familiarity with advertising and its purpose, but the ethical issues in this case went beyond this; the ads were deceptive in that Western medical opinion did not support the use of formula feeding in the Third World. But the most serious ethical problems arose because of the consequences of the use of baby formula; it exposed the infants to malnutrition, disease, and contaminated water. International agencies claimed many babies died as a result. This case makes clear that using advertising to exploit people's vulnerabilities puts an ethical obligation on the advertiser to ensure that no harm results.

Subliminal ads are ads that the target market cannot see, hear, or otherwise be aware of. For example, if a movie theater flashes "Drink Brand X Soda" on the screen so fast no one can perceive it, this is an attempt to manipulate people below their level of consciousness; as such, it tries to subvert rational decision making and so is unethical. Key's book titled *Subliminal Seduction: Ad Media's Manipulation of a Not So Innocent America,* popular in the 1970s, claimed that this technique was common and that large numbers of people were being brainwashed by it. Since then, experiments have failed to show that subliminal advertising works, and it is unlikely that it was ever widely used. Notwithstanding that, many legal jurisdictions have banned it.

Subliminal ads should not be confused with suggestive ads. As an example of a suggestive ad, consider a magazine ad that shows a couple passionately embracing in the background; in the foreground is a long cylindrical bottle of men's cologne obviously suggestive of a phallus. This is not subliminal; the viewer can clearly see what is going on. (In case the viewer needs confirmation, the letters "man's co. . . ." disappear strategically around the side of the bottle.) Suggestive advertising is not inherently unethical since there is no evidence that it manipulates below our level of awareness or that it subverts rationality.

ADVERTISING AND THE NATURAL ENVIRONMENT

Advertising affects the natural environment in three ways: ads use resources; some ads encourage destructive activities; and ads always encourage consumption, never nonconsumption.

Although radio ads and television commercials use a minimum of natural resources, print ads such as newspaper ads and inserts, flyers, and direct marketing mailings use vast amounts of paper. However, pulpwood for paper is a renewable resource if forests are harvested sustainably, and paper can be recycled, so reduced usage may not be ethically required. What is required is a sustainable paper industry, but is this the ethical responsibility of the advertisers? If advertisers insist on print media using sustainable paper supplies, the pulp industry would be hugely affected in a positive way. But the grounds for saying this is that the advertiser's ethical responsibility are not clear unless, of course, the advertiser claims to be an environmentally friendly company.

Some ads encourage activities destructive to the environment, such as the multitude of SUV ads that idealize off-road driving. Ethically, it is questionable whether advertisers should use such images. Sometimes, a negative environmental impact is inherent in the product advertised; for example, flying to the Caribbean on a vacation package uses petroleum, a nonrenewable and polluting natural resource. In such cases, environmental concerns should concentrate on the product, not just the advertising. What actions should be taken about such products is greatly debated, but the ads do not interfere with environmentalists who choose, for example, to vacation nearer home. Nor do they interfere with such environmentalists advocating this course of action to others.

Finally, critics of ads point out that consumer advertising always promotes consumption; reduced consumption is never advertised except occasionally by some advocacy groups that never have the money to compete with large corporations. Even government advocacy ads tend to emphasize recycling rather than reduced consumption; reduced consumption threatens jobs, taxes, and the economy. Environmentalists argue that, ethically, the developed countries ought to reduce their level of consumer consumption. Perhaps this is true, but the ethical responsibility cannot lie with the individual advertisers because they would be at a potentially fatal competitive disadvantage if they stopped advertising. This is a social and cultural problem that should only be changed by citizens through democratic processes and changes of their own behavior.

CORPORATE CONTROL OF THE MEDIA

Advertising critics claim that advertising gives corporate advertisers too much control of the programming and editorial content of the media; advertising biases mass media news coverage, and as a result, the media in North America only present what is in the interests of corporations for people to believe. For example, cigarette advertisers for decades threatened to and did pull their ads from any magazine or newspaper that carried articles on the health risks of cigarettes. Most magazine advertisers ask for advanced information on articles in the issues their ads will appear in; their ads are pulled if any article might create negative associations with their products.

Defenders of advertising do not deny that corporations sometimes withdraw ads or threaten to; they argue that corporations have a right to select where they advertise, and a fiduciary duty to shareholders and other stakeholders not to jeopardize the image of the corporation or its products. It can also be pointed out that newspapers and magazines that do not rely on corporate advertising are available to those who choose them; their subscription price is, of course, much higher (compare, e.g., the subscription prices of *Time* or *Newsweek* with the *Guardian Weekly*), but if people choose to be free of corporate influence they cannot expect to benefit from the subsidy that advertising gives much of the media.

IN DEFENSE OF ADVERTISING

The volume of criticism of advertising can make us lose sight of possible ethical defenses. Besides the economic role of advertising mentioned above, it can also be pointed out that advertising gives us information, introduces us to new products, presents us with images we can enjoy, creates symbols that allow us to express ourselves, subsidizes our media, and promotes human freedom by presenting to us vast numbers of products from which we can freely choose what we want to buy. Those who want to ban or strictly regulate all advertising should remember that advertising is a form of expression and that freedom of expression is a basic human right recognized in the UN Declaration of Human Rights and most national constitutions. However, that should not prevent the regulation of ad techniques or placements that cause specific harms. Those who worry about advertising should consider Schudson's point that ads are targeted primarily at people who are already heavy uses of a product-type and that the purpose of most advertising is not increase product-type usage, only brand switching. Ethical objections to ads have to make a case about specific ads on grounds of harm, viewer vulnerability, subversion of rationality, or plain dishonesty.

—John Douglas Bishop

Further Readings

Bishop, J. D. (2000). Is self-identity image advertising ethical? *Business Ethics Quarterly, 10*(2), 371–398.

Brenkert, G. (1998). Marketing to inner-city blacks: Powermaster and moral responsibility. *Business Ethics Quarterly, 8*(1), 1–18.

Goodrum, C., & Dalrymple, H. (1990). *Advertising in America: The first two hundred years.* New York: Harry N. Abrams.

Leiss, W., Kline, S., & Jhally, S. (1986). Social communication in advertising: Persons, products and images of well-being. New York: Methuen.

Mikkelson, B., & Mikkelson, D. P. (2002, August 18). *Subliminal advertising.* Retrieved October 21, 2005, from www.snopes.com/business/hidden/popcorn.asp

Schudson, M. (1984). Advertising, the uneasy persuasion: Its dubious impact on American society. New York: Basic Books.

Shields, V. R. (2002). *Measuring up: How advertising affects self-image.* Philadelphia: University of Pennsylvania Press.

Twitchell, J. B. (2000). *Twenty ads that shook the world.* New York: Three Rivers Press.

Williamson, J. (1978). Decoding advertisements: Ideology and meaning in advertising. London: Marion Books.

Wolf, N. (1990). *The beauty myth.* Toronto: Random House.

Advertising Ethics

PUBLIC RELATIONS ETHICS

The ethical issues of public relations arise because public relations is not just a set of techniques to disseminate information. There is always a perceptual objective to be achieved, and ethical dilemmas abound in how that objective is achieved.

Codes of ethics exist within the public relations profession at various levels—in trade associations (The Public Relations Society of America, The Council of Public Relations Firms, the International Association of Business Communicators, etc.), in public relations agencies, and within the public relations departments of companies. Except in the specialized area of government relations, there are few laws that govern how public relations professionals go about their objective of persuasion. Enforcement of codes is sporadic, and sanctions are few. The codes that exist cover a variety of issues (protecting confidentiality, avoiding cultural offense, financial management), but three areas remain ethically ambiguous: (a) truthfulness of information, (b) relations with the media, and (c) motivation of third-party support.

TRUTHFULNESS OF INFORMATION

The public relations industry makes a variety of statements about a commitment to supply information that is accurate and honest and known not to be false. Some of these statements go further to require that public relations professionals make an effort to confirm the accuracy of the information they are communicating and to correct any misinformation that is transmitted.

The ethical gray areas include what might be termed "lying by omission" or "being factually correct while leading to a misimpression." In both cases, there may be a commitment to "telling the truth" but perhaps not the whole truth. Indeed, only a slice of the truth might be presented, and this might be done in a fashion that knowingly leads the audience to a conclusion that they might not have reached if they had the "full story."

Such activities are very common in public relations (as they are in marketing), since public relations can involve "spin"—that is, finding the best thing to say and avoiding discussing the negatives. In some cases of regulated communications, such as FDA regulation of pharmaceutical information, there are both guidelines and a watchdog over this parsing of the truth. But even with regulation, the line between acceptable and unacceptable can be muddy.

RELATIONS WITH THE MEDIA

The public relations profession has a symbiotic relationship with the media. Public relations people want their messages and stories in the press, and journalists need information and access.

In some parts of the world, direct payments to journalists for press coverage are a matter of course. In most countries, however, such "pay-for-play" practices are forbidden by the ethical codes of the media. However, there are some subtle distinctions in what *pay* may mean. Many—but not all—media outlets forbid reporters from accepting any travel reimbursement or entertainment from a company or an agency. But reporters can be invited to speak at conferences, sometimes for honoraria; and moonlighting reporters have been known to accept writing or video-editing jobs through companies that they own.

Most media also create an institutional barrier between their desire to sell advertising to a company and the company's desire for good media coverage. Nonetheless, many public relations professionals know when purchasing of ads will help with favorable coverage, and many media are now offering advertising in "special issue sections" (e.g., a report on environmental issues) where advertisers also will get coverage.

In early 2005, a major industry scandal erupted when a syndicated "columnist/commentator" received a government contract for his advertising firm to help explain a government program. The work also included speaking well of the program as a commentator. While the controversy led to apologies and the discussion of new rules for government public relations contracts, the practice is not rare. Various experts who widely comment through their own columns or TV appearances as specialized reporters (e.g., "our travel reporter") have contracts with companies to provide favorable comment. No disclosure of these relationships is required by public relations codes of practice.

The 2005 scandal also led to a focus on video news releases (VNRs) issued by government agencies. A VNR is designed to be a fully produced news segment that a TV news show can simply slip into its news program. It includes a "reporter," who may or may or may not appear on camera, and some government VNRs may include an "interview" with a senior government official that is actually a scripted appearance. In the 2005 controversy, reform proposals ranged from forbidding government-produced VNRs altogether (even for important public information programs) to requiring a visual disclosure on the entire tape. Government has no ability to require such disclosure on VNRs produced by the private sector.

THIRD-PARTY SPOKESPEOPLE

Many public relations efforts involve motivating third parties (e.g., respected experts, happy consumers, celebrities, or interest groups) to carry a message to the media or directly to the intended audience. This may involve simply finding such people and encouraging them to make their views known. At the other end of the ethical spectrum is the paying of spokespeople, preparing and training them, writing their words, and "pitching" them to the media, all without disclosure of who is providing this support.

Strategies can also include the support of "coalitions," which are essentially front groups that will buy advertising, serve as spokespeople, and sometimes lobby a particular issue. Such support can include the re-creation of such groups or providing special grants to existing nonprofit groups to support specified activities on behalf of the company. Sometimes these relationships are publicly disclosed, sometimes not.

Disclosure is usually the ethical remedy suggested for these third-party practices, since it seems to be acceptable to pay a spokesperson or provide a VNR or even have a financial relationship with a business owned by a journalist if these relationships are fully disclosed. To date, however, the public relations industry— and some in the media industry—have resisted such a "sunshine" approach since the effectiveness of numerous public relations tactics would be greatly reduced if the mechanisms behind them were revealed.

—Jim Lindheim

Further Readings

Caywood, C. L. (1997). *The handbook of strategic public relations and integrated communications.* New York: McGraw-Hill.

Public Relations Society of America. (2000). *PRSA member code of ethics.* New York: Author.

White, J., & Mazur, L. (1994). *Strategic communications management.* Cambridge, UK: Addison-Wesley.

PART VII: Ethics of Advertising, Marketing, and Public Relations

APPENDIX A

Problematic Practices

SUGGESTED PAIRINGS TABLE*

Problematic Practices	Related Entries
Archer Daniels Midland	Sustainability Ethics of Management Ethical Issues in Pricing
Enron Corporation	Corporate Governance Ethics of Finance
Ethics and the Tobacco Industry	Adverting Ethics Consumer Rights Sustainability
Ford Pinto	Consumer Rights Utilitarianism
Merck & Co.	Corporate Social Responsibility Corporate Social Performance Consumer Issues
Nike, Inc.	Employee Protection & Workplace Safety Legislation Employee Rights Movement
Triangle Shirtwaist Fire	Employee Protection and Workplace Safety Legislation Employee Rights Movement
Tylenol Tampering	Consumer Protection Legislation Consumer Rights

---

This correlation table provides suggested pairings between the problematic practices that follow and the entries that appear throughout the text, so that instructors have an idea of which concepts are illustrated in the problematic practices entries.

ARCHER DANIELS MIDLAND

ounded in 1902 and incorporated in 1923, Archer Daniels Midland (ADM) is one of the largest agricultural processors in the world. It supplies many of the inputs for agricultural production, buys the crops from the field, processes them into food for humans and animals, fuels, and chemicals, and sells them all over the economy—and lobbies, very successfully, to obtain and retain the legislation that makes the entire operation profitable.

It *is* profitable. In the fiscal year ending June 30, 2005, ADM reported net earnings of $1,044 billion, or $1.59 per share, compared with $495 million, or $0.76 per share, in the previous year. Profits were up in Europe, South America, and Asia. So the board of directors declared a cash dividend of $0.085 per share on the company's stock—ADM's 315th cash dividend and 295th consecutive quarterly payment, 73 years of uninterrupted dividends. Clearly, they are doing something right.

In addition to being profitable, ADM tries to be environmentally friendly, and often succeeds. In the same fiscal year, ADM won two United States Environmental Protection Agency Presidential Green Chemistry Awards for a way to reduce volatile toxins in paints and a way to lower trans fats and oils in vegetable oils.

It is not always easy to be good. ADM stands at the heart of an enormous network of companies and activities, owning or controlling the entire agricultural enterprise through direct ownership or joint ventures with other companies. Its position entails that it controls the entire food chain, from the decision on what to plant, from the seed, through the machine that plants the seed and the pesticides and herbicides that help that seed to prosper, through the tending and harvest of the crop, through all processing and distribution of the products, to the very shelf in the supermarket (or repose in the chuckling fat of the fast-food French fries cooker). In the course of its vertically integrated enterprises, it is often difficult to discover the market price of a product that, for instance, is created from crops on an ADM farm and immediately sent back to another ADM farm to feed hogs. Just such a product is lysine, a corn-based dietary supplement for farm animals that is widely used across several countries. Yet it turns out to be possible for one to cheat, and price fix, on this product, for that's just what

ADM was caught doing in 1996; they ended up paying a record fine of $100 million for price-fixing. That wasn't the end of their problems: Two years later the government brought separate criminal charges against three top executives for conspiring in the crime, collected more fines, and sent the executives briefly to jail. Later, the European Union added its own penalties; in all, ADM had to budget over a quarter of a billion dollars for all expenses connected to the price-fixing incident.

ADM has maintained its agenda in Washington largely through very generous political contributions to both parties, amounting to some $2 million per year. A large part of its Washington lobbying agenda has been to urge, as the petroleum resources decline, the adoption of a provision requiring that ethanol should be a part of every gas station and oil reform. (The concern for oil scarcity has a lot to do with the fact that ethanol is produced from corn; at this point ADM controls more than 50% of the ethanol capacity in the world.) Conservatives and liberals alike have objected to this huge subsidy, but it continues.

—Lisa H. Newton

Further Readings

Archer Daniels Midland [Web site]. Retrieved September 17, 2005, from www.adm world.com

Lieber, J. B. (2000). Rats in the grain: The dirty tricks and trials of Archer Daniels Midland, the supermarket to the world. New York: Four Walls Eight Windows.

Thompson, P. B. (1995). The spirit of the soil: Agriculture and environmental ethics. London: Routledge.

ENRON CORPORATION

E nron Corporation's December 2, 2001, Chapter 11 reorganization filing was the largest bankruptcy in history, until it was exceeded in 2002 by WorldCom. Enron, headquartered in Houston, Texas, had grown quickly into a superficially giant and well-regarded company. It rapidly collapsed following the sudden disclosure of massive financial misdealing, which revealed the company to be a shell rather than a real business. During 2001, Enron stock fell to about $0.30—an unprecedented collapse for a blue-chip stock.

The Enron scandal helped propel passage of the McCain-Feingold Bipartisan Campaign Reform Act of 2002 (March). While Enron was neither the biggest nor the most important source of political funds, it had been active in making political contributions and attempting to influence legislators. Part of the Enron scandal involved political connections to President George W. Bush (former governor of Texas) and Vice President Dick Cheney (formerly CEO of a Texas-headquartered company). In May 2005, a U.S. appeals court dismissed a related lawsuit against the vice president on the grounds that an administration must be free to seek confidential information (including Enron) concerning energy policy.

Enron, quickly followed by WorldCom, helped propel the Sarbanes-Oxley Act of 2002 (July), the most significant change in U.S. securities laws since the early 1930s. As shocking as the sudden bankruptcy of a blue-chip company was, the subsequent revelations were worse: The traditional U.S. corporate governance watchdogs—attorneys, auditors, and directors—had either aided and abetted the responsible executives or been grossly negligent in the supervision of those executives. The United States and several other countries were rocked by multiple revelations of corporate scandals that ultimately also included analysts; auditors; banks; brokerages; mutual, hedge, and currency trading funds; and the New York Stock Exchange.

ARROGANCE, CORRUPTION, GREED, AND RUTHLESSNESS

Enron was not the first or the last or the largest of the corporate scandals in recent years. Nevertheless, Enron became, above all other companies, the emblem for management fraud, director negligence, and adviser misconduct. Enron is easily the most widely studied and best documented of the recent corporate frauds. Enron was a prolonged media event.

The high education levels and intelligence of Chairman Kenneth L. Lay (Ph.D. in economics), CEO Jeffrey K. Skilling (Harvard MBA and top 5% Baker Scholar), and CFO Andrew Fastow (Northwestern MBA) raised serious questions about business school treatment of ethics and law. In January 2005, the documentary movie *Enron: The Smartest Guys in the Room,* based on Bethany McLean and Peter Elkind's 2003 bestseller of the same name, premiered at the Sundance Film Festival in Utah. Spring 2005 releases took place in Austin and then Houston. The theme of the book and the movie is that smart guys can outsmart themselves as well as everyone else.

The most astonishing aspect of the Enron scandal was that a significant number of executives had engaged in improper actions despite the company having in place the key elements and best practices of a comprehensive ethics program. There was a detailed 64-page "Code of Ethics" with an introductory letter from Chairman Ken Lay and a "Statement of Human Rights Principles" together with a sign-off procedure on the code for each employee, an internal reporting and compliance system, visible posting of corporate values (banners in the headquarters building, signs in the parking garage, and so forth), and an employee-training video—*Vision and Values*—discussing ethics and integrity. Enron issued a 2000 annual report on corporate responsibility. The "Code of Ethics," like other Enron paraphernalia, was later auctioned on eBay. The Smithsonian Institution reportedly obtained a copy of the code for its permanent collection.

The publicized "values" of Enron were respect, integrity, communication, and excellence. The real "ethical" climate at Enron was a combination of arrogance (or hubris), corruption, greed, and ruthlessness. The gap between words and deeds at Enron was dramatic. This gap suggests that it is not particular corporate governance devices that matter most but the probity and integrity of individuals in relationship to the ethical climate within a company.

The executives were arrogant in attitude and conduct. The company strategy was one of revolutionizing trading by breaking traditional rules. The "vision" at Enron was to become the world's leading energy company—in reality, by any means necessary. There were rumors of sexual misconduct by executives. Expensive vehicles and power-oriented photogenic poses were commonplace.

The weight of evidence suggests that the lure of wealth had suborned the corporate governance watchdogs. It turned out that the directors must have been asleep at the switch or mesmerized by the rising stock price. It turned out that the external attorneys and auditors could not afford to lose such a successful client. Enron executives did not hesitate to bully the external safeguards, such as analysts, when and if necessary. A corruption machine was at work, whether intentionally or inadvertently.

In the 1987 film *Wall Street,* the character named Gordon Gekko announces that greed is good. Enron—whose logo became known as "the Crooked E"—epitomized that slogan. Greed is a morally disturbing paradox at the heart of the market economy. Bernard Mandeville, in the *Fable of the Bees, or Private Vices, Publick Benefits* (1714), argued that individual vices and not individual virtues produce public benefits by encouraging commercial enterprise. An economic actor engages in selfish calculation of interest or advantage. This consequentialist perspective emphasizes outcomes over intentions or means. The Enron executives carried this perspective to its logical extreme. Adam Smith's telling criticism in *The Wealth of Nations* of the East India Company's personnel suggests that he would hardly be surprised.

The company culture embodied ruthlessness toward outsiders and insiders alike. Skilling emphasized a process of creative destruction within the company. The rank and yank system of employee evaluation by peer review, reportedly installed by CEO Skilling, annually dismissed the bottom 20% of the employees—and perhaps corruptly rather than objectively. It has been reported that traders were afraid to go to the bathroom because someone else might steal information from their trading screen. In such a culture, no one would report bad news. In such a culture, individual achievement was everything and teamwork was nothing. Enron culture emphasized bonuses, hardball, take no prisoners, and tacit disregard for ethics and laws.

THE RISE OF ENRON

Ken Lay, then CEO of Houston Natural Gas, formed Enron in 1985 by merger with InterNorth. Lay had worked in federal energy positions and then in several energy companies. He was an advocate of free trade in energy markets and had experience in political influence peddling. Enron was originally involved in transmission and distribution of electricity and natural gas in the United States. It also built and operated power plants and gas pipelines, and similar industrial infrastructure facilities, globally. Allegedly, bribes and political pressure tainted contracts around the world—most notoriously a $30 billion contract with the Maharashtra State Electricity Board in India.

Jeff Skilling was a senior partner at McKinsey & Co. and in the later 1980s worked in that capacity with Enron. Skilling joined Enron in 1990 as chairman and CEO of Enron Capital & Trade Resources. In 1996, he became president and COO of Enron. The company morphed into an energy trading and communications company that grew to some 21,000 employees, and its stock price rose to about $85. Enron grew to the seventh largest publicly listed company in the United States. Strategy emphasized bold innovation in trading of power and broadband commodities and risk management derivatives—including highly exotic weather derivatives. Trading business involved mark-to-market accounting in which revenues were booked, and bonuses awarded, on the basis of effectively Enron-only estimates of the value of contracts. *Fortune* magazine named Enron "America's Most Innovative Company" for five consecutive years (1996–2000). Enron made *Fortune*'s "100 Best Companies to Work for in America" list in 2000. The company's wealth was reflected in an opulent office building in downtown Houston. Business school cases on Enron's business practices and culture were circulated for teaching purposes. Skilling served briefly as CEO of Enron from February to August 2001. Then, he abruptly resigned from Enron and Lay took over as CEO.

THE FALL OF ENRON

Following the bankruptcy filing, there were multiple investigations, including one commissioned by the Enron board of directors and directed by William C. Powers Jr., dean of the University of Texas at Austin's law school. The U.S. Department of Justice announced (January 9, 2002) a criminal investigation of Enron, and various congressional hearings began (January 24, 2002). The hearings also revealed the role of Sherron Watkins, a certified public accountant, who had warned Lay about Fastow's offshore devices after Skilling suddenly resigned. Watkins's experience helped propel into law the whistleblower protection elements of the Sarbanes-Oxley Act. The investigations emphasized two key matters, revealing how Enron had been built as an empty house of cards.

Enron was deeply involved in manipulating the California energy crisis. John Forney, a former energy trader, was indicted in December 2002 on

11 counts of conspiracy and wire fraud and pled guilty. Tape recordings revealed Enron traders on the phone asking California power plant managers to get a little creative in shutting down plants for repairs. Forney was a *Star Wars* fan. His "Death Star" strategy involved shuffling energy around the California power grid to generate state payments relieving congestion. Death Star deliberately created congestion. He named other devices JEDI (Joint Energy Development Investments) and Chewco (after the character of Chewbacca).

The other key revelation concerned CFO Andrew Fastow's creative use and alleged partial ownership of offshore special purpose entities (SPEs) or limited partnerships. These devices separated debt from revenues and kept mark-to-market losses off Enron's books temporarily. Fastow had been a *CFO Magazine* award for excellence winner. Fastow was indicted (November 1, 2002) on 78 counts, including fraud, money laundering, and conspiracy. He and his wife, Lea Fastow, former assistant treasurer of Enron, accepted a plea agreement (January 14, 2004) in exchange for testifying against other Enron defendants. Mr. Fastow received a 10-year prison sentence and a loss of $23.8 million; Mrs. Fastow received (for income tax evasion charges in concealing Mr. Fastow's gains) a 5-month prison sentence and 1 year of supervised release, including 5 months of house arrest. The Enron board had waived conflict of interest rules in its own Code of Conduct to permit Fastow to oversee some of these SPEs. Most important were the "Raptors" (after *Jurassic Park* creatures) or "LJM1" and "LJM2," named for Fastow's wife and two children. It was alleged that Fastow had engaged in unauthorized self-dealing and benefited directly from these supervised devices.

The Enron bankruptcy resulted in the criminal conviction for obstruction of justice and, thus, forced auditing license surrender of its auditor Arthur Andersen, which collapsed. The audit partner assigned to Enron, David Duncan, pled guilty to ordering large-scale destruction of work documents. Some 28,000 Arthur Andersen employees had to find other employment. On May 31, 2005, the U.S. Supreme Court unanimously overturned the firm's conviction on grounds that the trial judge's jury instructions were too vague and broad. Federal prosecutors decided in November 2005 not to retry the case. Duncan was allowed to withdraw his guilty plea, although other charges could be filed against him.

As of July 2005, there had been 16 guilty pleas and six convictions (one thrown out) in the Enron cases. Former Merrill Lynch bankers and Enron executives were convicted in the Nigerian barge trial. (One executive was found innocent.) Nonexistent barges (to be built) were flipped between Enron and

Merrill Lynch to generate paper profits and bonuses. In July 2005, three former executives of Enron Broadband Services (EBS) were acquitted of some charges; the jury deadlocked on other charges against them and two other defendants. The charges had argued intentional overpromotion of EBS's value. The judge dismissed the remaining charges against all defendants. In November 2005, a special grand jury issued three streamlined indictments against the five codefendants. Skilling was indicted in February 2004 and Lay in July 2004, both on multiple counts. Both pled not guilty; their trials had not commenced as of November 2005. The prosecution wanted to try with Lay and Skilling the former chief accounting officer of Enron Rick Causey. He had pled not guilty to more than 30 charges of fraud. He was indicted in January 2004.

EMPLOYEES AND SHAREOWNERS

Enron's bankruptcy had serious effects for many individuals and organizations. The Houston Astros paid Enron $5 million to rename Enron Field as Astros Field, subsequently changed to Minute Maid Park. *Playboy* (August 2002) featured a pictorial "The Women of Enron." David Tonsall, former Enron employee, became rapper "N Run" (i.e., Enron and "never run") on a December 2003 CD *Corporate America.*

Shareowners lost virtually everything. Several employees lost their jobs and their life savings that they had invested in Enron stock. Like former Arthur Andersen employees, former Enron employees may have damaged résumés. The Enron bankruptcy reorganization was a lengthy affair under a new management and bankruptcy examiner. The state of California is attempting recovery of monies from various parties. Eventually, shareowners and employees may begin partial financial recoveries from various parties, including banks and insurance companies. As of November 2005, Citigroup had settled for $2 billion, J. P. Morgan Chase for $2.2 billion, and the Canadian Imperial Bank of Commerce for $2.4 billion. These figures represent the largest securities class-action settlement on record, and there are still a number of other prominent defendant banks remaining. The U.S. bankruptcy court finalized a settlement in May 2005 of about $3,500 on average for more than 20,000 current and former employees (about $69 million total). Civil lawsuits are still proceeding against Lay, Skilling, Enron, and others. The directors of Enron (and WorldCom) personally paid damages.

—Duane Windsor

Further Readings

Berenson, A. (2003). *The number: How the drive for quarterly earnings corrupted Wall Street and corporate America.* New York: Random House.

Brewer, L., & Hansen, M. S. (2002). *House of cards: Confessions of an Enron executive.* College Station, TX: Virtualbookworm.com.

Bryce, R. (2002). *Pipe dreams: Greed, ego, and the death of Enron.* New York: PublicAffairs.

Cruver, B. (2002). *Anatomy of greed: The unshredded truth from an Enron insider.* New York: Carroll & Graf.

Eichenwald, K. (2005). *Conspiracy of fools: True story of the Enron scandal.* New York: Broadway Books.

Enron traders caught on tape [Electronic version]. (2004, June 1). *CBS Evening News.* Retrieved from www.cbsnews.com/stories/2004/06/01/eveningnews/main620626.shtml

Fox, L. (2003). *Enron: The rise and fall.* New York: Wiley.

Fusaro, P. C., & Miller, R. M. (2002). *What went wrong at Enron: Everyone's guide to the largest bankruptcy in U.S. history.* New York: Wiley.

Holtzman, M. P., Venuti, E., & Fonfeder, R. (2003). Enron and the raptors [Electronic version]. *CPA Journal.* Retrieved from www.nysscpa.org/cpajournal/2003/0403/features/f042403.htm

Jaedicke, R. K. (2002). The role of the board of directors in Enron's collapse. In *Hearing before the House Committee on Energy and Commerce, Subcommittee on Oversight and Investigation.* 107th Congress, testimony of R. K. Jaedicke, Enron Board of Directors, Chairman of Audit and Compliance Committee.

McLean, B., & Elkind, P. (2003). *The smartest guys in the room: The amazing rise and scandalous fall of Enron.* New York: Portfolio.

Persons of the year—The whistleblowers: Cynthia Cooper of WorldCom, Coleen Rowley of the FBI, Sherron Watkins of Enron. (2002, December 30, to 2003, January 6). *Time, 160*(27).

Rapoport, N. B., & Dharan, B. G. (Eds.). (2004). *Enron: Corporate fiascos and their implications.* New York: Foundation Press.

Smith, R., & Emshwiller, J. R. (2003). *How two Wall Street Journal reporters uncovered the lies that destroyed faith in corporate America.* New York: HarperBusiness.

Swartz, M. (with Watkins, S.). (2003). *Power failure: The inside story of the collapse of Enron.* New York: Doubleday.

Watkins, S. S. (2003). Ethical conflicts at Enron: Moral responsibility in corporate capitalism. *California Management Review, 45*(4), 6–19.

ETHICS AND THE
TOBACCO INDUSTRY

Health advocates assert that tobacco is the first or second leading cause of preventable death among humans, contributing to cancer, lung disease, and coronary heart disease, among other ailments, and that the addictive properties of cigarette ingredients prevent smokers who desire to quit from doing so. While cigarettes are the primary culprit, other tobacco products, such as cigars and pipe tobacco, are potentially equally or even more dangerous, but because they are less prevalent, they do not pose public health risks on the same scale as cigarettes. Smokeless (chewing) tobacco is said to cause other health problems, such as mouth cancer. The risks of tobacco use are not limited to users of tobacco, since carcinogens, or cancer- causing agents, can be passed on to others through second-hand smoke and from a pregnant or nursing mother to her child; cigarette smoking contributes to an inordinate share of building and house fires, and the health care costs associated with tobacco are borne by the public at large. As a result of these health and economic risks, governments and nongovernmental organizations have increasingly treated tobacco as a public health hazard and have sought to economically impair the tobacco industry through aggressive regulation and litigation, thus reducing its harmful impact.

For decades, the big tobacco companies sought to downplay the health risks of tobacco products and categorically to deny claims that their products were addictive. In stark contrast to the health realities, various brands of cigarettes were associated through advertisements with social sophistication and glamour, friendship, rugged outdoorsmanship, recreation, and, generally, the good life. Historically, tobacco's place in society was more complex, a traditional pleasure among the native peoples of the Americas transported by explorers to Europe and then by commercial sailors to the Middle East and Asia. In these regions, tobacco took hold among the populace but received a mixed reception among political and religious leaders, who saw it as a pagan vice. As the global market for tobacco grew, however, its economic value became clear, and it became a key commodity grown and exported by

European settlers in the southern United States as well as an exotic import from afar, hence the even contemporary references to "Turkish" and "Oriental" leaf and the famous Camel brand with images of the Near East. After industrialization, tobacco became an important enough commodity for political interests to coalesce to defend it from its detractors, for if big tobacco were suddenly to falter, the consequences for tobacco-dependent economic actors would be potentially catastrophic. At stake were the livelihoods of low-paid field laborers, high-paid executives, and those within the supply and distribution chains that linked them. Also at stake were an aesthetic view promoted by proponents of the smoking lifestyle and the search among researchers and developers for the perfect flavor. In recent years, faced with mounting regulatory pressure and litigation, big tobacco companies have become more transparent about the health risks and have been exploring new forms of innovation in product development and social responsibility to prop up their increasingly perilous economic reality. Fascinatingly, and possibly too late to flourish again, the tobacco industry has both been the target of the full range of ethical criticism that can be directed at business and demonstrated the potential for business to engage more constructively in the ethical debate on whether there is a place for dangerous products in the good life.

ETHICAL CRITICISM OF THE TOBACCO INDUSTRY

The ethical criticism directed at the tobacco industry begins with the fact that its products are unhealthy, whether or not consumed in moderation. While other consumer goods pose risks to consumer well-being—for example, household cleaners may contain hazardous chemicals; prepared snacks may be high in sodium, fat, or sugar; and consumer electronics pose modest dangers to the laypersons who install them—the direct costs to individuals and the associated external costs to society of smoking cigarettes are perceived by critics to disproportionately outweigh any compensating benefits. Used as directed, cigarettes are high-probability, high-impact risks that are not only fundamentally unsafe but even more unsafe the more they are used.

In a free society, consumers generally are perceived to have the right to "choose their poison," but another ethical concern posed by cigarettes is that consumers may not have unfettered choice. Critics have charged that in the past decades, tobacco companies concealed evidence about the health risks of their products; manipulated studies to understate those risks; adjusted product formulae to increase the potency of nicotine, an addictive ingredient; and publicly denied that their products were addictive to fend off public concern and oversight by drug regulators. Not only were consumers making decisions about smoking based on incomplete information; those smokers who wished to quit were in effect incapable of free choice while battling addiction. The concern for consumer choice is even more pronounced with minors, who, even with complete information available to them, may make irrational choices when bombarded with advertisements that speak louder of the attractiveness of the smoking lifestyle than volumes of less accessible scientific data speak of the risks. Critics have further charged that advertising in sports venues inaccurately implies that cigarettes can be integral to a healthy lifestyle and that using cartoon characters as spokespersons specifically encourages youth to smoke. Until the early 1990s, tobacco representatives commonly took the position that restrictions on advertising restricted free speech, but this debate has for the most part been settled in favor of substantial restrictions as a matter of public interest.

Less unique to the tobacco industry but relevant nonetheless is the vulnerability of tobacco products to counterfeiting, in which inauthentic products bear name brand packaging, and the gray market, in which authentic products are purchased inexpensively in one market and subsequently diverted to be sold at below-market prices in a more expensive market. Cigarettes are vulnerable to these schemes in part because price gaps are significant from market to market due to varying regulatory practices and tax premiums and partly because the per unit price is reasonably high relative to the physical size and weight of the product. While tobacco manufacturers may not accept responsibility for these business practices, critics have charged them with complicity and with keeping suspect company. Another affair in which tobacco's role was too coincidental to ignore concerned the leveraged buyout of the tobacco giant RJR Nabisco in 1988, in which some company executives sought personal financial windfalls that would have entailed actions that were of dubious value to the company and the well-being of its employees. This episode occurred at the tail end of a decade in which investment bankers and junk bond traders rose and fell and prefigured the accounting scandals of the turn of the next century, in which executives benefited at the apparent expense of other stakeholders.

CONSTRAINTS ON INDUSTRY GROWTH

At the heart of the tobacco controversy is the question of whether the mere fact of consumer demand for cigarettes justifies the continued supply. This economic question has been answered in the affirmative to justify the market for firearms, pornography, violent entertainment, and other ironically labeled consumer "goods." The question includes consideration of manufacturers' and marketers' potential moral obligation to attempt to shape consumer perceptions regarding what will promote social well-being. While most free market theorists would contend that companies taking on such a moral obligation would smack of paternalism, tobacco companies have nevertheless, through marketing and advertising campaigns, shaped consumer perceptions regarding the place of cigarettes in the good life. Critics have suggested that in doing so they have kept the demand for cigarettes artificially high by allowing nicotine addiction to perpetuate consumer dependence on them and by withholding data that would allow consumers to make informed choices.

Because tobacco products have been part of the fabric of social relations and consumer habits since well before the health risks were documented, they bred cultural dependence among consumers, which led to economic dependence among suppliers. In the recent heyday of the industry's growth, spanning the third quarter of the 20th century, this economic dependence was rather a matter of economic flourishing, with Philip Morris, RJR Nabisco, British American Tobacco, and some of their lesser-known competitors among the United States' and the world's most financially successful corporations, enjoying brand visibility, strong margins, a solid consumer base in developed countries, and prospects for continued growth in untapped markets. The ubiquitous availability of cigarettes in large retail outlets, convenience stores, restaurants, and vending machines—anywhere the multipack-a-day consumer could obtain them to satisfy the need—required a complex supply, distribution, and sales network that could get the cigarette from the tobacco fields to the space between the smoker's second and third fingers. Consumers' smoking habits supported, among others, growers and harvesters, processors, truckers and shippers, paper suppliers and packagers, advertisers and marketers, warehousers, sales agents, and retailers—from grocers to gas station clerks to restaurateurs, who stood to pocket more when diners who smoked lingered at the table longer, ordering a few extra drinks.

An extension of the economic argument in support of the tobacco industry has thus been that any interference in this complex economic system would have unintended, harmful consequences for all these actors. To illustrate the complexity of this system, consider that tobacco farmers long benefited from governmental subsidies and that debate over the continuation of those subsidies was complicated by the fact that ending them might actually increase tobacco production (to compensate for lower margins with higher quantity) and lower prices (leading to increased consumption). However, in recent decades, regulation of the tobacco industry, especially in the United States, has accelerated, catching up with and finally surpassing the rate at which the tobacco companies envisioned their own expansion.

This regulation includes taxes and tariffs on tobacco products, which have grown to the point that as much as 80% of the cost of a pack of cigarettes in countries such as Denmark and Portugal and routinely more than half the retail price in many developed countries including the United States goes to government entities. The justification for such high taxes includes the argument that high product costs deter excessive smoking and the right of the government to recover costs that it will inevitably have to incur for the provision of health care. Also, the demand for cigarettes among young people has been demonstrated to diminish significantly with price increases. Historically, however, the tobacco industry has argued, to little sympathy, that these taxes were discriminatory since smokers are on average poorer than nonsmokers and thus spend a disproportionate amount of their income to support their habit. Notably, the percentage of the retail price that goes to taxes tends to be substantially lower in less prosperous countries.

As far back as 1954, personal injury litigation in the United States has cited adverse health effects caused by the tobacco industry, but until the 1990s, such litigation was largely unsuccessful given the relative inconclusiveness of scientific data and the imbalance of legal resources brought to the cases by the tobacco companies in comparison with what individual plaintiffs could afford. However, by the mid-1960s, the antitobacco movement took an important, if isolated, step forward when in the wake of a surgeon general's report on tobacco health risks, the Federal Trade Commission (FTC) instituted a new rule that finally resulted in warning labels appearing on cigarette packs and advertisements concisely affirming the risks posed by the product. The tobacco companies contended that if tobacco products posed any dangers, then they were no different from many other consumer goods that pose dangers to those who use them, but the FTC countered that there were no safe levels of cigarette consumption.

Tobacco companies continued with a united front to balk in the absence of conclusive clinical evidence in support of the surgeon general's claims, appealing to an age-old philosophical debate over whether any scientific evidence can ever properly be deemed conclusive, denying first the apparent link between tobacco and lung cancer and eventually the apparent link between nicotine and cigarette addiction. Despite this resistance, the report was seminal in opening the door to new regulatory strategies requiring tobacco companies to take actions, such as disclosure of risks, seemingly contrary to their own interests. Concern for the welfare of minors later resulted in regulatory proposals to restrict the placement and content of cigarette advertisements. Notwithstanding the written warnings on their products, tobacco companies continued to challenge their validity in other forums, but by the 1980s, the FTC had approved a rule requiring rotating written warnings on cigarette packages and ads that somewhat more explicitly depicted the direct and indirect risks of cigarettes to consumer, including fetal, health. In 1993, when the Environmental Protection Agency declared smoke to be a carcinogen, it was clear that the industry was increasingly subject to the scrutiny of multiple regulators. Nevertheless, as recently as 1994, tobacco executives summoned to testify before Congress uniformly denied that cigarette smoking was addictive and were successful, at least temporarily, in stonewalling the Food and Drug Administration's (FDA's) attempts at appropriate regulatory oversight of tobacco. But the increasing tide of public concern and class action personal injury litigation led finally to a breaking of the ranks among the leading producers of tobacco, so that in 1996, Liggett, then the smallest of the five major tobacco companies in the United States, settled health claims with several states and publicly admitted the deadly potential of tobacco use. These and other developments culminated in the historic Master Settlement Agreement of 1998 (MSA) between participating manufacturers and 46 state attorneys general and six U.S. territories (the other states were covered in separate agreements). Among other provisions, the MSA spelled out restrictions on the placement and content of advertisements, particularly restricting any venues and branding characters that would appeal to young people; lobbying activity; cigarette pack sizes; merchandising; and other activities that in effect seek to expand the consumer market for tobacco products. In addition, the MSA contained provisions for public access to information; the establishment of a national foundation for further coordinated public education and study on tobacco health risks; and payments for Medicaid reimbursement—the original focus of the MSA, thus illustrating the enhanced power of litigation to twist the arm of big tobacco. Once again, however, unintended consequences have caused an ironic intersection of interests, as state budgets for even non-health-related expenditures have benefited from the influx of tobacco industry funds, which would dissipate if the industry were to collapse.

The incentive for tobacco companies to enter into a settlement so evidently contrary to their interests was to reduce the litigation burden and potential share price volatility associated with fighting numerous similar cases, but the MSA has not led to a cessation in litigation against the tobacco industry within the United States. Internationally, there are few, if any, legal systems as conducive to class action and product liability litigation as that of the United States, so while the momentum for legal action against tobacco companies has not waned, there remain questions about the extent of the international threat to tobacco industry interests. The 2005 World Health Organization Framework Convention on Tobacco Control has sought to provide model instruments for its 168 signatory countries to enact legislation to reduce the demand for tobacco products through price and nonprice measures and also to reduce its supply by inhibiting illicit trade activities and sales of tobacco to minors.

Local interests have also sought action against tobacco, as demonstrated by the 2003 ban in New York City on tobacco use in all workplaces and most public venues, such as restaurants and bars, which as a sign of the times stimulated more copycat legislation than did a similar 1985 ban in Vail and Aspen, Colorado. Whereas bars were once a smoker's haven and restaurant space was long governed by an imaginary demarcation between smoking and nonsmoking sections, smoking is now increasingly a private activity, or when done in public, it is relegated to places such as sidewalks, where the space between smokers and nonsmokers is less simple to define. Well before the New York City legislation in bars and restaurants, smoking was banned from other public spaces, such as airplanes, and many workplaces.

Investors have further punished tobacco companies through nonlegal means by filtering tobacco stocks out of so-called socially responsible investment funds. Along with alcohol, defense contracting, gambling, and firearms, tobacco industry stocks are routinely classified as "sin" stocks, which are excluded from socially responsible investing (SRI) portfolios. While SRI capital continues to be a relatively minor proportion of the overall investment capital, that proportion is gradually increasing and represents yet another squeeze on tobacco companies' operating margins.

PREVENTING ASPHYXIATION

Far from eliciting sympathy for tobacco companies, the pressures from outside
that seem to be contributing to the slow and painful asphyxiation of the
tobacco industry—witness the 50% reduction in smoking rates among men in
the United States, Canada, and the United Kingdom between 1960 and 2001—
are increasingly being applied to other consumer goods. Increasing consumer
consciousness of health and wellness has led to legislation demanding clearer
labeling on the nutritional content of foods and beverages. Packaged consumer
goods manufacturers have had to comply with good manufacturing practices
to ensure product safety from food-borne disease and potential allergen con-
tamination. Restaurants have come under formal and informal demands to use
healthy ingredients or to disclose the presence of trans fats in meals. Such
pressures have spawned self-regulation, such as voluntary action by soft drink
manufacturers and marketers to restrict school sales and serving sizes of high-
calorie, low-nutrition products.

These developments have their roots in the experience of the tobacco industry and its often innovative but ultimately futile attempts to resist adaptation to
social norms regarding two fundamental ethical questions. First, to what extent
do consumer goods manufacturers have moral obligations to support the well-
being of consumers beyond the economic laws of supply and demand? For a
long time, tobacco companies advanced a pure economic argument in defense
of their product, while critics gradually restricted the applicability of that argument to adults who were free to choose, a dwindling population. Second, what
should be the standard for truth telling and disclosure when scientific certainty
about the effects of product consumption is unattainable? Again, tobacco companies' defense proved only temporarily effective as scientific certainty about
tobacco-induced health risks drew ever closer.

As the ethical risks to the tobacco industry have increasingly become economic realities, tobacco companies have resorted to other forms of innovation to
improve corporate performance. One step has been product innovation, which
began with the introduction of filters in the early1950s, matured with the availability of so-called lite (low tar, low nicotine) product varieties, and more
recently has manifested itself in the pursuit of the smokeless cigarette. While
filters arguably made cigarettes marginally less unhealthy, lite cigarettes have
been the target of litigation contending that companies essentially set forth
deceiving claims about their relative safety for consumer health, and smokeless

cigarettes struggle to provide the same satisfaction to consumers who choose to smoke. Another form of product and marketing innovation has been to develop cigarette varieties and advertising campaigns aimed at a specific consumer demographic, though this approach has been criticized for preying on less well-informed consumers. Likewise, producers have sought to prioritize international growth, since regulation on tobacco products outside the markets in developed countries is not typically as restrictive and consumers may be less well-informed. This has continued to spawn seemingly disingenuous advertising and marketing practices, in which tobacco companies have complied with restrictions in developed countries while handing out free cigarettes in promotions in less regulated markets. Pursuing such growth, however, has proved risky as real-time media coverage has increased the risk to the reputation of companies seeking to hawk their wares to unsuspecting consumers while disapproving investors look on. Meanwhile, the introduction of measures such as the 2005 World Health Organization Framework Convention on Tobacco Control has helped international regulators catch up. Another corporate strategy has seen cycles of diversification and disaggregation. With the introduction of other packaged consumer goods into their product portfolios, tobacco companies were able to reduce the risk of concentration and volatility to which they were vulnerable when they were exclusively dependent on tobacco, while leveraging economies of production and distribution scale since food products and tobacco products are often sold in the same retail venues. However, those economies have waned as tobacco has been perceived at times as dragging down the food side of the business, or vice versa, as tobacco purists have argued that tobacco companies would do best to focus on their core customers.

Perhaps even more interesting to watch has been the innovative transformation of some tobacco companies into odd paradigms of corporate social responsibility. It is no longer unusual for tobacco companies to promote and undermine their own interests simultaneously, making their products available to those who choose to use them while offering help and comprehensive information to customers who seek to quit and actively engaging in youth smoking prevention initiatives. Interested in preserving the stability of market share among a dwindling pool of smokers, in some cases tobacco companies have come to invite regulators such as the FDA in rather than continuing the fight to keep them out. Long engaged in active lobbying of politicians, big tobacco now manages its reputation through corporate support for the arts, education, and other community-building initiatives. Not wanting to shed the heritage of foreign royalty and American presidents, who were active in the tobacco business, and unable to deny a history of nonparticipation in constructive debate about health and the public interest, tobacco companies have increasingly sought to refresh their image with a balanced approach to perpetuating the industry. This approach recognizes that (addiction aside) there are still and may always be individuals who enjoy smoking and have a right to do so, while it appears to accept accountability for creating a framework for compliance and social responsibility that encourages open dialogue to put the decision to smoke in the hands of the consumer. While there continue to be skeptics regarding the sincerity of this approach, in theory it addresses the fundamental ethical questions challenging the tobacco industry and other consumer goods manufacturers and marketers. It remains to be seen whether the tobacco industry is sustainable in the broad sense of the term—socially, since its products are harmful to the health of its target consumer; environmentally, as its products originate from the soil and subsequently pollute the air with carcinogens; and economically, while the verdict on its financial performance remains in doubt.

What is beyond reasonable doubt is that there are many lessons to be learned by all industries from the experience of the tobacco industry: first, that economic questions cannot be wholly emptied of ethical content; second, that the accelerating pace of information availability and regulatory sophistication will inevitably catch up with attempts to restrict adequate disclosure; and third, and a consequence of the other lessons, that the decision about what consumer goods are good for social well-being is not exclusively up to the manufacturer or its business partners, government regulators, or the individual consumer. What is good is not a simple question of right or wrong but must rather emerge as an outcome of constructive debate and continuing dialogue among all parties in pursuit of an elusive, uncertain conclusion.

—Christopher Michaelson

Further Readings

Carlyle, J., Collin, J., Muggli, M., & Hurt, R. (2004). British American Tobacco and Formula One. *British Medical Journal, 329*(7457), 104–106.

Collin, J., LeGresley, E., MacKenzie, R., Lawrence, S., & Lee, K. (2004). Complicity in contraband: British American Tobacco and cigarette smuggling in Asia. *Tobacco Control, 13*(Suppl. 2), ii96–ii111.

Feldman, E., & Bayer, R. (Eds.). (2004). *Unfiltered: Conflicts over tobacco policy and public health.* Cambridge, MA: Harvard University Press.

Gilmore, A., & McKee, M. (2004). Moving East: How the transnational tobacco companies gained entry to the emerging markets of the former Soviet Union—Part I: Establishing cigarette imports. *Tobacco Control, 13,* 143–150.

Kluger, R. (1996). *Ashes to ashes.* New York: Alfred A. Knopf.

Legacy Tobacco Documents Library, University of California, San Francisco [Web site]. Retrieved from http://legacy.library.ucsf.edu

MacKenzie, R., Collin, J., & Lee, K. (2003). *The tobacco industry documents: An introductory handbook and resource guide for researchers.* London: London School of Hygiene and Tropical Medicine.

Palazzo, G., & Richter, U. (2005). CSR business as usual? The case of the tobacco industry. *Journal of Business Ethics, 61,* 387–401.

Sloan, F., Ostermann, J., Picone, G., Conover, C., & Taylor, D. (2004). *The price of smoking.* Cambridge: MIT Press.

Smith, E., & Malone, R. (2003). Altria means tobacco: Philip Morris' identity crisis. *American Journal of Public Health, 93*(4), 553–556.

WHO Framework Convention on Tobacco Control. (2003). Retrieved November 25, 2006, from www.who.int

FORD PINTO

One of the best-known and infamous cases in corporate ethics and social responsibility involves the Ford Pinto. The case involved the decision by the Ford Motor Company during the 1970s not to recall its Pinto model, despite knowledge of a dangerous fuel tank design flaw and the potential loss of life that would result. It also involved, for the first time, charges that were brought against a corporation not just for negligence but for murder.

In 1976, Ford was the second largest manufacturer of automobiles, with revenues of $30 billion a year and net income of almost $1 billion. Due to concern over competition over subcompact vehicles from Germany and Japan, Ford President Lee Iacocca was determined to manufacture a car at or below £2,000 and for less than $2,000. Whereas normal development and production of an automobile takes more than three and a half years from start to finish, the Pinto was a rush project, beginning in 1968 and taking just over two years to reach the showrooms. As a result, engineering design decisions came after style decisions to a greater degree than normal. The Pinto's style required that the fuel tank be located behind the rear axle, leaving only 9 or 10 inches of "crush space" between the rear bumper and rear axle. In addition, bolt heads were exposed that were capable of puncturing a fuel tank on rear impact.

Crash tests revealed that when the Pinto was struck from behind at even slow speeds the fuel tank could be punctured, causing fuel leakage. Any stray sparks could then ignite the spilling gasoline, causing the car to become engulfed in flames. If the fuel tank design was to be modified however, or a rubber bladder installed, the vehicle could pass the rear impact test. The crash test information was forwarded to the highest levels of Ford management.

Despite being fully aware of this information, the company continued with the production of the Pinto and was able to justify the decision on the basis of several reasons. First, the company met all applicable federal safety standards. Second, the car was comparable in safety with other cars then being produced. Third, in the early 1970s consumers were more concerned with price than safety, leaving little incentive for firms to spend money promoting the safety of their vehicles. Fourth, changing the design would lead to little trunk space, an important selling feature for cars.

The fifth and most controversial reason for sticking with the design was based on a cost-benefit analysis conducted by Ford. An internal study suggested that it would be more cost effective to continue with the same fuel tank design rather than change it. The study indicated the cost to improve the design of all Ford vehicles using the flawed fuel tank to be $137 million ($11 per vehicle × 12.5 million vehicles), which was much greater than the cost to society of just over $49 million. Ford's estimate of the cost to society was based on a 1972 study by the U.S. National Highway Traffic Safety Administration, which estimated the cost of a human life to be approximately $200,000, with the cost of a serious burn injury being approximately $67,000. These amounts included categories such as future productivity losses, medical costs, property damage, legal costs, and employer losses. The amount of $49 million was based on the estimated cost to society of the expected 180 burn deaths (180 × $200,000), 180 serious burn injuries (180 × $67,000), and 2,100 burned vehicles (2,100 × $700).

Despite reported incidents of burning vehicles, Ford still decided not to recall the Pinto. In addition, the company managed to successfully lobby the U.S. government for 8 years not to implement a key government safety standard that would have required Ford to modify its fire-prone gas tank or even warn the public of the danger. Several high-profile deaths were reported in the media, and a civil suit was settled in 1978 when a jury awarded $125 million, later reduced to $6 million, for what the judge called Ford's callous indifference to human life. Following the death of three teenage girls in 1978, Ford went on trial in 1980 with the charge of criminal conduct, the first time a company experienced such a charge. It was only after the law became effective in 1977 that the Pinto was made with a rupture-proof fuel tank design. In 1978, Ford finally recalled all Pintos made between 1970 and 1976 and replaced the Pinto with the Ford Escort after 1980. Some estimate that more than 500 people died in burn deaths related to the Ford Pinto.

It's not clear whether Ford learned anything from the Pinto experience, based on its actions (or inaction) during the Ford Explorer versus Bridgestone/Firestone scandal in 2000 when many drivers and passengers died or were seriously injured due to rollovers and/or tire blowouts. Ford appears to have known of rollover problems for some time before taking any action and continued to blame Bridgestone/Firestone. On May 25, 2001, Ford placed advertisements in several newspapers such as *USA Today* signed by its CEO Jacques Nasser and Chairman Bill Ford stating that customer safety has always been and always will be their first priority. Based on the Ford Pinto case, however, many might suggest that Ford provided an example of a company that disregarded the safety of its customers out of concern for their bottom line.

—Mark S. Schwartz

Further Readings

Gioia, D. A. (1992). Pinto fires and personal ethics: A script analysis of missed opportunities. *Journal of Business Ethics, 11*(5/6), 379–390.
Velasquez, M. G. (1992). The Ford motor car. In *Business ethics: Concepts and cases* (3rd ed., pp. 110–114). Englewood Cliffs, NJ: Prentice Hall.

MERCK & CO., INC.

Merck & Co. Inc., a large U.S. public pharmaceutical company, has faced several important ethical and social responsibility tests over the years. Established in 1891, Merck discovers, develops, manufactures, and markets vaccines and medicines in more than 20 therapeutic categories. The company has approximately 60,000 employees and sells products in approximately 150 countries. Worldwide sales in 2005 were more than $22 billion. The firm has always had a "patient first" approach to doing business as indicated by George Merck, the son of the founder, who stated that Merck tries never to forget that medicine is for the people, not for the profits. This view is currently reflected in the company's values, which states that Merck's business is preserving and improving human life. Although the firm has faced many challenges, two of the more significant ethical and social responsibility issues confronted by Merck include whether to produce and distribute a drug to help cure river blindness and whether to recall its arthritis drug Vioxx.

In terms of the first major issue faced by Merck, river blindness is an eye and skin disease caused by a worm that is transmitted to humans through the bite of a fly. The baby or larval worms then move through the body migrating in the skin and the eye causing itching, severe skin disease, and after repeated years of exposure, blindness. Merck researchers discovered that it was highly likely that by spending tens of millions of dollars they could develop the cure for river blindness. The problem was that the millions of people afflicted by the disease lived in parts of the world (primarily Africa) where they could not afford to pay for the drug. Other pharmaceutical companies, foundations, governments, and health organizations were not interested in paying for the development of the drug. Other concerns related to the risk of side effects for humans that might then affect the sales of Merck's animal drug, or that the human drug might be diverted into the black market, undercutting sales of the animal drug. The company also risked creating a precedent both internally among its researchers and externally among the public that might be difficult to meet in the future in terms of developing other important drugs with little or no financial return expected.

Despite the costs and the risks, Merck, through the leadership of its CEO Roy Vagelos, decided to spend the money. The drug, known as Mectizan, was not only developed but also distributed by Merck for free for years beginning in 1987. The decision did end up having indirect financial benefits for the firm, which according to Dr. Vagelos related primarily to the recruitment of top researchers. In December 2002, the World Health Organization declared river blindness virtually eradicated as a world disease, with the program reaching 40 million people annually in more than 30 countries.

The second major ethical and social responsibility issue places Merck in a potentially more negative light. The issue involves what has been perceived as Merck's delayed decision to recall its arthritis drug Vioxx, despite apparent knowledge of numerous deaths caused by the drug. Merck pulled its $2.5 billion-a-year drug off the market on September 30, 2004, when a study indicated that it doubled the risk of heart attack and stroke in patients who took the drug for more than 18 months. The issue appears similar to that faced by A. H. Robins Company, which was eventually forced into bankruptcy in the mid-1980s after facing lawsuits due to its allegedly defective "Dalkon Shield" intrauterine birth control device.

Plaintiffs claim that Merck knew of the additional risk of heart attacks based on previous clinical studies, but failed to warn doctors and consumers of the risk. From 1999 to 2004, more than 20 million Americans took Vioxx. By the end of 2005, Merck faced close to 10,000 lawsuits in the United States. The firm is also being sued in Europe, Australia, Brazil, Canada, Israel, and Turkey. As of April 2006, Merck had already spent hundreds of millions of dollars to defend four cases, with two wins and two losses (with judgments against Merck for $253 million in Texas and $13.5 million in New Jersey). The company continues to refuse to pursue a global settlement and is appealing the cases it has lost. Some estimate that the company may have to defend more than 100,000 Vioxx lawsuits leading to possible liability of up to $50 billion (U.S.) for Merck, since epidemiologists estimate that 100,000 people might have suffered heart attacks because of the drug. It is still unclear how Vioxx will ultimately affect the future prospects of Merck, and whether Merck will be able to withstand the current legal assault.

—Mark S. Schwartz

Further Readings

Berenson, A. (2006, April 12). Merck jury adds $9 million in damages. *New York Times*. Retrieved from www.nytimes.com/2006/04/12/business/12vioxx.html

Bollier, D., Weiss, S., & Hanson, K. O. (1991). *Merck & Co. Inc.: Addressing Third World needs (A and B)*. Boston: Harvard Business School Press.

Merck Corporate. [Web site]. The Merck mectizan donation program. Retrieved from www.merck.com/about/cr/policies_performance/social/mectizan_donation.html

Merck Corporate. [Web site]. VIOXX information center. Retrieved from www.merck.com/newsroom/vioxx_withdrawal

Velasquez, M. G. (2006). *Business ethics: Concepts and cases* (6th ed.). Upper Saddle River, NJ: Prentice Hall.

NIKE, INC.

Nike, Inc. is a high-profile sporting goods and apparel company that engages in the design, development, and marketing of footwear, equipment, and accessory products worldwide under brand names such as NIKE, Cole Haan, Converse, Starter, Hurley, and Bauer. The company, which is headquartered in Beaverton, Oregon, sells its products through a mix of independent distributors, licensees, and subsidiaries in approximately 120 countries worldwide. Nike has experienced substantial financial and marketing success since its founding in the 1960s and is now the largest sporting goods company in the world (in terms of market capitalization). Despite its success, the company has been the target of much criticism in recent years for alleged abusive or "sweatshop" labor practices in its subcontractors.

Nike was founded as an athletic shoe company by Phil Knight and Bill Bowerman in 1962 under the name Blue Ribbon Sports. In 1972, the company changed its name to Nike, after the Greek goddess of victory. Knight had been a track athlete and business student at the University of Oregon, where Bowerman was his coach. While getting his MBA at Stanford, Knight devised a strategy for the manufacturing of athletic shoes overseas that would take advantage of lower-cost off-shore production capabilities. The plan was for Nike to be essentially a design, marketing, and distribution company with all the production performed by subcontractors operating overseas.

This strategy proved highly successful. Nike started subcontracting in Japan and then moved its sourcing operations to South Korea and Taiwan to take advantage of lower cost of production in these locations. As the economies of South Korea and Taiwan developed, Nike continued to move its sourcing operations to even cheaper locations such as China, Indonesia, and Vietnam.

In the fiscal year 2005, Nike had revenues of $13.7 billion and employed about 24,000 people directly and another 650,000 in more than 800 supplier factories worldwide. The company has operations in several locations including Oregon, Tennessee, North Carolina, and the Netherlands in addition to its Niketown and Nike Factory Store retail outlets. It has several subsidiaries: Cole Haan (casual luxury footwear and accessories), Bauer Nike Hockey

(hockey equipment), Hurley International (teen-oriented sports apparel for surfing, skateboarding, and snowboarding), Converse (athletic footwear), Nike IHM, Inc. (cushioning components used in Nike footwear), and Exeter Brands Group, which includes Starter and licenses other Nike brands. Nike became a publicly traded company in 1980, and its New York Stock Exchange ticker symbol is NKE.

One of the key components of Nike's strategy has been the use of celebrity athletes as endorsers for its products. Its endorsers have included some of the biggest names in sports such as Michael Jordan (after whom the famed "Air Jordan" shoes were named), Lance Armstrong, Tiger Woods, Kobe Bryant, and Jerry Rice.

In the late 1980s, Nike found itself at the center of controversy brewing over alleged sweatshop labor working conditions in its subcontractor factories in developing countries. Critics alleged that a number of labor-oriented problems existed in these factories including (1) wage and salary concerns—both the payment of low wages and the use of various schemes to cheat workers out of the wages to which they were entitled, (2) unsafe/unhealthy working conditions, (3) excessive working hours and forced overtime, (4) harsh and abusive disciplinary tactics, (5) the use of child labor, and (6) active opposition to unionization efforts by the workers. According to some critics, such as labor activist Jeff Ballinger, the opposition to unionization was the key concern because, it was reasoned, with effective union representation the other issues could be resolved.

Several incidents contributed to the notoriety Nike quickly acquired on these issues. There were several worker fatalities reported in Nike subcontractor factories in the early 1990s. In addition, reports started circulating of Nike's involvement with the use of child labor in its subcontractor factories. A picture purported to be of a child worker in a Nike subcontractor factory in Pakistan sewing soccer balls appeared in *Life* magazine in 1996. It was later learned that the photo was staged (soccer balls are sewn before they are inflated but the ball the child was holding had already been inflated). Nevertheless, Nike was perceived by the general public as a leading culprit in the exploitation of child labor. The company was lampooned in comic strips such as Doonesbury and by late night talk show hosts such as Jay Leno and David Letterman (e.g., one of the top 10 signs you are at a bad summer camp: you spend all day sewing swooshes on Nike sneakers). Critics also parodied Nike's "Just Do It" slogan by suggesting that Nike "Just Stop It."

There are several ironies related to Nike's strategy that contributed to the publicity this controversy received. The fact that Nike's shoes were high-prestige luxury items sold to well-to-do children (and sometimes not-so-well-to-do children) in the United States and other western countries contrasted sharply with working conditions being portrayed in the media and the perceived exploitation of child labor.

In addition, Jeff Ballinger, who had been working to organize Nike subcontractor factories in Indonesia in the late 1980s and early 1990s, was able to point out the disparity in the money Nike paid celebrity endorsers versus what workers were paid to make Nike shoes. In the August 1992 issue of *Harper's* magazine, Ballinger was quoted as saying that an Indonesian worker making Nike shoes in Java would have to work 44,492 years to make what Nike paid Michael Jordan in one year. This criticism was an example of how Ballinger and other critics were able to use Nike's celebrity endorsement strategy against the company. Although Ballinger would later concede that Nike was no worse than other firms in the industry, Nike's name became synonymous with the term *sweatshop labor* in the eyes of much of the general public.

Labor-affiliated critics of Nike's overall strategy and labor practices were concerned both with the loss of jobs to overseas production and what they referred to as a "race to the bottom." According to this line of argument, the exploitation of low-paid workers overseas in harsh working conditions put downward pressure on wages and working conditions of workers in the United States. Thus, it was both a matter of labor solidarity and self-interest that led union activists to criticize Nike's labor practices and to call for reforms.

The criticisms of Nike got traction on the nation's college campuses where chapters of Students Against Sweatshops began to form. Students and faculty involved began demanding to know who was making the college-branded gear (e.g., hats, sweatshirts, T-shirts) being sold in the college bookstores and under what conditions they were being made. About the same time, mid-1990s, a boycott of Nike products over sweatshop labor concerns began to pick up steam.

Both critics and supporters of Nike concede that Nike's problems were exacerbated by its initial response to the criticism. This was to disavow any responsibility for labor problems in its subcontractor facilities on the grounds that it did not make the shoes—they are made by its subcontractors. Nike subsequently enlisted former Atlanta Mayor and UN Representative Andrew Young to investigate its subcontractor factory operations in Vietnam. When a generally upbeat report was issued, Young was criticized for bias and sloppy research methods.

In November 1997, the *New York Times* stated that in an inspection report that was prepared for the company's internal use only, Ernst & Young wrote that workers at the factory near Ho Chi Minh City were exposed to carcinogens that exceeded local legal standards by 177 times in parts of the plant and that 77% percent of the employees suffered from respiratory problems. The article leaked several excerpts from this report that detailed the unsafe and unhealthy working conditions in Nike's factories.

While Nike was at the center of the controversy over alleged sweatshop labor practices, other firms and parties became embroiled in it as well. When morning talk show host Kathie Lee Gifford's line of clothing was criticized for being made with abusive labor practices, she investigated the allegations herself and confirmed some of the charges. Ms. Gifford then became an advocate for improving working conditions in the apparel industry.

As the criticism mounted regarding the use of sweatshop labor in the apparel and footwear industries, the federal government got involved. During the Clinton Administration, the White House convened a meeting of industry, labor, and activist representatives to address issues of sweatshop labor in the apparel industry. Originally called the Apparel Industry Partnership, this group came to be known as the Fair Labor Association whose purpose was to promote adherence to international labor standards and improve working conditions worldwide.

A turning point in Nike's response to critics was Phil Knight's appearance at the National Press Club in May 1988. In his speech, Knight conceded that Nike bore responsibility for conditions in its subcontractors' factories and that many of the critics' complaints about those factories were valid. Furthermore, he pledged to reform Nike's labor practices with respect to child labor, worker development, and safe working conditions. More specifically, Knight promised to raise the minimum age of all sneaker workers to 18 and apparel workers to 16, adopt clean air standards, advance microloans to workers, and expand its monitoring program. Following this speech Nike undertook a number of institutional changes to carry out Knight's promises. Notably, Nike changed its response to this controversy from defensive to proactive and began to take the lead in efforts to reform working conditions in poor countries. In addition, Nike has become more proactive in addressing criticisms of the company. Nike representatives have participated in forums at professional associations such as the Academy of Management and the International Association of Business and Society. Nike has also welcomed researchers into its factories and it has hosted college study abroad groups visiting countries in which its subcontractors operate. How much of this response was due to a sincere belief that the company had acted wrongly in the treatment of its sub-contractor workers and how much was due to business expediency to silence the critics is uncertain.

Nike is one of the first companies to publicly publish a list of its active subcontractors/suppliers in an effort to establish transparency and also to gain efficiency for monitoring and inspections by collaborating with other companies who use the same subcontractors. As of May 2005, Nike is also recognized by four institutions that gauge according to their own specific criteria whether a company should be considered a socially responsible investment. These are *FTSE4 Good Index Series, Dow Jones Sustainability Index, Ethibel Investment Register,* and *KLD Broad Market Social*^{SM} *Index.*

Furthermore, Nike has also published a 113-page Corporate Responsibility Report FY 04 freely available on its Web site. While the company painstakingly details its efforts at engaging its five most important stakeholders, namely consumers, shareholders, business partners, employees, and the community, it recognizes that for the future they need to focus on the following priority issues with respect to workers and factories: freedom of association; harassment, abuse, and grievance procedures; payment of wages; hours of work; environment; and safety and health. The report notes that its biggest challenge is in China, which accounts for 180,000 contract workers in more than 110 factories. China accounts for 36% of its manufactured footwear and has a large and fast-growing domestic market for Nike goods. However, upholding its code of conduct in China is a difficult problem for Nike due to local laws that prevent independent labor organizing. Several other problems exist, such as the lack of clarity about the law and its monitoring, falsification of information related to wages by factories, and social problems caused by temporary migration of workers from rural China to manufacturing provinces. Nike believes that engagement with its stakeholders, including the Chinese government, and building partnerships in China is the long-term solution to improving labor conditions there.

Because Nike has been so closely tied to the sweatshop labor controversy, the underlying debate about the ethics of sweatshop labor is particularly relevant to the Nike case. Many critics have argued that companies like Nike have a responsibility to see to it that their subcontractors provide better than market-derived or legally mandated wages and working conditions in their operations in developing countries. Others though have argued that if such companies were to do so, there would be less incentive to invest in these developing countries and the benefits of economic growth would be forfeited.

As of this writing, critics and supporters of Nike are still very far apart on the quality of working conditions and the extent of labor abuses in Nike sub-contractor factories. However, there does seem to be fairly widespread agreement that the criticisms leveled against the company have brought about an improvement in these conditions since the controversy started.

—Richard E. Wokutch and Manisha Singal

Further Readings

Arnold, D. G., & Bowie, N. E. (2003). Sweatshops and respect for persons. *Business Ethics Quarterly, 13*(2), 221–242.

Ballinger, J. (1992, August). The new free trade heel: Nike's profits jump on the backs of Asian workers. *Harper's Magazine, 285,* 46–47.

Maitland, I. (1997). The great non-debate over international sweatshops. *British Academy of Management Annual Conference Proceedings, September,* 240–265.

Nike homepage. Retrieved November 28, 2005, from www.nikebiz.com

Spar, D. L. (2002). *Hitting the wall: Nike and international labor practices.* Boston: Harvard Business School. (Original work published 2000)

Greenhouse, S. (1997, November 8). Nike shoe plant in Vietnam is called unsafe for workers. *New York Times,* p. A1.

Wokutch, R. E. (2001). Nike and its critics. *Organization & Environment, 14*(2), 207–237.

TRIANGLE SHIRTWAIST FIRE

The Triangle Shirtwaist Factory is best known as the site of a deadly fire that blazed for 18 minutes in the late afternoon of March 25, 1911. On the ninth floor of the Asch Building, which housed the factory just off Washington Square in New York City, hundreds of young women and girls were trapped by fire. Thirty or more workers jumped to their death on the pavement below, while more than 100 working girls burned on the factory floor. The resulting public outrage prompted the creation of the New York Factory Investigating Commission. This commission launched an era of remedial factory legislation.

Throughout the late 19th and early 20th centuries immigrant girls and women were recruited to work in the garment industry sweatshops. Italian, Jewish, Polish, and Slavic women worked long hours in these unventilated and minimally heated factories. Although female workers were actively recruited into the recently organized International Ladies' Garment Workers' Union (ILGWU), the founders of the union believed that women had neither the ability nor the commitment to sustain leadership roles in the union.

The garment industry was thriving as working women became eager consumers of ready-made clothing. As profit opportunities grew for factory owners, they cut wages, put more workers in smaller spaces, and introduced strict workplace monitoring to reduce pilferage and wasted time. Firsthand accounts of life in the factories describe them as cramped and filthy. In November 1909, a mass meeting of factory workers convened in New York to demand better wages and improved working conditions. When the male leaders hesitated to commit to a plan, a 15-year-old Ukrainian-born girl stood up and called on her fellow workers to strike. The response to her call began the Uprising of the Twenty Thousand.

Within 2 days, 20,000 to 30,000 factory workers in New York went on strike. The walkout quickly spread to Philadelphia and became an important milestone in the women's labor movement. For 3 months the workers picketed in the cold, withstanding the hardships of weather and lost wages in hopes of improved conditions, hours, and wages in the sweatshops. In February 1910, an arbitrated settlement was reached with most of the factory owners, although some refused to sign the agreement. One of these was the Triangle Shirtwaist Factory, where Clara Lemlich, the instigator of the Uprising, worked.

Triangle's ninth-floor factory rooms had inadequate fire escapes, no sprinklers, and exit doors locked from the outside to prevent worker theft of materials. When fire broke out, spreading quickly through hanging fabric and paper patterns, 500 women and girls were trapped inside. A few escaped by running to the roof, or getting the last run of the elevator downstairs, but many resorted to jumping out the windows, crashing to the ground as appalled observers watched. By night, 146 corpses were piled on the 26th Street pier.

In December 1911, the owners of the Triangle Shirtwaist factory went on trial for manslaughter. Despite enormous public outrage and grief, the all-male jury returned a verdict of not guilty, in response to the judge's insistence that the owners could only be found guilty if the jury believed that they knew the workshop exit door to the stairway was locked. However, over the subsequent 3 years, 36 new laws were enacted following the recommendations of the Factory Investigating Commission to reform the state labor code and mandate safer working conditions in factories. One commission member was Frances Perkins, who later became secretary of labor in the Roosevelt administration.

—Robbin Derry

Further Readings

Blewett, M. H. (1991). *We will rise in our might: Workingwomen's voices from nineteenth-century New England.* Ithaca, NY: Cornell University Press.

Fishback, P. V. (1987). Liability rules and accident prevention in the workplace: Empirical evidence from the early twentieth century. *Journal of Legal Studies, 16,* 305–328.

Kessler-Harris, A. (1982). *Out to work: A history of wage-earning women in the United States.* Oxford, UK: Oxford University Press.

McEvoy, A. F. (1994). *The Triangle Shirtwaist factory Fire of 1911: Social change, industrial accidents, and the evolution of common-sense causality* (ABF Working Paper #9315). Chicago: American Bar Foundation.

Perkins, F. (1946). *The Roosevelt I knew.* New York: Viking Press.

Stein, L. (1962). *The Triangle fire.* New York: J. B. Lippincott.

TYLENOL TAMPERING

One of the most significant examples of business ethics and corporate crisis management involved the actions of Johnson & Johnson (J&J) during the Tylenol tampering crisis. In the fall of 1982, a subsidiary of United States–based J&J, McNeil Consumer Products, learned that seven people in Chicago had died from taking Extra-Strength Tylenol capsules that had been laced with cyanide. The management was convinced that the tampering did not occur at its plants, meaning that it must have taken place once the product had reached Illinois. J&J faced a dilemma, how best to handle the crisis without damaging the reputation of the company, when the company had quickly established that it could not be held liable for the tampering.

Reports on the firm's decision-making process during the crisis indicate that the company placed the safety of its customers first, before considering profit implications. A nationwide voluntary recall took place, involving approximately 31 million bottles of Tylenol, representing more than $100 million in sales. Consumers were told not to use any type of Tylenol product until the cause of the tampering had been established. Production and advertising of Tylenol ceased. The company offered to exchange all Tylenol capsules that had been purchased for Tylenol tablets. Relations were quickly established with the Chicago police, the FBI, and the Food and Drug Administration (FDA). A toll-free crisis phone line was set up for concerned consumers. Senior executives, including CEO James Burke, were readily accessible to the media. As part of a longer-term response, the company reintroduced Tylenol capsules with new triple-seal tamper-resistant packaging. Despite the firm having its market share drop from 33% to 18%, it wasn't too long before the company was able to recover its position. Following a second tampering incident in 1986, J&J made the decision to offer Tylenol in a caplet form, as opposed to a capsule form. No one was ever convicted of the tampering incidents and subsequent deaths.

Probably the most significant aspect of how J&J handled the crisis was the apparent corporate culture that existed at the time. According to J&J executives, turning to the firm's credo enabled the firm to make the right early decisions that led to the comeback phase. The credo, initially written in 1943, stated that the firm had obligations to society beyond merely profit maximization or enhancing shareholder value.

As a direct consequence of the Tylenol murders, U.S. Congress approved in 1983 a new "Tylenol Bill" that made maliciously tampering with consumer products a federal offense. In 1989, the FDA set national requirements for all over-the-counter products to be tamper-resistant.

Unlike many other firms, which often fail to react quickly on discovering potential danger to their stakeholders, J&J is remembered as a company that possessed an ethical corporate culture enabling the firm to handle the Tylenol tampering crisis quickly, openly, and honestly. By doing so, J&J was able to protect and enhance its corporate reputation into the future.

—Mark S. Schwartz

Further Readings

Hartley, R. F. (2005). Johnson and Johnson's Tylenol scare: The classic example of responsible crisis management. In R. F. Hartley (Ed.), *Business ethics: Mistakes and successes* (pp. 303–314). Hoboken, NJ: Wiley.

Johnson, C. H. (1989). A matter of trust. *Management Accounting, 71*(6), 12–13.

Kaplan, T. (2006). The Tylenol crisis: How effective public relations saved Johnson and Johnson. In J. W. Weiss (Ed.), *Business ethics: A stakeholder and issues management approach* (pp. 89–96). Mason, OH: Thomson/South-Western.

Snyder, L., & Foster, L. G. (1983). An anniversary review and critique: The Tylenol crisis/reply. *Public Relations Review, 9*(3), 24–35.

APPENDIX B

Business Ethics Organizations

Center for Ethical Business Cultures

The Center for Ethical Business Cultures works to encourage current and future business leaders to build ethical cultures in their organizations and high standards of integrity in their communities.

http://www.cebcglobal.org/

Council for Ethical Leadership

The Council for Ethical Leadership is a worldwide association of leaders in business, education, and other professions working together to strengthen the ethical fabric of business and economic life. The Council identifies and responds to issues important for ethical economic practices and assists in the resolution of these issues.

http://www.businessethics.org/

Ethics Resource Center

ERC is a nonprofit, nonpartisan research organization, dedicated to independent research that advances high ethical standards and practices in public and private institutions.

http://www.ethics.org/

European Business Ethics Network

The European Business Ethics Network, EBEN, is the only international network dedicated wholly to the promotion of business ethics in European private industry, public sector, voluntary organizations, and academia.

http://www.eben-net.org/

Institute of Business Ethics

The IBE was established to encourage high standards of business behavior based on ethical values. The UK-based institute works to raise public awareness of the importance of doing business ethically and collaborate with other UK and international organizations with interests and expertise in business ethics.

http://www.ibe.org.uk/

Institute for Global Ethics

The Institute for Global Ethics is dedicated to promoting ethical behavior in individuals, institutions, and nations through research, public discourse, and practical action.

http://www.globalethics.org/

International Association for Business and Society (IABS)

IABS is a learned society devoted to research and teaching about the relationships between business, government, and society.

http://www.iabs.net/

International Business Ethics Institute

The International Business Ethics Institute focuses on fostering global business practices to promote equitable economic development, resource sustainability, and just forms of government.

http://www.business-ethics.org/

Society for Business Ethics

The Society for Business Ethics (SBE) is an international organization of scholars and others interested in the field who are engaged in the academic study of business ethics.

http://www.societyforbusinessethics.org/

APPENDIX C

Business Ethics Periodicals

This appendix presents a selected guide to periodicals that are for researchers, practitioners, and the interested layperson. The reader seeking articles on business ethics will find a number of significant research journals and annual series. In addition, there are many trade magazines (those read by primarily businesspeople) and popular press sources. Other "born digital" resources, such as online-only journals, society newsletters, and Web sites also may be useful, peripherally. The publications discussed here are primarily English language, although their contents may be international in scope. Also highlighted are the electronic databases currently most effective for finding articles in these periodicals and the few research-related born digital resources.

CORE ACADEMIC JOURNALS

Relatively few academic journals are devoted to business ethics and cover a full range of topics and methodological approaches associated with the field. Generally, the three publications doing both are the field's core journals *Journal of Business Ethics, Business Ethics Quarterly,* and *Business & Society.* Their readership predominantly consists of theorists and practitioners.

All three contain articles that are theoretical, empirical, or literature reviews. Other regular features include book reviews, thematic issues, conference announcements, and calls for papers. The publishers' Web sites for these three journals offer free e-mail alerts for the tables of contents of each new issue, as do several of the other journals mentioned later in this appendix.

Journal of Business Ethics (JBE) began in 1982 as a quarterly, but has expanded to seven volumes per year (28 issues), with a circulation of approximately 7,500 institutional subscriptions worldwide. Its audience is academics and anyone else interested in business ethics topics. From 1997 to 2003, articles that focused on education were published separately in *Teaching Business Ethics* (ISSN 1382–6891, Kluwer). Currently, this topic is reincorporated into *JBE*. Similarly, the *International Journal of Value-Based Management* (ISSN 0895–8815, Kluwer, 1988–2003) became integrated into *JBE*. (ISSN 0167–4544; Springer; URL: http://springer link.metapress.com/openurl.asp?genre=journal&issn=0167-4544)

Business Ethics Quarterly, launched in 1991, is the official publication of the Society for Business Ethics and has a paid circulation of more than 1,050. Six to twelve double-blind peer-reviewed articles appear per issue. The intended audience is researchers, teachers, and business practitioners who are interested in conceptual and methodological aspects of business ethics, especially those approaches that address international business, economics, and values. (ISSN 1052–150X, Philosophy Documentation Center; URL: www.pdcnet.org/beq.html)

Business & Society: A Journal of Interdisciplinary Exploration has appeared quarterly since 1960 and presently has a circulation of more than 700. This official publication of the International Association of Business and Society focuses on social issues in management and business ethics. The articles address ethics and values, business-government relations, corporate governance, environmental management, and international issues. In addition to research and book reviews, it provides relevant dissertation abstracts. (ISSN 0007–6503, Sage; URL: http://bas.sagepub.com)

OTHER SCHOLARLY JOURNALS

Since business ethics research is often interdisciplinary in nature, many useful articles appear in the periodicals of other fields. Also, material can be found in journals that focus entirely on a single topic within the field of business ethics. Below is a selected list of significant peer-reviewed journals of both kinds, presented in alphabetical order. Which titles among them are most important depends on the reader's focus and research interests. Some of the most highly regarded research titles among this group are *Academy of Management Review, Business & Society Review, Business Ethics: A European Review,* and *Organization Science.* Typical supplemental contents are conference announcements and book reviews.

Academy of Management Review, a highly regarded management journal, has appeared quarterly since 1976 and features a number of articles each year on ethics-related topics. In addition to research, book reviews, and announcements, there is a Publications Received list. (ISSN 0363–7425, Academy of Management; URL: http://aom.pace.edu/amr)

Business & Professional Ethics Journal, published quarterly since 1981, contains articles that compare professions or cover ethics topics in areas like marketing, health care management, human resources, and global labor. Half of the issues reprint selected papers from international conferences. More recently, the journal has appeared irregularly and incorporates the publication *Professional Ethics* (ISBN 1063–6579, 1992–2004). (ISSN 0277–2027, University of Florida Center for Applied Philosophy and Ethics in the Professions; URL: www.ethics.ufl.edu/BPEJ)

Business and Society Review: Journal of the Center for Business Ethics at Bentley College has appeared quarterly since 1972. Each issue has about a dozen articles by academics and practitioners that contain scholarly research, commentary, policy analysis, or book reviews. Some issues are thematic. (ISSN 0045–3609, Blackwell; URL: www.blackwellpublishing.com/journals/BASR)

Business Ethics: A European Review is considered a top business ethics journal by many, appearing quarterly since 1992. It covers current issues and emerging concerns, from a European perspective, on topics related to the ethical practices of corporations and individuals. The audience is academics and businesspeople. (ISSN 0962–8770, Blackwell; URL: www.blackwell-synergy.com/loi/beer)

Corporate Governance: An International Review (CGIR), produced bimonthly since 1992, publishes research on trends in the development and improvement of organizations' governance, boards, and directors. *CGIR* frequently includes articles about ethics-related issues. (ISSN 0964–8410, Blackwell; URL: www .blackwellpublishing.com/journals/CORG)

Corporate Governance: The International Journal of Business and Society, published five times a year since 2001, includes articles on real-world performances of boards and CEOs and corporate social responsibility. Articles are research, policy analysis, or case studies, occasionally gathered into thematic issues. (ISSN 1472–0701, Emerald; URL: www.emeraldinsight.com/cg.htm)

Corporate Reputation Review: An International Journal, appearing quarterly since 1996, produces articles on reputation management, highlighting best practices and current trends. Article treatments include research, case and industry studies, and policy analysis. (ISSN 1363–3589, Palgrave Macmillan; URL: www.henrystewart.com/corporate_reputation_review)

Electronic Journal of Business Ethics and Organization Studies, is an online journal published in Finland, semiannually since 1996. It contains research, primarily in English, and is open access (free to readers) online. (ISSN 1239–2685, University of Jyväskylä, Business and Organization Ethics Network, School of Business and Economics; URL: http://ejbo.jyu.fi/index.cgi?page=cover)

Ethics in Film is an online journal, begun in 2005, that focuses on using film to teach ethics, including business ethics examples. (ISSN not available, Center for Business and Society, University of Colorado; URL: www .ethicsinfilm.com)

Greener Management International: The Journal of Corporate Environmental Strategy and Practice, produced quarterly since 1993, has articles and case studies with an international scope that focus on environmentally sustainable business practice. Recent examples of thematic issues have included sustainable performance and business competitiveness, chemical risk management, and greening supply chain management. (ISSN 0966–9671, Greenleaf; URL: www.greenleaf-publishing.com)

International Journal of Business Governance and Ethics, published quarterly since 2003, focuses with interdisciplinary perspectives on aspects of corporate social responsibility and ethical decision making within organizations. (ISSN 1477–9048, Inderscience Publishers; URL: www.inderscience.com/ijbge)

Journal of Business Ethics Education (JBEE) began publishing quarterly in 2004. Currently, it is the only journal exclusively devoted to articles on teaching business ethics, since content for the former *Teaching Business Ethics* is now reincorporated into *JBE,* and the *Journal of Management Education* is more broadly focused. *JBEE* contains research articles and curriculum materials. (ISSN 1649–5195, Senate Hall and Carnegie Bosch Institute; URL: www.senatehall.com/journals.php?journal=5)

Journal of Corporate Citizenship, produced quarterly since 2001, publishes articles that link theory with practice about corporate citizenship, addressing

global and local perspectives. (ISSN 1470–5001, Greenleaf; URL: www
.greenleaf-publishing.com/jcc/jccframe.htm)

Journal of Management Education has appeared bimonthly since 1975 with
articles on teaching business students and managers. Ethics-related items
appear in nearly every issue. Articles may be theoretical and empirical
research, essays, reviews of instructional materials, as well as teaching tools,
such as exercises and assignments that use discussion, case method, role
playing, and writing. The December issue has an annual index. (ISSN 1052–
5629; URL: www.sagepub.com/journal.aspx?pid=181)

Journal of Public Policy and Marketing (JPPM) published semiannually since
1982, *JPPM* contains articles on social, ethical, public policy, and economic
aspects of marketing. (ISSN 0748–6766, American Marketing Association;
URL: bear.cba.ufl.edu/centers/jppm)

Organization Science, one of the top research journals in management,
began publishing in 1990. Its bimonthly issues focus on systems and
behavior in organizations, drawing from the fields of management, sociology,
psychology, economics, and communications. Usually, there are several
ethics-related articles per year. (ISSN 1047–7039, Institute for Operations
Research and the Management Sciences; URL: www.marketingpower.com/
content1056C342.php)

Review of Social Economy, published quarterly since 1948, is the official
publication of the Association for Social Economics and concentrates on
topics like the relationships between social values, economics, and ethics.
Themes include social justice, poverty, income distribution, gender,
environment, and humanism. (ISSN 0034–6764, Routledge; URL: www
.tandf.co.uk/journals/titles/00346764.asp)

Teaching Business Ethics appeared quarterly from 1997 to 2003 and is now
incorporated into *Journal of Business Ethics* (see above). (ISSN 1382–6891,
Kluwer Academic)

Zeitschrift fuer Wirtschafts und Unternehmensethik (Journal of Business,
Economics and Ethics), begun in 2000, is published three times per year.
Theoretical and empirical articles are primarily in German, but some are in
English, and all articles have English abstracts. (ISSN 1439–880x, Rainer-
Hampp-Verlag; URL: www.zfwu.de)

ANNUAL BOOK SERIES

Annual series have been a key format for distributing business ethics articles, especially before many journals published ethics-related articles regularly. Below is a selected list of the most relevant ones, presented in alphabetical order.

Annual Editions: Business Ethics has run from 1989 to present, reprinting articles from diverse academic journals and popular magazines that focus on basic concepts drawn from many perspectives. (ISSN 1055–5455, McGraw-Hill/Dushkin; URL: www.dushkin.com/annualeditions/ae-list.mhtml)

IABS Proceedings, published since 1990, includes papers presented at annual meetings of the International Association for Business and Society, the producers of *Business & Society.* (ISSN not available; URL: www.iabs.net)

International Business Ethics Review covers international aspects of corporate social responsibility. The International Business Ethics Institute of Washington, D.C., has turned out three to five academic articles annually since 1997 but began more frequent publication in 2005. The print copies are free on request. (ISSN not available; URL: www.business-ethics.org/iberpub.asp)

Issues in Business Ethics has appeared irregularly since 1990, producing single-topic volumes that are collections of previously unpublished scholarly articles on ethics in international management. (ISSN 0925–6733, Springer-Verlag Dordrecht; URL: www.springer.com/sgw/cda/frontpage/0,11855,5–40385–69–33114156–0,00.html)

JAI Press (now called JAI/Elsevier) generates several annual titles, each with original research articles. The most notable include the following:

> *Research in Ethical Issues in Organizations* (ISSN 1529–2096, 1999 to present)

> *Research on Professional Responsibility and Ethics in Accounting* (ISSN 1574–0765, 1995 to present; called *Research on Accounting Ethics* prior to 2004)

> *Research in Corporate Social Performance and Policy* (ISSN 0191–1937, 1978–1998)

JAI also publishes *Advances in Bioethics, Research in Social Problems and Public Policy,* and others. (URL: www.elsevier.com/wps/find/books_browse.cws_home?pseudotype=SER)

Ruffin Series in Business Ethics, appearing biennially since the 1990s, publishes the papers delivered at the renowned lecture series at the Darden School sponsored by the University of Virginia's Olsson Center for Applied Ethics and the Ruffin Foundation. (ISSN not available, Philosophy Documentation Center; formerly published by Oxford University Press, 1998–2004; URL: www.pdcnet.org/ruffin.html)

Soundings: A Series of Books on Ethics, Economics and Business has appeared irregularly since 1987, produced by the University of Notre Dame Press. (ISSN not available; URL: www3.undpress.nd.edu/dyn/series/36)

Transparency International, based in Berlin, Germany, has two annual publications that are available free online: *Global Corruption Report,* www .globalcorruptionreport.org, and *Corruption Perceptions Index,* www.icgg .org/corruption.cpi.html (copublished with the International Center for Corruption Research).

TRADE JOURNALS, NEWSLETTERS, AND THE POPULAR PRESS

Some periodicals are used primarily for locating news, trends, commentary, and case study material. Below is an alphabetical list of selected publications that are geared toward researchers, businesspeople, students, and the public:

Business Ethics: The Magazine of Corporate Responsibility (BE), formerly *Business Ethics Magazine,* publishes quarterly with a circulation of about 10,000 (current issue is free online). *BE* covers trends and includes special features like reports on teaching ethics in MBA programs, interviews with corporate leaders, awards, and an annual ranking of the "100 Best Corporate Citizens." (ISSN 0894–6582, New Mountain Media; URL: www.business-ethics.com)

The Conference Board's *Research Reports* and *Executive Action Reports* frequently include publications that address ethics topics, with items such as "Why Ethical Leaders are Different," "Using Ethical Analysis to Guide Offshoring," and "Corporate Citizenship Reporting: Best Practices." (ISSN 0732–572X; URL: www.conference-board.org/publications)

Compact Quarterly: Corporate Citizenship in the World Economy is the official newsletter (free online) of the United Nations' Global Compact, which began in 1999 as an initiative promoting corporate responsibility worldwide by encouraging company participation in adhering to principles promoting human rights, labor standards, the environment, and anticorruption. (ISSN not available, United Nations; URL: www.enews builder.net/globalcompact)

CQ Researcher, a weekly, frequently publishes issues on business ethics topics that are particularly good for basic overviews of subjects currently appearing in the U.S. and international news. Each issue includes a chronology of the topic, pro/con arguments, and essays. Past issues have addressed the following: "Whistleblowers," "Disabilities Act," "Religion in the Workplace," "Lobbying Boom," "Corporate Crime," "Child Labor and Sweatshops," "Drug Company Ethics," "Asbestos Litigation," "Diversity in the Workplace," and "Contingent Work Force." (ISSN 1056–2036, Congressional Quarterly; URL: www .cqpress.com/product/Researcher-Online.html)

Ethics Newsline, free online, summarizes each week's ethics-related news, and includes features like statistics, quotes, research reports, commentary, charts, and illustrations. (ISSN not available, Institute for Global Ethics; URL: www .globalethics.org/newsline/members/index.tmpl)

Ethics Today, produced by the Ethics Resource Center, Washington, D.C., is a monthly free e-mail newsletter and accompanying Web site that contains news, white papers, research reviews, and educational resources on organizational ethics (formerly *Ethics Journal,* ISSN 1060–0698, 1991–1996). (ISSN not available; URL: www.ethics.org/erc-publications/newsletter.asp)

Ethikos: Examining Ethical and Compliance Issues in Business has come out semimonthly since 1987, focusing on corporate ethics programs and reporting on experiences with corporate compliance programs (incorporates *Corporate Conduct Quarterly,* ISSN 1061–8775, 1991–1999). (ISSN 0895–5026, Ethics Partners, Inc.; URL: www.singerpubs.com/ethikos)

European Business Ethics Newsletter, biannual since 2003 (free online), publishes news and announcements related to the activities of the European Business Ethics Network. (ISSN none available; URL: www.ebenuk.org/ info_resources.html)

Philosophy for Business, appearing monthly since November 2003 (free online) from the International Society for Philosophers, features articles and book reviews for a broad audience about the philosophical aspects of business. (ISSN not available; URL: www.isfp.co.uk/businesspathways)

Society for Business Ethics Newsletter has been published twice a year since 2004 (free online) by the producers of *Business Ethics Quarterly* and includes items like conference calendars, calls for papers, job announcements, and other association business. (ISSN not available; URL: www.societyforbusinessethics.org)

RESEARCH DATABASES

Online databases allow simultaneous searching of hundreds of periodicals, across a broad chronological range. They save the researcher time by searching widely for relevant articles, covering both the journals typically devoted to business ethics and those from allied fields that occasionally produce ethics-related articles.

More than 12 commercial services may be used effectively to locate articles on business ethics. The major, broad-based management databases are the primary choices to research business-ethics-related topics because they cover the largest range of relevant academic literature, as well as news, commentary, case studies, and policy analysis articles. The leading databases cover six or more journals that are central to business ethics, along with a significant number of other academic and trade journals of secondary importance to the field. They are as follows:

ProQuest's ABI/Inform Global

EBSCO's Business Source Premier

Another strong resource, the *Bibliography of Business Ethics Articles* (www.isbee.org/biblio/EthicsArticles.php), is available online at no charge. Created and maintained as a project of the International Society of Business, Economics, and Ethics, it contains about 4,000 citations (dating from 1992 to present) that are handpicked from nine central business-ethics-related journals. This bibliography of high-quality sources is easily accessible, although it has limitations, compared with commercial databases, in terms of the range of journals, the citation-only format, how fast new content is added, and its search engine's features.

Secondary choices for research databases on business ethics topics are the major interdisciplinary academic databases or those others that are dedicated to specific disciplines (e.g., philosophy, psychology). They contain fewer of the periodical titles that publish business ethics research. Listed in order of most-to-least coverage are

Expanded Academic,

International Bibliography of the Social Sciences,

Business Periodicals Index,

Emerald Insight,

Business and Company Resource Center,

Philosopher's Index,

PAIS International,

Social Science Index,

IBZ/Internationale Bibliographie der Geistes- und Sozialwissenschaftliche Zeitschriftenliteratur (International Bibliography of Periodical Literature in the Humanities and Social Sciences),

IBR/Internationale Bibliographie der Rezensionen Geistes- und Sozialwissen schaftliche Literatur (International Bibliography of Reviews of Scholarly Literature in the Humanities and Social Sciences),

Dietrich's Index Philosophicus, and

Social Science Citation Index.

Other highly specialized databases may be useful occasionally, depending on the research topic. Examples are *Communication Abstracts, Criminal Justice Abstracts, Environmental Science and Pollution Management, POESIS, PsycINFO, Religion Index, Risk Abstracts,* and *Worldwide Political Science Abstracts.*

A notable feature of commercial databases is that they provide a controlled vocabulary that not only assists searching by subject (e.g., corporate social responsibility) but also by specific article treatments, so that researchers can combine their subjects with keywords such as "case studies," "peer review," "editorial," or "statistical" (keywords vary by database). Free Internet search engines, even Google Scholar, currently do not offer this kind of powerful search refinement feature.

Google Scholar does outperform the commercial databases in one area: The contents published in annual book series, many of which are original research articles, currently are ignored by these commercial database sources, with the exception of the *Ruffin Series,* which is available through *ABI/Inform* and

POESIS. Google Scholar is providing some incomplete, but promising, indexing that uncovers the material in these annual series. Comprehensive tracking of items in annuals, however, is best done from each publisher's Web site.

MISCELLANEOUS DIGITAL RESOURCES

Useful Web sites that support business ethics research come in a variety of forms, with links to business ethics periodicals, news, or other documents. BELL: The Business Ethics Link Library (http://libnet.colorado.edu/Bell/front page.htm) is a comprehensive collection of resources compiled by the business library at the Leeds School of Business, University of Colorado, that primarily provides many dozens of examples of the codes of ethics of business and organizations. BELL also serves as a useful first stop for links to ethics periodicals, education programs, and other ethics and corporate social responsibility online resources. In addition to the already-mentioned newsletters by the Ethics Resource Center, European Business Ethics Network, and the Society for Business Ethics, there presently are two well-established English language Internet sites that contain news, commentary, announcements, and the occasional case study. They are the business ethics section of Management Logs, www.managementlogs.com/business_ethics.html, a Web log by more than 12 international contributors, and *RISQ: Review of International Social Questions,* www.risq.org/category4.html, a publication by 18 international researchers, journalists, and policy makers. These sites host journalistic reporting and interviews and have supplemental features like notifications for new content, useful links, and interactive discussions. More sites such as these are likely to appear as interest in and the study of business ethics become more widespread.

—Adele L. Barsh

Further Readings

Urlich's periodicals directory. (Annual). New Providence, NJ: R. R. Bowker. Retrieved from www.ulrichsweb.com/ulrichsweb